PSYCHOANALYTIC ASSESSMENT: THE DIAGNOSTIC PROFILE

AN ANTHOLOGY OF

The Psychoanalytic Study of the Child

PSYCHOANALYTIC ASSESSMENT: THE DIAGNOSTIC PROFILE

Foreword by Anna Freud

NEW HAVEN AND LONDON
YALE UNIVERSITY PRESS
1977

Set in Baskerville type.
Printed in the United States of America by The Colonial Press Inc., Clinton, Mass.

Published in Great Britain, Europe, Africa, and Asia (except Japan) by Yale University Press, Ltd., London. Distributed in Latin America by Kaiman & Polon, Inc., New York City; in Australia and New Zealand by Book & Film Services, Artarmon, N.S.W., Australia; and in Japan by Harper & Row, Publishers, Tokyo Office.

Library of Congress Cataloging in Publication Data

Main entry under title:

Psychoanalytic assessment.

Bibliography: p.
Includes index.
CONTENTS: Theory of development assessment: Freud, A. Assessment of childhood disturbances. Freud, A. The concept of developmental lines. Freud, A. The symptomatology of childhood. [etc.]
1. Mentally ill children — Diagnosis. 2. Psychological tests for children. 3. Child analysis. I. The Psychoanalytic study of the child.
RJ503.5.P74 618.9'28'9075 75-32280
ISBN 0-300-01980-7
ISBN 0-300-01981-5 pbk.

CONTENTS

FOREWORD

ANNA FREUD

The papers included in this Monograph have been assembled for the benefit of readers who are interested in the diagnostic studies carried out in the Hampstead Clinic. Since the tool used for these explorations was the Developmental Profile of the child under investigation, it is only natural that the expansion and applications of this schema form the main subject matter of this book.

Since Part I documents in detail the theoretical considerations that led to the setting up of the Profile schema, it is unnecessary to repeat the motives here. Suffice it to say that its primary objective was to curb any diagnostician's tendency to be one-sided or superficial, i.e., to overemphasize overt manifestations such as disturbed behavior and symptoms to the neglect of underlying factors and conditions. Guided by the subheadings of the Profile which are ordered according to metapsychology, the diagnostician is prompted to organize his findings with the dynamic, genetic, and economic viewpoints in mind—that is, to think psychoanalytically. The resultant diagnostic picture cannot fail to contain more than the habitual enumeration of symptomatology. It will determine the child's developmental status and assess any abnormality against the background of normal psychological growth.

Once this method had come into use for the problem children diagnosed at the Clinic, its application inevitably was extended to other age groups: to the diagnostic services for adults, adolescents, and infants. This required the modification and enlargement of some of the subsections of the Profile (see Part II).

The Profile has many uses and practical applications, some of which are demonstrated in Part III of this monograph. Assessment by Profile of the blind, the atypical, the borderline cases, the psychoses permits us to indicate precisely where in the mental apparatus or structure of the personality pathology is located. It then becomes possible to make meaningful comparisons between the impaired mental functioning in the various disorders.

The Profiles also proved to be an important tool for the purpose of measuring success or failure of analytic treatments. Profiles can be drawn up at any stage of the child's analysis or after its termination. Comparisons between the diagnostic and terminal Profiles are indispensable for distinguishing between superficial, behavioral improvements and basic cures, the changes becoming especially apparent in the Profile sections dealing with anxiety level, defense organization, superego maturity, frustration tolerance, and sublimation potential.

Profiles drawn up at decisive developmental stages open up a variety of research possibilities. They seem almost a must in longitudinal studies of personality development. Drawn up early in a child's life and at later stages of his development, they allow us to assess the more permanent characteristics of an individual and provide early indications of subsequent pathological development—areas in which we still have much to learn. Profiles can thus be used for prospective and retrospective assessments of development.

As a less ambitious application, even simple case presentations are more instructive if they are organized in accordance with the Profile headings.

Although diagnosis before treatment has never been a major interest of psychoanalysts, there has been a growing concern about the discrepancy between the metapsychological thinking which underlies the analyst's therapeutic work and the phenomenology of the diagnostic categories which the analyst borrows from psychiatry. The search for a nosology based on psychoanalytic concepts has been going on for some time now. Assessment by Profile is one attempt among others to bridge the gap between these two divergent approaches.

ACKNOWLEDGMENTS

Most of the work reported in this volume was carried out at the Hampstead Child-Therapy Course and Clinic, which is at present supported by the G. G. Bunzl Fund, London; The Field Foundation, New York; Foundation for Research in Psychoanalysis, Beverly Hills, Calif.; Anna Freud Foundation, New York; Freud Centenary Fund, London; The Grant Foundation, Inc., New York; The Andrew W. Mellon Foundation, New York; Paul Mellon Fund, New York; National Institute of Mental Health, Bethesda, Maryland; The New-Land Foundation, Inc., New York; Leo Oppenheimer and Flora Oppenheimer Haas Trust, New York.

PART I

THEORY OF DEVELOPMENTAL ASSESSMENT

1

ASSESSMENT OF CHILDHOOD DISTURBANCES

ANNA FREUD, LL.D., D.Sc., M.D.

(1962)

When diagnosing the mental disturbances of children, the child analyst is confronted with difficulties which are due to the shifting internal scene in a developing individual and which are not met with in adult psychiatry.

One of these difficulties concerns the fact that, during development, symptoms, inhibitions, and anxieties do not necessarily carry the same significance which they assume at a later date. Although in some cases they may be lasting, and thus the first signs of permanent pathology, in other cases they need be no more than transient appearances of stress which emerge whenever a particular phase of development makes specially high demands on a child's personality. After adaptation to that particular phase has been achieved, or when its peak has passed, these seemingly pathological appearances either may disappear again without leaving much trace, or make way for others. In either case, what is left behind may be no more than an area of heightened vulnerability. These semblances of "spontaneous cures" are the equivalent of what used to be called "outgrowing" of difficulties, a phrase which, though outmoded, is in reality still quite appropriate.

Another difficulty for the diagnostician is bound up with the

---

This short article is a preliminary communication, extracted from an extensive study of normal and abnormal child development, the publication of which is in preparation by the author. The "Diagnostic Profile" contained in it has to be considered as a tentative draft, open to amendment and revision of all its parts, after their usefulness has been tested against clinical material over a prolonged period.

well-known fact that there are no childhood alternatives to the adult's efficiency or failure in sex and work, vital factors which are used in adult psychiatry as indications of intactness or disturbance. Although in what follows efforts will be made to outline some "age-adequate tasks" for children, these are by no means of similar diagnostic significance.

Since, thus, neither symptomatology nor life tasks can be taken as reliable guides to the assessment of mental health or illness in childhood, we are left with the alternative idea[1] that the capacity to develop progressively, or respectively the damage to that capacity, is the most significant factors in determining a child's mental future. Accordingly, it becomes the diagnostician's task to ascertain where a given child stands on the developmental scale, whether his position is age adequate, retarded or precocious, and in what respect; and to what extent the observable internal and external circumstances and existent symptoms are interfering with the possibilities of future growth.

But even this more circumscribed task, namely, to place the case of a given child in the correct position on the scale of normal or pathological development, is admittedly difficult, all the more so since, besides psychoanalysis, several other disciplines such as descriptive and dynamic psychiatry, psychology, and the social sciences have a stake in it. For the child analyst the appraisal of the child serves not only practical but also theoretical aims. To the first category belong the decision for and against treatment and the choice of therapeutic method; to the second, the attempts to formulate clearer pictures of the initial phases of those mental disorders which are known now principally in their later stages; to distinguish transitory from permanent pathology; and in general to increase insight into the developmental processes themselves.

The analyst's requirement for the latter purposes is a comprehensive metapsychological picture of the child (i.e., one containing structural, dynamic, economic, genetic, and adaptive data). This order cannot be filled with the comparatively meager facts elicited from the children or their parents at their first contact with the Clinic. Therefore, the task of assessment, which begins with the

[1] Suggested by me in "Indications for Child Analysis" (1945).

diagnostic team, is continued by the child analyst, i.e., it passes from the stage of initial diagnostic procedure into the stage of therapy. Since in analysis the method of therapy coincides with the method of exploration, the whole bulk of analytic material can be utilized for the latter purpose or, as happens in analytic teamwork in the Clinic, be handed back to the diagnostician to confirm, correct, and expand his first impressions of the case.

In what follows we attempt to outline the setting up of a metapsychological framework of this kind, i.e., of a "*developmental* profile" in which the result of the analyst's diagnostic thinking is broken up into its component parts. Profiles of this kind can be drawn up at various junctures, namely, after the first contact between child and Clinic (preliminary diagnostic stage), during analysis (treatment stage), and after the end of analysis or follow-up (terminal stage). If this is done, the profile serves not only as a tool for the completion and verification of diagnosis but also as an instrument to measure treatment results, i.e., as a check on the efficacy of psychoanalytic treatment.

At the diagnostic stage the profile for each case should be initiated by the referral symptoms of the child, his description, his family background and history, and an enumeration of the possibly significant environmental influences. From these it proceeds to the internal picture of the child which contains information about the *structure* of his personality; the *dynamic* interplay within the structure; some *economic* factors concerning drive activity and the relative strength of id and ego forces; his adaptation to reality; and some genetic assumptions (to be verified during and after treatment). Thus, broken up into items, an individual profile may look as follows:

Draft of Diagnostic Profile

I. Reason for Referral (Arrests in Development, Behavior Problems, Anxieties, Inhibitions, Symptoms, etc.)

II. Description of Child (Personal appearance, Moods, Manner, etc.)

III. Family Background and Personal History

IV. Possibly Significant Environmental Influences

V. Assessments of Development

A. *Drive Development*

1. Libido.—Examine and state
   (a) with regard to *phase development:*
   whether in the sequence of libidinal phases (oral, anal, phallic; latency; preadolescence, adolescence) the child has ever proceeded to his age-adequate stage, and especially beyond the anal to the phallic level;
   whether he has achieved phase dominance on it;
   whether, at the time of assessment, this highest level is being maintained or has been abandoned regressively for an earlier one;
   (b) with regard to *libido distribution:*
   whether the self is cathected as well as the object world, and whether there is sufficient narcissism (primary and secondary, invested in the body, the ego, or the superego) to ensure self-regard, self-esteem, a sense of well-being, without leading to overestimation of the self, undue independence of the objects, etc.; state degree of dependence of self-regard on object relations;
   (c) with regard to *object libido:*
   whether in the level and quality of object relationships (narcissistic, anaclitic, object constancy, preoedipal, oedipal, postoedipal, adolescent) the child has proceeded according to age;
   whether, at the time of assessment, the highest level reached is being maintained or has been abandoned regressively;
   whether or not the existent object relationships correspond with the maintained or regressed level of phase development.
2. Aggression.—Examine the aggressive expressions at the disposal of the child:
   (a) according to their quantity, i.e., presence or absence in the manifest picture;

(b) according to their quality, i.e., correspondence with the level of libido development;

(c) according to their direction toward either the object world or the self.

B. *Ego and Superego Development*

(a) Examine and state the intactness or defects of ego apparatus, serving perception, memory, motility, etc.;

(b) Examine and state in detail the intactness or otherwise of ego *functions* (memory, reality testing, synthesis, control of motility, speech, secondary thought processes. Look out for primary deficiencies. Note unevennesses in the levels reached. Include results of Intelligence Tests);

(c) Examine in detail the status of the *defense organization* and consider:

whether defense is employed specifically against *individual drives* (to be identified here) or, more generally, against drive activity and instinctual pleasure as such;

whether defenses are *age adequate,* too primitive, or too precocious;

whether defense is *balanced,* i.e., whether the ego has at its disposal the use of many of the important mechanisms or is restricted to the excessive use of single ones;

whether defense is *effective,* especially in its dealing with anxiety, whether it results in equilibrium or disequilibrium, lability, mobility or deadlock within the structure;

whether and how far the child's defense against the drives is dependent on the object world or independent of it (superego development);

(d) Note any secondary interference of defense activity with ego achievements, i.e., the price paid by the individual for the upkeep of the defense organization.

C. *Development of the Total Personality*

(Lines of Development and Mastery of Tasks)

While drive and ego development are viewed separately for purposes of dissection, their action is seen as combined in the *lines of development* which lead from the individual's state of infantile immaturity and dependence to the gradual mastery of his own body and its functions, to adaptation to the object world, reality and the social community, as well as to the building up of an inner structure. Whatever level has been reached by a given child in any of these respects represents the end point of a historical sequence which can be traced, reconstructed, scrutinized for defects (this to be done during and after treatment), and in which ego, superego, as well as drive development have played their part. Under the influence of external and internal factors these lines of development may proceed at a fairly equal rate, i.e., harmoniously, or with wide divergences of speed, which lead to the many existent imbalances, variations, and incongruities in personality development. (See, for example, excessive speech and thought development combined with infantilism of needs, fantasies and wishes; good achievement of object constancy combined with low frustration tolerance and primitive defense system; or complete dependence for feeding, defecation, etc., combined with fairly mature intellectual and moral standards.)

At the time of diagnosis, the status of these developmental lines can be investigated by using for the purpose of examination any one of the many situations in life which pose for the child an immediate problem of mastery. Although such tasks may seem simple and harmless when viewed from the outside, the demands made by them on the personality show up clearly when they are translated into terms of psychic reality. Such translations are the indispensable prerequisites for assessing the meaning of successful mastery as well as for understanding failure and for allotting it correctly to the right sources in either the drives or the ego agencies.

Examples of such situations as they may occur in the life of every child are the following:

separation from the mother;
birth of sibling;
illness and surgical intervention;
hospitalization;
entry into nursery school;
school entry;
the step from the triangular oedipal situation into a community of peers;
the step from play to work;

the arousal of new genital strivings in adolescence;
the step from the infantile objects within the family to new love objects outside the family;

(For one particular situation of this kind, namely, "Entry into Nursery School," the psychological significance of the event has been traced in detail, taking into account the demands made on all parts of the personality. [See A. Freud, 1960a, 1963, 1965.])

VI. Genetic Assessments (Regression and Fixation Points)

Since we assume that all infantile neuroses (and some psychotic disturbances of children) are initiated by libido regressions to fixation points at various early levels, the location of these trouble spots in the history of the child is one of the vital concerns of the diagnostician. At the time of initial diagnosis such areas are betrayed:

(a) by certain forms of manifest *behavior* which are characteristic for the given child and allow conclusions as to the underlying id processes which have undergone repression and modification but have left an unmistakable imprint. The best example is the overt obsessional character where cleanliness, orderliness, punctuality, hoarding, doubt, indecision, slowing up, etc., betray the special difficulty experienced by the child when coping with the impulses of the anal-sadistic phase, i.e., a fixation to that phase. Similarly, other character formations or attitudes betray fixation points at other levels, or in other areas. (Concern for health, safety of parents and siblings show a special difficulty of coping with the death wishes of infancy; fear of medicines, food fads, etc., point to defense against oral fantasies; shyness to that against exhibitionism; homesickness to unsolved ambivalence, etc.):

(b) by the child's fantasy activity, sometimes betrayed accidentally in the diagnostic procedure, usually only available through personality tests. (During analysis, the child's conscious and unconscious fantasies provide, of course, the fullest information about the pathogenically important parts of his developmental history);

(c) by those items in the symptomatology where the relations between surface and depth are firmly established, not open to variation, and well known to the diagnostician as are the symptoms of the obsessional neurosis with their known fixation points. In contrast, symptoms such as lying, stealing, bed wetting, etc., with their multiple causation, convey no genetic information at the diagnostic stage.

For the diagnostician trained in the assessment of adult disturbances, it is important to note that infantile regression differs in various respects from regression in the adult; it does not always require fixation points and it does not need to be permanent. As "temporary regression" it takes place along the developmental lines mentioned before, and forms part of normal development as an attempt at adaptation and response to frustration. Such temporary regression may give rise to pathology, but the latter will be short-lived and reversible. For purposes of assessment the two types of regression (temporary or permanent, spontaneously reversible or irreversible) have to be distinguished from each other, only the former type justifying therapy.

VII. Dynamic and Structural Assessments (Conflicts)

Behavior is governed by the interplay of internal with external forces, or of internal forces (conscious or unconscious) with each other, i.e., by the outcome of conflicts. Examine the conflicts in the given case and classify them as:

(a) external conflicts between the id-ego agencies and the object world (arousing fear of the object world);
(b) internalized conflicts between ego-superego and id after the ego agencies have taken over and represent to the id the demands of the object world (arousing guilt);
(c) internal conflicts between insufficiently fused or incompatible drive representatives (such as unsolved ambivalence, activity versus passivity, masculinity versus femininity, etc.).

According to the predominance of any one of the three types it may be possible to arrive at assessments of:

(1) the level of maturity, i.e., the relative independence of the child's personality structure;
(2) the severity of his disturbance;
(3) the intensity of therapy needed for alleviation or removal of the disturbance.

VIII. Assessment of Some General Characteristics

The whole personality of the child should be scrutinized also for certain general characteristics which are of possible significance for predicting the chances for spontaneous recovery and reaction to treatment. Examine in this connection the following areas:

(a) the child's frustration tolerance. Where (in respect of developmental age) the tolerance for tension and frustration is unusually low, more anxiety will be generated than can be coped with, and the pathological sequence of regression, defense activity, and symptom formation will be more easily set in motion. Where frustration tolerance is high, equilibrium will be maintained, or regained, more successfully;

(b) the child's sublimation potential. Individuals differ widely in the degree to which displaced, aim-inhibited, and neutralized gratification can recompense them for frustrated drive fulfillment. Acceptance of these former types of gratification (or freeing of the sublimation potential in treatment) may reduce the need for pathological solutions;

(c) the child's over-all attitude to anxiety. Examine how far the child's defense against fear of the external world and anxiety caused by the internal world is based exclusively on phobic measures and countercathexes which are in themselves closely related to pathology; and how far there is a tendency actively to master external and internal danger situations, the latter being a sign of a basically healthy, well-balanced ego structure;

(d) progressive developmental forces versus regressive tendencies. Both are, normally, present in the immature personality. Where the former outweigh the latter, the chances for normality and spontaneous recoveries are increased; symptom formation is more transitory since strong forward moves to the next developmental level alter the inner balance of forces. Where the latter, i.e., regression, predominate, the resistances against treatment and the stubbornness of pathological solutions will be more formidable. The economic relations between the two tendencies can be deduced from watching the child's struggle between the active wish to grow up and his reluctance to renounce the passive pleasures of infancy.

IX. Diagnosis

Finally, it is the diagnostician's task to reassemble the items mentioned above and to combine them in a clinically meaningful assessment. He will have to decide between a number of categorizations such as the following:

(1) that, in spite of current manifest behavior disturbances, the personality growth of the child is essentially healthy and falls within the wide range of "variations of normality";

(2) that existent pathological formations (symptoms) are of a transitory nature and can be classed as by-products of developmental strain;

(3) that there are permanent regressions which, on the one hand, cause more permanent symptom formation and, on the other hand, have impoverishing effects on libido progression and crippling effects on ego growth. According to the location of the fixation points and the amount of ego-superego damage, the character structure or symptoms produced will be of a neurotic, psychotic, or delinquent nature;

(4) that there are primary deficiencies of an organic nature or early deprivations which distort development and structuralization and produce retarded, defective, and nontypical personalities;

(5) that there are destructive processes at work (of organic, toxic, or psychic, known or unknown origin) which have effected, or are on the point of effecting, a disruption of mental growth.

2

THE CONCEPT OF DEVELOPMENTAL LINES

ANNA FREUD, LL.D., D.Sc., M.D.

(1963)

The diagnostic Profile which we have set up serves the systematic assessment of childhood disturbances by seeing the picture of any given child against the background of a developmental norm into which the state of his inner agencies, his various functions, conflicts, attitudes, and achievements have to be fitted. In our psychoanalytic theory such developmental sequences are laid down so far as certain circumscribed parts of the child's personality are concerned. With regard to the development of the sexual drive, for example, we possess the sequence of libidinal phases (oral, anal, phallic, latency period, preadolescence, adolescent genitality) which, in spite of considerable overlapping, correspond roughly with specific ages. With regard to the aggressive drive we are already less precise and are usually content to correlate specific aggressive expressions with specific libidinal phases (such as biting, spitting, devouring with orality; sadistic torturing, hitting, kicking, destroying with anality; overbearing, domineering, forceful behavior with the phallic phase;

Like last year's article on "Assessment of Childhood Disturbances," this paper is extracted from a more extensive study of child development as a preliminary communication.

The individual lines of development have been discussed in detail with the Diagnostic Research Committee of the Hampstead Child-Therapy Clinic, and I have incorporated suggestions and amendments made by John Bolland, Liselotte Frankl, Ilse Hellman, Martin James, Maria Kawenoka, Humberto Nagera, Joseph Sandler, Ruth Thomas, Doris Wills.

inconsiderateness, mental cruelty, dissocial outbursts with adolescence, etc.). On the side of the ego, the analytically known stages and levels of the sense of reality, in the chronology of defense activity and in the growth of a moral sense, lay down a norm. The intellectual functions themselves are measured and graded by the psychologist by means of the age-related scales of the various intelligence tests.

On the other hand, it is true that we need more for our assessments than these selected developmental scales which are valid for isolated parts of the child's personality only, not for its totality. What we are looking for are the basic interactions between id and ego and their various developmental levels, and also age-related sequences of them which, in importance, frequency, and regularity, are comparable to the maturational sequence of libidinal stages or the gradual unfolding of the ego functions. Naturally, such sequences of interaction between the two sides of the personality can be best established where both are well studied, as they are, for example, with regard to the libidinal phases and aggressive expressions on the id side and the corresponding object-related attitudes on the ego side. Here we can trace the combinations which lead from the infant's complete emotional dependence to the adult's comparative self-reliance and mature sex and object relationships, a gradated developmental line which provides the indispensable basis for any assessment of emotional maturity or immaturity, normality or abnormality.

Even if perhaps less easily established, there are similar lines of development which can be shown to be valid for almost every other area of the individual's personality. In every instance they trace the child's gradual outgrowing of dependent, irrational, id- and object-determined attitudes to an increasing ego mastery of his internal and external world. Such lines—always contributed to from the side of both id and ego development—lead, for example, from the infant's suckling and weaning experiences to the adult's rational rather than emotional attitude to food intake; from cleanliness training enforced on the child by environmental pressure to the adult's more or less ingrained and unshakable bladder and bowel control; from the child's sharing possession of his body with his mother to the adolescent's claim for independence and self-determination in body management; from the young child's egocentric view of the world and his fellow beings to empathy, mutuality, and companionship with his contemporaries; from the first erotic play on his own and his mother's body by way of the transitional objects (Winnicott, 1953) to the toys, games, hobbies, and finally to work, etc.

Whatever level has been reached by any given child in any of these respects represents the results of interaction between drive and ego-superego development and their reaction to environmental influences, i.e., between maturation, adaptation, and structuralization. Far from being theoretical abstractions, developmental lines, in the sense here used, are historical realities which, when assembled, convey a convincing picture of an individual child's personal achievements or, on the other hand, of his failures in personality development.

Prototype of a Developmental Line: From Dependency to Emotional Self-Reliance and Adult Object Relationships

To serve as the prototype for all others, there is one basic developmental line which has received attention from analysts from the beginning. This is the sequence which leads from the newborn's utter dependence on maternal care to the young adult's emotional and material self-reliance—a sequence for which the successive stages of libido development (oral, anal, phallic) merely form the inborn, maturational base. The steps on this way are well documented from the analyses of adults and children, as well as from direct analytic infant observations:

(1) The biological unity between the mother-infant couple, with the mother's narcissism extending to the child, and the child including the mother in his internal "narcissistic milieu" (Hoffer, 1952), the whole period being further subdivided (according to Margaret Mahler, 1952) into the autistic, symbiotic and separation-individuation phases with significant danger points for developmental disturbances lodged in each individual phase;

(2) the part object (Melanie Klein), or need-fulfilling, anaclitic relationship, which is based on the urgency of the child's body needs and drive derivatives and is intermittent and fluctuating,

since object cathexis is sent out under the impact of imperative desires, and withdrawn again when satisfaction has been reached;

(3) the stage of object constancy, which enables a positive inner image of the object to be maintained, irrespective of dissatisfactions and frustrations;

(4) the ambivalent relationship of the preoedipal, anal-sadistic stage, characterized by the ego attitudes of clinging, torturing, dominating, and controlling the objects;

(5) the completely object-centered phallic-oedipal phase, characterized by possessiveness of the parent of the opposite sex, jealousy and rivalry with the parent of the same sex, protectiveness, generosity, curiosity, bids for admiration and exhibitionistic attitudes; with girls a phallic-oedipal (masculine) relationship to the mother precedes the oedipal relationship to the father;

(6) the latency period, i.e., the postoedipal lessening of drive urgency and the transfer of libido from the parental figures to contemporaries, community groups, teachers, leaders, impersonal ideals, and aim-inhibited, sublimated interests, with fantasy manifestations giving evidence of disillusionment with and denigration of the parents ("family romance," twin fantasies, etc.);

(7) the preadolescent prelude to the "adolescent revolt," i.e., a return to early attitudes and behavior, especially of the part-object, need-fulfilling, and ambivalent type;

(8) the adolescent struggle around denying, reversing, loosening, and shedding the tie to the infantile objects, defending against pregenitality, and finally establishing genital supremacy with libidinal cathexis transferred to objects of the opposite sex, outside the family.

While the details of these positions have long been common knowledge in analytic circles, their relevance for practical problems is being explored increasingly in recent years. As regards, for example, the much-discussed consequences of a child's separation from the mother, the parents or the home, a mere glance at the unfolding of the developmental line will be sufficient to show convincingly why the common reactions to, respectively, the pathological consequences of, such happenings are as varied as they are, following the varying psychic reality of the child on the different levels. Infringements of the biological mother-infant tie (phase 1), for whatever reason they are undertaken, will thus give rise to separation anxiety (Bowlby, 1960) proper; failure of the mother to play her part as a reliable need-fulfilling and comfort-giving agency (phase 2) will cause breakdowns in individuation (Mahler, 1952) or anaclitic depression (Spitz, 1946), or other manifestations of deprivation (Alpert, 1959), or precocious ego development (James, 1960), or what has been called a "false self" (Winnicott, 1954). Unsatisfactory libidinal relations to unstable or otherwise unsuitable love objects during anal sadism (phase 4) will disturb the balanced fusion between libido and aggression and give rise to uncontrollable aggressivity, destructiveness, etc. (A. Freud, 1949). It is only after object constancy (phase 3) has been reached that the external absence of the object is substituted for, at least in part, by the presence of an internal image which remains stable; on the strength of this achievement temporary separations can be lengthened, commensurate with the advances in object constancy. Thus, even if it remains impossible to name the chronological age when separations can be tolerated, according to the developmental line it can be stated when they become phase-adequate and nontraumatic, a point of practical importance for the purposes of holidays for the parents, hospitalization of the child, convalescence, entry into nursery school, etc.[1]

There are other practical lessons which have been learned from the same developmental sequence, such as the following:

that the clinging attitudes of the toddler stage (phase 4) are the result of preoedipal ambivalence, not of maternal spoiling;

that it is unrealistic on the part of parents to expect of the preoedipal period (up to the end of phase 4) the mutuality in object relations which belongs to the next level (phase 5) only;

that no child can be fully integrated in school before libido has been transferred from the parents to the community (phase 6). Where the passing of the oedipus complex is delayed and phase 5 is protracted as the result of an infantile neurosis, disturbances in

[1] If, by "mourning" we understand not the various manifestations of anxiety, distress, and malfunction which accompany object loss in the earliest phases but the painful, gradual process of detaching libido from an internal image, this, of course, cannot be expected to occur before object constancy (phase 3) has been established.

adaptation to the group, lack of interest, school phobias (in day school), extreme homesickness (in boarding school) will be the order of the day;

that reactions to adoption are most severe in the later part of the latency period (phase 6) when, according to the normal disillusionment with the parents, all children feel as if adopted and the feelings about the reality of adoption merge with the occurrence of the "family romance";

that sublimations, foreshadowed on the oedipal level (phase 5) and developed during latency (phase 6), may be lost during preadolescence (phase 7), not through any developmental or educational failure, but owing to the phase-adequate regression to early levels (phases 2, 3, and 4);

that it is as unrealistic on the part of the parents to oppose the loosening of the tie to the family or the young person's battle against pregenital impulses in adolescence (phase 8) as it is to break the biological tie in phase 1, or oppose pregenital autoerotism in the phases 1, 2, 3, 4, and 7.

Some Developmental Lines toward Body Independence

That the ego of an individual begins first and foremost as a body ego does not imply that bodily independence of the parents is reached earlier than emotional or moral self-reliance. On the contrary: the mother's narcissistic possessiveness of her infant's body is matched from the child's side by his archaic wishes to merge with the mother and by the confusion concerning body limits which arises from the fact that in early life the distinctions between the internal and external world are based not on objective reality but on the subjective experiences of pleasure and unpleasure. Thus, while the mother's breast, or face, hands or hair, may be treated (or maltreated) by the infant as parts of his own organization, his hunger, his tiredness, his discomforts are her concern as much as they are his own. Although for the whole of early childhood, the child's life will be dominated by body needs, body impulses, and their derivatives, the quantities and qualities of satisfactions and dissatisfactions are determined not by himself but by environmental influence. The only exceptions to this rule are the autoerotic gratifications which from the beginning are under the child's own management and, therefore, provide for him a certain circumscribed measure of independence of the object world. In contrast to these, the processes of feeding, sleeping, evacuation, body hygiene, and prevention of injury and illness have to undergo complex and lengthy developments before they become the growing individual's own concern.

From Suckling to Rational Eating

A long line has to be passed through before a child arrives at the point where, for example, he can regulate his own food intake actively and rationally, quantitatively and qualitatively, on the basis of his own needs and appetites and irrespective of his relations to the provider of food, and of conscious and unconscious fantasies. The steps on the way are approximately as follows:

(1) Being nursed at the breast or bottle, by the clock or on demand, with the common difficulties about intake caused partly by the infant's normal fluctuations of appetite and intestinal upsets, partly by the mother's attitudes and anxieties regarding feeding; interference with need-satisfaction caused by hunger periods, undue waiting for meals, rationing or forced feeding set up the first—and often lasting—disturbances in the positive relationship to food. Pleasure sucking appears as a forerunner, by-product of, substitute for, or interference with feeding;

(2) weaning from breast or bottle, initiated either by the infant himself or according to the mother's wishes. In the latter instance, and especially if carried out abruptly, the infant's protest against oral deprivation has adverse results for the normal pleasure in food. Difficulties over the introduction of solids, new tastes, and consistencies being either welcomed or rejected;

(3) the transition from being fed to self-feeding, with or without implements, "food" and "mother" still being identified with each other;

(4) self-feeding with the use of spoon, fork, etc., the disagreements with the mother about the quantity of intake being shifted often to the form of intake, i.e., table manners; meals as a general battleground on which the difficulties of the mother-child relationship can be fought out; craving for sweets as a phase-ade-

quate substitute for oral sucking pleasures; food fads as a result of anal training, i.e., of the newly acquired reaction formation of disgust;

(5) gradual fading out of the equation food-mother in the oedipal period. Irrational attitudes toward eating are now determined by infantile sexual theories, i.e., fantasies of impregnation through the mouth (fear of poison), pregnancy (fear of getting fat), anal birth (fear of intake and output), as well as by reaction formations against cannibalism and sadism;

(6) gradual fading out of the sexualization of eating in the latency period, with pleasure in eating retained or even increased. Increase in the rational attitudes to food and self-determination in eating, the earlier experiences on this line being decisive in shaping the individual's food habits in adult life, his tastes, preferences, as well as eventual addictions or aversions with regard to food and drink.

The infant's reactions to the changes in phase 2 (i.e., to weaning and to the introduction of new tastes and consistencies) reflect for the first time his leaning toward either progression and adventurousness (when new experiences are welcomed) or a tenacious clinging to existing pleasures (when every change is experienced as threat and deprivation). It is to be expected that whichever attitude dominates the feeding process will also become important in other developmental areas.

The equation food-mother, which persists through phases 1-4, provides the rational background for the mother's subjective conviction that every food refusal of the child is aimed at her personally, i.e., expresses the child's rejection of her maternal care and attention, a conviction which causes much oversensitiveness in handling the feeding process and underlies the battle about food on the mother's side. It explains also why in these phases food refusal and extreme food fads can be circumvented by temporarily substituting a stranger, i.e., a noncathected or differently cathected person, for the maternal figure in the feeding situation. Children will then eat, in hospital, in nursery school, or as visitors, but this will not cure their eating difficulties at home, in the presence of the mother. It explains also why traumatic separations from the mother are often followed by refusal of food (rejection of the mother substitute), or by greed and overeating (treating food as a substitute for mother love).

The eating disturbances of phase 5, which are not related to an external object but are caused by internal, structural conflicts, are not affected by either the material presence or the material absence of the mother, a fact which can be utilized for differential diagnosis.

After phase 6, when the arrangements for food intake have become the mature individual's personal concern, the former food battle with the mother may be replaced by internal disagreements between the manifest wish to eat and an unconsciously determined inability to tolerate certain foods, i.e., the various neurotic food fads and digestive upsets.

From Wetting and Soiling to Bladder and Bowel Control

Since the desired aim on this line is not the comparatively intact survival of drive derivatives but the control, modification, and transformation of the urethral and anal trends, the conflicts between id, ego, superego, and environmental forces become particularly obvious.

(1) The duration of the first phase, during which the infant has complete freedom to wet and soil, is determined not maturationally but environmentally, i.e., by the mother's timing of her interference, in which she in her turn is under the influence of personal needs, familial, social, or medical conventions. Under present conditions this phase may last from a few days (training from birth based on reflex action) to two or three years (training based on object relatedness and ego control).

(2) In contrast to phase one, the second phase is initiated by a step in maturation. The dominant role in drive activity passes from the oral to the anal zone, and due to this transition the child stiffens his opposition to any interference with concerns which have become emotionally vital to him. Since in this phase the body products are highly cathected with libido, they are precious to the child and are treated as "gifts" which are surrendered to the mother as a sign of love; since they are cathected also with aggression, they are weapons by means of which rage, anger, disappointment can be discharged within the object relationship. In correspondence to this double cathexis of the body products, the toddler's entire attitude toward the object world is dominated by ambivalence, i.e., by violent swings

between love and hate (libido and aggression not fused with each other). This again is matched on the ego side by curiosity directed toward the inside of the body, pleasure in messing, molding, play with retaining, emptying, hoarding, as well as dominating, possessing, destroying, etc. While the trends shown by the children in this phase are fairly uniform, the actual events vary with the differences in the mother's attitude. If she succeeds in remaining sensitive to the child's needs and as identified with them as she is usually with regard to feeding, she will mediate sympathetically between the environmental demand for cleanliness and the child's opposite anal and urethral tendencies; in that case toilet training will proceed gradually, uneventfully, and without upheavals. On the other hand, such empathy with the child in the anal stage may be impossible for the mother due to her own training, her own reaction formations of disgust, orderliness, and punctiliousness, or other obsessional elements in her personality. If she is dominated by these, she will represent the demand for urethral and anal control in a harsh and uncompromising manner and a major battle will ensue, with the child as intent to defend his right over unrestricted evacuation as the mother is on achieving cleanliness and regularity and with them the rudiments and *sine qua non* of socialization.

(3) In a third phase the child accepts and takes over the mother's and the environment's attitudes to cleanliness and, through identification, makes them an integral part of his ego and superego demands; from then onward, the striving for cleanliness is an internal, not an external, precept, and inner barriers against urethral and anal wishes are set up through the defense activity of the ego, in the well-known form of repression and reaction formation. Disgust, orderliness, tidiness, dislike of dirty hands guard against the return of the repressed; punctuality, conscientiousness, and reliability appear as by-products of anal regularity; inclinations to save, to collect, give evidence of high anal evaluation displaced to other matters. In short, what takes place in this period is the far-reaching modification and transformation of the pregenital anal drive derivatives which—if kept within normal limits—supply the individual personality with a backbone of highly valuable qualities.

It is important to remember in respect to these achievements that they are based on identifications and internalizations and, as such, are not fully secure before the passing of the oedipus complex. Preoedipal anal control remains vulnerable and, especially in the beginning of the third phase, remains dependent on the objects and the stability of positive relations to them. For example, a child who is trained to use the chamberpot or toilet in his home does not exchange them automatically for unfamiliar ones, away from the mother. A child who is severely disappointed in his mother, or separated from her, or suffering from object loss in any form, may not only lose the internalized urge to be clean but also reactivate the aggressive use of elimination. Both together will result in incidents of wetting and soiling which appear as "accidents."

(4) It is only in a fourth phase that bladder and bowel control become wholly secure. This is brought about when the concern for cleanliness is disconnected from object ties and attains the status of a fully neutralized, autonomous ego and superego concern.[2]

From Irresponsibility to Responsibility in Body Management

That the satisfaction of such essential physical needs as feeding and evacuation[3] remains for years under external control and emerges from it in such slow steps corresponds well with the equally slow and gradual manner in which children assume responsibility for the care of their own body and its protection against harm. As described at length elsewhere (A. Freud, 1952), the well-mothered child leaves these concerns largely to the mother, while he allows himself attitudes of indifference and unconcern, or, as a weapon in a battle with her, downright recklessness. It is only the badly mothered or the motherless who adopt the mother's role in health matters and play "mother and child" with their own bodies as the hypochondriacs do.

On the positive progressive line, here too, there are several consecutive phases to be distinguished from each other, though our present knowledge of them is more sketchy than in other areas.

(1) What comes first, as a maturational step in the first few months of life, is an alteration in the direction of aggression from being lived out on the body to being turned toward the external

[2] See H. Hartmann (1950) on "secondary autonomy of the ego."
[3] Also sleep.

world. This vital step sets limits to self-injury from biting, scratching, etc., although indications of such tendencies can be seen in many children as genuine remnants also at later ages.[4] The normal forward move happens partly due to the setting up of the pain barrier, partly due to the child's answering to the mother's libidinal cathexis of his body with a narcissistic cathexis of his own (according to Hoffer, 1950).

(2) What makes itself felt next are the advances in ego functioning such as orientation in the external world, understanding of cause and effect, control of dangerous wishes in the service of the reality principle. Together with the pain barrier and the narcissistic cathexis of the body, these newly acquired functions protect the child against such external dangers as water, fire, heights, etc. But there are many instances of children in whom—owing to a deficiency in any one of these ego functions—this advance is retarded so that they remain unusually vulnerable and exposed if not protected by the adult world.

(3) What comes last normally is the child's voluntary endorsement of the rules of hygiene and of medical necessities. So far as the avoidance of unwholesome food, overeating, and keeping the body clean are concerned, this is inconclusive here since the relevant attitudes belong to the vicissitudes of the oral and anal component instinct rather than to the present line. It is different with the avoidance of ill-health or the compliance with doctor's orders concerning the intake of medicines, and motor or dietary restrictions. Fear, guilt, castration anxiety, of course, may motivate any child to be careful (i.e., fearful) for the safety of his body. But when not under the influence of these, normal children will be remarkably uncompromising and obstructive in health matters. According to their mothers' frequent complaints, they behave as if they claimed it as their right to endanger their health while they left it to the mother to protect and restore it, an attitude which lasts often until the end of adolescence and may represent the last residue of the original symbiosis between child and mother.

[4] Such remnants should not be confused with the later "turning of aggression against the self" which is not a defect in maturation but a defense mechanism used by the ego under the impact of conflict.

Further Examples of Developmental Lines

There are many other examples of developmental lines, such as the two given below, where every step is known to the analyst, and which can be traced without difficulty, either through working backward by reconstruction from the adult picture, or through working forward by means of longitudinal analytic exploration and observation of the child.

The Line from Egocentricity to Companionship

When one describes a child's growth in this particular respect, a sequence can be traced which runs as follows:

(1) a selfish, narcissistically orientated outlook on the object world, in which other children either do not figure at all or are perceived only in their role as disturbers of the mother-child relationship and rivals for the parents' love;
(2) other children related to as lifeless objects, i.e., toys which can be handled, pushed around, sought out, and discarded as the mood demands, with no positive or negative response expected from them;
(3) other children related to as helpmates in carrying out a desired task such as playing, building, destroying, causing mischief of some kind, etc., the duration of the partnership being determined by the task, and secondary to it;
(4) other children as partners and objects in their own right, whom the child can admire, fear, or compete with, whom he loves or hates, with whose feelings he identifies, whose wishes he acknowledges and often respects, and with whom he can share possessions on a basis of equality.

In the first two phases, even if cherished and tolerated as the baby by older siblings, the toddler is by necessity asocial, whatever efforts to the contrary the mother may make; community life at this stage may be endured but will not be profitable. The third stage represents the minimum requirement for socialization in the form of acceptance into a home community of older siblings or entry into a nursery group of contemporaries. But it is only the fourth stage which equips the child for companionship, enmities and friendships of any type and duration.

The Line from the Body to the Toy and from Play to Work

(1) Play begins with the infant as an activity yielding erotic pleasure, involving the mouth, the fingers, vision, the whole surface of the skin. It is carried out on the child's own body (autoerotic play) or on the mother's body (usually in connection with feeding) with no clear distinction between the two, and with no obvious order or precedence in this respect.

(2) The properties of the mother's and the child's body are transferred to some soft substance, such as a nappy, a pillow, a rug, a teddy, which serves as the infant's first plaything, the "transitional object" (according to Winnicott, 1953) which is cathected both with narcissistic and with object libido.

(3) Clinging to one specific transitional object develops further into a more indiscriminate liking for soft toys of various kinds which, as symbolic objects, are cuddled and maltreated alternately (cathected with libido and aggression). That they are inanimate objects, and therefore do not retaliate, enables the toddler to express the full range of his ambivalence toward them.

(4) Cuddly toys fade out gradually, except at bedtime, when—in their capacity as transitional objects—they continue to facilitate the child's passing from active participation in the external world to the narcissistic withdrawal necessary for sleep.

In daytime their place is taken increasingly by play material which does not itself possess object status but which serves ego activities and the fantasies underlying them. Such activities either directly gratify a component instinct or are invested with displaced and sublimated drive energies, their chronological sequence being approximately the following:

(a) toys offering opportunities for ego activities such as filling-emptying, opening-shutting, fitting in, messing, etc., interest in them being displaced from the body openings and their functions;
(b) movable toys providing pleasure in motility;

(c) building material offering equal opportunities for construction and destruction (in correspondence with the ambivalent trends of the anal-sadistic phase);

(d) toys serving the expression of masculine and feminine trends and attitudes, to be used

  (i) in solitary role play,

  (ii) for display to the oedipal object (serving phallic exhibitionism),

  (iii) for staging the various situations of the oedipus complex in group play (provided that stage 3 on the developmental line toward companionship has been reached).

Expression of masculinity can be taken over also by the ego activities of gymnastics and acrobatics, in which the child's entire body and its skillful manipulation represent, display, and provide symbolic enjoyment from phallic activities and phallic mastery.

(5) Direct or displaced satisfaction from the play activity itself gives way increasingly to the pleasure in the finished product of the activity, a pleasure which has been described in academic psychology as pleasure in task completion, in problem solving, etc. By some authors it is taken as the indispensable prerequisite for the child's successful performance in school (Bühler, 1935).

The exact manner in which this pleasure in achievement is linked with the child's instinctual life is an open question still in our theoretical thinking, although various operative factors seem unmistakable such as imitation and identification in the early mother-child relationship, the influence of the ego ideal, the turning of passive into active as a mechanism of defense and adaptation, and the inner urge toward maturation, i.e., toward progressive development.

That pleasure in achievement, linked only secondarily with object relations, is present in very young children as a latent capacity is demonstrated in a practical manner by the successes of the Montessori method. In this nursery-school method the play material is selected so as to afford the child the maximum increase in self-esteem and gratification by means of task completion and independent problem solving, and children can be observed to respond positively to such opportunities almost from the toddler stage onward.

Where this source of gratification is not tapped to the same degree with the help of external arrangements, the pleasure derived from achievement in play remains more directly connected with praise and approval given by the object world, and satisfaction from the finished product takes first place at a later date only, probably as the result of internalization of external sources of self-esteem.

(6) Ability to play changes into ability to *work*[5] when a number of additional faculties are acquired, such as the following:

(a) to control, inhibit, or modify the impulses to use given material aggressively and destructively (not to throw, to take apart, to mess, to hoard), and to use them positively and constructively instead (to build, to plan, to learn, and—in communal life—to share);

(b) to carry out preconceived plans with a minimum regard for the lack of immediate pleasure yield, intervening frustrations, etc., and the maximum regard for the pleasure in the ultimate outcome;

(c) to achieve thereby not only the transition from primitive instinctual to sublimated pleasure, together with a high grade of neutralization of the energy employed, but equally the transition from the pleasure principle to the reality principle, a development which is essential for success in work during latency, adolescence, and in maturity.

Derived from the line from the body to the toy and from play to work and based predominantly on its later stages are a number of allied activities which are significant for personality development such as daydreaming, games, and hobbies.

Daydreaming

When toys and the activities connected with them fade into the background, the wishes formerly put into action with the help of material objects, i.e., fulfilled in play, can be spun out imaginatively

[5] What is attempted here is not a definition of work with all its social as well as psychological implications, but merely a description of the advances in ego development and drive control which seem to be the necessary forerunners of any individual's acquisition of the capacity to work.

in the form of conscious daydreams, a fantasy activity which may persist until adolescence, and far beyond it.

Games

Games derive their origin from the imaginative group activities of the oedipal period (see stage 4, d, iii) from which they develop into the symbolic and highly formalized expression of trends toward aggressive attack, defense, competition, etc. Since they are governed by inflexible rules to which the individual participant has to submit, they cannot be entered successfully by any child before some adaptation to reality and some frustration tolerance have been acquired and, naturally, not before stage 3 on the developmental line toward companionship has been reached.

Games may require equipment (as distinct from toys). Since this is in many instances of symbolic phallic, i.e., masculine-aggressive, significance, it is highly valued by the child.

In many competitive games the child's own body and the body skills in themselves play the role of indispensable tools.

Proficiency and pleasure in games are, thus, a complex achievement, dependent on contributions from many areas of the child's personality such as the endowment and intactness of the motor apparatus; a positive cathexis of the body and its skills; acceptance of companionship and group life; positive employment of controlled aggression in the service of ambition, etc. Correspondingly, functioning in this area is open to an equally large number of disturbances which may result from developmental difficulties and inadequacies in any of these areas, as well as from the phase-determined inhibitions of anal aggression and phallic-oedipal masculinity.

Hobbies

Halfway between play and work is the place of the hobbies, which have certain aspects in common with both activities. With play they share a number of characteristics:

(a) of being undertaken for purposes of pleasure with comparative disregard for external pressures and necessities;
(b) of pursuing displaced, i.e., sublimated, aims, but aims which are not too far removed from the gratification of either erotic or aggressive drives;

(c) of pursuing these aims with a combination of unmodified drive energies plus energies in various states and degrees of neutralization.

With working attitudes as described above, the hobbies share the important feature of a preconceived plan being undertaken in a reality-adapted way and carried on over a considerable period of time if necessary in the face of external difficulties and frustrations.

Hobbies appear for the first time at the beginning of the latency period (collecting, spotting, specializing of interests), undergo any number of changes of content, but may persist as this specific form of activity throughout life.

Correspondence between Developmental Lines

If we examine our notions of average normality in detail, we find that we expect a fairly close correspondence between growth on the individual developmental lines. In clinical terms this means that, to be a harmonious personality, a child who has reached a specific stage in the sequence toward emotional maturity (for example, object constancy), should have attained also corresponding levels in his growth toward bodily independence (such as bladder and bowel control, loosening of the tie between food and mother), in the lines toward companionship, constructive play, etc. We maintain this expectation of a norm even though reality presents us with many examples to the contrary. There are numerous children, undoubtedly, who show a very irregular pattern in their growth. They may stand high on some levels (such as maturity of emotional relations, bodily independence, etc.) while lagging behind in others (such as play where they continue to cling to transitional objects, cuddly toys, or development of companionship where they persist in treating contemporaries as disturbances or inanimate objects). Some children are well developed toward secondary thought, speech, play, work, community life while remaining in a state of dependency with regard to the management of their own bodily processes, etc.

Such imbalance between developmental lines causes sufficient friction in childhood to justify a closer inquiry into the circumstances which give rise to it, especially into the question how far it is determined by innate and how far by environmental reasons.

As in all similar instances, our task is not to isolate the two factors and to ascribe to each a separate field of influence but to trace their interactions, which may be described as follows in the present case:

We assume that with all normally endowed, organically undamaged children the lines of development indicated above are included in their constitution as inherent possibilities. What endowment lays down for them on the side of the id are, obviously, the maturational sequences in the development of libido and aggression; on the side of the ego, less obviously and less well studied, certain innate tendencies toward organization, defense, and structuralization; perhaps also, though we know less still about this, some given quantitative differences of emphasis on progress in one direction or another. For the rest, that is, for what singles out individual lines for special promotion in development, we have to look to accidental environmental influences. In the analysis of older children and the reconstructions from adult analysis we have found these forces embodied in the parents' personalities, their actions and ideals, the family atmosphere, the impact of the cultural setting as a whole. In the analytic observation of young infants it has been demonstrated that it is the individual mother's interest and predilection which act as stimulants. In the beginning of life, at least, the infant seems to concentrate on development along those lines which call forth most ostensibly the mother's love and approval, i.e., her spontaneous pleasure in the child's achievement and, in comparison, to neglect others where such approval is not given. This implies that activities which are acclaimed by the mother are repeated more frequently, become libidinized, and thereby stimulated into further growth.

For example, it seems to make a difference to the timing of speech development and the quality of early verbalization if a mother, for reasons of her own personality structure, makes contact with her infant not through bodily channels but through talking. Some mothers find no pleasure in the growing infant's adventurousness and bodily unruliness and have their happiest and most intimate moments when the infant smiles. We have seen at least one such mother whose infant made constant and inordinate use of smiling in his approaches to the whole environment. It is not unknown that early contact with the mother through her singing has consequences for the later attitudes to music and may promote special musical aptitudes. On the other hand, marked disinterest of the mother in the infant's body and his developing motility may result in clumsiness, lack of grace in movement, etc.

It has been known in psychoanalysis long before such infant observations that depressive moods of the mother during the first two years after birth create in the child a tendency to depression (although this may not manifest itself until many years later). What happens is that such infants achieve their sense of unity and harmony with the depressed mother not by means of their developmental achievements but by producing the mother's mood in themselves.

All this means no more than that tendencies, inclinations, predilections (including the tendency to depression, to masochistic attitudes, etc.) which are present in all human beings can be eroticized and stimulated toward growth through forming emotional links between the child and his first object.

The disequilibrium between developmental lines which is created in this manner is not pathological as such, though it becomes a pathogenic agent where the imbalance is excessive. Moderate disharmony does no more than produce the many *variations of normality* with which we have to count.

3

THE SYMPTOMATOLOGY OF CHILDHOOD

A Preliminary Attempt at Classification

ANNA FREUD, LL.D., D.Sc., M.D.

(1970)

The Misleading Quality of Manifest Symptomatology

Analysts have always been proud of the distinction that theirs is a causal therapy, aiming directly at the conflicts and stresses which are hidden in the patients' personalities and underlie their symptomatology. Inevitably, with this approach they find themselves at cross-purposes with many of the adult neurotics under analysis who are intent only on being relieved of the suffering caused by painful anxieties and crippling obsessions, and who regard these as the only logical starting point for investigation; or with the parents of child patients who are concerned only with removing the disturbing manifestations in the child and completely disregard the pathological turn in the child's development which is revealed by the disturbances that trouble them.

Naturally, neither the adult neurotics themselves nor the parents of these endangered children possess the analyst's knowledge of the deceiving nature of overt symptomatology. They lack the experience of how quickly anxieties can be shifted from one apparently all-important object to another; or how easily one particular compulsion can be substituted for by a different one. Therefore, they cannot appreciate that symptoms are no more than symbols, to be taken merely as indications that some mental turmoil is taking place in the lower strata of the mind. Many symptoms, important and unassailable as they seem if untreated, give way fairly easily to many types of therapy. But if they are removed by measures which do not reach to their roots, their place may be taken almost instantaneously by other pathological formations which, although overtly different, express the same latent content and may be no less aggravating for the individual's life.

On the other hand, symptoms are negligible in the analyst's view only for the purposes of the technique of therapy; in their eyes, too, symptoms have retained full significance so far as diagnostic classification is concerned. Whether a patient is assessed as a hysteric or phobic subject, as suffering from an obsessional neurosis or a paranoid state, is decided wholly on the basis of his manifest symptomatology, i.e., on the overt evidence of bodily conversions, anxiety attacks, avoidance mechanisms, compulsive acts, ruminations, projections, etc.

There is an incongruity here between the analyst's therapeutic thinking, which is metapsychological, i.e., directed toward the dynamic, economic, genetic, and structural aspects of psychic functioning, and his thinking as a diagnostician, which proceeds on the basis of concepts and categories which are descriptive.[1] The difference between these viewpoints is so fundamental that it has caused many analysts to withdraw their interest altogether from diagnostic assessment as from an area which is neither essential nor very significant for their field of work, and has caused some others to regard all their patients' abnormalities as mere variations of the many vagaries and complexities of human behavior.[2]

But before subscribing to a diagnostic nihilism of this extreme kind, the attempt seems worthwhile to bridge the gap between the two contrasting approaches and to use the vast array of overt symptoms themselves for the purpose of forging links between them. There is no reason, after all, why the very classification of symptomatology should not go beyond enumeration and description and why probing into dynamic clashes and genetic antecedents should be ex-

1 Or, at best, on the basis of unconscious content converted into conscious symbols.

2 An outstanding example of the latter is Karl Menninger who is known to condemn all psychiatric labels and classifications as unjustified offenses against the patient's human dignity, i.e., as "name-calling."

cluded from it, to be reserved for scrutiny within the analytic procedure. It is inevitable, of course, that such a different mode of classification will sacrifice the neatness and order of any system based on phenomenology. It is only to be expected that in many instances there will be no one-to-one correlation between underlying unconscious constellation and manifest symptom. The former, as shown in Part I of this paper, can give rise to a variety of manifestations; the latter, as demonstrated in Part II, are the result of a variety of causes. Far from this being confusing for the analyst, it can only help to sharpen his diagnostic acumen.

When one is dealing with the psychopathology of childhood, a descriptive survey of symptomatology is even less rewarding. As is well known, in the immature personality, isolated symptoms are no reliable guide to any specific type of underlying pathology, nor are they a measure of its severity. Symptoms may be no more than the child's answer to some developmental stress and as such transitory, i.e., liable to pass away together with the maturational phase which has given rise to them. Or symptoms may represent a permanent countercathexis against some threatening drive derivative and as such be crippling to further development. Or symptoms, though pathological in origin, may nevertheless be ego-syntonic, and merged with the structure of the child's personality to a degree which makes it difficult to distinguish between such manifestations as outward evidence of ongoing pathological involvement or as more or less normal, stable features of the individual's character. There is no doubt that in any classification system based on phenomenology, these widely different classes of symptom appear as if on a par.

Moreover, if we scrutinize what children's clinics list under the heading of "referral symptoms," we feel doubtful whether in all instances these manifestations deserve to be classified as symptomatology, or whether the meaning of the term "symptom" is not extended here beyond its proper use. What is grouped together in such surveys are on the one hand the true signs or residues of present or past pathological processes; on the other hand such complaints by parents and disruptions of the child's life as, for example, multiplicity of fears; disturbances of intake, digestion, and elimination; sleep, respiratory or skin disturbances; aches and pains, motor disturbances; unusual sexual behavior; self-injurious acts and habits; disturbances of mood, affect, and object relatedness; failure of learning processes and/or poor quality of other ego functions; behavior disorders including antisocial reactions; moral indifference; failures of adaptation; failure to comply with parental demands or to fulfill parental expectation in general; etc.

Although an enumeration of this kind promises a first orientation in the field, and seems to satisfy the clinicians' immediate need at the stage of intake of cases, what it does, in fact, is to defeat its own purpose. By remaining strictly on the descriptive level, regardless of genetic roots, dynamic, structural, and economic complications, such an initial approach discourages analytic thinking and blocks the road to diagnostic assessment proper instead of facilitating it. Last but not least, it provides no clue for the diagnostician with regard to the choice of adequate therapeutic method.[3]

There is no warning implied in such a phenomenological survey that many of the items listed in it may belong genetically to any one of two, three, or more analytic categories. A *behavior disorder,* such as lying, for example, may be rooted in the child's stage of ego development, i.e., express the immature individual's inability to distinguish between reality and fantasy, or may signify a delay in acquiring and perfecting this important ego function. But, equally, lying may betray the level and quality of the child's object relations and express his fear of punishment and loss of love. As fantasy lying it may be evidence of persistent denial of unpalatable realities, with the function of reality testing fundamentally intact. As a feature of the child's character, it may denote weakness or failure of superego function.[4]

Disturbance of elimination such as extreme withholding of feces may have its roots in a very early vulnerability of the digestive system (i.e., psychosomatic); or it may be symbolic of the child's imitation of and identification with a pregnant mother (hysterical); or it may signify his revolt against inappropriate forms of toilet training (behavioral); or it may express phallic sexual needs and fantasies on a regressed anal level (obsessional).

Similarly, *enuresis* may be the sign either of simple failure of

[3] This may be the explanation why many clinics for children provide only one type of treatment, i.e., once weekly psychotherapy.

[4] See also Hedy Schwarz, "On Lying" (unpublished manuscript).

control in a generally impulsive personality structure,[5] or a highly complex reaction on the level of penis envy and castration anxiety. *Learning failures* may point to developmental arrest or, conversely, to blocking and inhibitions interfering with basically intact intellectual functions. *Antisocial reactions*, such as aggressive outbursts, may be the mark of defusion or insufficient fusion between libido and aggression; or of insufficient control of drives in an impulsive character; or of a violent defensive reaction against underlying passive-feminine leanings in boys striving overtly for masculinity.

In short, manifest symptoms may be identical so far as their appearance is concerned, but may differ widely in respect to latent meaning and pathological significance. According to the latter, they may require very different types of therapeutic handling.

Ideally, the solution for the analytic clinician in the children's field is a classification of symptoms which, on the one hand, embodies consideration of the various metapsychological aspects, while, on the other hand, maintains links with and pointers to the descriptive diagnostic categories as they are in common use. It is obvious nevertheless that no complex system of this kind will lend itself to the quick, almost automatic application to which diagnosticians are used so long as they remain within the framework of phenomenology. What is needed to make such a new classification of symptomatology profitable is, already at the diagnostic stage, a thorough investigation of the child's personality which makes it possible to pinpoint each symptom's relevance with regard to developmental level, structure, dynamic significance, etc.

I. Symptomatology Proper

As indicated above, for a first attempt of ordering the clinical material, it seems useful to separate symptoms, in the narrow sense of the term, from other signs of disturbance and other reasons for a child's referral for diagnosis and treatment. In this restricted field it becomes more possible to survey the relevant range of pathological processes and to correlate them with the various forms of mental illness which correspond to them.

[5] See J. J. Michaels (1955).

1. SYMPTOMS RESULTING FROM INITIAL NONDIFFERENTIATION BETWEEN SOMATIC AND PSYCHOLOGICAL PROCESSES: PSYCHOSOMATICS

At the beginning of life, before somatic and psychological processes are separated off from each other, bodily excitations such as hunger, cold, pain, etc., are discharged as easily via mental pathways in the form of unpleasure, anxiety, anger, rage, as mental upsets of any kind are discharged via disturbances of the body surface, of intake, digestion, elimination, breathing, etc. Such "psychosomatic" reactions are developmentally determined at this time of life. It is important for later events which particular bodily outlets are given preference by the individual since this choice gives rise to increased sensitivity and vulnerability in the organ system concerned, i.e., the skin, the respiratory system, the intestinal system, the sleep rhythm, etc.

Normally, this easy access from mind to body (and vice versa) diminishes with advancing ego development and the opening up of new, purely mental pathways of discharge by means of action, thought, speech. Where it remains more than usually open, on the other hand, it accounts directly for the range of *psychosomatic symptomatology,* i.e., for *asthma, eczema, ulcerative colitis, headaches, migraine,* etc.

It is also responsible for the creation of the so-called "somatic compliance" which, in later and more complex hysterical symptom formation, facilitates the conversion of mental processes into physical manifestations with symbolic meaning.

2. SYMPTOMS RESULTING FROM COMPROMISE FORMATIONS BETWEEN ID AND EGO: NEUROTIC SYMPTOMATOLOGY

Since basic psychoanalytic training takes place in the area of theory and therapy of the neuroses, analysts feel most knowledgeable about the specific structure of neurotic symptomatology. In fact, so far as the neuroses are concerned, the term "symptom" has become synonymous with the conception of the ego acting as intermediary and finding solutions for the clashes between drive derivatives on the one hand and other, rational or moral, claims of the individual on the other hand. The complex route of symptom formation along a line of danger-anxiety-regression-defense-compromise has become familiar.

The resulting symptomatic structures may prove ego-dystonic and continue to produce mental pain and discomfort; or they may be accepted as ego-syntonic and become part of the individual's character. The latter outcome depends largely on economic factors, i.e., on the varying degrees to which elements from id, ego, and superego sides are embodied in the final symptomatic result. It depends also on the ego's willingness to become distorted itself by accommodating the pathological manifestation within its structure. This last-mentioned solution, not to treat the symptoms as a foreign body, is one often adopted by children.

Since compromise formations of this kind depend for their existence on established boundaries between id and ego, unconscious and conscious, we do not expect to find neurotic symptoms in the unstructured personality, i.e., in early infancy. Neurotic symptom formation waits until the ego has divided itself off from the id, but does not need to wait until ego and superego also have become two independent agencies. The first id-ego conflicts, and with them the first neurotic symptoms as conflict solutions, are produced with the ego under pressure from the environment, i.e., threatened not by guilt feelings arising internally from the superego but by dangers arising from the object world such as loss of love, rejection, punishment.

The neurotic manifestations of this phase are *hysterical* in nature so far as the body areas involved have oral or oral-aggressive value and the symptom implies a primitive defense against these drive representatives (*affection of single limbs, motor disturbances, aches and pains, food fads and avoidances, vomiting*). They are *obsessional* in nature so far as they defend against anal-sadistic strivings (first appearance of *compulsive cleanliness, orderliness, repetitiveness, avoidance of touch*).

With the emergence and dissolution of the phallic-oedipal strivings and the superego as an independent source of guilt these isolated symptoms become organized into the syndromes which form the familiar infantile neuroses, i.e., the full-blown *phobias* (of animals, of separation, of doctor, dentist, of the lavatory, of school, etc.) as well as the true *obsessional neuroses,* complete with *doubting, repeating, rituals,* bedtime *ceremonials, ruminations, compulsive ac-*

tions. Crippling *inhibitions, ego restrictions,* and *self-injurious tendencies* appear as character defenses against aggression at this time.

3. SYMPTOMS RESULTING FROM THE IRRUPTION OF ID DERIVATIVES INTO THE EGO

Neurotic symptomatology comes about only where the border between id and ego is intact. This may be lacking for a variety of reasons: the ego may be constitutionally weak; or the id strivings may be constitutionally increased in intensity; damage may have been done to the ego through traumatic events which have put it out of action; or through phase-determined alterations of the inner equilibrium. In any case, the result will be failure to control id content and the entrance of id elements into the ego organization, with disruptive consequences for the latter.

Where the irrupting elements are part of primary process functioning and take the place of the rational secondary process thinking which is characteristic for the ego otherwise, the corresponding manifest symptoms such as *disturbances of thought and language, misidentifications, delusions,* etc., are significant for the differential diagnosis between neurosis and psychosis; if only partially in evidence, they are a hallmark of the borderline states between the two diagnostic categories.

Where the irrupting elements are from the area of the drives, the resulting symptoms consist of the *undefended* (or unsuccessfully defended) *acting out of drive derivatives* with disregard for reality considerations which is characteristic for certain types of delinquency and criminality.

The combination of both leakages from the id produces those ominous types of abnormal behavior which on the one hand carry the individual beyond the confines of what is legally permissible and, on the other hand, characterize him as mentally ill and for this reason absolved from responsibility for his actions.

4. SYMPTOMS RESULTING FROM CHANGES IN THE LIBIDO ECONOMY OR DIRECTION OF CATHEXIS

Although all symptom formation implies pathological upsets to the dynamics and structural aspects of the personality, these may be secondary to alterations in the economy of the libido and the direction of its employment.

Where, for example, the narcissistic cathexis of the self is increased unduly, the corresponding symptomatic results are *egotism, self-centeredness, overvaluation* of the self, in extreme cases *megalomania*. Where such cathexis is decreased unduly, the symptoms are *bodily neglect*, *self-derogation*, *inferiority feelings*, *depressive states*, *depersonalization* (in childhood).

Direction of cathexis may be altered in three respects with corresponding symptomatology. Narcissistic libido may move from the individual's mind to his body, where the increased cathexis of specific body parts creates *hypochrondriacal* symptoms. Object libido may be withdrawn from the external world, changed into narcissistic libido, and employed wholly in cathexis of the self. Or, conversely, all narcissistic libido may be added to the existing object libido and become concentrated on an external love object with consequences for its overvaluation; in extreme cases for complete *emotional surrender* to it.

5. SYMPTOMS RESULTING FROM CHANGES IN THE QUALITY OR DIRECTION OF AGGRESSION

What is significant for symptomatology in this respect are the changes in intensity as well as the frequent changes in aim direction, from mind to body, from self to object, and vice versa.

The former, the quantitative changes, are brought about mainly by the vagaries within the defense organization, in childhood by the varying quality of the defense mechanisms which are employed, from crudely primitive to highly sophisticated. These decide about the availability or nonavailability of the necessary aggressive contributions to ego functioning and to sublimations. Some of the resulting symptomatic manifestations are *inhibitions* and *failure* in play, learning, and work.

The type of defense used against aggression is also responsible for the swings between *self-injuriors behavior,* which corresponds to aggression turned against the self, and violent *aggressive-destructive outbursts* against animate and inanimate objects in the environment.

6. SYMPTOMS RESULTING FROM UNDEFENDED REGRESSIONS

In our work with children we have become alerted to a type of pathological manifestation which equals a prestage of neurotic symptom formation, but remains abortive so far as the infantile neuroses are concerned. Its point of origin is the phallic phase, its precipitating cause is danger and anxiety arising from the oedipus and castration complexes, followed by regression to oral and anal fixation points.

While in neurotic symptom formation such regressions are rejected by the ego and defended against, in these cases they are accepted and treated as ego-syntonic, i.e., they do not give rise to further conflict. The result is a lowering of all aspects of the personality (drive activity as well as ego functioning). The clinical pictures which correspond to this are *infantilism* and a form of *pseudodebility*, accompanied by behavioral symptoms such as *whining, clinging,* prolonged *dependency, passive-feminine traits* in boys, *inefficiency,* etc.

7. SYMPTOMS RESULTING FROM ORGANIC CAUSES

The foregoing enumeration leaves to the last those disturbances of psychic function which have an organic origin such as brain damage due to prenatal influences or to birth injury or to later inflammatory processes or to traumatic accidents. A whole range of symptoms is attributable to these causes such as a *delay in developmental milestones, difficulties in locomotion,* difficulties with *speech, poor* quality of *intellectual functions, interference with concentration, flatness or lability of affect, distractability,* etc. Many of these symptoms bear a close resemblance to the result of inhibitions, compromise formations, or any other of the categories described above, and the correct diagnosis is difficult in those cases where the neurological tests prove inconclusive. Doubtless, mistakes in differential diagnosis occur here in both directions, either mental or organic damage being discounted unjustifiably, or a combination between the two factors being overlooked.

What should also be added here are those symptomatic manifestations or deviations from the norm which are the direct or indirect consequence of physical handicaps, whether inborn or acquired ones. It is well known by now that where vision is missing, ego development is thrown into confusion, the balance between autoerotism and object relatedness disturbed, aggression inhibited, passivity enhanced, etc. Where hearing is absent or grossly defective, not only speech development but secondary process thinking and, with it, higher development of the personality are interfered with. Missing limbs, spasticity bring with them their own psychopathology which needs to be explored further.

II. Other Signs of Disturbance and Other Reasons for a Child's Clinical Referral

As discussed before, not all the manifestations which lead to a child's clinical examination are evidence of true pathology, nor do they all form part of recognized clinical pictures. There are other disturbances, upsets, and malfunctions, and, consequently, other reasons for referral. What they all have in common is that they represent interferences with normal processes, with adequate growth and development, with reasonable behavior, with contentment and enjoyment of life, with adaptation to environmental conditions and requirements. Since the causes for them are diffuse, and the same overt manifestation may be due to a variety of underlying constellations, the attempt seems justified to approach their classification from a different angle. The method adopted before consisted of following certain psychic processes ongoing in the depth to their various expressions on the surface of the mind. The procedure applied to what follows is the opposite one, namely, to start out from the surface signs of disturbance and, from there, to trace back the links to whichever upheaval, involvement or failure may be responsible for them.

1. The Fears and Anxieties

The mere number of children who are referred to clinics with fears and anxieties of all kinds and intensities justifies the attempt to classify these manifestations as such, i.e., apart from the active role which they play in the formation of a variety of clinical syndromes.

It is well known to analysts, of course, that anxiety, experienced by the ego, is a regular accompaniment to development in childhood, occasioned on the one hand by the helplessness of the immature being, on the other hand by structuralization, higher development, and the resultant rising tension between the inner agencies. Its absence rather than its presence in the picture is considered as an ominous sign. Nevertheless, even though anxiety is normal and the disturbance in many instances no more than a quantitative exacerbation of expectable reactions, anxiety states remain one of the most common and potent causes of suffering in childhood.

To arrive at their understanding, these manifestations have to be viewed from a number of angles. For example, their classification can be, and has been, attempted from the *developmental* point of view, by creating a chronological sequence according to which the common fears and anxieties are allocated to the various instinctual phases in which they arise and, connected with these, the external or internal dangers toward which they are directed. Classification has also been carried out from the aspect of *dynamic* vicissitude, i.e., from the side of the defenses employed to keep fear and anxiety in check, and the *economic* factors which determine the success or failure of these coping mechanisms. What has been done most frequently by analytic authors, without doubt, is to explore the role played by the various kinds of anxiety in *structural* conflict and the responsibility which has to be ascribed to them for the swings between mental health and illness since it is at their instigation that the ego's defensive mechanisms and, following on them, the ego's compromises with the id are put into action.

Obviously, it is the diagnostician's task to explore each of these avenues in greater detail.

(i) *The Chronology of Fears and Anxieties*

Where the clinician arrives at ordering the child's manifest fears and anxieties according to the developmental stages in which they arise and according to the dangers represented by these stages, many of the quantitative increases in them can be understood as due to unsatisfied developmental needs or to unjustifiable developmental interferences (see Nagera, 1966).

The initial stages of ego development, in this view, become correlated with the so-called *archaic fears* of the infant. These are inevitable while the ego has no resources of its own to cope either with the massive stimuli which arrive from the environment or with the equally disturbing tensions in the inner world. These fears increase in intensity and range when a child's ego is unusually sensitive or when a child's mother is unusually unable to provide the comfort and reassurance to which the infant is entitled at this stage. Where ego development is slow, the archaic fears last beyond infancy. Their undue persistence and prominence can be taken as diagnostic indicators for retardation or arrest in the area of ego functioning.

The symbiotic stage, i.e., the phase of biological unity between infant and mother, is relevant for the arousal of *separation anxiety,* i.e., fear of object loss, whenever this unity is threatened. Separation anxiety becomes overwhelming if the infant experiences actual separations from the mother, or if in other ways the mother proves unreliable as a stable object. Separation anxiety can be prolonged unduly, which points diagnostically to fixation in the symbiotic phase or arrests in it.[6]

When the parental objects become representatives of the demand for drive control, the child's difficulty of complying with this arouses *fear of rejection* by the object and fear of the loss of the object's love. As such, these fears are signs of beginning moral adjustment and positive prestages of superego development; their nonemergence points to developmental failure in these respects. They become excessive for environmental reasons if the parents commit errors in either the timing or the harshness of their demands. But even where no blame can be attached to the environment in this respect, oversensitivity of the ego or excessive dependency on being loved can bring about the same result for internal reasons.

The arrival of a boy in the phallic phase, which as such is a welcome event, commonly reveals itself at the same time in a heightened fear for the intactness of his sex organ, i.e., in *castration anxiety*. The frequent exacerbations of this correspond directly to the strivings of the oedipus complex and depend on the defenses and compromise formations which the ego employs to deal with them. Castration

[6] There are fears of object loss in later childhood which manifest themselves as difficulties in separating from the parental objects, especially the mother. Although phenomenologically identical, they are different in dynamic and structural respects, i.e., due to internal rejection of aggression and death wishes directed against the parents.

anxiety represents a specific threat for development owing to the drive regressions initiated by it and their further role for neurosis and character formation.

The child's first moves from family to community and his new dependency on the opinions of his peers give rise to an additional *fear,* that of *social disgrace,* which is especially experienced in school.

According to the individual child's structural development, i.e., with the establishment of the superego's independence and authority (whenever this happens), the advance from anxiety to *guilt* is made as the crowning step in this chronology of infantile fears.

Obviously, such a chronology of fears and anxieties is helpful as a diagnostic tool since observation of the presenting disturbance leads directly to the corresponding phase of development in which the child's mental upset is rooted. Nevertheless, it fails to serve the diagnostician in other respects, since it does not include an important anxiety which neither originates in any particular phase nor bears the characteristics of any one, but persists through the whole period of development and reappears at all times of later life, not for reasons of fixation or regression but whenever the inner structural balance is upset. This anxiety denotes the ego's concern for the intactness of its own organization, at whatever level; it is due to economic reasons, i.e., to the uneven distribution of energy between id and ego; and it gains in intensity whenever the strength of the drive derivatives increases or ego strength diminishes for some reason.

In contrast to other anxieties, this *fear of the id* is not favorably influenced by the lightening of external pressure. Much to the parents' disappointment, it is increased rather than decreased by excessive educational leniency or by educational nihilism.

When fear of the id is more than usually in evidence, it arouses the diagnostic suspicion of a borderline or prepsychotic state.

(ii) *The Manifest and Latent Content of Fears and Anxieties*

While in these childhood cases described, the affect of anxiety is manifest and brought directly to the clinician's notice, the latent meaning of the fear is obscured by the fact that almost any type of anxiety can find symbolic expression in almost any mental representation, or can remain free-floating and unattached. Nevertheless, in most instances it is possible to correlate fear and symbol as follows:

Archaic fears:	of darkness, noise, strangers, solitude, etc.
separation anxiety:	of annihiliation, starvation, loneliness, helplessness, etc.
fear of loss of love:	of punishment, rejection, desertion, earth quakes, thunderstorms, death, etc.
castration anxiety:	of operation, mutilation, doctor, dentist, illness, poverty, robbers, witches, ghosts, etc.

On the whole, these symbols are also interchangeable and, by themselves, an insufficient guide to diagnosis.

(iii) *Defense against Anxiety, Absence of Defense, Its Role within the Structure*

So far as a classification of the various fates of anxieties is concerned, the study of childhood cases is more productive than that of adult ones since the defensive moves against anxiety are more often incomplete, i.e., partly unsuccessful. This allows both sides to be visible on the conscious surface, on the one hand the manifest expression of the anxiety affect, on the other hand the ego's attempts to deal with the danger situations and their affective consequences by means of denial or avoidance, displacement or projection, repression, reaction formation, or any other available defense mechanism or defensive move, or a combination of several of them.

There is also the possibility for defense against anxiety to be lacking altogether, or to be wholly unsuccessful, in which case the affect reigns supreme in the form of *panic states* and full-blown *anxiety attacks*.[7] The occurrence of these is indicative that the child's ego has failed to acquire the important ability to reduce harmful panic anxiety to structurally useful signal anxiety, i.e., to the much smaller amount which is necessary to set defense in motion. Panics and anxiety attacks are not only extremely painful for the total personality of the child, they are, in fact, actually harmful for the

[7] For the clinician it is important to differentiate between such states and the common temper tantrums of childhood, which are manifestly similar but different as regards origin.

ego which is swamped by them. Similar to true traumatic events, they temporarily put ego functioning out of action and thereby constitute a threat to the stability of the ego organization.

Classification of anxiety according to defense activity also provides clues for predicting the direction in which the child's further course is set: toward more or less normal adjustment; toward social or dissocial character formation; toward hysterical, or phobic, or obsessional or paranoid symptom formation or character development, etc.

2. THE DELAYS OR FAILURES IN DEVELOPMENT

It is well known by now that the developmental age of a child does not need to coincide with his chronological age and that fairly wide discrepancies in this respect are within the normal range. Children may be either fast or slow developers throughout. One also frequently sees that they change their rate of growing between one developmental phase and the succeeding one.

Nevertheless, a large number of children arrive in the clinic with the "referral symptoms" of unsatisfactory development, which, on clinical examination, may be found to range from the merest delay to the complete cessation of all forward movement on the lines of progress. A child's failure to reach the expected level of growth may show up anywhere within the structure of his personality. It may concern the so-called milestones in the first year of life, i.e., the advances in motor development, the beginning of speech, etc. On the side of the drives it may concern a lagging behind on the prephallic libidinal and aggressive stages, in extreme instances a failure to reach the phallic-oedipal level at all. So far as the ego is concerned, the arrest may reveal itself in the quality of object relatedness, for example, in the persistence of anaclitic relationships at a time of life when object constancy is to be expected; or in the retardation of functions such as control of motility, reality testing, memory, learning capacity which remain below par; or in the defense organization which may remain at a primitive level of functioning via somatization, denial, projection, avoidance, etc., instead of advancing to repression, reaction formations, and sublimations. The superego may be retarded either with respect to its autonomy, or its effectiveness, or with regard to the quality of its content, i.e., the crudeness of the internalized commands and prohibitions.

Developmental irregularities and failures of this kind confront the clinician with many problems, foremost among them the need to differentiate between the causes for them. Retardation of milestones in the first year of life raises the suspicion of *organic* damage (see Part I, 7). Delay in drive development may either be due to *constitutional* factors or may be determined *environmentally* by inadequate response from the parental objects. Ego retardation is frequently due to poor *endowment* but, as the study of many underprivileged children has revealed, equally often the consequence of lack of proper *environmental* stimulation. Arrested superego development may be part of general ego retardation (and share its causations); or it may be due to the lack of adequate objects in the child's *environment;* or to separations from them; or to *internal* failure to form relations to objects; or to the *qualities* of the parental personalities with whom the child identifies. Traumatic experiences may at any time endanger progress in any direction or, at worst, bring forward development to a complete standstill.

It remains as a task then to distinguish between these developmental delays and failures and another type of damage to development which, though superficially similar, is different in kind. While the former refer to expected developmental steps not being taken, the latter represents the undoing of developmental achievements after they have been acquired and is due to regressions and inhibitions, i.e., based on conflict (see Part I,2, neurotic symptomatology). Although the differential diagnosis here is important, and becomes all-important when the choice of therapy comes into question, confusion—especially between the effects of arrest and regression—is frequent. There are few criteria to guide the clinician when, for example, he has to decide whether a boy has retreated from the phallic to the anal level (due to castration anxiety), or whether he has never reached the phallic stage; whether a child's superego has never proceeded beyond a primitive, crude level or whether it has become so at a later, more sophisticated stage of development, due to aggression turned inward and/or sexualization of its demands, etc. The most reliable hallmarks of neurosis are anxiety, guilt, and conflict, while in contrast to this the various types of developmental arrest may remain internally undisputed, especially in those cases where the arrest affects more than one sector of the personality. But this diagnostic indicator too cannot be trusted in all instances. Retarded children frequently react with anxiety and a semblance of guilt to the disapproval of their disappointed parents, while neurotic children are well able to deny conflict and guilt and thereby make them disappear from the manifest picture.

3. THE SCHOOL FAILURES

While all developmental failures are apt to arouse the parents' concern, usually they seek clinical advice most urgently when the child lags behind in age-adequate intellectual achievement and becomes a school failure. While the parents' concern exists regardless of the origin of the defect, in clinical examination it proves most important to distinguish between the different types of causation which can be subsumed under almost any of the different diagnostic categories discussed above.

Thus, learning difficulties, although they may be identical in their manifest appearance, may have to be allocated to any of the following categories:

- to *arrested development,* affecting either the person of the child as a whole, or the ego in general, or the ego's intellectual function in particular;
- to *undefended ego regression,* either global or particular to the intellect;
- to *sexualization or aggressive symbolization,* either of the learning process as such, or of the particular subject to which the learning difficulty is attached;
- to *defense* against the symbolic dangers implied, especially by means of *inhibition* and ego restriction;
- to *symptom formation* of the neurotic types and its crippling effect on ego activity in general and sublimation in particular.

4. FAILURES IN SOCIAL ADAPTATION

In this respect, as in the previous one, there is a marked discrepancy between the parents' concern which is easily alerted when a child fails to respond to moral standards, and their ignorance with regard to the causes which, either singly or combined, lead to the asocial, or dissocial, or delinquent or even criminal behavior which is produced.

On the basis of the reasoning which has gone before, failures in social adaptation can be seen in the following lights:

as the logical outcome of adverse environmental circumstances such as neglect, lack of stability in object relations, separations and other traumatic events, undue parental pressure, failure of parental guidance, etc.;

as the result of defects in the ego functions and the defense organization due to developmental arrests or neurotic regressions;

as the result of economic alterations in the balance between id and ego;

as the result of defects in the superego, caused by failures in object relatedness, identifications, internalizations, or by aggression used in its entirety against the external world instead of being in part at the disposal of the superego;

as the result of faulty ego ideals, due to deviant parental models for identification.

In fact, causation of social failure is extremely varied in its nature, ranging, as it does, from the purely environmental to the near-psychotic. This has led to doubts among clinicians and some law teachers whether it is permissible at all to use the terms "dissociality" or "delinquency" as diagnostic labels, instead of speaking merely of dissocial or delinquent actions committed by individuals who may belong to any number of diagnostic categories.[8]

5. ACHES AND PAINS

What remains are the multiple aches and pains of childhood for which no organic cause can be found in physical examination. They alarm the parents, and distress the child. Incidentally, they also lead to innumerable absences from school and, if massive, may constitute a serious threat to formal education. They are also the most frequent reason for a child's medical referral to a child guidance clinic or, in general, for a pediatrician's interest in the intricacies of child psychology.

[8] See, for example, Joseph Goldstein of the Yale Law School who opposes violently the use of "delinquency" as a meaningful diagnostic term.

According to the metapsychological classification of symptoms in Part I of this paper, the various aches and pains of nonorganic origin can be traced back to three or four of the categories enumerated there:

to category 1, so far as they are the direct somatic expression of mental processes;

to category 2, so far as the affected body parts are symbolic of mental content and as such involved in mental conflict;

to categories 3 or 4, so far as the affection of the body part is due to changes of cathexis, either qualitative or quantitative.

The diffuse aches and pains of childhood can be characterized accordingly as either psychosomatic, or hysterical, or hypochondriacal. It hardly needs stressing that these different origins have a significant bearing on the evaluation of the presenting symptom, on the therapeutic approach to it, as well as on the prognosis with regard to its transience or permanency.

Conclusions

The Diagnostic Profile, as it is in use in the Hampstead Child-Therapy Clinic at present, is intended to draw the diagnostician's concentration away from the child's pathology and to return it instead to an assessment of his developmental status and the picture of his total personality. The present attempt at classifying the symptomatology of childhood may serve to amend and amplify this procedure by returning to the symptoms themselves a measure of diagnostic significance. If symptoms are viewed merely as manifest phenomena, dealing with them remains arid so far as analytic interest is concerned. If the clinician is alerted to see opening up behind these the whole range of possible derivations, causations, and developmental affiliations, the field becomes fascinating, and scrutinizing a child's symptomatology becomes a truly analytic task.

Besides, so far as work with children is concerned, diagnostic assessment is more than a mere intellectual exercise for the clinician. It is, in fact, the only true guide to the choice of therapeutic method.

As matters stand now, the form of treatment available for a disturbed child depends usually not on the specific category of his disorder but on the resources of the department or clinical facility to which he has been referred: institutional or foster parent provision if he is taken in care; residential treatment if, legally, found out of control; weekly psychotherapy if referred to a child guidance clinic; family psychiatry, where this is the clinic's orientation; full-scale child analysis in a psychoanalytic clinic. It is only too frequent that the specific type of treatment applied is insufficiently matched with the specific type of disorder which should have been ascertained. Where this happens, children find themselves in institutions while they are in urgent need of individual, one-to-one relationships to develop their libidinal potentialities. Or they find themselves adopted, or in foster care, in spite of being far removed from the possibility of producing the child-to-parent attitudes which are an indispensable requirement of these situations. Or they receive analysis when education and guidance are needed; or guidance, when only analysis can solve their internal conflicts.

It is also futile to expect that any single method, whether superficial or deep, educational or therapeutic, will prove effective with disorders which are as different from each other as, for example, the neurotic compromise formations and the developmental arrests; or, so far as the learning failures are concerned, those caused by arrest, by undefended regression, and by inhibitions. Arrested children have to be treated educationally on their own mental level, an approach which fails disastrously where the therapeutic need is for the undoing of regressions or of lifting conflicts to consciousness, i.e., of freeing in the child an existing intellectual potentiality. Where the diagnostician remains on the phenomenological level and remains oblivious of the underlying fundamental differences, such therapeutic misapplications become inevitable.

The same plea for therapeutic differentiation (following diagnostic differentiation) is justified where the child's fears and anxieties are concerned. It is as futile therapeutically to reassure a child in the throes of castration anxiety and guilt as it would be futile to approach separation anxiety at the symbiotic stage with analytic efforts. Fear of loss of love can be diminished by removal of external pressure, but only in those instances where its origin is due largely to environmental causes; not in others. Where fear of the id is present, as said before, parental leniency acts as an aggravating factor, not as a relieving one.

Where children commit delinquent acts, it is perhaps more obvious than with other disturbances that treatment has to be selected according to the cause being either environmental, or developmental, or neurotic, or psychotic. No single type of therapy, however elaborate, or costly, or easily available, can possibly fit these widely different circumstances.

It is reasonable to expect that any step forward in the refinement of diagnostic assessment will, in the long run, lead to improvements in matching disorder and therapy in the children's field. The present paper is meant to represent a move in this direction.

Appendix

THE SYMPTOMATOLOGY OF CHILDHOOD

I. Symptomatology Proper

1. Symptoms resulting from the initial nondifferentiation between somatic and psychological processes=psychosomatic manifestations.
2. Symptoms resulting from compromise formations between id and ego=neurotic manifestations.
3. Symptoms resulting from the irruption of id derivatives into the ego=infantile psychosis, borderline states, delinquent states.
4. Symptoms resulting from changes in the libido economy or direction of cathexis=upsets in self and object valuation, depressive states, autism, emotional surrender.
5. Symptoms resulting from changes in the quality or direction of aggression=inhibition of functioning, accident proneness, self-injury, aggressive outbursts.
6. Symptoms resulting from undefended regressions=infantilisms, pseudodebility.
7. Symptoms resulting from organic causes:
   (a) from brain damage = delay of milestones, reduced quality of ego functioning, affective changes, etc.;
   (b) from sensory or anatomical handicaps = deviations in drive and ego development, multiple upsets of inner equilibrium.

II. *Other Signs of Disturbance*

1. The fears and anxieties (origin, content, defense, bearing on pathology).

2. The delays and failures in development (organic, constitutional, environmental, traumatic; differentiation from regressions).

3. The school failures (developmental arrest, undefended ego regression, sexualization or aggressive symbolization and defense against it, neurotic inhibition, ego restriction, neurotic symptom formation).

4. Failures in social adaptation (environmental, developmental, economic, structural, neurotic, psychotic).

5. Aches and pains (psychosomatic, hysterical, hypochondriacal).

[Anna Freud also discussed issues related to the central topic of this chapter in other writings (1960b, 1968, 1974a, 1974b).]

PART II

EXTENSIONS OF THE DEVELOPMENTAL PROFILE

4

ASSESSMENT OF ADOLESCENT DISTURBANCES

The Application of Anna Freud's Diagnostic Profile

MOSES LAUFER, Ph.D.
(1965)

The Diagnostic Profile prepared by Anna Freud (1962) for the assessment of childhood disturbances is based on a psychoanalytic theory of childhood development. This Profile, which is now used in all diagnostic work at the Hampstead Child-Therapy Clinic, enables the psychoanalyst to assess behavior in structural, dynamic, economic, genetic, and adaptive terms. Further, it enables the clinician to judge the available diagnostic observations as being part of a normal internal process, as a sign of psychopathology, or as indicating possible future vulnerability to mental disturbance.

When this Profile was used in the assessment of adolescent disturbances, it was found that some sectors of the Profile needed to be changed and expanded. These changes reflect the expected differences between childhood and adolescent development. Expressed more broadly, a Profile for the assessment of adolescent disturbances should reflect a psychoanalytic theory of adolescent development.

However, there is also a similarity between childhood and adolescence: both periods are developmental stages. In both instances, therefore, we may be observing either temporary manifestations of internal stress or signs of future pathology. Yet, the problems with

---

The author is Director, Centre for the Study of Adolescence/Brent Consultation Centre, and a part-time staff member of the Hampstead Child-Therapy Clinic, London.

which the ego must deal in adolescence are qualitatively different from those which exist in childhood. These are related to

(a) the reaction to the physical primacy of the genitals;

(b) the changing relationship to the original objects;

(c) the finding of a heterosexual love object; and

(d) the integrating of preoedipal identifications, oedipal identifications, and present internal as well as external expectations of behavior.

At every stage of childhood the inadequacy of earlier conflict solutions makes itself felt as a distorting influence; but when these solutions are tested in adolescence in the context of the person's new sexual role, they may fail completely in crucial areas, and in this way they may hinder development to adulthood. Identifications which may have served their purpose well in the oedipal and preoedipal periods may be found to be inadequate in helping the person change the internal relationship to the oedipal objects or to take on the role of sexual partner. For example, the male child who, during the oedipal period, identified with a passive father may find that in adolescence this oedipal model is not only insufficient but may be a hindrance in his relation to a new love object.

Again, if we compare childhood and adolescence, we note that in childhood both the content and the functions of the structures are being determined. In adolescence, on the other hand, we observe mainly a change in the functions within each structure as well as a change in the relation of the structures to each other. In childhood, including latency, we are mainly concerned with the child's ability to progress further in both drive and ego development, or with interferences due to intersystemic or intrasystemic conflicts. The psychic structures are still incomplete in their development, and it is our task in diagnosis to see whether structuralization is proceeding or can be expected to proceed normally, or whether this process seems to be impaired. In adolescence we are examining something different. We no longer see structural development in the same way as in the child. Instead, what we observe is the *result* of either successful or faulty structuralization, which now, in addition, must be evaluated in the context of physical genitality. Changes may still take place, but they occur in the functions and the relation of the functions to each other, rather than in the content of the structures. The commonly held belief that adolescents easily give up old standards and earlier identifications and readily adopt new criteria upon which to base their present behavior refers to new ego identifications, and not to change in the content of the superego, which is determined at the stage of internalization (Laufer, 1964). These factors taken together imply that, in the assessment of adolescent disturbances, some areas of mental functioning must be viewed differently than they were in the child. Temporary id and ego regression, the use made of defenses, the role of the object world, extreme mood swings, must be seen not only structurally and genetically, but in relation to factors that are specific for adolescence.

These various new factors which affect behavior in adolescence are at the same time responsible for the fact that it is extremely difficult to distinguish between transitory disturbance and vulnerability to future pathology. The application of the Diagnostic Profile enables us to examine our observations more closely, and to organize the available data in such a way that we can be more precise about diagnosis and prediction.

Anna Freud constructed the Profile for the assessment of childhood disturbances. In adapting its use for adolescence several sections needed to be changed. These changes reflect our expectations of the normal development of each of the psychic structures in adolescence and highlight areas that are especially relevant in the assessment of adolescent disturbances. In what follows I have outlined the additional considerations and changes and I have also tried to show which sections coincide or differ in the Childhood and Adolescence Profiles.

For practical purposes, the Profile is a frame of reference which in many cases can be completed only gradually. Even though many of the answers may not be available at the diagnostic stage, the Profile presents those questions which are of special importance in assessment.

This article is a provisional draft, subject to amendment as its usefulness is tested against clinical data. At a later date, parts of this Profile will be elaborated to include a more detailed discussion of some aspects of adolescent development.

Provisional Draft of Diagnostic Profile

(Describe the material on which the Profile is based.)

I. Reason for Referral

In the Childhood Profile, the reasons for referral include arrests in development, behavior problems, anxieties, inhibitions, symptoms, etc.

It is always assumed that the referral of the child is initiated by the parents, the school, or social agency. However, in the referral of the adolescent, the family may or may not be involved or the adolescent may seek help on his own. His attitude to future help may depend on the manner in which the adolescent has first sought help. For these reasons, this section includes items which are not relevant for the child.

Note whether the referral is from the adolescent himself, or from parents, school, or other organizations. State the adolescent's *manifest* reason for seeking help, as well as the reasons given by those responsible for the initial referral. If the adolescent has referred himself, state whether his complaints are about himself or about the environment as the cause of the trouble.

State also the *latent* reason for the adolescent's attendance. (The latent reason for the child's referral could be related to factors not directly having to do with the child, e.g., parental problems, projection onto the child of a history of illness, etc. For the adolescent, the latent reason has often to do with his concern about his sexual role and development to adulthood, e.g., concern about homosexuality, impotence, inability to continue a love relationship, inability to change the relationship to the original objects.) Note also whether the adolescent sees the manifest difficulty as the main problem, even though there may be a much more serious latent problem.

II. Description of Child

This heading, used in the Childhood Profile, can remain the same for the adolescent. Note his personal appearance, moods, manner, etc.

While the child's external appearance reveals the way he is taken care of and cathected by the parents, the adolescent's appearance reveals his attitude to his own body. It is of diagnostic help to include here any observable incongruity in behavior, e.g., an inhibited manner compared to clothing which exhibits the body; a capacity for verbalization, but an inability to describe how he feels. The diagnostician should also include his own reaction to the adolescent.

III. Family Background and Personal History

The information available in this section of the Childhood Profile is generally quite extensive. Usually when the child is referred, it is possible (as well as accepted procedure) to obtain information about the child from a variety of sources—parents, school, social agencies, doctor, etc.

In the Adolescence Profile, however, this section may either contain a good deal of information or it may be very sparse. The amount of information depends partly on the manner in which the referral has taken place. Moreover, the possibility of obtaining historical data depends on whether the adolescent has sought help on his own or whether he has been referred in a formal way. Some adolescents find it easy to provide historical information, whereas others are quite unable to supply any at all. One should distinguish between those adolescents who do not wish to give historical facts and those who have little or no conscious recollection of them.

In some circumstances, it may be advisable to avoid collecting information in a set way from the adolescent. This section will then have to be completed at a later date. On the other hand, when it is possible to obtain information, a "Description of the Latency Period" should be included as part of the adolescent's personal history.

IV. Possibly Significant Environmental Influences

This section remains the same as in the Childhood Profile. We can, however, assume that the information about the child may well be more complete, simply because of the sources from which the material could be available.

Chronologically, one may note here which external factors may have had a special impact on the person's life, e.g., illnesses, hospitalizations, events which may have been traumatic, crises in the history of the family. What environmental influences does the adolescent himself emphasize? All *possible* influences should be included in this section, even if one is not able to state at this point whether these influences actually had a special meaning in the life of the person.

V. Assessments of Development

In the Childhood Profile, this section concentrates on the development of the psychic structures and functions within each structure. This is shown in the headings used. For example, the section dealing with "Drive Development" includes not only "libido" and "aggression," but libido is examined from the point of view of phase development and libido distribution (including cathexis of the self and cathexis of objects). "Ego and Superego Development" includes an examination of the ego apparatuses, ego functions, defense organization, and secondary interference with ego achievements. This is followed, in the case of the child, with an examination of the "Lines of Development and Mastery of Tasks." In this section of the Adolescence Profile, I have suggested a number of changes which will be described in what follows:

A. *Drive Development*

1. Libido

(a) Examine with regard to *phase development:*

In the Childhood Profile, there is an examination of the development of the libidinal phases to an age-adequate stage, especially beyond the anal to the phallic level. In this respect the Adolescence Profile is similar, with the emphasis now being on signs of puberty and adolescence. Therefore, state the signs indicating that the person has reached puberty and adolescence; whether he has achieved phase dominance; whether, at the time of assessment, he seems to have the ability to maintain the highest level reached, or whether there are signs of regression and to which level.

In adolescence, the drive organization develops progressively to the point where genitality serves as the most important means of gratification. Although phase dominance may not be established until the person is well into adolescence, there are earlier signs which enable the diagnostician to know whether preoedipal drive manifestations are such that they endanger the establishment of phase dominance. In the male adolescent, the physical ability to produce semen may act as an encouragement for further libidinal development. In the female adolescent, menstruation would be a sign of physical maturity, but it may be extremely difficult to judge the level of libidinal development reached until she has had sexual intercourse. The move from the clitoral to the vaginal stage may be accomplished easily, or it may be held up. In diagnostic assessments, one would have to differentiate between the level of drive development reached and drive development which is secondarily interfered with due to defense activity.

Phase dominance in adolescence does not mean that pregenital libidinal signs are nonexistent. Normally, the adolescent will seek satisfaction on a variety of libidinal levels, which he will give up for genitality only in late adolescence. Assessment of phase dominance must therefore be a quantitative one, i.e., whether genitality serves as the most important means of gratification. Temporary id regression results in drive expression characteristic of preoedipal libidinal levels, but this in itself is not a criterion for the assessment of the level of drive development which has been or is likely to be reached. However, the degree to which satisfactions from each level participate in his libidinal life can tell us whether phase dominance has been or is likely to be achieved, and whether this dominance can be regained following temporary regression. Such an assessment enables us to know whether satisfaction from any of the component instincts is interfering or will interfere with normal heterosexuality.

(b) with regard to *libido distribution:*

(i) Cathexis of the self

In the Childhood Profile, the main questions are whether the self is cathected, and whether there is sufficient narcissism (primary and secondary, invested in the body, the ego, or the superego) to ensure self-regard, self-esteem, a feeling of well-being. Does this lead to overestimation of the self and undue independence of the object, etc.? To what degree is self-regard dependent on the object world?

Although we need not raise many additional questions in the Adolescence Profile, the cathexis of the self may be affected by some specific factors that are relevant in adolescence but not in childhood. When the person reaches physical genitality, the role of the outside world takes on a different meaning. Demands and expectations of contemporaries become more important. Structurally, the superego is now a more defined system; therefore it may be helpful to see how each of the superego functions (conscience, ego ideal, self-criticism) participates in the cathexis of the self. Dependence on or independence of the object world has a different meaning now than during childhood. Is this related to oedipal objects, oedipal substitutes, or to contemporaries? Does it detach the adolescent from the outside world? Does his estimation of himself assist him in his relation to the external world? Does it result in withdrawal? If there is withdrawal, this should be examined as follows—is it to something or from something; is it from activity; is it into fantasy; is it into autoerotic activity? During periods of withdrawal, does the object world still remain important, or is the cathexis withdrawn from the object world?

(ii) Cathexis of objects

In the Childhood Profile, this section examines the level and quality of object relationships reached by the child; whether the highest level reached is being maintained; whether or not the existent object relationships correspond with the maintained or regressed level of phase development.

It is, of course, equally important in the assessment of the adolescent to enquire into the level and quality of object relationships, but at the same time there are some factors which are exclusive to adolescence. During this period, for example, a variety of object relationships can exist simultaneously, each having an important part to play in maintaining libidinal phase development and in assisting the adolescent to detach himself from the original objects. The object can act as a means of allowing for regressive manifestations and either help or hinder the libidinal detachment from the oedipal objects. In examining the level and quality of object relationships which exist, it is important to note not only the kind of relationships that exist but also which ones seem to be dominant.

The phases of adolescence should show alteration in cathexis of objects. The boy or girl who has just entered adolescence continues to have a variety of relationships serving different libidinal and ego purposes—including control of regression, overcoming superego demands, detachment from the oedipal objects. However, the late adolescent should primarily cathect those objects which can be instrumental in helping him to establish his sexual role. This means that the narcissistic type of object choice (including homosexuality) need not be a sign of pathology in the early adolescent, whereas a continuation of such an object choice in late adolescence may be viewed as a sign of failure to give up these earlier means of narcissistic supply and as a hindrance to further emotional development.

2. Aggression

The Childhood Profile examines the aggressive expressions (a) according to their quantity (presence or absence in the manifest picture), (b) according to their quality (correspondence with the level of libido development), (c) according to their direction, toward either the object world or the self.

For the adolescent, there is some slight change needed here to include the specific expressions which may be diagnostically meaningful. For example, in (c), when examining the direction of the aggressive expressions toward either the object world or the self, we should divide the object world into "within the family" and "outside the family."

In addition, for the adolescent, one should state whether there has recently been a change in the aggressive manifestations or whether the present picture seems to be similar to what existed before. One should also differentiate between physical harm to oneself and aggression which may be lodged in the superego and which may show itself in mood swings, etc.

One of the difficulties which may be encountered here is that mood swings need not be due to aggression lodged in the superego; they may be occasioned by other immediate problems which the adolescent is trying to solve. For example, the adolescent may go through a period of some withdrawal while he is trying to detach himself from the oedipal objects and has not yet been able to cathect other objects. The mood observed at such times would not necessarily be due to aggression. Furthermore, the adolescent must have some aggression available in order to free himself from the oedipal objects, and here too one should differentiate between this kind of aggression and that which is lodged in the superego.

B. *Ego and Superego Development*

In the Childhood Profile, this section includes an examination of (a) ego apparatuses, (b) ego functions, (c) defense organization, (d) secondary interference of defense activity with ego achievements.

For the Adolescence Profile, this section is divided into two separate sections, (1) *Ego Development* and (2) *Superego Development.* In addition, under "Ego Development," there are two new headings which do not appear in the Childhood Profile—"Affects" and "Identifications." These changes reflect a number of theoretical assumptions about adolescence which do not in the same way apply to childhood. They also show some of the specific demands made upon the ego during this period, and help us to assess the manner in which the ego deals with these demands. These points will be discussed in the relevant sections.

[1.] *Ego Development*

(a) There is no change in this section. Examine and state the intactness or defects of *ego apparatus,* serving perception, memory, motility, etc.

(b) The questions in the Childhood Profile relate to the intactness of *ego functions* (memory, reality testing, synthesis, control of motility, speech, secondary thought processes). Any primary deficiencies and unevennesses in the levels reached are noted. Intelligence test results are included.

For the Adolescence Profile, it is equally important to examine the intactness of the ego functions. But when we try to determine the level of development reached by the different ego functions, we have to begin by asking how the adolescent is dealing with the new age-appropriate demands. Our expectations of development vary with the age of the adolescent. Although the ego of the early adolescent and that of the late adolescent may be dealing with similar problems, the relative importance of these problems to the ego varies a great deal from one phase to the next. For example, although the adolescent of fourteen or fifteen normally chooses as friends contemporaries who can help him in establishing his sexual role, they may also have been chosen because they enable him to accept temporary regression or to find new ways of fighting old superego demands. The adolescent of nineteen will normally still have to deal with these same problems, but the relative importance of the problems has now changed. Regression, for example, will now mean something quite different to the ego; the superego disapproval will be much more severe; and the defenses employed may be aimed at avoiding any temporary regression or superego condemnation. Similarly, identifications will be used differently: now they are important for purposes of integrating the remnants of the positive oedipal relationship (through the elaboration of the ego-ideal content of the superego), whereas in early adolescence they were a normal means of defying the oedipal object.

This means that some ego functions in adolescence may be under greater pressure than others, and for this reason it is necessary to differentiate between levels reached and temporary regression of specific ego functions. Of special importance are reality testing, synthesis, and secondary thought processes. Although the other ego functions such as speech, control of motility, and memory should be examined as well, it may be that in assessment the latter should be given less weight than the former. At the same time, one should note the unevenness in development of ego functions.

Note also the signs of *secondary ego autonomy*. For example, has a disturbance affected the entire ego organization or only specific areas of ego functioning? Or, even though there is some disturbance present, has the adolescent been able to continue with his interests, or has he given up doing things? For example, a sudden severe drop in school functioning is usually taken as an ominous diagnostic sign.

(c) In the Childhood Profile, this section deals with the status of the *defense organization*. Here one considers:

whether defense is employed specifically against *individual drives* or, more generally, against drive activity and instinctual pleasure as such;

whether defenses are *age adequate,* too primitive or too precocious;

whether defense is *balanced,* i.e., whether the ego has the use of many of the important mechanisms or is restricted to the excessive use of single ones;

whether defense is *effective,* especially in its dealing with anxiety; whether it results in equilibrium or disequilibrium, lability, flexibility, or deadlock within the structure;

whether and how far the child's defense against the drives is dependent on the object world or independent of it (superego development).

In the Adolescence Profile, it is necessary to ask the same questions about the defense organization. At the same time, however, there exist a number of factors which are specific for the adolescent and therefore alter the manner of assessment. Although the adolescent uses every means available to him to assist the ego in coping with instinctual demands, with superego demands, and with what is experienced as the demands from contemporaries, we can learn a great deal about the capacity of the ego by examining the *hierarchy* of defense mechanisms used and the specific content against which they are directed. For example, the early adolescent normally uses primitive defenses without their affecting his relation to reality. However, if these primitive defenses are the only ones available in late adolescence, we may conclude that adolescence has brought about no significant internal change, and that there is now, or will be, deadlock in the personality. The adolescent who in situations of anxiety uses such defenses as projection, identification with the aggressor, or regression functions on a lower level than the adolescent who uses the more sophisticated defenses such as reversal of affect, intellectualization, displacement, or even reaction formation.

In assessing the adolescent, we would ask whether defense is used mainly against:

(i) drive demand in general, or specific drives;
(ii) superego demand, and which superego functions are felt by the ego as producing demand;
(iii) demands and expectations of contemporaries;
(iv) infantile object ties;
(v) masturbation;
(vi) fantasy content;
(vii) specific kinds of object relationships.

We can assume that, normally, every adolescent tries to ward off superego demand, infantile object ties, and fantasy content from preoedipal and oedipal levels. Such defense activity is age adequate and serves the purpose of progression to adulthood. But if the adolescent wards off drive demands in general, demands and expectations from contemporaries, and masturbation, we can assume that his relation to his own body and to external reality is much more disturbed. If the defenses used are such that they do not allow for temporary ego regression, we may be able to conclude that he will solve none of his age-adequate problems, that there will be no significant structural changes, and that adolescence is merely another stage on the way to a mental disturbance in adulthood.

We know that a picture of equilibrium during adolescence is itself a sign of danger, and one should note the ego's general attitude to internal pressure.

Has the ego internal means at its disposal in dealing with anxiety and drive demand, or must the ego rely on external objects for this purpose? The adolescent may use one or the other of his contemporaries as an auxiliary ego or superego in helping him to cope with specific kinds of internal demands; or the adolescent may regard his contemporaries as an additional threat toward id and ego regression and may then withdraw from contact with them.

We should also inquire whether the current picture is a familiar one in the history of the adolescent, or whether a sudden change has taken place.

(d) This section remains the same as in the Childhood Profile. Note any *secondary interference* of defense activity with ego achievements, i.e., the price paid by the individual for the upkeep of the defense organization.

(e) *Affects.* (This section is added in the Adolescence Profile.) Examine the different affects available to the ego. Does a person respond to different internal and external situations with a variety of affects appropriate to them or is his response limited to a single affect, e.g., guilt, general anxiety, depression, feeling of shame, cynicism?

Although the availability of affect is a guide to the understanding of ego development at all stages of life, it is characteristic of the adolescent that he normally becomes able to express various kinds of affect much more easily than did the child. In addition, the adolescent becomes aware of his feelings and of their progressively becoming independent of the external world. This is in contrast to the child who normally feels that behavior and feelings are externally determined and who ordinarily is not expected to have some distance from his feelings.

In initial interviews with adolescents, a clear description of the availability and appropriateness of affect may give us a crucial clue to the underlying problem and can often be used by the diagnostician to decide which kind of help would be of greatest benefit.

Affects are one of the most certain indications of what parts of the personality are involved in conflict. At the same time, the range of affect available to the ego signifies whether it has one or many means of discharge for different internal and external situations. Affect differentiation also means that there is greater development from primary- to secondary-process thinking and functioning, that the ego is the master of affect rather than passive in the face of it. One should distinguish between mastering of affect and defensive control of affect—a distinction which constantly needs to be made in the assessment of behavior in adolescence.

For the adolescent specific affects may stand for a specific kind of danger situation. For example, a particular affect may represent his continued attachment to the oedipal objects, or it may be experienced as a sign of danger involving regressive manifestations. We should therefore distinguish between defense against affect and lack of availability of appropriate affect due to faulty structural development. The adolescent may use reversal of affect defensively, or he may try to present a picture of complete neutrality, as if affect did not exist. These methods may be a temporary means of dealing with specific kinds of anxiety, or they may be resorted to so extensively that they begin to distort the person's relation to the external world.

(f) *Identifications.* (This section is added in the Adolescence Profile.) Identifications in adolescence may either encourage progression or participate in pathology. They play a special part throughout adolescence, and their detailed scrutiny can significantly aid the diagnostician in determining which parts of the structure are under special stress. For example, does the adolescent identify mainly with oedipal substitutes, with contemporaries, or with impersonal ideals and ideologies? Does some of his behavior show us that identifications are now being used for the purpose of:

(i) controlling regression;
(ii) maintaining the repression of ego-dystonic thoughts and wishes;

(iii) detaching himself from the oedipal objects;
(iv) overcoming his awareness that earlier identifications (which helped to resolve the oedipal conflict) are now inadequate;
(v) dealing with the activity-passivity conflict;
(vi) coping with demands of the superego.

Which identifications are now most important—those which are used defensively, in a transitory way, or those which assist in structural rearrangement?

(Identification may be only one way of dealing with the activity-passivity conflict. More primitive means of handling the activity-passivity conflict would be by repetition of the event or identification with the aggressor. On a higher level, where there is more structuralization, the identifications would show up in sublimations.)

The part played by identifications should normally diminish in importance as the adolescent moves closer to adulthood. The early adolescent needs to use identifications as an aid in controlling regression and in dealing with superego demands, whereas the late adolescent may use them in his attempt to establish his sexual role.

One of the crucial problems with which the ego in adolescence must deal is the testing of earlier identifications in a new context. The behavior of the adolescent is often described as chaotic, unpredictable, infantile, adult, or both. Such manifest behavior may, to some extent, be indicative of the adolescent's efforts to close the gap between the earlier identifications and the more recent ego identifications related to demands and expectations of contemporaries (Laufer, 1964).

[2.] *Superego Development*

This heading becomes a separate section in the Adolescence Profile because the points included here are especially relevant to adolescence. They can help the diagnostician to see how much structural conflict exists and which functions are involved.

(a) Examine each of the functions of the superego (conscience, ego ideal, and self-criticism), stating which of the functions seems to be most highly cathected.

(b) Which of the functions of the superego seems most important in determining the superego's relation to the ego?

(c) Are the superego functions independent of the object world, or is the behavior partly a reflection of the effort to compromise between superego expectations and external expectations of contemporaries?

(d) Do the identifications act as an auxiliary to the superego? Which superego function utilizes identifications in this way?

(e) Does a change in the relationship to the oedipal objects bring with it an overthrow of superego demands and expectations and result in a feeling of loss of object and loss of earlier identifications?

C. *Development of the Total Personality* (Lines of Development and Mastery of Tasks)

This section in the Childhood Profile is used to determine the stages reached in the mastery of various tasks and to judge whether or not these stages are age adequate. Anna Freud (1963) states: "Whatever level has been reached by any given child in any of these respects represents the results of interaction between drive and ego-superego development and their reaction to environmental influences, i.e., between maturation, adaptation, and structuralization. Far from being theoretical abstractions, developmental lines, in the sense here used, are historical realities which, when assembled, convey a convincing picture of an individual child's personal achievements or, on the other hand, of his failures in personality development." Those lines of development which reflect the child's "gradual outgrowing of dependent, irrational, id- and object-determined attitudes to an increasing ego mastery of his internal and external world" are (i) from dependency to emotional self-reliance and adult object relationships; (ii) areas of ego development related to body independence—from suckling to independent eating; from wetting and soiling to bladder and bowel control; from irresponsibility to responsibility in body management; (iii) from egocentricity to companionship; (iv) from the body to the toy and from play to work.

Clearly, these developmental lines cannot in the same way be applied to the adolescent. We are no longer examining ongoing development of a child's personality; we are now looking at the *Functioning of the Total Personality.*

The diagnostician attempts to determine whether the adolescent can make the step to adulthood in an emotional sense and the extent to which such progress may be impeded. To get a complete picture of the total life of the adolescent, the following areas should be examined:

1. *Social Relationships.* The relations to the outside world, to adults, contemporaries, people in authority, etc., are of special importance in adolescence. Various kinds of relationships can exist simultaneously, but their quality and meaning should change as the person progresses through this period. For example, at the beginning of adolescence, the person may have a variety of relationships, each representing different needs at various libidinal and ego levels. As the person gets older, some of these relationships can be expected to lose in importance.

For this reason we should ask such questions as: are the relationships mainly narcissistic; anaclitic; to part or whole objects; related mainly to idealization; functioning as auxiliary ego or superego; on the preoedipal or oedipal level; on the genital level; a means of avoiding being alone, etc.? What part do social relationships now play in helping establish one's sexual role? Which kinds of relationships seem dominant?

2. *Frustration Tolerance.* How readily can the adolescent tolerate frustration? What kinds of frustration cannot be tolerated? Does frustration bring about regression and certain forms of defense activity?

The diagnostician should try to differentiate here between the inability to tolerate frustration and heightened anxiety due to this inability.

3. *Attitude to Anxiety.* Does the ego react to specific kinds of anxiety or to anxiety in general? Certain situations may induce special anxiety and be experienced by the adolescent as special dangers. Which are these?

Is there fear of the external world, or is the anxiety specifically related to internalized aspects? Is the ego active or passive in the face of anxiety situations?

4. *Sublimations.* In the child one can evaluate his potential, whereas in the adolescent one should be able to see the result, if any, of aim-inhibited and neutralized gratification.

5. *Attitude to School or Work.* How well does the adolescent function in these areas? Is there a discrepancy between performance

and ability? Has there been a recent change in attitude and performance compared to previously?

6. *Attitude to the Future.* Adolescence is a period of life in which the "future" is of special importance. The child's concept of "future" contains different expectations. They center on the oedipal objects; approval from them for specific kinds of achievement; the wish to take on a role similar to the parent of the same sex; the ego's ability to control drive demand. To be "grown up" means for the child to be like the parent of the same sex.

For the adolescent, the "future" is determined by different criteria. They concern his sexual role with real objects and his choice of work. His attitude to the future must now take into account the various superego demands, the oedipal and preoedipal identifications, the fate of the earlier ambivalence, the internally determined reaction to success or failure, the internal reaction to one's adult sexual role.

For diagnostic purposes it is helpful to trace the changes which may have taken place in the attitude to the future. For example, what did the child, in latency, want to be as an adult? How much was this related to reality? Is the present attitude to the future the same as existed in childhood, or is there a change which reflects specifically adolescent hopes, etc.?

7. *Attitude to Achievements.* Are achievements valued, and if so, are they directed toward internal or external approval? Are they pursued mainly for the sake of oedipal objects or for reasons of competition? On which level does the adolescent compete?

8. *Ability for Self-Observation.* Has the adolescent the ability to observe his behavior, his difficulties, the impact he has on the object world? Can his ego temporarily detach itself from the immediate experience to see what is going on?

9. *Verbalization.* Is the adolescent able to express himself verbally (how he feels, what he thinks about)? Can he verbalize affect? Or content?

10. *Comparison of the Various Sectors.* Comparison may show whether there is balance or imbalance and in which areas. Is the picture of balance or imbalance similar to what existed before adolescence, or has there been a sudden change in the personality?

VI. Genetic Assessments (Regression and Fixation Points)

In the Childhood Profile, the information collected here is meant to help the diagnostician locate the libidinal regressions and fixation points in the history of the child. Knowledge of these can be gained (a) by certain forms of manifest behavior characteristic for the given child; (b) by the child's fantasy activity; (c) by those items in the symptomatology where the relations between surface and depth are firmly established.

In the Childhood Profile Anna Freud (1962) stressed the need to distinguish between infantile regression and regression in the adult; ego regression "does not always require fixation points and it does not need to be permanent. As 'temporary regression' it takes place along the developmental lines mentioned before, and forms part of normal development as an attempt at adaptation and response to frustration. Such temporary regression may give rise to pathology, but the latter will be short-lived and reversible. For purposes of assessment the two types of regression (temporary or permanent, spontaneously reversible or irreversible) have to be distinguished from each other, only the former type justifying therapy."

Whereas preadolescence is normally characterized by massive regressions, i.e., repetitions of the past, adolescence should bring with it a change in the kind of regressions that take place. In adolescence, regression can serve a number of purposes: it may be a means of retreating from a danger situation and therefore a way of avoiding anxiety; it may be a temporary means of withdrawing from internal and external demands, but it is now undertaken with the ego's and superego's participation and mainly for purposes of temporary respite rather than to avoid anxiety; it may be the means of allowing for fantasy activity (which in turn can be used to avoid anxiety or as trial action to prepare the ego to handle new reality situations).

For the diagnostic assessment of adolescents, it is of utmost importance to determine both the quantity and quality of the regression; under which circumstances this takes place; whether it seems to be of a temporary or permanent nature; and whether the regression to pregenital fixation points offers so much instinctual gratification that the latter may override genital satisfaction as the main means of satisfaction.

Although this information often is not available at the time of diagnosis, we can gain some knowledge about these questions during the diagnostic procedure (as is the case in diagnosis of the child) without necessarily endangering the possibility of future work with the adolescent. In this respect the following items are significant:

(a) repetitive forms of behavior;
(b) withdrawal and certain kinds of activities which accompany this withdrawal;
(c) forms of impulsive behavior;
(d) daydreams;
(e) certain symptoms, which are independent of the adolescent process, and which analytically can be linked to specific fixation points—obsessional symptoms, obesity, etc.;
(f) addictions, food fads;
(g) overconcern about parents;
(h) masturbation fantasies, usually available only during treatment, would be our most certain way of knowing about regression and fixation points;
(i) the affect accompanying the above points may help us to decide whether the regression should be viewed as a sign of pathology.

Although instinctual regression in adolescence predictably takes place in the normal person and changes its quality as the adolescent gets older, there are nevertheless some genetic factors which could make the person more prone to pathology. We know that psychopathology (whether in the child, the adolescent, or the adult) always involves regression to fixation points at various levels. The strength of the fixation is therefore one factor that makes the person more prone to pathology. Another factor is the satisfaction or lack of satisfaction available through genital strivings. Still another is the ego's ability to cope with regression—to permit it but at the same time to have the means of re-establishing its more mature level of functioning.

VII. Dynamic and Structural Assessments (Conflicts)

In the Childhood Profile, we ask whether conflicts are mainly externally or internally determined. Is the conflict between the ego and the object world; is it between ego-superego and id; is it related to internal conflicts?

In adolescence, too, there are demands from the external world, but we can say that behavior is determined primarily by internal factors. Development of the personality can no longer be considered in the same way as before adolescence. The content of the ego and superego as separate structures has already been established, although final structuralization may take place only during adolescence. The object world is still of crucial importance, but it may now be used as a means of strengthening the structures, or it can be experienced as an additional demand for specific forms of behavior. In whichever way the object world is used, the diagnostician must weigh the part played by each of the structures in determining behavior, but he must also take into account that the adolescent has to cope with society as well as with himself. Therefore, conflicts should be classified as follows:

(a) Conflicts which are felt to be between the ego and object world. Although the superego may play an important part here, the conflicts may be felt to be with oedipal objects, with external demands, etc. One should also take into consideration that the adolescent may be exposed to such real external pressures that to be in conflict with them is a sign of ego strength.

(b) Internalized conflicts between ego and superego. From the material available, is it possible to determine on which level the earlier internalized conflicts are being repeated; e.g., is the conflict related to the oedipal level; attachment to mother; sadomasochistic aspects?

(c) Internal conflicts (activity-passivity; masculinity-femininity; unresolved ambivalence).

VIII. Assessment of Some General Characteristics

Included in this section are (a) the child's frustration tolerance; (b) the child's sublimation potential; (c) the child's over-all attitude to anxiety; (d) progressive developmental forces versus regressive tendencies. These points are meant to assist the diagnostician to predict the chances for spontaneous recovery and reaction to treatment.

These "General Characteristics" cannot in the same way be applied in the assessment of the adolescent because during this developmental phase the entire personality structure is in flux: we simply cannot distinguish between what is permanent and what is transitory. In the Adolescence Profile, the points mentioned above have therefore been included under "Functioning of the Total Personality" (Section V, C), in addition to some items which are specific for assessment in adolescence, e.g., attitude to the future, attitude to achievements, self-observation, and verbalization. The inclusion of all these points under "Functioning of the Total Personality" gives the diagnostician a picture of how the adolescent reacts to specific stresses and what part the ego plays in solving them.

IX. Diagnosis

The first important diagnostic conclusion about both child and adolescent is the distinction between transitory disturbance and pathology. When we are dealing with the adult, we assess the outcome of internalized conflict (Anna Freud et al., 1965). With the adolescent, in contrast, we try instead to examine the interaction of the forces which are creating the disturbance; we try to determine whether there already is a deadlock or whether the disturbance represents a temporary defensive measure. In this sense, the psychiatric categories used to describe adult pathology are not suitable in the classification of adolescent disturbances. The diagnostic categories used in the Childhood Profile are based on metapsychological concepts; they reflect the degree of disturbance and enable us to decide whether outside intervention is required. The following categories are distinguished: (i) behavior which falls within the wide range of "variations of normality"; (ii) pathological formations which are a reflection of the developmental process and are transitory in nature; (iii) behavior which reflects permanent regression and results in ego and superego damage; (iv) primary deficiencies of an organic nature or early deprivations which distort development and structuralization; (v) destructive processes (of organic, toxic, psychic, known or unknown origin) which have effected, or are on the point of effecting, a disruption of mental growth.

The fact that we encounter such great difficulties in distinguishing between transitory disturbance and pathology in adolescence means that we are still unsure how to assess various forms of behavior or what criteria to use to reach a diagnostic conclusion. It is also an indication of the unknown factors which can influence the outcome. Therefore, although the categories used in the Childhood Profile can, with only slight change, be directly applied to diagnosis in adolescence, I suggest some amplification.

All our observations must first be viewed in relation to the ego's ability to deal with the new internal demands (changing the relationship to the oedipal objects, and establishing one's sexual role). Therefore, with regard to the drives, we would have to assess whether the satisfaction from any of the component instincts interferes or will interfere with normal heterosexuality. Although the fantasies can supply some answers, they should themselves be viewed as participating in future pathology only if they interfere with heterosexuality and with ego achievements.

Furthermore, we need to assess whether the present disturbance affects the entire ego organization or whether it is confined to isolated areas. Although there may be temporary regression of some ego functions, the function of reality testing remains crucial. Is there the ability to continue to distinguish between internal and external reality? The degree of distortion of external reality should be assessed; e.g., what is the adolescent's image of the parents and how does this compare to the real parents; how does he view his contemporaries and their expectations? The availability of affects and their appropriateness provide clues enabling us to assess the degree of structural conflict and to predict whether the adolescent will be capable of dealing with the immediate developmental problems. The way in which he uses identifications can tell us whether there is the possibility of structural rearrangement, or whether internalized conflict is so rigidly fixed that there is already a deadlock which makes further progressive development impossible. Vulnerability to narcissistic injury would reflect the degree to which narcissistic equilibrium depends on external objects as well as the extent to which achievements are independent of the object world.

A description of the latency period could help to establish whether interference with ego functions and achievements had existed at that time. We could then distinguish more clearly between behavior which is a continuation from the latency period and will change little during adolescence and behavior which is due to adolescence and will result in structural rearrangement. In some persons, when they reach adolescence, the new demands seem to have almost no impact on their ego. While there may be some slight outward changes in the personality, these adolescents have in fact found no new means of dealing with the heightened anxiety that we expect to occur in this period. The rigidity and limited availability of defenses have created some kind of deadlock long before adolescence, with the result that adolescence does not contribute to maturity but is another stage on the way to a character disturbance in adulthood. At the other extreme, there are persons who, when they reach adolescence, change beyond recognition. This change may be due to the person's ability to use earlier identifications and various defenses in such a way that he can give up the earlier means of narcissistic satisfaction. Ego achievements and superego expectations and ideals now become more important sources of self-esteem. On the other hand, a complete change in adolescence could also be due to the person's inability to give up precisely these earlier means of narcissistic supply. It is as if the adolescent tries, by overthrowing the superego demands and expectations, to disprove the existence of the emotional tie to the oedipal objects. Adolescence can be described as a period of narcissistic crisis, and our inquiry should enable us to find out how the adolescent deals with this crisis.

X. Recommendations (Including Initial Aims of Treatment)

(This is a new section, added to the Adolescence Profile.)

A number of special factors should be taken into account when we consider any recommendation for the adolescent. There are times when the adolescent experiences what seems to be a transitory problem and when help of some kind is advisable. There are other circumstances in which treatment at the present time is not advisable, even though we have no difficulty in diagnosing the existence of a pathological condition.

Similarly, considerations concerning the intensity of treatment at this period should take into account not only the degree and nature of psychopathology and the adolescent's attitude toward it, but also his ability to cope with the demands of treatment—the ego's capacity for insight, his ability to participate in a treatment alliance—as well as the cooperation that can be expected from the family, and the external pressures existing at that time.

The recommendations for treatment should include a statement about the aims of treatment. For example, if analysis is recommended, what structural changes should one expect or aim for; should we prepare for a long introductory period and why; will there have to be any variation in classic technique; should the family be involved or not? Or will help offered be mainly supportive, without intending to bring about much insight into the disturbance? Should we encourage changes in the environment, so that the adolescent will be in a better position to deal himself with his internal demands?

The aims, as stated, may have to be reformulated at a later date, but they should at this point reflect what we consider to be the major areas of the adolescent's personality which require help, as well as the limitations that exist because of either internal or external factors.

[The author discussed related problems of assessment in other papers (1968, 1975).]

5

METAPSYCHOLOGICAL ASSESSMENT OF THE ADULT PERSONALITY

The Adult Profile

ANNA FREUD, LL.D., D.Sc., M.D.,
HUMBERTO NAGERA, M.D.,
and W. ERNEST FREUD, B.A.

(1965)

The need for a Profile of adult patients has made itself felt in our clinical work for some time, especially for those cases where a child and one or the other parent are in treatment simultaneously.

Our original Profile schema was devised for neurotic child patients in order to facilitate the organization of the material available about them under psychoanalytically meaningful headings (before, during, or after therapy). When the Profile was subsequently applied beyond the scope of the neurosis, a number of sections had to be amplified to embrace all the details relevant to the individual's specific pathology. In the case of the blind, this involved above all the headings concerned with phase development, fixation and regression. In the case of the borderline children, so far the sections containing information about cathexis of self and cathexis of objects have been provided with subdivisions to trace in more minute detail the location of pathology. When the Profile schema was applied to the characterization of the adolescent, it had to be widened to accommodate the variations of superego development, ideal formation, and the identity problems, which form an essential part of the adolescent's upheaval.[1]

While the Profile schema as such profited from these expansions and gained so far as its scope of application was concerned, the basic

---

1 See M. Laufer in this Volume.

rationale underlying it remained untouched. For all the categories of disturbance enumerated above, assessment by Profile is made on the basis of developmental considerations, i.e., the individual is examined for his position on the progressive sequences relevant to drive development, ego and superego development, and the age-adequate developments of internal structuralization and adaptation to the environment. Pathology is evaluated in all instances according to its interference with orderly and steady progress in these respects.

This basic rationale changes with the application of the Profile schema to the adult personality. In this instance assessment is concerned not with an ongoing process but with a finished product in which, by implication, the ultimate developmental stages should have been reached. The developmental point of view may be upheld only in so far as success or failure to reach this level or to maintain it determines the so-called maturity or immaturity of the adult personality. For the rest, normality is judged by the quality of functioning (in sex, work, and sublimations), the pleasure in life derived from it, and by the quality of the individual's object and community relations. Pathology reveals itself through permanent symptomatology which interferes with any of the above aims, by suffering for internal causes, by the individual's incapacity to relate realistically to his environment, or by both.

Since childhood and adult Profiles are not identical in orientation, the comparison between such assessments of parent and child will have to be restricted to the sections which are most similar. Nevertheless, the schemas may prove invaluable for the correlation of items such as the importance within the individual structure of particular drives, the quality of the defense organization, the content of ideal self and superego, the developmental phase governing the quality of object relationships, etc.

As regards the application of what follows to individual case material, the analytic clinician has to be advised as well as warned. It would be a grave misunderstanding of what the authors have in mind if the Profile were treated as a questionnaire, if it were allowed to dominate the interviewer's attitude during diagnostic examination, if it were shared with the patient, or if its headings were merely filled in with information given by him. What the Metapsychological Profile sets out to be is of a completely different order—namely, a framework for the analyst's thinking, and a method to organize findings after they have been elicited, assimilated, and digested by him. Where a Profile is set up after diagnostic investigation, it is only natural that there will be many blanks and unanswered questions in the analyst's mind; these will be filled gradually as an analysis proceeds, to be most completely answered when analytic treatment has been terminated. Profiles set up at these different junctures will reflect the analyst's growing familiarity with the material and, by their increase in completeness, give evidence of his advances in awareness of existing problems, complications, and solutions.

Metapsychological Assessment of the Adult Personality
Adult Profile

(State the material on which the Profile is based.)

I. Reason for Referral

Symptoms, anxieties, inhibitions, difficulties, abnormalities, breakdowns in functioning, acting out in the environment, inability to fulfill inherent potentialities, arrests in development leading to faulty ego and superego structuralization, etc.

An attempt is to be made, where possible, to distinguish between the manifest and the latent reasons for which the patient seeks help.

II. Description of the Patient as Directly or Indirectly Conveyed in the Interview

Personal appearance, moods, manner, affects, attitudes, etc.

III. Family Background (Past and Present) and Personal History

(As provided by patient or derived from other sources.)

IV. Possibly Significant Environmental Circumstances

(Interviewer's as well as patient's evaluation where available:)

(a) in relation to the timing of referral;
(b) in relation to the over-all causation of the disturbances as evaluated by the patient himself as well as by the interviewer;
(c) in relation to the links between individual and family pathology and their interaction.

V. Assessment of Drive and Ego-Superego Positions

A. *The Drives*

1. *Libido.*—Examine and state

(a) *Libidinal Position*

Describe the present libidinal position of the patient against the ideal normal position that he should have reached. Ideally, for women, a passive feminine position; for men, an active masculine one, with no more than the normal admixture in terms of bisexuality. At the time of assessment it is important to determine if the highest level has ever been reached, if it is being maintained, or if it has been abandoned regressively for an earlier one. Where the adult position has not been reached, it is important to assess the quality and quantity of interference contributed by previous phases.

(b) *Libido Distribution*

(i) *Cathexis of the Self*

whether the self is cathected, and whether there is sufficient narcissism (primary and secondary), invested in the body, the ego, or the superego, to ensure regard for the self, self-esteem, a sense of well-being, without leading to overestimation of the self. If possible, consider the regulation of narcissism; note whether this is brought about through identification, object dependence, magical means, work, etc. In the adult some information in relation to the cathexis of the self can be obtained in areas such as the patient's personal appearance, clothes, etc. (while the child's appearance in this respect reflects the adult's attitude toward him).

(ii) *Cathexis of Objects* (past and present; animate and inanimate)

The disturbances observed here should be described from the point of view of their predominant origin in one of the following phases: narcissistic, need-fulfilling, object constancy, preoedipal, oedipal, postoedipal, adolescence. As in previous sections evaluation should start at the highest level, i.e., at the level where the objects are considered and treated as partners in their own right. State:

—whether the individual in question has been able to choose his or her *sexual partner* and how far his object needs are met by the partner;

—whether the attitude necessary for *motherhood* and *fatherhood* has been achieved and on what level;

—whether and how far the infantile oedipal relationships have been outgrown or still dominate the picture;

—what part is played by *other human relationships* such as friendships, alliance to groups, or their avoidance, working relationships, etc.;

—above all, what part is played on the one hand by heterosexual object cathexes and on the other hand by homosexual object cathexes;

—whether too much libido is withdrawn from the real object world and sexual satisfaction sought in masturbation (accompanied by object-directed fantasies);

—whether and how deeply the individual is attached to objects which serve as substitutes for or extensions of ties with other human beings such as *animals, property, money*, etc.

2. *Aggression*

Note to what degree aggression is under control while being at the service of the personality in sexual life, work, and sublimatory activities.

Examine the defenses against aggression for relevant information. Aggression thus has to be assessed:

(a) according to quantity, i.e., presence or absence in the manifest picture;

(b) according to quality, i.e., correspondence with a given libidinal position;

(c) according to the direction or distribution, i.e., toward the object world (within or outside the family) or the self or both. In the latter case, state whether directed to the body or through the superego to the ego;

(d) according to the methods and defense activity used in dealing with it.

B. *Ego and Superego*

(a) Examine and state the intactness or defects of ego apparatus serving perception, memory, motility, etc.

(b) Examine and state in detail the intactness, or otherwise, of ego functions, as they are at present (memory, reality testing, synthesis, control of motility, speech, secondary-thought processes, etc.). If possible compare the present state of ego functions with functioning before the onset of the disturbance.

(c) Examine and state whether danger is experienced by the ego as coming from the external world, the id, or the superego, and whether consequently anxiety is felt predominantly in terms of fear of annihilation, separation anxiety, fear of loss of love, castration fear, guilt, etc.

(d) Examine in detail the status of the defense organization and consider:

—whether defense is employed specifically against individual drives, affects, and anxieties (to be identified here) or more generally against drive activity and instinctual pleasure as such;

—whether the patient's defense organization is mature, i.e., dependent on his own superego structure;

—whether it has remained immature, or regressed to pre-superego stages, i.e., whether id control is dependent on the object world;

—whether the defense mechanisms predominantly used are

archaic or of a higher order (for example, denial, projection versus reaction formation, sublimation);

—whether defense is balanced, i.e., whether the ego has at its disposal the use of many of the important mechanisms or is restricted to the excessive use of specific and primitive ones.

—whether defense is effective, especially in its dealing with anxiety, whether it results in equilibrium or disequilibrium, lability, mobility, rigidity, or symptom formation within the structure.

(e) Note all secondary interferences of defense activity with ego functioning, i.e., the price paid by the individual for the upkeep of the defense organization.

(f) Examine the status of the superego with regard to:

—its degree of structuralization (arrested, faulty, mature, etc.);

—its sources (where obvious);

—its functions (critical, aim- and direction-giving, satisfying);

—its effectiveness (in relation to ego and id);

—its stability (under the impact of internal and external pressure);

—the degree of its secondary sexual or aggressive involvement (in masochism, in melancholia, etc.).

C (A + B). *Reaction of the Total Personality to Specific Life Situations, Demands, Tasks, Opportunities, etc.*

Drive and ego development that were viewed separately for purposes of investigation in the earlier sections of the Profile are here seen in interaction with each other, as well as in reaction to specific situations, such as: the totality of the patient's attitude to his sex life; his success or failure in work; attitude to social and community responsibilities; his disturbed or undisturbed capacity for enjoying companionship, social relationships, and the ordinary pleasures of life; his vulnerability and ability or failure to withstand disappointments, losses, misfortunes, fateful events, environmental changes of all kinds, etc.

VI. Assessment of Fixation Points and Regressions

As character disturbances, neuroses, and some psychotic disturbances—in contradistinction to the atypical personalities—are assumed to be based on fixations at various early levels and on drive regressions to them, the location of these points is one of the vital concerns of the diagnostician. At the time of initial diagnosis such areas are betrayed:

(a) by the type of the individual's object relationships, the type of drive activity, and the influence of these on type of ego performance in cases where these are manifestly below adult level;

(b) by certain forms of manifest behavior which are characteristic of the given patient and allow conclusions to be drawn about the underlying id processes which have undergone repression and modification but have left an unmistakable imprint. The best example is the overt obsessional character where cleanliness, orderliness, punctuality, withholding and hoarding, doubt, indecision, slowing up, etc., betray the special difficulty experienced by the patient when coping with the impulses of the anal-sadistic phase, i.e., a fixation at that phase. Similarly, other character formations or attitudes betray fixation points at other levels or in other areas. Unrealistic concerns for health, safety of the marital partner, children, parents or siblings show a special difficulty of coping with death wishes; fear of medicines, food fads, etc., point to defense against oral fantasies; shyness to defense against exhibitionism, etc.;

(c) by the patient's fantasy activity. Some adult patients may occasionally be more willing than children to communicate some of their fantasy life at the diagnostic stage. Personality tests may reveal more of it (during analysis the patient's conscious and unconscious fantasy provides, of course, the fullest information about the pathogenically important parts of his developmental history);

(d) by those items in the symptomatology where the relations between surface and depth are firmly established, not open to variation, and well known to the diagnostician (such as the symptoms of the obsessional neurosis with their known fixation points); in contrast, symptoms with multiple causation such as anxiety attacks, insomnia, vomiting, some forms of headaches, etc., convey no clear genetic information at the diagnostic stage.

VII. Assessment of Conflicts

By examining the conflicts which are predominant in an individual's personality, assessments can be made of

—the level of maturity, i.e., the relative independence of the patient's personality structure;

—the severity of disturbance, if any;

—the intensity of therapy needed for alleviation or removal of the disturbance.

According to quality, conflicts, which should be described in detail, may be graded as follows:

(a) *External Conflicts*

In the adult direct clashes between id and external demands occur only where ego and superego development are defective. Conflicts between the total personality and the environment (refusal to adapt to, creative attempts to modify the environment) can occur at any stage after adolescence and are not pathogenic.

(b) *Internalized Conflicts*

In the fully structured mature adult, disharmonies between instinctual wishes and external demands are mediated via ego and superego and appear as internalized conflicts. Occasionally such conflicts are externalized and appear in the guise of conflicts with the environment.

(c) *Internal Conflicts* between insufficiently fused or incompatible drive representatives (such as unsolved ambivalence, activity versus passivity, masculinity versus femininity, etc.).

VIII. Assessment of Some General Characteristics with a Bearing on the Need for Analytic Therapy and the Ability to Profit from It

An all-round metapsychological view of the patient will assist the analyst in assessing on the one hand the patient's need for internal change, and on the other hand his chances to effect this in psychoanalytic treatment.

As regards the need for internal change the following points may be considered relevant:

—whether the patient's id and ego agencies have been separated off from each other too completely by excessive use of repression, and whether better communication needs to be established between them;

—whether the ego's sphere of influence has been restricted unduly by the defenses and needs to be enlarged;

—whether ego mastery over the impulses is weakened for other than defensive reasons (ego defects, psychotic core, etc.) and whether improvement will depend in the first instance on the strengthening effect that therapy has on the ego resources;

—whether the superego structure is archaic and, through analysis of its sources, needs to be replaced by a more mature one;

—whether the libidinal and aggressive energies or only libido or aggression are bound up in countercathexes, conflicts, and symptom formation, and need to be released for constructive use.

The following characteristics, attitudes, and circumstances seem of relevance to either a positive or negative reaction to analytic therapy:

On the positive side:

—whether there is insight into the detrimental nature of the pathology, including the desire to be cured;

—whether there is ability for self-observation, self-criticism, and capacity to think and verbalize;

—whether the patient has a sufficiently high level of object relationship and a sufficient quantity of free object libido to establish a meaningful transference relationship to the analyst, and whether this relationship will serve also as a treatment alliance and withstand all the ups and downs of the resistances;

—whether there is enough frustration tolerance to cope with the necessary restrictions on wish fulfillment in the transference setting;

—whether there is enough tension tolerance to cope with the additional anxiety likely to be released by exposing conflicts and weakening defenses during the analytic process;
—whether the patient has on previous occasions shown ability to persevere in the face of difficulties;
—whether there are (past or present) areas of established sublimations which attest to the patient's capacity to displace and neutralize energies and to accept substitute satisfactions;
—whether in the absence of established sublimations there is evidence of a sublimation potential which has been interfered with by pathology;
—whether there is flexibility of libido (as contrasted with adhesiveness);
—whether there is a positive, optimistic general outlook on life (as contrasted with a crippling pessimism).

On the negative side:

—whether there is dangerously low tolerance for frustration and anxiety, coupled with the unwillingness to renounce secondary gains of the pathology;
—whether the patient's pathology is part of a pathological family or professional setting and cannot be altered without causing major upheavals and breakups in the external life situation;
—whether there are extreme self-punishing, self-destructive, and masochistic attitudes that are satisfied through the pathology and oppose improvements, i.e., which cause negative therapeutic reactions.

Example of an Adult Profile[2]

Mr. C. H.
Age: 34 years old,
Married, 3 children.

Based on:

1. Interview with a psychiatrist (Dr. A.). 1.31.1963.
2. Forty-one weekly reports to the Freud Centenary Fund Scheme for Adult Analysis, covering the period from March, 1962 to December 27, 1962.

[2] The Profile has been prepared by Dr. H. Nagera.

I. Reason for Referral

Analysis for this patient was suggested by the therapist of his daughter Alice; Mr. C. H. had been seen for some time at regular weekly or fortnightly intervals. Alice, who is four years old, had been in psychoanalytic treatment for almost two years. *Her* main complaint is a sleeping disturbance consisting of waking up and crying.

During the interview with Mrs. X (the child's therapist) Mr. H. came to realize that he tends to avoid arguments. He similarly avoids decisions leaving them to somebody else. If he has to make a decision in business, he later worries about the consequences but does not want to know what the consequences are.

He finds it difficult to deal with figures in authority and does not take well to instructions. "I always fight against them as I did at school. I would not wear the school tie and cap; I am against authority and in my political thinking I am rather left but not a communist; my father has always been rather the same."

When Dr. A. asked if there was any relation between his seeking treatment and the fact that his daughter was in treatment, the patient answered: "If something is suggested by the therapist who sees me and my wife regularly, I always make suggestions why it ought to be done, or why it will depend on my wife whether or not it will be done." The patient added that he would not have thought of having psychoanalysis if his daughter had not been in treatment. Nevertheless, he always thought he should have some help.

Dr. A.'s opinion of the patient was that "there is a very positive indication for full psychoanalytic treatment." He further expressed the opinion that this patient's basic conflicts were around his repressed oedipal rivalry and his inhibition of aggression. Once Mr. H. could free himself from the latter, Dr. A. felt, there would be an improvement in his masculinity that might bring the wife as the next patient.

II. Description of the Patient as Directly or Indirectly Conveyed in the Interview

The patient is medium height, neither thin nor fat, and has rather dark skin and dark hair. He is very punctual and usually rather anxious, restless, and a bit jerky at times, though quite capable of settling down quietly. He is rather careless of his personal appearance, as shown by his dirty hands and nails. His clothes tend to be somewhat dirty as well.

He is polite and well mannered in his behavior, especially during the initial interview. He expresses himself well and uses some technical psychoanalytic words. He works as an insurance agent for a company which does a great deal of business in this and in other countries. The patient works in the department that deals especially with foreign countries.

He describes himself as having few friends. At work he feels he has made no progress whatsoever. He attributes this to the difficulties he has in dealing with people in authority, etc. He has been employed in the present capacity for the past eight years. His net earnings are £1,200.

The patient is not particularly religious but likes to keep the forms up to a point; he observes a number of Jewish holidays mainly because of the children.

III. Family Background (Past and Present) and Personal History

Past

Mr. H. comes from a very poor Jewish background. His father, now sixty-nine, works as a tailor. His mother is sixty-eight. She is very ill, having recently had an operation for cancer. Her sight has been very poor for many years.

There is a brother three years younger than the patient (thirty-one at present), married, active, outgoing, successful.

The mother is described by the patient as the strong character of the family, in contrast to the weak father. She is experienced as an overpowering character who completely controlled and dominated the father and the family.

She is further described by the patient as having had a tendency to cheat and lie, playing him and his brother against each other in order to make them behave as she wanted. For example, she is said to have moved the clock ahead several hours to try to get the children to sleep early. Mr. H. and his brother were aware of the mother's trick because of the light and activity outside.

Mr. H. feels she was always nagging and trying to make them

feel guilty. His childhood is seen as full of rules and prohibitions coming from the mother.

He thinks the mother was always hoarding, always taking home whatever other people were going to throw away, even if she had no use for it, and the objects were not even in a good condition.

The father is seen mainly as a weak and passive man by the patient. Both parents had great hopes and expectations (scholastically) for Mr. H. He feels that in this respect he has been a complete disappointment to them.

Present

Mr. H. was married about eleven years ago. His wife is thirty years old, described as very efficient, the organizing and executive power in the family. She comes from a much wealthier Jewish home. Mr. H. feels his father-in-law has no time for him because he is poor and unsuccessful. He feels his wife is now subjected to economic restrictions and anxieties that were unknown to her before.

Mrs. H. is usually affectionate and in general the relationship is not bad. The patient thinks his wife is a somewhat anxious woman, and from his description she appears somewhat obsessional. She apparently is not able to go to bed in the evening (no matter how late it may be) until she has completely cleaned up the house and finished all other household work in the most meticulous and obsessional manner. The patient frequently tries (because of the late hour) to get her to leave the unessential things for the next day, but she is quite unable to do so.

The patient is on reasonably good terms with his brother-in-law, the only sibling of his wife; he is very much preferred and favored economically by Mrs. H.'s father.

Mr. and Mrs. H. have three children, a boy, Joseph, who is nearly seven years old and had a diagnostic interview not long ago because of learning difficulties. No treatment was advised at the time but special educational help. Alice, a little girl of four, is in treatment because of her sleep disturbances, and there is a third child only one year old.

Personal History

Nothing is known of his early developmental history.

The patient is known to have grown up in tight economic and

rather crowded conditions. He has many memories of listening to primal-scene noises up to the time when he was an adolescent. He remembers being annoyed by it and thinking of his father: "Why doesn't he leave her alone?" On the other hand, apart from this exposure to primal scene, Mr. H.'s mother seems to have looked after Mr. H.'s body care until rather late in the patient's life. He believes he remembers being bathed by his mother until he was about twelve years old. At that time he was bathed occasionally by the father as well.

Mr. H. studied for two years at a university but was in effect dismissed because of his examination failures. Even at that time he had great difficulty concentrating because of his excessive fantasy life. He did his National Service in the Medical Corps for two to three years.

IV. Possibly Significant Environmental Circumstances

1. The mother's personality and the severe restrictive atmosphere at home.
2. Excessive exposure to primal scene and body stimulation through being bathed until a late age.

V. Assessment of Drive and Ego-Superego Positions

A. The Drives

1. *Libido*

(a) *Libidinal Position*

This patient is able to perform sexually in an active masculine position under favorable circumstances. He described his sexual life during his interview with Dr. A. as regular and satisfactory.

Further material elicited during treatment seems to point to the fact that this ideal state of affairs is frequently interfered with for a number of different reasons and on one occasion, so far as is known, led to temporary impotence. Thus, Mr. H. has mentioned how worried he was about not being potent at the time of his marriage, and he was in fact temporarily impotent at that time. Mr. H.'s complaints about his not being able to give his wife more money for the home and entertainment, etc., are, on another level, a reference to his dissatisfaction with his potency.

At the beginning of his married life he remained for some time very concerned about his ability to satisfy his wife sexually. He felt that his wife did not enjoy sexual intercourse. He had to ask her frequently about this. She reassured him that everything was fine. He does not worry consciously about it any more, though his wife's reactions during intercourse lead him to believe that she does not really enjoy her sexual life.

The main sources of interference in this area can be enumerated as follows:

(i) *The homosexual components of the patient's bisexual conflict.*—Mr. H.'s passive, feminine fantasies are perhaps best shown in the following examples. He had been reading a French book describing several intercourse positions. He was very excited by the one where intercourse was performed with the woman on top. He proposed it to his wife, who rejected the idea. He said his wife would have been the male in this relationship. At this point Mr. H. felt that he had my weight on him, commenting with great embarrassment that he thought in this fantasy he wanted the analyst on top of him. Mr. H. remembered how much pleasure he got when being bathed by his father at quite a late age. He always felt rejected and disappointed because his father sent him out of the room when he took his own bath. He wanted to remain to help bathe the father and look at him. Mr. H. thinks he was between ten and twelve at that time.

Some of this is now transferred to the relationship to his son Joseph (who is about seven). When treatment started Mr. H. used to get into bed with his son every morning. He explained it as being Joseph's wish resulting from his jealousy of the excessive amount of attention that Alice is said to be receiving. He still bathes Joseph frequently.

The patient described how on his way to the Underground after a session he was suddenly seized by the idea that he wanted to be loved by the analyst. He found the thought very disturbing and went on to explain that he did not really wish me to love him in a homosexual way but that he wanted me to admire him.

He described how he always finds himself in conflict with people in authority (males) while at the same time wishing to be admired and loved by them. Analysis thus is felt by the patient as a submissive experience in which he is forced to play a passive-feminine role lying on the couch while the analyst is behind him.

Mr. H. remembers having once made an overt homosexual advance by stroking a man's hair. The man was very annoyed and he was most embarrassed. This seems to have taken place during late adolescence.

(ii) *Fantasies of being damaged and castrated.*—A fantasy of having a damaged penis seems to play an important role in Mr. H.'s feeling of "insufficiency and inferiority" and in what he calls his "not being able to do well in life." Mr. H. remembers this preoccupation as going back many years. He says he remembers the following incident from his childhood. He was being bathed by his mother while another woman (a friend of his mother?) was also present. His mother then expressed some concern about his penis. He is not sure, but he thought that she meant that there was something wrong with it or perhaps that it was too short.

(iii) *Interference due to important fixations at the oedipal level with incomplete solution of the oedipal conflicts.*—For description and examples see under Section VI, Fixations and Regressions.

(iv) *Interferences due to fixation at the anal-sadistic level of libidinal development; these make sexuality into somewhat of a dirty, objectionable activity.*—Sexuality has strong anal connotations for Mr. H. These types of conflict frequently find expression through the symbolism of coal, getting dirty, cleaning the bunker, etc., either in his dreams or fantasies.

(v) *Interference coming from his conflicts with the aggressive drive in general and with anal sadism and phallic aggression in particular.*—See under Section V, 2. Aggression.

(b) *Libido Distribution*

(i) *Cathexis of the Self*

Mr. H. has on the whole a rather poor opinion of himself. He feels ashamed because he failed at the university and has not done well for himself in life, economically or otherwise.

He attempts to compensate for his feelings of inferiority, inadequacy, and failure by a very rich fantasy life and frequent withdrawal into it. He describes himself as the "Walter Mitty" type. The fantasies occur in great numbers, the content covering a wide range, but the central theme is always connected with being successful. He is, for example, a most famous surgeon or psychoanalyst, etc., and sees himself performing difficult operations with great success. They bring fame, wealth, admiration, and great respect. (It is not without interest to note that his father wanted the patient to be a doctor. He is aware that the fantasy serves both to gratify the father's wish and to attract his admiration.)

(ii) *Cathexis of Objects* (past and present; animate and inanimate)

Mr. H. has been able to choose an appropriate sexual partner in life and there is no doubt that he can consider and treat his wife as a partner in her own right. This level of functioning with his wife and others is interfered with by his strong ambivalence and anal sadism as well as other conflicts. Although there is a basically positive attitude toward the children and fatherhood, a number of conflicts interfere in this area. Thus, the children, especially Joseph, are seen as oedipal rivals in a battle for his wife's affection and sexual favors. On the other hand, he sees them partly as extensions of the self and hopes that they will restore his damaged self-esteem through their achievements and successes. For the same reason any shortcomings and failures of the children are felt as his own failures.

Finally, the infantile oedipal relationships have not been outgrown to a sufficient degree and consequently tend to interfere at times with a more mature and adequate relationship to his wife, children, friends, colleagues, boss, etc. Examples illustrating this point can be found under Section VI, Assessment of Fixation Points and Regressions. This patient's very significant attitude to money will also be described there.

2. *Aggression*

Conflicts in this area constitute one of the essential problems of this patient's psychopathology. They are extremely important in their own right also because they make a contribution to other conflictive areas.

Aggression is expressed mainly verbally and in fantasy, with frequent death wishes at the slightest provocation. Some of the aggression finds its way into provocative, teasing, stubborn behavior (anal-sadistic) with certain objects. Some of it seems to find an outlet in somewhat careless driving and speeding (phallic aggression). A great deal is directed toward the object world in the forms described above, but a certain amount is turned against the self, especially on certain specific occasions, as some of the examples will show. Projection, repression, and turning against the self are three favored mechanisms to deal with it.

(i) *Aggression Finding Outlet in Fantasy*

This can be seen in his fantasy of being called by the Foreign Office to work for them. He was expected to deal with a "foreign agent" (the analyst). He killed this man in the fantasy.

(ii) *Expressed Verbally*

His aggression breaks through in meetings with colleagues at work where he presents his points of view with so much provocation and hostility that they become unacceptable. Most of the time he tends to remain silent out of the fear of saying something improper and being criticized for it.

He tends to express some aggression verbally, for example, in the relationship to his brother. The brother was going on holidays. Mr. H. said that the brother was so lucky that even the weather was good for him. He did hope that something would spoil it.

(iii) *Aroused by Oedipal Rivalry with His Brother*

The oedipal rivalry with the brother has become more manifest during treatment. Mr. H. claims that he was not fully aware of its intensity before. He recounted a recent incident when his brother paid the taxi for their mother to go from the hospital to her home. He felt the brother was "buying his way" at home; this was unfair because he cannot afford the money to do the same. At such moments he felt he could strangle his brother.

(iv) *As Shown in the Transference with Examples of Projection*

Frequently when Mr. H. feels annoyed or angry with the analyst he gets rid of the feeling by attributing it to the analyst. Thus, he finds that the analyst's face looks angry or his voice sounds angry.

Aggression has only rarely been expressed against the analyst. For example, the patient once stated in an angry voice that had he had the money, he might not have chosen me as an analyst. The sequence that followed is very illustrative of the type of conflict the patient has with his aggression and the type and form of defense activity that is called into operation. No sooner had he said this than he felt very perturbed because he had been offensive to me. A few seconds later he resorted to "projection" to dispose of what was obviously a very disturbing feeling. He started saying with much feeling that he felt that the analyst was trying to provoke him, but he would not be provoked at all, etc. (The analyst had been silent all this time.)

During treatment Mr. H. developed a fear of driving because he was afraid of having an accident in which he would smash a car. Soon Mr. H. connected this fantasy with his having noticed the analyst's new car and his feelings of envy. It was the analyst's car that he wanted to smash, the analyst having now become the successful brother, who can get a new car frequently and thus bid for the mother's admiration.

(v) *Aggression and Careless Driving, Death Wishes against Wife and Children*

In one of his sessions, Mr. H. told of a car accident, withholding a certain amount of information related to it because he thought the analyst would feel that he was a careless father who endangered the lives of his family. What he left out of his account was that his children were in the car when the accident took place. This accident seems one which, though the other party could be held responsible, really occurred because Mr. H. did not take the necessary steps or care to prevent it. It appears that it was due partly to his death wishes against his wife and children (the car was hit where they were sitting and then turned over). At this point Mr. H. talked with great distress about his many conscious death wishes toward his family.

He is in a way surprised that he is not more frequently involved in accidents since there are roads where he knows he ought to stop and does not; he just takes the chance.

(vi) *Death Fantasies Relating to His Brother-in-law and Mother, and Defense Activity of Turning Aggression against the Self*

Mr. H. frequently has fantasies about his brother-in-law's death, which he thinks will induce his wife's parents to turn their attention to her and himself. He will then be treated as a son and receive the benefits of their economic help that are at the moment given mostly to the brother-in-law.

Mr. H.'s abundant death wishes have always included his mother. When the seriousness of her illness became known and led to hospitalization and operation, Mr. H.'s guilt rose to a pitch, his death fantasies now having found support in reality. He started to turn them against himself and on a number of occasions was nearly run over by cars because he was distracted by thoughts and fantasies that interfered with his attention while crossing roads, etc.

(vii) *Conflict around Phallic Aggression*

One example of his conflict around phallic aggression could be observed when he was in the Army. He remembered "being in a panic and feeling sick" when there were exercises where he had to use the bayonet—body fights between two groups of soldiers, having to push the bayonet into the body of dummies, etc. The above material appeared in relation to a slip of the tongue. At the time his son wanted a penknife. This distressed Mr. H. greatly. He thought Joseph wanted it to fight with the other boys at the school: "I thought Joseph wanted it to fight with the other boys, *not to fight with the other girls.*" The slip shows the unconscious link in Mr. H.'s mind of this type of aggression and phallic sexuality.

B. EGO AND SUPEREGO

(a) and (b) *Ego Apparatus and Ego Functions*

There are no known defects in this patient's ego apparatus and no primary deficiencies are observable in relation to his ego functioning.

(c) and (d) *Defense Activity* is used against libidinal and aggressive strivings as well as against certain painful affects (guilt, feelings of inferiority, etc.).

The patient tends to use a large number of defenses, including some rather primitive ones like denial and projection, which are used frequently and excessively. On the whole the defense organization is not successful in dealing with the many conflicts active in this patient and has led to a number of undesirable restrictions and faulty adjustments of the ego structure.

(i) *Withdrawal into Fantasy.*—He remembers that this tendency was already present and occupied a great deal of his mental activities when he was eighteen or nineteen years old. The patient feels that it was this constant fantasying that spoiled his academic efforts at the university. He remembers that he sat for hours with his book, but he could not concentrate. These fantasies seem to have taken the place of early masturbatory activities. He now has the same feeling of shame and guilt about them that he remembers having when he masturbated. Similarly, he feels that he now gets the same pleasure out of these fantasies that he did out of his earlier masturbation. Masturbation was always a tremendous conflict. He was always trying to stop himself from doing it but was quite unable to do so. This is what now happens with his fantasies.

(ii) *Identification with His Parents.*—(1) He has very high expectations of his children, but especially of his son Joseph. (2) Mr. H. still bathes Joseph, who is about seven years old, as his own mother and father used to do with him up to a very late age. (3) The patient recounted with guilt that on several occasions Alice actually walked into the room while Mr. H. and his wife were having intercourse. On many occasions his daughter has walked around the house in the middle of the night while they were having intercourse. Mr. H. seems to be forced to expose his children to the primal scene (sometimes look, more frequently listen), just as he was exposed to it himself.

(iii) *Identification with His Father.*—He never buys on Hire Purchase because that is against his principles. He does not remember his father buying anything through it. He cannot do it either.

(iv) *Passive into Active.*—Separation is difficult, even on week ends sometimes. He deals with this by turning passive into active. He felt he did not want to come one day and while he was on his way to the analytic session he made a mistake in the Underground and passed the right station.

Mr. H. reacts strongly to breaks in his treatment for holidays. At such points he feels he wants to stop coming to his treatment before the holiday arrives.

(v) *Passivity.*—He is extremely passive and leaves every decision, jobs at the house, etc., to his wife, who seems quite happy to take on these responsibilities.

(vi) *Displacement.*—This is frequently used to deal with aggression. The object to whom it is directed is thus frequently changed. At home aggressive feelings related to the wife are often directed to the children.

(vii) *Rationalization.*—For example, he makes all sorts of excuses to himself so that he can phone home two or three times every day and keep in control.

(viii) *Intellectualization.*—Included here and in the case of the previous defense is his use of analytic reading for defensive purposes.

(ix) *Externalization.*—At the time of the break for holidays Mr. H. externalizes his own fears and anxieties concerning the separation. He describes in great detail how upset his daughter is because of the coming holiday in her treatment.

Externalization of superego sometimes leading to projection is frequently observable. After a session when he talked about his sexual fantasies relating to a ten-year-old girl, his scoptophilia, and his death wishes, he said that he observed that at the beginning of that session my face was pale while at the end of it it was red. He attributed it to my having become very angry with him and my having to control myself in order not to recriminate him for his "thoughts," etc.

(x) *Intellectualization and Isolation of Affect.*—These two frequently combined defense mechanisms are used when he is talking about his sexual life or some other distressing event. He then sounds like a professor addressing his students in a cold fashion about sexual matters.

(xi) *Denial.*—He has to pretend to himself and others that he could not care less about getting in touch with his parents and especially his mother, when in fact he makes quite sure that his wife does so regularly and keeps him informed.

Denial was used as well to deal with his mother's illness and hospitalization (cancer operation). He constantly claimed that he did not care what might happen to her. In some cases the denial became a reversal of affects, Mr. H. claiming that he would be better off when she is gone, etc. At the same time he was obviously very disturbed because of his mother's illness and went to see her at the hospital practically every day. Interpretation of this denial and reversal frequently brought him close to tears.

At the time of the Profumo affair Mr. H. denied having any interest in it. In fact he says he has a rather "puritanical attitude" to these questions. He never buys or reads the *News of the World,* etc. Later it transpired that though he does not buy the paper himself, he regularly goes to his father-in-law's house, where *News of the*

World is available, and there reads it with great enjoyment. Moreover, he is frequently the one who starts discussion of this affair at work.

He has to deny any awareness or knowledge of the economic situation of his wife's parents in order to control the hate he would feel for his father-in-law if he admitted that the father-in-law is capable of helping him financially but never does so. He similarly attempts to avoid fantasies in which he takes the favored position of his brother-in-law after the latter's death, etc.

(xii) *Projection.*—Mr. H.'s mother-in-law likes to come down for a few days whenever the H.'s are on holiday. Mr. H. finds this unbearable. He thinks she comes because she cannot trust him at all. He thinks she feels he is not capable even of finding a *reasonably safe* and convenient place to take the family on holiday: that is why she really comes down, to check up that everything is all right. Mr. H. himself refers to this as being paranoid, but sometimes he feels convinced of the truth of such judgments.

Mr. H. said that he knew that in his first interview (facing the analyst) I thought he was a homosexual. He based this statement on my having asked twice during his interview whether he had three children. He interpreted this as my doubting his masculinity. (For another example, see under Aggression. After trying to be offensive to the analyst, he felt the analyst was trying to provoke him.) Similar examples are abundant and can be found in his relationship to colleagues and superiors. After having meant to be offensive to them, he begins to feel persecuted.

(e) *Secondary Interference of Ego Functions*

Mr. H.'s excessive use of denial and particularly of projection (the latter especially to deal with his aggression) frequently interferes with his reality testing and reality adaptation. These factors further complicate his relationship to colleagues and superiors and badly handicap his opportunities of improving his position in his firm.

Similarly, his excessive withdrawal into fantasy interferes with his ability to work. When he was at the university, it was partly the reason for his failure. It worries him that he can drive for long periods in this dreamy state paying no proper attention to conditions on the road.

(f) *Superego Structure*

Mr. H. has a well-developed superego structure and on the whole a rather severe one. Its severity seems partly the result of identifications with a strict mother, seen even stricter than she is in reality because of the projection of his own aggressive impulses onto her.

He reacts with extreme guilt to fantasies in which he sees himself married to rich women and consequently without any economic difficulties. Similarly, he shows great guilt and anxiety because of his aggressive fantasies and death wishes. He is very distressed that even in fantasy he can think such things, especially since he feels that whatever is wrong at home is largely his fault.

Mr. H.'s behavior at work is frequently aimed at showing himself in a bad light, as an extremely inefficient person. By such means he manages to keep isolated, never making any progress at work. By these and other similar mechanisms he seems to deal with intense unconscious guilt and need for punishment, thus being forced to make a failure out of himself in spite of his potentialities.

A great deal of this guilt comes from the oedipal rivalry with his father. His superego seems to demand that he must not outgrow or do much better than his parents did, especially his father. This is shown in the following two examples:

When he was about to buy a carpet for his bedroom, he talked about the unpleasant feeling he gets because his parents never had such a thing in their home.

Similarly, he cannot buy through the Hire Purchase because his father never did and doing so may bring material comforts that his parents never had.

C (A + B). REACTION OF THE TOTAL PERSONALITY TO SPECIFIC LIFE SITUATIONS, DEMANDS, TASKS, OPPORTUNITIES, ETC.

Mr. H. is unable to make full use of his potentialities at his work. He is reduced to the performance of activities well below his capabilities. His character difficulties make it difficult for him to relate to superiors, people in authority, and even colleagues.

He has very few friends, and at work he relates to a very limited number of persons.

Adaptation and capacity to enjoy his sexual life: As described elsewhere.

Capacity to enjoy leisure: Mr. H. finds week ends somewhat of a strain. It seems that at present this is due mainly to the fact that a week end implies many hours of close contact with the family and especially with his son Joseph, whom he sees as a rival and who tends to annoy and irritate him. Sometimes he finds it difficult to control himself in relation to the boy.

As for holidays, the only ones about which I have direct knowledge were not enjoyable for Mr. H. for a number of reasons. It is difficult to decide, on the basis of my scanty knowledge, how much his complaints are rationalizations or justified reality-adapted complaints about the places.

Capacity to enjoy companionship, social relationships, the ordinary pleasures of life, etc.: His capacities in these respects are limited by his conflicts in general and especially by those around aggression; the need for control and the type of his character disturbance further interfere here. Thus his ability to enjoy companionship and social relationships is limited, as is the case with the ordinary pleasures of life. He feels restless at the thought of having things easy or having more out of life than his very restricted parents did.

VI. Assessment of Fixation Points and Regressions

Mr. H. shows at present a great deal of drive activity pertaining to the anal and phallic-oedipal phases of drive development. There is very little, if any, relevant material that points to the oral phase. My general impressions through Mr. H.'s own description of himself, incomplete as it has to be, favor the conclusion that such activity is mainly the result of strong fixations acquired when going through such phases rather than the result of later regressive moves. This is based on the fact that his anal character traits have remained in the foreground, playing a most important role throughout his development up to the present. There are indications that a similar situation existed at the phallic-oedipal level and that the conflicts typical of this phase remained largely unsolved. These have shaped his personality and conflicts in their present form.

On the other hand, there are no indications in the history of this patient that conflicts in later life led to qualitatively relevant regressive moves to previously existing fixation points and earlier modes of drive gratification.

With this patient one has the impression that these early difficulties, especially the anal ones, found their way into the character structure, leaving a permanent imprint there in the form of an anal character of a not very desirable type or quality. Furthermore, the difficulties at the anal level have contaminated to some degree the phallic and genital levels of sexual development. Thus, sexual intercourse is somehow considered as a dirty activity.

A number of examples follow to show the indicators to fixation at the pregenital levels.

Anal

Mr. H. shows a clear-cut tendency to argue for the sake of arguing. This is a typical component of the transference relationship; every interpretation will at first be rejected. He can accept it only at a later stage and after satisfying the strong tendency to argue.

He needs to keep absolute control of what goes on at home. He has to be consulted about the most trivial things before his wife can make any decisions. Similarly, he phones home two or three times a day to arrange everything.

Some compulsive doubting is present, showing the strong anal components of his personality structure. This appears combined with strong ambivalent feelings as in the following example. He was trying to write a letter of thanks to his child's therapist because of her suggestion that he should come to treatment. He wrote several drafts of the letter and was never satisfied. Finally, he typed one of them, placing it in an envelope to have it posted. He did not send it and after some time had to open the envelope and type a different letter again. This behavior was repeated for several days. The compulsive doubting was related here to his ambivalence about treatment. This made him doubt that he expressed his thanks properly in the letter.

His ambivalence is clearly shown in most of his relationships, but especially in that with his brother. His anal ambivalent feelings in relation to him are exacerbated by his oedipal rivalry since the brother is believed to be more successful and admired by the mother. Mr. H. tries not to invite his brother to parties when the mother is going to be there.

Mr. H.'s attitude to money is very revealing. He is very secretive about it. At the time he was buying a carpet for his bedroom he hid from the analyst the fact that he had £80 to buy it. He pretended for some time that he had no money for it. Mr. H. connected this behavior with his need to keep this secret from his mother, who would otherwise want to *take this money away* from him. He also fears that his wife always wants to take whatever little money he has. He had similar feelings in relation to the analyst.

Anal provocative and teasing behavior is a characteristic trait of Mr. H.'s relationships to relatives, friends, bosses, etc. He will not come down for breakfast when called, forcing his wife to call and shout at him repeatedly that breakfast is getting cold. He knows this behavior annoys his wife very much.

His scholastic failure is partly a result of his anal defiant attitude against the parents' ambitions.

The relationship to the mother and others is still on a sadomasochistic level; if she says "white," he will automatically think in terms of "black" and the other way around. This is also observable in the transference, as described above. Further, he is somewhat stubborn and obstinate.

He frequently has a rather grubby and dirty appearance. His shirt, nails, and especially his suit were for many months somewhat dirty (now he wears a new suit).

Phallic-Oedipal

In the following fantasy Mr. H. sees himself as a prominent analyst who is consulted by two women from the Hampstead Clinic about a child. In the fantasy he was very pleased with himself because he was as good as I and was much admired by these two women, one of them being Alice's therapist (to make clear the oedipal connotation of this fantasy, see below the fantasy in which Mrs. X and I are a couple, have intercourse, and exclude him from the relationship). This fantasy is in fact one of a series in which he is admired by the mother and considered to be as good as the father.

Similarly, oedipal rivalry (related to both father and brother) is expressed in terms of colleagues who are preferred and promoted by "the firm" (mother). These people represent the father or brother who are admired and favored by the mother, while Mr. H. feels like a small child who cannot quite understand why the mother prefers the father, whom he envies and whose place he wants to take.

Fantasies of "having a successful business," "getting a better position," becoming "the head of an important firm," "getting control of the firm," etc., stand symbolically for taking his father's position in the relationship to the mother. His constant dissatisfaction is due partly to his oedipal rivalry and fantasies. The guilt and the fear of retaliation that go with it seem to interfere with his ability to make any actual progress in his work, as pointed out in the Superego section.

At a later stage in treatment Mrs. X and the analyst were made into the parental couple that excluded him from their sexual activities. He had fantasies that Mrs. X and I would meet during the holiday and have intercourse.

His son Joseph is seen as an oedipal rival competing for the favor of his wife.

Recently, his father showed some interest in a book Mr. H. was reading. The book is somewhat "sexy." He was very annoyed with his father and felt that he was watching his sexual activities.

At present Mr. H.'s oedipal rivalry is expressed mainly in the relationships to his son, his brother, superiors, etc. His father has so far largely been spared, partly because of defensive reasons Mr. H. shows strong positive feelings for him (partly perhaps as the result of his primary conflict around bisexuality, though it is not really possible at this time to point out with certainty what is primary and what defensive). In any case, for the moment the father has been rendered an inoffensive, weak, helpless creature. There are, nevertheless, a few indications that somewhere in Mr. H.'s mind there is the image—fantasied or real—of a violent, dangerous man. This could be seen in one or two recently recovered memories which showed that the father had been in quite a rage.

VII. Assessment of Conflicts

Conflicts in this patient are internalized. They involve id, ego, and superego structures, and concern both the libidinal and aggressive drives.

On the libidinal side they concern especially an insufficiently resolved oedipal situation and certain aspects of the patient's anal component instincts (other aspects having been taken directly into the personality structure in the form of character traits which, though perhaps undesirable, are not conflictive as far as the patient is concerned, e.g., his obstinacy).

On the aggressive side there is a massive conflict with practically all forms of aggressive expression. On the whole the conflicts described and the defense activity used in the attempt to cope with them have led to a number of ego restrictions, to an inability to utilize his full potential, and to certain character distortions, rather than to symptom formation of a more typical neurotic nature.

Similarly, there is abundant evidence of important conflicts of an internal nature such as unsolved ambivalence, active-passive conflicts and masculine-feminine ones. It is very difficult to say at this stage how much of the active-passive and masculine-feminine types of conflict is primary in nature and how much secondary and defensive.

As already described, he depicts himself as a very passive man, quite contented to leave every decision to his wife but at the same time insisting on being consulted. His passive-feminine and passive-active conflicts showed themselves clearly in the transference relationship in which he falls into a passive submissive position; he then feels compelled to reject all of the analyst's interpretations, though he admits that with a part of his mind he fully agrees with them. On the other hand, he wants the analyst to do everything for him, to love and to admire him, "to be on top of him."

His fantasies of occupying the position of a woman during intercourse while making his wife into a man lying on top of him have already been referred to. Other examples have been referred to elsewhere.

As to ambivalence, several examples have been given under Section VI, Assessment of Fixation Points and Regressions.

VIII. Assessment of Some General Characteristics with a Bearing on the Need for Analytic Therapy and the Ability to Profit from It

On the positive side:

—whether there is insight into the detrimental nature of the pathology, including the desire to be cured

This patient has always had some awareness of being in need of help but would not have looked for it himself at this stage. Particularly during adolescence and early adulthood, he was fully aware of how his conflicts and marked withdrawal into fantasy ruined his chances at the university. It was then that he started reading psychological books and articles in an attempt to understand and solve his problems. As already mentioned, he came to treatment through his daughter's treatment and the daughter's therapist's advice. He did not experience neurotic suffering or anxiety but instead had an awareness of the limitations and restrictions in his character and personality.

—whether there is ability for self-observation, self-criticism, and capacity to think and verbalize

The patient has given signs of a reasonably good capacity for self-observation. Self-criticism may be somewhat exaggerated, especially in relation to certain aspects of his personality or fantasy life. He can verbalize a good deal of his inner life without showing any marked tendency to act out.

—whether the patient has a sufficiently high level of object relationship, and a sufficient quantity of free object libido to establish a meaningful transference relationship to the analyst, and whether this relationship will serve also as a treatment alliance and withstand all the ups and downs of the resistances

The patient has reached the necessary level in terms of object relationships so as to make the type of transference relationship that he can be expected to establish during the analytic procedure a potentially useful one for therapeutic purposes. In other words, it can be expected that the object-constancy quality of his potential relationship to the therapist will be largely predominant since there are few signs, if any, of his having to use his object on a need-satisfying basis. Furthermore, there is every evidence that there is enough free object libido available at the present time to make it possible to expect the establishment of an appropriate transference relationship. There is no evidence of depression, ongoing intense mourning, etc.

—*whether there is enough frustration tolerance to cope with the necessary restrictions on wish fulfillment in the transference setting*

There was nothing in this patient's history to make us doubt his ability to tolerate the frustrations and anxieties involved in the analytic treatment.

—*whether there is enough tension tolerance to cope with the additional anxiety likely to be released by exposing conflicts and weakening defenses during the analytic process*

During the few months he has been in analysis he has shown himself able to cope in these respects.

—*whether the patient has on previous occasions shown ability to persevere in the face of difficulties*

This patient has the capacity to persevere. His failures are due rather to the nature of his character and conflicts which interfere with the achievement of positive results, sometimes in spite of strenuous efforts.

—*whether there are (past or present) areas of established sublimations which attest to the patient's capacity to displace and neutralize energies and to accept substitute satisfactions*

His achievements in terms of actual sublimations, etc., are somewhat limited. The patient's situation is that so far he has not fulfilled his potential, being in fact very critical of himself for it. The solution of his oedipal conflicts and especially of the conflicts around aggression may lead to a better utilization of this energy for constructive and sublimatory activities with an over-all improvement of his performance. There is no doubt that he has a potential capacity to accept substitute gratifications and once the situations of conflicts, fixations, etc., are helped by analysis, we can expect this to come to the foreground.

—*whether in the absence of established sublimations there is evidence of a sublimation potential which is interfered with by pathology*

Mr. H. has a reasonably good potential for sublimation. At present his capacity to make use of it is very much interfered with by the nature and content of some of his early neurotic conflicts, e.g., guilt about doing better than his father, etc. Similarly, some undesirable character traits (themselves an attempt at solution of some of his early neurotic conflicts) further interfere with the use of his sublimation potential, for example, his extreme obstinacy, stubbornness, and negativism.

—whether there is flexibility of libido (as contrasted with adhesiveness)

On the whole he shows no tendency to an excessive adhesiveness of the libido. He is most probably within the limits we observe in the large majority of cases.

—whether there is a positive, optimistic general outlook on life (as contrasted with a crippling pessimism)

Mr. H. is the sort of man who has a mainly positive constructive outlook, in spite of obvious handicaps, shortcomings, and past failures. He has come to analysis to improve his relationship with his family and the handling of his children, especially with the hope of being able to do better for himself in the future.

On the negative side:

In the case of this patient, there are no important secondary gains to be renounced. There is the question, already posed at the diagnostic interview, of the impact which important changes in the patient's personality and character structure might have on the patient's wife. The limited treatment period here covered has confirmed the fact that certain changes in the patient's attitudes and behavior brought about by the analysis are reacted to by the patient's wife with anxiety, aggressive outbursts, and depression. The patient himself has a distinct fear of changes that may interfere or create difficulties in his family relationships. Finally, though there is some evidence of self-punishing, self-destructive, and masochistic attitudes, they do not appear to be excessive or extreme and there is no reason to assume that they will tend to interfere unduly with therapeutic progress or lead to negative therapeutic reactions.

6

The Baby Profile

W. ERNEST FREUD

(1967, 1971)

The various departments and research projects of the Hampstead Child-Therapy Clinic have for some time been working with the diagnostic Profile developed by Anna Freud (1962) for the assessment of childhood disturbances. This original Profile has been expanded (A. Freud, 1963) and adapted for use with adolescents (Laufer, 1965) and adults (A. Freud et al., 1965). It was therefore natural to venture into assessment of early infancy.

My own interest in this was greatly enhanced when a five-and-a-half-year-old girl was referred for diagnostic assessment. This child had been known by our Well-Baby Clinic staff almost since birth, had then graduated to our toddler group, and from there to our nursery school. It was most rewarding to make a Profile on the basis of these earlier observations contained in our records. For once, it was possible to perceive the whole range of development in detail. I was struck by features which had been evident from very early in life (e.g., the child's tension, on which all observers had commented) and by later features which seemed closely connected with those earlier ones (e.g., her constant state of anxiety). It was tempting to regard one as the forerunner of the other and to establish causal links.[1]

In early January 1967, we formed the Well-Baby Research group to tackle this project.[2] The data on which we drew are the Well-Baby

---

[In order to present the Baby Profile as a unit, two papers (1967, 1971) by the author have been combined. A part of the 1967 paper which has not been included here contains clinical illustrations and a discussion of the kind of inferences one can draw from observations. For other publications relevant to the Baby Profile see W. E. Freud (1968, 1975) and W. E. Freud and I. Freud (1974).]

[1] Sally Provence's paper (1966) is an example of a most impressive achievement in this direction.

[2] The members of this group were: Dorothy Burlingham, Liselotte Frankl, Anna Freud, Irene Freud, W. Ernest Freud, Hanna Kennedy, E. Model, Humberto Nagera, Marjorie Sprince, and

Clinic records—direct observations of mother and infant who are seen both at home and in the Well-Baby Clinic by multiple observers. In addition, mothers and sometimes the fathers are interviewed.

In attempting to design a Baby Profile we started with existing relevant knowledge—the metapsychological assessment Profile used for children. Since early infancy obviously differs from later childhood, the various sections of the child Profile are not equally applicable and useful. However, they do provide a general framework which can then be elaborated or revised. This, as one would expect, proved easiest with the initial Profile sections, which deal mainly with environmental aspects (Part 1).

The general aim of the Baby Profile is to convey a global, overall picture of an infant's personality from the impressions of one or more observers (hence the importance of an overall final summary in section XV). As on a photograph, it should at least adumbrate areas of actual and potential strength and weakness. Of necessity, the younger the infant, the more of the mother will be in view.[3]

With regard to Part II of the Baby Profile, frequent revisions were necessary. It soon became apparent that revision and improvement were better viewed as ongoing rather than finite tasks.[4] This not only is in keeping with the conception of Profiles as vehicles for open-ended metapsychological research but also takes account of the special conditions pertaining to the Baby Profile, where we are frequently dealing with manifestations at the point of emergence from biological and physiological phenomenology.

Opinions were divided on whether one single schema would suffice to do justice to the profusion and complexity of the many ongoing changes that occur during the first 12 to 18 months of life[5] or whether a number of different schemas should be devised to take account of chronological diversity. The overriding need was for a method that could, in a preverbal setting, simultaneously view manifestations from

the Well-Baby Clinic's pediatrician, Josefine Stross. Also collaborating on the project were Phyllis Cordell and Kerry Kelly Novick. I am greatly indebted to all of them for their enthusiastic support and interchange of ideas; without them the project would not have been possible.

[3] Such assessment of the mother's personality (or, for that matter, of the father's) can of course be supplemented with the aid of the Adult Profile (Anna Freud et al., 1965).

[4] It is understood that categories should not be multiplied beyond necessity. The sequence of sections, however, may remain open to debate.

[5] We have left open the actual age range for the applicability of the Baby Profile and the specific age at which it might be preferable to begin to use the child Profile.

an observational and from a conceptual point of view. Many of the phenomena confronting us are due to internal stimuli that cannot be observed and must therefore be inferred. Normally we can see what is there, but if we look closer and receive some help, we can see more; and here Sigmund Freud's simile is relevant: "a student who is looking through a microscope for the first time is instructed by his teacher as to what he will see; otherwise he does not see it at all, though it is there and visible" (1916–1917, p. 437). One of the aims of the Baby Profile is to achieve just that—to point to facets and manifestations of early development which might otherwise be overlooked or escape attention (Anna Freud, 1953, p. 9).

One of the consequences of seeing more has been an increased awareness of what still remains to be understood. Those relatively uncharted areas highlighted by the Baby Profile probably merely reflect what has occupied most psychoanalytic thinkers at one time or another. There is the challenge of understanding the intricate processes of ego formation (section IX), especially the unfolding development of defenses (section IX, D). In section IX, C, on the State and Functioning of the Mental Apparatus, we have been unable to do much more than list a number of aspects that contribute to ego building and eventually will develop into ego functioning. Many representative, meaningful, and convincing clinical examples are needed to illustrate these processes and to clarify precisely when a phenomenon should cease to be regarded as a forerunner or antecedent and can be recognized as a function, however precariously established. The following example illustrates this dilemma.

Observation: Don (age 6¾ months): In the course of a Well-Baby Clinic visit the mother (a highly intelligent professional woman) told us that Don had got the knack of bringing empty cardboard boxes within reach of his grasp by hitting their tops with his hands until they turned over toward him. In the bath he tried to do the same to a plastic floating duck, but there the duck floated further away. He then became very angry and hit the water. This has happened several times.

Comment: We infer that on the basis of memory Don has established a firm and reliable connection between actions performed by him and specific results. Should his understanding of cause and effect be regarded as a forerunner of the synthetic function, or should it be viewed as an example of integrative thinking?

Similar problems were encountered in other areas, e.g., aggression (VIII, C, 2). For purposes of mental health the directional aspect seems the most important one, but can one speak of direction inward or outward before a distinction between the two has been established? The implications of too much inward-directed aggression are far-reaching. The primitive fear of one's own aggressive impulses forms the basis for a cruel superego in the adult, who as a result may be crippled by self-punitive tendencies that may also interfere with analytic treatment (Lampl-de Groot, 1967). When, how, and why are quantities of aggression, which should find an outlet toward the object world, deflected and directed toward the body (section VIII, C, 2, a, ii), and at what age does an infant stop responding primarily with his body and begin to respond with changes of mood and his mind? Many other areas of uncertainty could be cited.

We believe that systematic, metapsychologically sophisticated infant observation holds the key to a deeper understanding of many of the unsolved problems, although we realize that some of these and other questions can in the last resort be answered only through *longitudinal* studies. But precisely because of these considerations the Baby Profile is tremendously important in that it records a baseline of observations in a systematic schema that can be linked to comparable psychological tools designed for later ages, even though the "docking device" with the Child Profile may not yet have clicked perfectly into place. With the addition of the Baby Profile to the already existing Child, Adolescent, and Adult Profiles, we now have a continuous series of metapsychological instruments which permit, on the one hand, overall monitoring of unfolding development from the very beginning of life and, on the other, retrospective assessment of observational data.[6] It is obvious that the systematic correlation of manifestations from earliest infancy with those encountered in the later stages of development and in adulthood should yield rich findings, the implications of which for prediction, prophylaxis, and therapy need not be elaborated.

[6] We have not overlooked that adequate validation and verification of these metapsychological tools may have to await the completion of a sufficient number of representative longitudinal studies.

While the detailing of these correlations will have to await the outcome of further research, the short-term applications of the Baby Profile have already shown a number of welcome and encouraging results. As a teaching aid the schema has decisively influenced both the orientation and the organization of our infant observations, which in turn enhanced the quality of Baby Profiles. The comprehensiveness of the schema has affected the observations of normal, disturbed, and handicapped (blind) babies in their homes as well as in the Well-Baby Clinic.

In addition to monitoring normal development, the Baby Profile is ideally suited for the earliest spotting of incipient pathology, an area with enormous research possibilities (E. Kris, 1950, 1951). By explicitly drawing attention to the many aspects that can be involved in a disturbance, the schema has proved no less useful in helping to sort out transient difficulties (e.g., in the areas of feeding and sleep, and of providing optimal conditions for speech development). In addition, it has led to more sophisticated formulations of predictions (M. Kris, 1957). It is probably fair to say that the availability of the Baby Profile has subtly revolutionized the way in which we ask questions, which in turn has had a beneficial influence on our research work.

The Baby Profile has facilitated the quest for much more detailed knowledge about the infinitesimal and scarcely perceptible developmental sequences, which should in time lead to a refinement of our thinking on "critical" phases, so that optimal states of readiness for inevitable events, such as weaning, can be pinpointed more easily and matched with optimal timing of intervention. Conversely, and even more important, the application of the Baby Profile has spotlighted phases of minimal readiness when interference must at all cost be avoided.

Furthermore, the Baby Profile offers the prospect of more accurately dating when certain manifestations first emerge in different infants, thus highlighting the wide range of variations in individual differences. It should also teach us more about the development of affects, as the following observation of an infant (12 days old) illustrates.

During a pause in the breast feeding, the mother sat the baby girl up, facing her, and spoke to her in a very soft sing-song voice, smiling at her, and saying, "Is that good, is that what you want? Ye-es, ye-es," and as she crooned the word, the baby seemed to mimic her with a head movement and mouth movements of her own, never taking her eyes off her mother's. (Soon thereafter she had a bowel movement.)

There is much that the Baby Profile can help us understand about the so-called prognostic pointers (section XIV), to find out how reliable and how phase-specific they are. How early and in which form can they be picked up, and under what conditions are they liable to change?

In summary, our experiences with the Baby Profile have proved it to be unique as a teaching aid and invaluable for organizing infant observations in a systematic way. Even if it cannot be expected to answer all questions, it is usually instrumental in helping one see problems in better perspective. It is an ideal foundation for longitudinal studies and has brought welcome results in short-term applications. It should remain open to revision and modification.

If science can be thought of as a method by which we are leap-frogging into new discoveries, then the Baby Profile is offered as one more stepping stone into the unknown.

Draft of the Baby Profile

Part I

I. Reason and Circumstances for Approaching Well-Baby Clinic

II. Description of Parents or Parent Substitutes

III. Description of the Infant

IV. Family Background (past and present)

V. Before Birth—mother

This section is subdivided into "Physical" and "Psychological." The *Physical* section deals with conception and pregnancy. The *Psychological* section covers: the mother's anxieties, her expectations (e.g., of the kind of labor she would have), and what aspirations she has for a child (whether she wants a boy or a girl and what they should be when they grow up, from handyman to prime minister; from typist to ballerina, or housewife with a large family of children).

VI. History of Birth (physical and emotional)—The Newborn Period up to Six Weeks (pediatrician's impression)

As an aside I would say that in this area we usually find that the most important details are not known and impossible to get, even from the maternity hospital. Yet, this is an area that offers immense possibilities for lavishly endowed research projects to initiate and collect observations on some factors which are often crucial to the whole of the infant's later development (see, e.g., the pilot studies by G. Bibring, 1959; and G. Bibring et al., 1961).

In this section we also look at such items as the *separation of the baby from the mother after delivery* (whether he is brought to her only for feedings or whether there is a rooming-in arrangement); the separation of mothers from their premature babies; maternity hospital visiting facilities; the mother's affective state (e.g., postpuerperal depression); the support she gets from the *father.*

It seems to us that the father has not been accorded the place he deserves since the days when it was fashionable to mention couvade (the practice in some primitive societies of the father retiring to bed during the time the mother has the child) (Reik, 1919) and when Ruth Mack Brunswick (1940) described the little boy's wish for a baby. Directly and indirectly he complements (sometimes negatively) the mother's handling of the child.[7] We are therefore interested in the differences in fathers: from the father who dissociates himself physically or emotionally on learning that the mother has become pregnant (to the extent of deserting her or instituting a divorce) to the father who eagerly attends all prenatal lectures with the mother in the maternity hospital and is even prepared to substitute for her by attending the lecture on his own if she is unable to go.

We all know fathers who tend to become a second mother to the baby and other fathers who become more of a second baby to the mother, adding to the strain on her. In between there are fathers who remain relatively neutral, neither burdening the mother nor helping her very much.

We would like to know what the father did during the mother's stay in the hospital—a period in which his behavior can range from sprucing up the home to rushing into an affair with another woman.

[7] I focus here only on the father's role as it directly bears on the mother's handling of the child. It is of course obvious that the relationship which the parents have to each other is of tremendous importance and also has an impact on the child.

When it comes to caring for the child, does the father help the mother, does he take over the child's care completely, or does he have no part in it; e.g., does *he* get up in the night and walk up and down with the baby over his shoulder until the infant falls asleep, or does he keep strictly to his bed on such occasions? Does he play with the baby in the daytime, does he pram him, is he proud of him, or is he ashamed? There are great variations and each tells us something about the marital relationship and about an important part of the baby's environment.

VII. Present Environmental Circumstances and Management

In the areas of feeding, cleanliness, comfort, motility, positioning, general contact, sound contact, smiling contact—fostering pleasure or unpleasure. Some aspects of management should be evaluated in greater detail in the context of the Mother-Infant Interaction during feedings (VIII, A, 2, c).

1. Auxiliary Ego—Assessment of the Mother's Manifest Responses to the Baby

My first approach resulted in the scheme for assessment that is presented in the diagram entitled *Auxiliary Ego.* As regards the *efficiency* of the infant's auxiliary ego, my approach was to assess how much the mother can and does help the baby to maintain pleasure-unpleasure equilibrium, in the vital areas of sleep, feeding (intake, processing, output), cleanliness, comfort, motility.

Unpleasure

The spectrum ranges (center to left) from *removing* of unpleasure (e.g., removal of tension, later leading to binding of free-floating anxiety by simple ministrations)—to *maintaining* unpleasure (e.g., through misinterpreting the baby's needs, or the baby's sounds and signals)—to *creating* unpleasure and pain (e.g., through applying age-inadequate frustrations, untimely or unsmooth weaning; through being out of tune or lacking "empathy"; through ignorance or inexperience; through her own pathology such as sadomasochistic involvement).

Pleasure

At the other end of the spectrum (center to right) one would find: *maintaining* pleasure—*creating* pleasure (actively fostering and eliciting

AUXILIARY EGO

Diagram illustrating the range of possibilities at the disposal of the Auxiliary Ego for influencing pleasure-unpleasure equilibrium in the infant.

UNPLEASURE					PLEASURE
creating	maintaining	removing	Passively tolerating either. (Mother incapacitated, e.g., by illness, withdrawal or depression.)	maintaining and supporting (following the infant's need)	actively fostering and eliciting (by stimulation and encouragement)
	Unpleasure			Pleasure	

This diagram is not meant to be a rating scale, nor does the space allocated to the various sections reflect their relative importance.

pleasure by stimulation and encouragement; e.g., how the mother positions herself in relation to the child, how she holds him, what kind of general contact she has with him, what kind of body, skin, sound, and speech contact; what is the quality of her presence or absence, her smiling contact, her furthering of his motility, her provision of age-adequate stimulation).[8] Going to extremes, *overstimulation* leads right back to the other end of the spectrum, i.e., creating unpleasure.

In the middle range (center) the mother *passively tolerates either* pleasure or unpleasure in the child when she is incapacitated, e.g., by illness, withdrawal, depression.

What complicates prognostic assessments is that some of the relatively stable features in a mother may nevertheless be subjected to change, apart from those variations that occur in response to the child's ongoing development (Coleman, Kris, and Provence, 1953). For instance, drastic and traumatic life experiences, such as the death of a grandparent, change of residence to another continent, war, emigration, or other "psychic traumatization through social catastrophe" may trigger off changes in mothering.

Such unpredictable influences on the mother are more than matched by the unpredictability of development in the child. One

[8] For lively descriptions of such situations see Joyce Robertson (1962, 1965).

crucial but often neglected factor that should make us cautious is: development need not necessarily be straightforward, but can just as well take place in somewhat "unexpected" directions. One and the same stimulus (e.g., separation from the mother) may become a trauma, causing regression, or it may become a spur to further development. The two trends can sometimes also be observed in the same child concurrently, e.g., when there is ego development alongside libidinal regression. Another possibility is that the child may develop an unduly strong attitude of self-mothering (we have seen several such children for diagnostic assessment).

2. AUXILIARY EGO—ASSESSMENT OF THE MOTHER'S LATENT ATTITUDES

Proceeding from the surface to the depth, we attempt a metapsychological appraisal of the mother. It is probably no coincidence that, in order to arrive at a Profile for the baby, we first had to go into the opposite direction, via the Profile of the adult. The simplest explanation of this apparent paradox would seem to be that in the assessment of the adult personality we can draw on a wealth of metapsychological formulations, whereas in evaluating the small infant we may have to develop formulations as we go along.

Be that as it may, it seemed easy enough to spot certain features in the mother which could not fail to affect her handling of the child.[9] We started with a *working hypothesis* which could easily be tested by comparing later events with earlier ones. It states: Ideally, mothering should occur solely according to the actual needs of the child (e.g., a cry for hunger leading to provision of food). It is the mother's task to observe and assess the child's signals correctly and to carry out her ministrations with appropriate, i.e., optimal cathexis. When, however, the mother's objective observation and assessment of the child are interfered with by contributions from her inner psychic reality, it is more than likely, first, that undue delay occurs from the time the infant communicates a need to the time it is met; and, secondly, that ministrations will no longer be applied solely according to the child's needs.

[9] The following formulation by Marianne Kris (1957) is pertinent: "Knowing that neurotic behavior is repetitive and relatively immune to outside events, we tend to select as having predictive value those characteristics of the mother's personality which reflect the greatest inflexibility. We assume that her behavior with the child is then dominated by her own inner conflicts which make her less aware of the child's needs and therefore less responsive to clues from the child—in other words, that she will, with her pathology, disturb the natural rhythm of the child's evolving endowment and narrow its potentialities" (p. 186). See also Augusta Bonnard's formulation: the mother's psychic reality is the external reality of the child.

In other words, the infant is then handled with inappropriate cathexis (undercathexis, or overcathexis, or cathexis of a different quality). Where such "inappropriate" ministrations by the mother impinge on a particular vital area in the child (e.g., feeding, sleep, motility), mothering goes beyond the child's need or falls short of it. A special kind of cathexis is then created in that vital area of the child. It need be no more than something like a greater readiness or sensitivity or potential for vulnerability, but it is thought that such specially sensitized areas may become potentially particularly fertile grounds for later fixations.[10]

We want to know which aspects of the mother's personality are likely to lend themselves to interference with the child's needs or demands. The factors that were thought likely to contribute their share are, in ascending order of importance, the following: defenses, fixation points, unresolved conflicts, anxieties.

I shall end the environmental section of the Profile with a statement made by Anna Freud: "Investigations into the first year of life and the consequences of the earliest mother-child relationship had revealed that much may be acquired by the infant that had been considered as innate before" (1958, p. 86). It is my hope that through the development and application of the Baby Profile the frontiers of what is regarded as innate may become delineated more clearly and in greater detail.

Part II

VIII. Assessments of Development

(Assessments at time of observation. Note changes in relation to earlier observations.)

A. BODY NEEDS AND FUNCTIONS

1. *Sleep*

Sleeping arrangements (location, clothing)
Favorite sleeping position

[10] It is interesting to recall that in 1958 Anna Freud said: "I agree with Ernst Kris that we cannot predict from outside observations, and at the time of occurrence, which events will prove important for future pathology. I should like to add that we do not know either which aspect or element of a given experience will be selected for cathexis and emotional involvement" (p. 114). Perhaps we are now a step nearer to pinpointing the relative impact of the quality of the mother's handling.

Sleeping pattern (length, quality, and times of sleep)—note age-adequateness or otherwise
Falling asleep (peaceful, restless, difficulties)
Waking from sleep (e.g., peaceful, grizzly)—note especially behavior after waking up in the morning
Vulnerability of sleep (state reasons, if possible)
Parents' attitude(s) toward sleep

2. *Feeding*

(a) *Mother*

Physical condition (breasts, nipples, difference between breasts)
Attitude to feeding (manifest and latent)
Were there any physical and mental complications before, during, and after delivery, that might affect feeding?

Food Supply

Breast milk—supply (sufficient or otherwise)
Formula—specify
Mixed feeding—specify
Demand feeding vs. schedule feeding—state approximate times
Reasons for delay in feeding (was it avoidable or unavoidable?)
Underfeeding, overfeeding, forcing food against the baby's needs
Consistency or inconsistency in handling in the feeding situation

(b) *Infant*

Note reactions anticipatory to feeding, to delays, to food intake, and the age-specific changes in all of them.

Signs of Hunger or Thirst

Crying
Distress
Tension[11]
Absence of signs

Patterns of Food Intake

Sucking reflex, its history from birth
Chewing and biting
Hints at congenital activity pattern[12]

[11] See also *Signs of Tension Reduction, Pleasure, and Unpleasure during and after the Feeding Process*, below.

[12] "The Congenital Activity Type is a descriptive term, referring to the amount of activity a newborn infant shows in response to certain stimuli" (Fries and Woolf, 1953, p. 48).

Passive or active feeder
Beginnings of self-feeding
Differentiation: emerging likes and dislikes (note also the mother's preferences and dislikes)

Activities during Feeding
Rooting
Crying or pleasurable sounds
Eyes (on what do they focus during feeding?)
Legs
Hands and fingers
Body movements
Sucking—reaction to interference (e.g., when finger is removed)

Signs of Tension Reduction, Pleasure, and Unpleasure during and after the Feeding Process[13]
In the mouth area (specify, if possible)
Relaxation—body (specify, if possible)
Sounds that convey pleasure
Note any signs of unpleasure in connection with alleviation of hunger or thirst

Reactions to Interruptions of Feeding
Interrelations between Feeding and Sleeping[14]
Interrelations between Feeding and Elimination[15]
Major and Minor Interferences in the Infant's Feeding Process
Immaturity at birth
Deformities (e.g., cleft palate, harelip)
Illness (e.g., pyloric stenosis)
Sore gums or thrush
Teething
Sucking
Biting
Wind
Vomiting
Others

(c) *Mother-Infant Interaction during Feeding*

[13] See also *Signs of Hunger or Thirst*, above.
[14] See also VIII, A, 1, above.
[15] See also VIII, A, 3, below.

This whole section should include observations of the ways in which mother and infant are in tune or out of tune with each other's needs and rhythms. Allowance should be made for the child's changing states of maturity.

(i) Physical
Note the manner in which the mother handles and holds the infant (comfortably or awkwardly), the amount of skin contact, and the scope for independent movement that is allowed. Note also the infant's position as regards comfort and distance from the mother as well as his reactions to being held or not held.

(ii) Psychological (Dialogue)
Note the extent to which the feeding situation is a very intimate and special occasion between mother and infant. If the feeding situation is colored by ambivalence on the mother's part, and by something like rejection of food or handling on the infant's part, note the partner's reaction.

(d) *Retrospective Assessment regarding Food Intake, and Prediction*
From your knowledge of the infant's development up to the time of observation, what do you think accounts for his present reactions in the feeding situation?
From your assessment of the present feeding situation, attempt a prediction of its effects on later development.[16]

3. *Elimination*
Consistency
Frequency and regularity
Physical interferences
Interventions (necessary and unnecessary)
Mother's attitude (manifest and latent)

4. *Other Needs*
Note how the following needs are met:
Protection against inappropriate stimuli
Provision of adequate stimulation
Provision of comfort and methods of comforting, holding, cuddling, rocking[17]

[16] In this context, see M. Kris (1957).
[17] See also VIII, A, 2, c, above.

Stability and flexibility of routine and arrangements
Maintenance of appropriate body temperature
Skin contact and stimulation
Unrestricted movement and exercise
Needs for other physical comfort
Other needs (not mentioned above)

Comment on the general success or failure of fulfillment of the infant's body needs.

B. PLEASURE-UNPLEASURE INDICATIONS[18]

Note manifestations and give reasons for considering them as either pleasurable or unpleasurable.

Examine them according to:
Sources
Reactions
Intelligibility
Overall balance or imbalance

C. DRIVE DEVELOPMENT

1. *Libido*

(a) *Regarding Oral Zone and Phase*

(i) Oral excitation in the feeding process
Sucking, biting, chewing, tasting, etc.
Oral greed or disinterest

(ii) Pleasure sucking
Finger and/or hand sucking
onset
finding
mode
time and frequency
Tongue sucking
first noted
frequency
exclusive or complementary
Other objects for sucking
dummy, bedclothes, etc.
Related activities

[18] Further elaboration will be found in section X.

drooling
blowing bubbles
other mouth play

Reaction to interference with sucking

The following two sections are viewed more as a sideline to actual libidinization.

(iii) Pleasurable use of the mouth for approach, grasping, "perceiving," and exploring
Comment on the presence or absence of these manifestations, as well as on any other significant circumstances in this area.

(iv) Sound production for pleasure
Add a general comment on orality, with reference to the *intensity* and *extent* of observed manifestations (e.g., are they evenly spread, or have you noted anything excessive?).

(b) *Regarding Manifestations from Other Zones*

(i) Anal zone
Signs of anal excitation
Pleasure-unpleasure

(ii) Phallic zone
Masturbation, erections

(c) *Regarding Libido Distribution*

(i) Prestages of self-cathexis
The notion of primary narcissism (investment of the individual's body and/or self, and/or parts of the self, with libidinal cathexis) is a theoretical concept derived from the analysis of adults. It is not easy to find evidence for it from direct observation of the infant. All that can be observed at this stage are the outward manifestations of fluctuating states having positive and negative qualities, i.e., signs of well-being, contentment, pleasure from gratification, etc., or their opposite, i.e., signs of restlessness, discomfort, unpleasure, and pain.
We assume that the preponderance of the first-named states leads to a gradually increasing investment of the

body and of the emerging self with positive libido, i.e., to primary narcissism, whereas the preponderance of the latter states interferes with this outcome. Popularly, these are summarized under the headings of "happy" or "fractious" baby.

The Profile-maker should note manifestations of either category and draw conclusions from them.

(ii) Prestages of object relationship

We assume that at the beginning of life no distinction is made between the experience of gratification and comfort and its provider, i.e., that what is cathected libidinally is the pleasurable experience as such. This would be borne out by observations that there is a stage in which most infants indiscriminately accept ministrations so long as the manner in which they are given remains the same. We call the relationship created on this basis anaclitic, i.e., a libidinal relationship based on need satisfaction.

What begins in this way as purely internal experiences within the child changes gradually into experiences occurring as interactions between the child (or parts of him) and agencies in the external world (or part of them—breast, bottle, the mother's body parts). From then onward the libidinal importance of gratifying experiences (their investment) is transferred increasingly to the person(s) who provide(s) them.

The Profile-maker should note, therefore, when and how the infant reacts to all changes—whether in the prevailing mood of the familiar caretaking person, or a change to another caretaking person, or changes in their manner of handling him and dealing with routine ministrations, or any other changes. If possible, an attempt should be made to indicate the main aspect of change to which the infant responds.

(iii) Further steps in object relatedness

We expect such precursors of object relatedness to lead in due course to constancy of object relationships. The term "constancy" has by now acquired two separate connotations: in one sense it denotes the ego's ability to maintain and retain an internal representation of the object, or part object, independently of the object's presence or absence in the external world; in the other sense it denotes the ability to retain the libidinal cathexis of this internal representation, independent of the presence or absence of needs.

Once object constancy in both senses has been achieved, the relationship to the object is not undone by temporary experiences of frustration, separation, loss, disappointment, etc., but merely changed in quality. For several years in the course of development there will be a considerable overlap between the anaclitic prestage of object love (step 1) and object love proper (step 2). There will also be frequent regressions from the higher to the lower level.

The Profile-maker should at all times note the quality of the observed object relationship as well as its fluctuations between the two levels.

2. *Aggression*

Description of observed manifestations is most important for this section.

(a) *Definition*

Manifestations of the discharge of aggression can appear in the service of angry or unpleasurable tendencies and affects. Although such manifestations contain a fusion of libidinal and aggressive components, we are, in this part of the Profile, focusing on aggressive aspects only.

Discharge of angry or unpleasurable affects may show itself in various ways:

(i) Nondirected:
as restlessness, sleeplessness, fractiousness, etc.

(ii) Directed toward the body:
in external self-injury (biting, scratching, pulling own hair)
in internal "psychosomatic" disturbances such as gastrointestinal, respiratory, vascular, urinary, dermatological, neuromuscular (spasms, convulsions). The organic etiol-

ogy of such disturbances has to be considered side by side with the nonorganic causes.

(iii) Directed toward the object world:
as anger, rage, or motor attack (such as biting, hitting, kicking, scratching)
where external discharge of angry or destructive affects is blocked, we should look for repercussions elsewhere.[19]

(b) *Examination of the Circumstances in Which Aggressive Manifestations Occur*
Examination of the *total* setting usually facilitates clarification of precipitating causes. The aggressive manifestations may be triggered off by tiredness, boredom, unpleasure, pain, anxiety, teasing, response to the caretaking adult, or by something else. Where aggressive manifestations are thought to be reactions to *frustration*, evaluate the capacity to delay urgency of gratification, i.e., comment on the minimum amount of frustration or interference required to trigger off intense manifestations of aggression.
Usually the mother, who is familiar with the infant and acquainted with the circumstances, will know with a high degree of certainty what is likely to be involved. In the Well-Baby Clinic reactions to interferences such as undressing, examination, dressing are instructive.

(c) *Study of the Range of Expressions of Aggression at the Disposal of the Infant*
Global reactions (involving the whole body)[20]
Localized and psychosomatic expressions
Vocal expressions
Mimic facial expressions[21]

(d) *Rate of Recovery from the Effect(s) of Build-up and Discharge of Aggression*
(Note any aftereffects)

IX. Ego Development

A. State and Functioning of the Sensory Apparatus

Visual, auditory, tactile, taste, olfactory, skin sensations, propriocep-

[19] Further elaboration will be found in section X.
[20] See E. Kris (1939).
[21] See Darwin (1872).

tors, kinesthetic

B. STATE AND FUNCTIONING OF THE MOTOR APPARATUS

1. *Reflex and Random*
2. *Directed Coordinated Motility (Distinction between Id Control and Ego Control)*

Initially, in the absence of a functioning ego, motility appears to be exclusively under id control in the service of fulfilling body needs and id impulses. With advancing ego functioning, motility gradually comes under ego control, although this is still in the service of direct gratification of instinctual needs.

Note what aims motor activity serves.

C. STATE AND FUNCTIONING OF THE MENTAL APPARATUS

Many mental activities contribute to the emergence of the gradually unfolding ego and its adaptation to the external and internal world. Comment on the following aspects of *ego building* which eventually develop into ego functioning: perception; attention (intensity and span); exploration and responding; laying down of memory traces—recognition, thinking, memory (recognition and recall); distinction between self and nonself; reality orientation, linking up of psychic experience (forerunner of synthetic function?); forerunner of speech (babbling, comprehension), speech, etc.

D. PRIMITIVE REACTIONS TO UNPLEASURE (PRECURSORS OF DEFENSES?)

Reactions to unpleasure foreshadow later defense. We are therefore interested in noting reactions to unpleasure from whatever source. It is difficult to discern defense activity, or even to assume its existence, before the emergence of a rudimentary ego. The baby's manner of reacting may, however, suggest or foreshadow the kind of defense he is likely to adopt in the future.

Such reactions are, e.g., protest, avoidance, withdrawal, regression, somatization.

E. FORERUNNERS OF IDENTIFICATION

Imitation, introjection, passive into active, etc.[22]

X. AFFECTIVE STATES

In the first few weeks of life we expect to see no more than the

[22] See also X, F.

variations of mood which reflect either pleasurable or unpleasurable states (as described in section VIII, B). Gradually these widen into discernible expressions of other affects.

What appears in the pleasure range are affects, such as contentment, serenity, joyfulness; their counterparts in the unpleasure range are anxiety, unhappiness, anger, and rage. The chronological appearance of these various affects may differ widely from infant to infant.

A. RANGE OF AFFECTS

Note how many different affects can be observed at each stage of development.

B. SITUATIONS IN WHICH AFFECTS APPEAR

Note which experiences of the infant give rise to an affective response. Examples are: reactions to fulfillment or frustrations of needs and to disappointments in objects, changes of position, handling by strangers.

C. AVAILABILITY OR ACCESSIBILITY OF AFFECTIVE RESPONSES

Describe whether the infant can, or cannot, experience and react with the appropriate affect in specific situations. Where applicable, note which affects are not available to the infant. Note whether affects are expressed via the body or in other ways.

D. APPROPRIATENESS OF AFFECTIVE RESPONSES

Describe whether the affective response seems appropriate in intensity to the stimulus that provokes it, i.e., whether it seems excessive or too weak. As regards quality, note whether affective responses are inappropriate, such as when joy appears where the normal reaction should be sadness.

E. TRANSIENCE OR PERSISTENCE OF THE AFFECTIVE RESPONSES

Describe whether there is recovery from the affective state within a reasonable time after an affective response has been triggered off or if there is a tendency for the affect to persist and linger on excessively.

F. THE INFANT'S REACTION TO HIS PERCEPTION OF OTHER PEOPLE'S AFFECTIVE STATE

Note the infant's tendency to perceive and respond to affective states in the mother, such as happiness, impatience, worry, unhappiness, depression, anxiety, anger. Note also whether such empathy extends to other people besides the mother. Consider such reactions as possible forerunners of later imitation and identification.

XI. Forerunners of Fixation Points (Vulnerable Areas or Specific Libidinizations)

In this section consider anything that can be regarded as setting up something like a greater readiness, sensitivity, or potential for vulnerability, i.e., anything that is thought to create specially sensitized areas which may become potentially particularly fertile grounds for later fixations.

Examples may be found either in very early and persistent autoerotic activities (sometimes carried on via a transitional object), or in physically overstimulating experiences affecting the skin, the mucous membranes, the intestines. Note especially any painful illnesses in early life and nursing, medical, or surgical interventions.

XII. Forerunners of Tendencies to Regression

Some oscillation between forward and backward developmental moves can already be discerned at a very early age, at which time they are to be viewed as within the range of normality. Note their frequency, rate, the occasions which give rise to them (if any), and the recovery rate from regressive moves.

Note also whether an established pattern in these alternating moves can be discerned and look for changes in this.

XIII. Forerunners of Conflicts

In considering the very young infant we do not think in terms of either external or internal conflicts. The question of *external* conflicts does not arise before the infant has learned to distinguish between himself and the outer world. *Internal* conflicts are not expected to occur before a personality structure has been established, i.e., before the inner agencies have been separated off from each other. Nevertheless, forerunners of both types of conflict can be discerned even at these early stages.

With regard to the external world, note the manner in which the infant responds to the type of maternal care and handling to which he is subjected. We distinguish in this respect between "compliant," "determined," or "difficult" babies. Naturally, in early infancy these modes of behavior are primarily the infant's means for the expression of object relationship. Nevertheless, they allow for some speculation regarding the tendency toward peaceful acceptance of or opposition to environmental influences.

As regards the internal world, we find clashes between competing needs, such as finger sucking and feeding, simultaneous anger and rejection of the object with clinging to it.

XIV. General Characteristics, with Special Prognostic Relevance for Future Pathological or Normal Development

When dealing analytically with older children, we have learned to look out for certain general characteristics in their personalities which seem to be significant for their establishing, maintaining, or regaining mental health. We do not know at present whether these characteristics are inborn or acquired early in life; nor do we know whether they are open to influence either by life experience or by analytic treatment. In any case, it seems important to us, wherever they appear, to trace them back to their first appearance within the personality.

A. The infant's threshold of tolerance for the frustration of needs and wishes

Individual infants differ remarkably with regard to the degree to which they can tolerate frustration. What is reacted to violently by some, such as postponement of fulfillment, disappointment, is taken in stride by others. A low threshold in this respect exposes the child to greater quantities of unpleasure. This leads to increased pressure toward the immediate discharge of tension which in the long run will militate against the gradual modification and taming of instinctual drives.

B. The infant's threshold of tolerance for anxiety

Note here how easily anxiety is released and whether or not, or to which degree, the infant is devastated by the experience of anxiety. Note also the rate of recovery from any experience of anxiety; i.e., whether and for how long the anxiety state outlasts its causation. This is of specific importance with regard to later neurotic development. The more anxiety an individual produces, and the less he can tolerate, the quicker he will resort to defensive measures and symptom formation, once his ego has acquired the capacity to ward off dangers.

C. The infant's ability to accept substitute gratification

While some infants cannot be satisfied except by the direct fulfillment of their unmodified wishes, others will be content with substitutes which are offered to them. This latter capacity is important because it foreshadows the individual's later *sublimation potential*, which opens up innumerable pathways for discharge, reduces unpleasure, and facilitates aim-inhibited gratification, contentment, and achievement. Where an individual does not develop beyond primitive, crude instinctual and material needs and wishes, he is exposed to increased disappointments with markedly decreased opportunity for the relief of tension.

D. Balance Between Progressive and Regressive Tendencies

While noting the oscillations between forward and backward developmental moves (see XII), the observer is asked to pay special attention to any imbalance between them. The child's further normal development depends to a large degree on the intactness of the progressive tendencies, i.e., on his wish and ability "to move forward and complete development."[23]

Where this force is outweighed by the clinging to early pleasures and by moving back to them whenever difficulties arise at later stages, normal growth can be severely interfered with.

XV. Summing Up of the Developmental Status

In this final summing up of impressions, convey a concise and clinically meaningful opinion which will be of use for later comparison and reference. Comment on the personality picture of the child, and on the salient features in his development, such as precocity or retardations in any directions. Also take special note of any unevenness in development. Infants may be either uniformly well developed or forward in some respects and lagging behind in others.

From your assessment attempt a prediction of later development. If applicable, include recommendations for influencing discernible traits of adverse development.

[23] See E. Bibring (1937) and Anna Freud (1965).

7

Special Problems of Blind Infants

Blind Baby Profile

DOROTHY BURLINGHAM

(1975)

In our attempts to apply the Developmental Profile (Anna Freud, 1965) to blind children, we found that special provisions must be made for the fact of blindness. While many of the developmental factors that the Baby Profile (W. E. Freud, 1967, 1971) assesses are the same, others are unique to the blind. In this paper I shall concentrate on the latter. In singling out specific areas for observation and evaluation, I have a double purpose in mind. On the one hand, careful attention to these areas will help in the completion of a Baby Profile for the Blind, which in turn might aid us in deciding some of the unanswered questions concerning the development of the blind. On the other hand, the detailed understanding of the blind baby's specific needs can serve as a practical guide to help mothers of such infants.

All mothers of blind and physically handicapped children need guidance with the tremendous problems they face, but we can help them only if we ourselves understand the special requirements of blind babies.

Family Background

In all our contacts with infants we attempt to learn a great deal about the background of the parents, their personal characteristics, their relationship to each other, and their past experiences. With parents of a blind infant it is especially important to determine whether similar abnormalities have occurred on either side of the family. If they have, we should attempt to find out whether the parents have been warned

---

The material used in this paper stems from the author's work with the Study Group for the Blind at the Hampstead Child-Therapy Course and Clinic, London: Annemarie Curson, Alice Goldberger, Anne Hayman, Hansi Kennedy, Elizabeth E. Model, and Doris Wills.

beforehand by either pediatrician or obstetrician that blindness may be transmitted to their child. We have two significant examples where mothers blind from an early age and married to blind husbands ignored all warnings and did not see why they should not claim the right to produce children. This contrasts very sharply with the almost ubiquitous tendency of mothers to blame themselves unreasonably for the child's handicap.

For this reason, when we examine the personal history of a sighted mother, we must pay special attention to the period of her pregnancy because it is of the utmost importance to find out whether she undertook any action which might have played a part in her producing a blind child, whether this was at the time of conception or in the intervening period before she gave birth. Regardless of whether rational or irrational, her belief that some action or behavior on her part is responsible for her baby's blindness will have a profound effect on the mother's sense of guilt and attitude to the infant.

In looking at the period after birth, we need to focus on six aspects that are especially significant for a mother's relationship to a blind infant:

1. The length of time during which the mother regards the baby as normal
2. The actual moment at which either mother or pediatrician recognizes the visual defect
3. The actual manner in which mother, or father, or both are informed of the finding
4. The mother's or parents' (as well as grandparents') manifest and latent reactions to the information and subsequent changes in their attitudes to the baby
5. The length of time during which the mother was estranged from the baby (if she so was) and the duration of her concentration on the handicap
6. The extent of the parents' eventual return to the baby as a person and the manner of recognizing his specific needs.

Body Needs and Functions

Sleep

It is obvious that blind babies will take longer than normal ones to establish a sleeping pattern with distinction between day and night. Such a delay in the sleeping pattern might even prove significant for the early diagnosis of defective vision.

It is well known that even sighted children may develop the habit of waking in the night, wishing to play, much to the distress of their parents. It is only logical that this happens much more frequently with the blind for whom there is no alternation between light and darkness.

It is worth investigating whether, in contrast to this, it is easier for blind children to fall asleep when they are put to bed because one of the distractions, namely, visual stimulation, is absent from the situation.

On the other hand, the baby's favorite sleeping positions, the specific sleeping arrangements (location, clothes), and the parental attitudes to sleep, though they should be noted, may be expected to be similar to those found in sighted children. Parents of blind infants also want them to sleep at specific times.

Feeding

In the interaction between mother and blind child during feeding the absence of visual contact is of overriding significance. The observer should note how far the mother replaces this with skin contact or vocal contact, the extent to which the baby listens to the mother's ministrations and seeks communication with her, and the degree to which the mother is able to recognize and respond to these approaches.

Rooting or pleasurable sounds, signs of hunger or thirst—any mother would be pleased to answer to such signs: these areas have nothing to do with vision and a mother concerned about her baby, sighted or blind, would be relieved by such signs. The indications of hunger and thirst, the patterns of food intake, passive or active feeding would be similar for blind and sighted, but other factors are not.

Since the blind baby cannot watch the approach of food to his mouth, it should be noted especially in what manner the mother inserts the nipple, bottle, or spoon into the baby's mouth and whether there is a moment of hesitation on the mother's part in the expectation that the infant will react to the approach of breast or bottle. We should also note any changes in the mother's handling before she is aware of her baby's blindness and after she has this knowledge.

Instead of noting the infant's watching of the feeding operations, the observer must give the same attention to the infant's listening to them.

Special note should be made of mouth movements toward food and body postures since we do not know how far these are occasioned only by the sight of food and how far other sensory avenues, for example, smell, play a part here. Such clues to self-feeding as hand-reaching movements toward the mother and toward food, grasping, will have to be expected to occur later than in the sighted.

We can assume that interruptions of the feeding process are even more unpleasurable to the blind since nipple, bottle, or spoon, when removed from physical contact with the blind infant, disappear completely from his awareness.

Other Needs

Protection against Inappropriate Stimuli and Provision of Appropriate Stimulation

Although most of the needs listed for sighted children apply equally for the blind, there are some quantitative and qualitative differences for which the Profile will have to make provision. One is that the role of auxiliary ego which every mother has to play is an extended one; the blind child is altogether more vulnerable and needs more protection and assistance. The other concerns the blind infant's extreme need for response and stimulation. This is not easy for the mothers since as sighted individuals they are more alerted to a visual interchange and get discouraged if they receive no response to their efforts of attracting the baby visually. The observer should note here whether this causes the mother to withdraw or whether she is inventive in finding other modes of interaction and stimulation.

Stability and Flexibility of Routine Arrangements

It may be important to keep in mind here that blind infants profit more than the sighted from the stability of routine arrangements and less from their flexibility. Since they are prone to be frightened of anything new and lack reassurance by the mother's glance, routine as the recurrence of expected events is helpful and gives the infant a feeling of security.

Prestages of Object Relationships

It is obvious that with the blind the anaclitic relationship lasts longer than with sighted children. Security is found in the mother's closeness and in her ministrations. Interruptions of the anaclitic relationship are therefore all the more disastrous for the blind.

The means by which the blind baby recognizes his mother, on the other hand, are far from obvious. It would be very important to know which perceptual modalities the infant uses, whether it takes a longer time for him to know that a different person is feeding him, and whether, on the contrary, he is more sensitive to such changes than sighted children.

Indications of Pleasure and Affects

Pleasure-Unpleasure Signs

While the reaction to unpleasure would be the usual ones, such as withdrawal and crying, we cannot expect the blind infant to show the normal manifestations of pleasure since his concentration on listening, even if pleasurable, and the immobility required for listening prevent the visible manifestations of pleasure from appearing. It may well be that observers are misled into thinking that the blind infant is indifferent when in reality he is engaged with pleasurable acoustic impressions (Burlingham, 1972).

All infants derive much pleasure from sucking their fingers. However, in the blind infant, the last phase in finding the hands—looking at them before bringing them to the mouth—is missing. This may make a difference in the important developmental step of hand-mouth coordination and has to be taken into account.

We should also observe carefully whether the blind infant develops other means of gratification.

Pleasurable Use of the Mouth for Approach, Grasping, Perceiving, and Exploring

The use of the mouth should be especially noted and described in even greater detail than normally. For exploration and differentiation, its use can be quite extraordinary. Blind children find the mouth the finest tool for differentiating and for acquiring knowledge of objects (spatial relations, surfaces, texture, shape); therefore it is of importance to know when and how this ability and preference develops, whether the blind's use of the mouth as a tool persists into later stages because it is rewarding, while the sighted give it up at an early age when other methods take its place. In any event, the persistent use of the mouth in the blind, despite its pleasurable elements, should not be interpreted solely as a manifestation of oral gratification, because it substitutes for and serves the purposes of important ego functions.

At a later age, I observed a little girl who in examining a room went along the wall, stopping to feel everything she met and could reach; she felt the floor with her feet and hands and finally with her tongue. Similarly, I know of a blind woman who, when she wanted to examine a fine detail of an object, secretly felt it with her tongue.

Availability or Accessibility of Affects

Just as the pleasure manifestations of the blind infant differ from those of the sighted, his affective responses require special attention.

It is my impression that the blind's affective responses are less strong or wide in range than those of the sighted. This is probably due to lack of response or withdrawal on the part of the mother, as a result of which there may be reduced input of stimulation. But even if the mother is highly inventive in stimulating the infant, the absence of vision greatly reduces the input of the many diverse signs, gestures, and facial expressions by which the sighted recognize and respond to affective expressions.

In contrast, the blind infant's limited understanding of what is going on around him gives rise to specific affects expressing this. Thus we should be alert to look for signs of bewilderment, fear, and confusion, which in the blind occur frequently.

For these reasons, it is especially important not to make hasty judgments concerning the inappropriateness of affects in the blind. So often the observer is unaware of what the infant is reacting to, or why he shows the opposite reaction from the expected one. Very careful study is therefore required to determine not only the nature of the affective response but also its probable source—whether pleasure or distress or lack of affective manifestations occur in response to external or internal stimulations.

Motility and Aggression

Aggression

When we look for signs of aggression in blind infants we should note in particular its lack where aggression would be expected; for instance, distress rather than aggression as a response to frustration. There is great fear of showing aggression when the dependence on the caretaking person is all-important. Only subtle ways of showing aggression are then permissible and tolerable.

Motility

Like the sighted, the blind infant becomes more active and more mobile in relation to the opportunities for pleasurable discharge, which are stimulated by the caretaking person. While the avenues of discharge available to the blind do not differ from those of the sighted, it is very interesting that for the blind the feet seem to play a far more important role than the hands. The blind baby's use of the legs as a means of discharging libidinal and aggressive drives should therefore be explored. Moreover, a possible delay in the use of the hands in general (Fraiberg, 1968; Wills, 1968) should be noted.

The early preponderant use of the legs contrasts with the marked delay in motility, which becomes apparent at a later stage when the child has some awareness of the dangerous consequences of moving into the unknown. When the blind toddler has learned to walk, he will do so, but he will stay in the same place.

Despite the normal maturation of the motor apparatus a certain retardation of motility in the blind is expectable for several reasons. There is for the blind infant no known environment—such as walls, furniture, windows—which on the one hand gives stability and on the other tempts the growing toddler to move toward things or around them. Movement for the blind occurs in a vacuum. Although sound provides a certain amount of orientation, this is not sufficient.

This lack of environmental stimulation is further reinforced by the mother's protective attitude which is designed to guard the child's endangering himself as soon as independent movement is possible. These two influences act together as a delaying force.

State and Function of the Mental Apparatus

It is evident that when vision is absent, one or more of the other senses will be called on to take over some of its functions. In many respects, however, the development of the other senses has to be stimulated and taught. The substitution of sensory modalities brings disorder into the usual sequence of the development of the sensory apparatus as well as the ego functions dependent on them. We must therefore take into account that—

1. Perception and attention are dependent on the use of listening
2. Exploration and recognition rely on touch
3. Reality orientation takes place via sensations called forth by sound, touch, vibrations, and probably also odor. These need to be integrated with each other before one can expect the blind child to have some awareness, for instance, of space
4. Memory traces are laid down by means of acoustic and other sensory modalities and will therefore differ greatly from visual memory traces.

The diminished sensory input requires a far greater intellectual effort on the part of the blind to arrive at the same degree of understanding that the sighted have of the environment. Special attention needs to be given to whether the infant is helped or hindered in this respect by the parents' efforts.

In this context, I also want to reemphasize that a blind child's apparent withdrawal from the external world need not be a reaction to unpleasure or a sign of lacking interest. Quite the contrary, it is a prerequisite for intensive listening and therefore a normal manifestation.

Forerunners of Fixation Points

There is no doubt that blind children more than others have a notable fixation in the stage of autoerotism. Again, this is partly attributable to the fact that they, much more than others, are "left to their own devices." Lacking perceptual stimulation and frequently also stimulation from the mother (who tends to pay less attention to a quiet baby), the blind infant spends much time in such autoerotic activities as rocking and swaying.

In the blind, the eyes often become a libidinized area, and their investment is significantly increased by examinations of and surgical interventions to the eye, restriction of touch after operations, which are so frequently necessary. Such experiences should be carefully noted.

Altogether blind infants have greater difficulty in progressing from the familiar and known to the unfamiliar and unknown. This in itself may create the semblance of fixation on a particular stage of development.

General Characteristics

In the Profile for sighted children we list general characteristics that have special prognostic relevance for the assessment of their development. These are not applicable to the blind and have to be replaced by others. Frustration tolerance can serve as an example. As with all handicapped children, frustration in the blind is the order of the day and a basic fact of their lives to which the children adapt in some way or other.

Instead I suggest a number of characteristics that might have special prognostic relevance for the blind's normal or abnormal development—

1. The infant's ability to make use of his remaining senses
2. The infant's ability to respond to appropriate stimulation
3. The infant's ability to express needs and wishes
4. With advancing ego development his intellectual ability to use the meager sensory data at his disposal for adequate orientation.

Summary

In selecting certain sections of the Profile for comment, I have tried to underscore two basic considerations in assessing the blind. On the one hand, we need to give special attention to those areas which are most affected by the impact of blindness; on the other, the usual behavioral manifestations we observe may have a different meaning in the blind.

The amendments I propose are a first step toward constructing the Baby Profile for the Blind. As our knowledge of blind babies increases, others will be added.

An early application of the Blind Baby Profile would be very helpful in assessing the normal or abnormal development of the blind, in sorting out the factors that are due to blindness, or to additional brain damage, and those that derive primarily from external sources and therefore can be influenced by appropriate guidance.

PART III

USES AND APPLICATIONS

8

THE DEVELOPMENTAL PROFILE

Notes on Some Practical Considerations Regarding Its Use

HUMBERTO NAGERA, M.D.

(1963)

The following pages describe some aspects of the work of the Diagnostic Research Group at the Hampstead Clinic.[1] In general our aims were to conduct an inquiry into the difficulties of diagnosing infantile disturbances, and to re-evaluate initial diagnostic impressions and predictions which were recorded after the initial interviews and in the Diagnostic Conference. This initial material was compared with that gained from the same children after psychoanalytic treatment. It was hoped that as a result of this research, errors in assessment would be reduced and a more satisfactory and systematic technique for evaluating the initial findings would be evolved.

Several different approaches to the problem have been followed, but this paper is concerned with only one of these: the Developmental Profile as outlined by Anna Freud (1962). The Profile is not yet a finished product, and has undergone numerous modifications and adaptations in the course of our work.[2]

[1] The Diagnostic Research Group has been engaged in research for some years and has been headed by Dr. L. Frankl (Physician-in-charge at the Hampstead Child-Therapy Clinic).

[2] A three-year research program has recently been started in order to attempt to improve and develop further the Developmental Profile through the constant application of it to our clinical material.

The Profile can be considered to be a way of thinking; more precisely, a metapsychological way of thinking and of organizing clinical material within the psychoanalytic frame of reference. It collects from the mass of information available, clinical or otherwise, that which is relevant and necessary to gain a proper picture, as complete as possible, of a given personality at a given moment of development. It tends to discard the irrelevant, and at the same time highlights the areas in which the available information is incomplete though essential for the proper understanding of a child's whole personality and conflicts.

This very point is one of the assets of the Profile. It largely solves the difficult question of how much and what kind of information is needed for a proper diagnostic evaluation of any specific case. By its very nature, the Profile is a metapsychological cross-section of a personality structure at a given moment.

Attention should be paid to the fact that, in the Profile, *pathology is seen against the background of normal development and its possible variations.* This is, of course, of particular importance in child diagnosis, because the child, unlike the adult, is not yet a finished product.

The picture we may gain of a normal child and of his reactions will be different at different ages and stages of development. His capacity to react is different as he develops. Many phenomena seen in children represent aspects of development and are normal or nearly so at certain ages. Thus, for example, sleeping disturbances appear quite commonly in the second year of life. Similarly the child may deal with frustration or aggression by temper tantrums before more appropriate ways have been achieved developmentally. At a particular age, however, both symptoms lack the ominous quality they would have at a later age [Nagera, 1966a, 1966b].

The developmental orientation of the Profile has a further advantage: by constantly forcing us to examine what is normal or pathological at different ages, it makes possible a clearer understanding and conceptualization of normal development.

As a concrete illustration of the Profile, I shall present the material of the diagnostic study of Arthur Z., eleven and a half years old. The information will be described and discussed under the main headings of the Profile.[3] Examples will be given to illustrate some of the arguments and the many possibilities opened up by this approach. In addition, I hope to show the correlation existing among the various headings and I will attempt to convey something of our present experience in the use of the Profile.

Developmental Picture and Guide to Diagnosis[4] (Profile at the Diagnostic Stage)

Material Used:

Social History, June 11, 1954—Mrs. Mason
Psychiatric Interview, June 15, 1954—Dr. L. Frankl
Intelligence Test Report, June 25, 1954—Miss D. Wills

I. Reasons for Referral

The mother felt that the child was retarded on account of persistent thumb sucking (which occurs only when he is at home and not when he is out). He has difficulties in school where he does not cooperate and is not progressing properly. He is frequently absent from school due to slight rise in temperature, stomach pains, sickness, etc. His health has been checked several times and is fine.

II. Description of the Child

Arthur has a slight negroid appearance because of his crinkly hair and thick lips. He is a nice-looking lad, wears glasses, and is the size of a thirteen- or fourteen-year-old boy.

3 The first four sections of the Profile are self-explanatory. Section III, Family Background and Personal History, is related to the subsection, External Conflicts, which occurs in Section VII. These initial four sections are intended to give a full picture of the child and his background.

4 At Hampstead the diagnostic procedure varies according to the nature of the case involved. Broadly speaking, however, it consists of a social history, a psychiatric interview with the child, and psychological tests where indicated (but always, where possible, an intelligence test). Additional psychiatric interviews with parents and other relatives may be carried out as necessary.

A word needs to be said about our use of psychological test results. At the very beginning of the application of the Developmental Profile to our cases, we utilized mainly descriptions of the child's behavior in the test situation. The I.Q. was stated, but no special attention was paid to the content of the child's responses except where it gave information about the status of certain ego functions (relevant for this heading in the Profile). This procedure was followed because initially we wanted to base our assumptions as much as possible on purely clinical grounds. A much wider use of the test results (content) is of course perfectly valid and useful, and we are presently organizing a pilot study on this very aspect.

He can be quite independent (in spite of difficulties over separation) and will go anywhere alone. He will go skating or bicycling with his friends, though he is described as not making friends easily and being rather reserved.

Arthur tends to copy his little brother who is said to play with imagination. He likes his mother to read to him and prefers little-girl stories.

III. Family Background and Personal History

Arthur comes from a Jewish nonorthodox background.

Mother: She has been in analytic treatment with Dr. W. She became increasingly depressed when the husband was away during the War. At that time, when Arthur was about two years, she started working to cope with her misery. When she was pregnant with her second child, Arthur was three years nine months to four years six months old. She found him so irritating that she could not stand him. Arthur was then sent to a kindergarten.

It seems as if a certain amount of seduction goes on between Arthur and his mother. There are references to his making jokes about girls and laughing about nude pictures with his mother. He giggles saying "ooh" whenever he sees his mother not fully dressed.

Father: He is now established in business. He was away during the War when Arthur was between one year eight months to two years six months. At that time Mr. Z. is said to have returned home after two months of convalescence following a nervous breakdown.

He was himself a difficult child, separating from his mother with difficulty. The father likes bathing the children on week ends (Arthur is now eleven and a half years) and has always cooperated a great deal in the care of Arthur.

Siblings: There is a seven-year-old brother. Arthur tends to copy this younger brother who is said to be imaginative. Arthur is now very jealous of him and constantly hits and teases him.

Friends: He is said not to make friends easily. While he did not refer to any special friend, he mentioned that he went out on his bike with a school friend and that he played with others in the street.

Personal History: The mother was well during the pregnancy. Arthur was born three weeks premature, but the birth is said to have been easy. The mother described him as a beautiful and happy baby. He was breast fed for six months; was fed to the hour; and was weaned to the bottle at six months, refusing it at first.

He walked at a year; talked between two to two and a half years with slight setbacks when he went to the nursery. He has sucked his thumb since birth.

His toilet training is described as having been difficult. Arthur used to retain his bowel movements and still does so. He had bowel movements only at home. Frequently his pants were slightly soiled and still are nowadays. He achieved urinary control at the age of two years, though there were occasional accidents later.

IV. Possibly Significant Environmental Influences

1. Mother's and father's seductive attitude toward the children.

2. There have been a number of enforced early and later separations (and withdrawal on the mother's side due to her depression) that may have played a role in Arthur's difficulties. He tended to react to these experiences with extreme distress and regression.

For example, when during the War Arthur's mother became depressed due to the absence of her husband, Arthur (then aged two and a half) was sent to a nursery. There he never settled in, stood in a corner, sucked his thumb, bit and scratched the other children. There was a setback in talking as well. He was kept at this place for three months.

At the end of this third year he was sent to kindergarten. The mother, who was then pregnant again, referred to her not being able to stand the child at the time. He had always to be dragged screaming to the kindergarten.

At the age of five he went to a progressive school, where he was again not able to settle. He started soiling, wetting, and developed a tic in one eye.

V. Assessment of Development

GENERAL COMMENTS

This section has three main subsections: the development of drives (libido and aggression); of ego and superego; and of the total personality.

In regard to libido development, the essential point is the determination of whether a child has ever reached the phallic (oedipal) phase, at about the age of three or four. The type of object relationship is included here; attention should be paid to the way in which libido and aggression are used in relation to the objects and the self, and how objects are used in general.

In a similar way, we can ask at a later age whether the child has ever entered latency or puberty; whether this is a normal latency or puberty or one disturbed by neurotic conflicts or in some other way.

It is important in this context to distinguish the phallic phase from isolated phallic manifestations which may occur even though the bulk of the libido is still at an earlier stage. For example, we may have penis envy for purely narcissistic reasons in a two-year-old girl. We speak here of phallic dominance as a phase, and not as isolated phallic manifestations while another phase is dominant.

Has regression from the phallic phase taken place and, if so, to where? Of course, a relationship exists between this heading and that of Section VI, Regression and Fixation Points, since one of the prerequisites for regression is the existence of previous developmental points at which the libido has remained fixated.

It is not always easy to determine clearly how much of the libido one sees at a particular pregenital fixation point is present there as the result of regression and how much has always remained fixated at that point and has never moved forward. In brief, how much can be attributed to regression and how much to fixation? We have gained the impression that in many cases it is possible to have a relative, quantitative, idea of how much of the libido seen at a particular point may be attributed to fixation and how much to regression as a consequence of conflicts at later stages. A thorough developmental history of the child is necessary here [Nagera, 1964].

In this connection, several possibilities may exist. Take, for instance, a child who was able to pass through the pregenital phases without too many difficulties and who shows what may be called the usual and normal fixation points at the oral and anal level. Further, let us suppose that as a result of the conflicts of the oedipal situation and because of castration fear the child regresses from the phallic level to the anal and oral levels.

The developmental history may show the picture of a child with no more than slight signs, if any, of fixations at the earlier levels. These may not be very outstanding, but at a certain point in development, for example, at the age of five years, as a consequence of the regression mentioned above, we can begin to observe the appearance of libidinal manifestations appropriate to the oral and anal phases, either as symptoms or as pieces of behavior which were previously absent.

If one pays proper attention to the details of the social history and in particular the developmental history, it will be seen that this picture differs markedly from that of another child in whom thumb sucking (or some other oral manifestation, e.g., excessive clinging and demandingness) had been present throughout his development, far beyond the age at which such behavior corresponds to a specific stage of development and is therefore accepted as normal. The picture also differs from that of a child who shows in some way that his character bears the imprint of difficulties in one particular phase of development. The latter child may have moved through to the phallic phase, but the manifest signs of fixation to the early levels will at no point have disappeared from his developmental picture. If at a later stage conflict induces a regression of libido from the phallic phase, reinforcing the libido already present at earlier levels, one may be able to assess how much is attributable to this reinforcement through regression and how much to the ever-present fixations (though only in relative terms).

The outcome of further regression is an intensification of such manifestations as thumb sucking, clinging, and demandingness, or indeed of whatever signs of the anal or oral phases are present. What we observe is a reinforcement and intensification of the manifestation previously present.

Such a distinction is naturally of prognostic importance. It is no doubt easier to help the forward movement of libido which has regressed than of libido which has always been arrested at earlier stages. In assessing the total personality it is of value to have a relative estimate of how much of the libido was able to move forward to the phallic phase, even though it may at present be seen in a regressed state. It is important to know that at some time most or part of the libido has moved forward and had made its contribution at the proper time to the development of the ego and to the personality as a whole. This is in contrast to those cases in whom, through excessive fixation, large amounts of libido have remained arrested and were unable to contribute to normal development at the time when that contribution was required.

We believe that through collecting the material of a sufficient number of cases, light will be thrown on how, when, where, and why the libido makes its contribution to proper development. The same argument applies to the aggressive drive which will be dealt with below.

Finally, an examination of the libido is required in regard to its distribution in the self, objects, etc. Similarly, whenever relevant and possible, the statements as to the mechanisms and self-esteem regulation and well-being can be included.

I return now to the assessment of development in the case of Arthur Z.

CASE ILLUSTRATION

A. *Drive Development*

1. *Libido*

(a) *With regard to phase development*

Arthur has reached the phallic-oedipal phase. (He giggles and says "ooh" whenever he sees his mother not fully dressed; he makes jokes about girls and laughs about nude pictures with his mother; used to write "like love letters" to mother when away from her at nine years, etc.) There is evidence that he has very strong fixation points at the oral and anal levels to which large amounts of his libido are now regressed.

The latency period is being interfered with by the lack of a proper solution of the oedipal conflict and the regression that has followed. It can be said that latency is further complicated by a certain amount of seduction and stimulation exerted particularly, though not exclusively, by the mother. This factor makes it all the more difficult for him to renounce the pleasure he experiences when he succeeds in inducing his mother to care for him and look after him physically as if he were a younger child (being dressed, bathed, etc.).

(b) *With regard to libido distribution*

(i) *Cathexis of self:* The cathexis of the self in Arthur's case seems to be interfered with in certain circumstances (like in the test situation where he showed an unusual degree of diffidence and self-criticism). He would present perfectly correct solutions, saying he was sure they were wrong: "I am not very good at this. . . ."

Similarly, the excessive use of turning aggression against the self may point either to a low narcissistic cathexis of the self (in relative terms) that allows and accounts for the choice and excessive use of this mechanism of defense or at least to a secondary interference with that cathexis when pressure on the side of the aggressive drive rises and defense has to be enforced.

(ii) *Cathexis of objects:* Arthur has, of course, reached the stage of object constancy, but that stage is constantly interfered with due to very strong and early fixations at the oral level.

2. *Aggression*

GENERAL COMMENTS

Here we look for the presence or absence of aggression on the surface, since we still know little about the vicissitudes of the different phases.

Quantitative, qualitative, and directional considerations are appropriate here.

The types of defense utilized to deal with aggressive drives should be noted and included here if relevant, or under the heading Ego, Defenses.

We hope that in time the systematic collection of information under this heading, and the correlation of that information with other aspects covered by the Profile, coming as it does from children of all ages and from all sorts of pathology, will ultimately make a contribution to our knowledge of the vicissitudes and development of the aggressive drive.

In Arthur's case the following material is recorded under the subheading of aggression.

CASE ILLUSTRATION

Arthur has not achieved adequate control of his aggressive impulses. Arthur's aggression breaks through frequently, particularly in the relationship with his mother. Whenever he is frustrated by her in any way, he attacks her and screams and yells with temper. On the other hand, at school he finds it difficult to read in a loud voice.

There is constant teasing and hitting of the brother.

He deals with aggression partly by turning it against himself (hurting himself frequently) and by means of his passivity.

B. *Ego and Superego Development*

GENERAL COMMENTS

This is the second main subheading in Section V, Assessment of Development. Under this heading are four main subdivisions: (1) ego apparatuses; (2) ego functions; (3) defenses; and (4) secondary interference of defenses with ego functions.

Ego development, like drive development, must be viewed against the background of normal development. One must constantly make allowances for the fact that there are variations or deviations in the normal development of ego function, and that, developmentally speaking, the child is not yet a finished product. Because of this, temporary regressions in ego functions or in libidinal development must under certain conditions be considered as normal.

Further allowance must be made for the processes of interaction between the child's endowment or innate capacity and the function of the environment as the releasing agent for the development of these innate capacities and as the stimulating agent for further ego development. For every infant and every environment (mainly represented by the mother at this early stage), the types of interaction will vary greatly.

The releasing and stimulating role of the mother depends of course on her interests and the possibilities for cathexis she provides. This factor plays a large role in the many variations of development which occur within normal limits.

It has previously been mentioned that there exists a link between the stage of libidinal development and the contribution made by it to further ego development.

(1) Under the subheading Ego Apparatuses, the intactness or defects of the ego apparatus are examined.

(2) Under the subheading Ego Functions, we look for the intactness of the various functions, always bearing it mind the age and stage of development of the particular child. We assess these functions against the background of our picture of normal development.

Particular attention should be paid to the existence of primary or developmental deficiencies.

When this point in the Profile has been reached we are able to categorize a very large number of cases diagnostically, i.e., those with an arrested libidinal or ego development. The value of the information recorded under this subheading for differential diagnosis and for prognosis cannot be overemphasized.

A good developmental history allows us to follow when certain functions appear, what their character is, and how they have developed since early in life. This is most useful for clarifying whether there is a "primary disturbance" based on an ego defect (organic damage being the possible substrate in many cases), or whether there is a "developmental disturbance" of the particular function or functions under consideration. In the latter case the cause might well be the lack of proper and adequate mothering. In this case the environment has failed in its releasing and stimulating function necessary for the proper development of the ego functions and apparatus (the extreme cases being those described by Spitz [1945] as "hospitalism").

The final picture presented by both types of cases may be similar, particularly if in the brain-damaged or deficient cases the neurological examination happens to be negative. Yet in one case there is an organic substrate, while in the other case there is a more functional defect (which nevertheless might be as irreversible as the first).

Both types of cases have a poor prognosis. The outcome depends not only on the extent of the damage but also on the particular functions affected and the degree to which this has occurred. In these cases analytic treatment will be limited since we cannot undo the organic defect, nor can we provide at a later date the stimulation and care which was required earlier.

A careful developmental history within the social history will help us here, and will at times allow us to make a differential diagnosis. For this purpose we should at the same time consider heading E in Section VII, Dynamic and Structural Assessment (Conflicts): External Conflicts, as well as the heading Background in Section III. There we will find descriptions of the sort of mothering the child has had in early life. Such details as normal siblings, coupled with the absence of information which might make us suspect the early mother-child relationship, and so on, will assist us. In other cases, the typical picture of the institutionalized child will complete our diagnosis.

On the other hand, in many cases of arrested ego development (of whatever nature), it is not possible to show or to point to conflicts of an internalized character (conflicts between superego, ego, and id), but only to conflicts of an internal nature (between opposites in the id) and to those of an external character. At a given age the absence of or incomplete picture of internalized conflicts can be a strong indicator of this type of problem, as shown by the lack of development in the structural sense. Furthermore, some of our cases used and needed their objects as auxiliary egos, to deal with fear and anxiety. They showed "an obsessionallike" organization. Any small change in the daily routine aroused extreme distress and anxiety. These cases are not obsessionals in the true meaning of the word but resemble them due to the incapacity of their egos to deal with any new situation or any change. These children were not withdrawn or autistic, but were quite able to cathect objects as long as they were approached at the level to which they had been able to develop. This latter point is important for the differential diagnosis of withdrawn or autistic children.

Some of these children showed phallic manifestations and reactions, but the ego development that should go with it and the rich fantasy life (oedipal) that should accompany these phallic reactions in normal children were never present. This is of great significance for the purpose of differential diagnosis. These cases represent the more or less extreme end of a scale which comprises all sorts of grades. The diagnostic procedure, and especially the prognostic evaluation, becomes more difficult as we approach the other end of the scale.

(3) Our third subheading under Ego and Superego Development deals with defenses, which we scrutinize in terms of their age adequacy.

Denial, identification, and projection are primitive defenses. Complete denial is adequate for a two-year-old but very abnormal later on. By the time of latency most of the primitive defenses should be in the background; one would then expect to see repression, reaction formation, sublimation, identification with the aggressor, turning passivity into activity, etc.

In adolescence all the primitive defenses seem to reappear for a time. Personal problems are now looked at impersonally, expressed in racial, social struggles, etc. (externalization). Attention should be paid to the excessive and untimely use of specific defenses, the availability of a variety of defenses, and the ego's effectiveness in dealing with the drives in an adequate form. We should examine the type of defense not only in relation to its age adequacy but also in regard to the economic factor involved; whether, for example, the types of defense used require permanent and large expenditure of energy in the form of countercathexis. It should be borne in mind that the ego can use functions and mechanisms not normally meant for that purpose in a defensive fashion at a given time.

(4) Secondary Interference of Defenses with Ego Functions is the

fourth subheading in the section Ego and Superego Development. Here we try to describe how the type of defense used by the ego interferes with some ego functions, though basically they were intact and properly developed. As soon as the defenses which interfere with these ego functions can be removed during the course of treatment the functions will reappear intact, in contrast with the primary defective functions.

It is easy to see, for example, that excessive use of withdrawal into fantasy will to a greater or lesser degree affect such functions as attention, perception, apperception, concentration, memory, thought processes. At a given age this implies a severe interference with schooling and the process of learning. Other defenses will affect different functions. Excessive use of projection interferes with reality testing and thought processes. Aggression turned against the self may temporarily interfere with motility and result in accident proneness. Regressive processes, particularly on the side of the ego, can imply a serious disturbance of very many ego functions.

If in a given case there is no particular conflict or type of defense that would explain the existing state of affairs, it is of great value when the Profile discloses a marked inhibition or lack of proper functioning of the ego as a whole. This suggests some sort of arrest in development; by looking to the other headings in the Profile, it becomes possible to find pointers to the real causes of disturbance.

We may ask: how will the faulty functioning of one function affect the development of the others? How does the ego attempt to compensate for this, and what is the result in terms of the final structure? This developmental approach which traces the lines of development of specific ego functions is bound to provide answers to these questions. The same approach is also valid in relation to the secondary interference of defenses with ego functions at different ages and stages of development, and to the manner in which this interference affects further development.

CASE ILLUSTRATION

1. *Ego Apparatuses*

Arthur's ego apparatuses seem to be intact. There are no symptoms or signs of primary defects there.

2. *Ego Functions*

There are no signs either of primary deficiencies in his ego functions. Arthur is a highly intelligent boy, who cannot at present make full use of his very good potentialities. He has an I.Q. of 137. Nevertheless his schoolwork is poor and his learning capacity seems to be impoverished in spite of his high I.Q. There is no doubt that there is an important secondary interference of his defensive system with many of his ego functions.

3. *Defenses*

Arthur's defense organization consists mainly of repression, regression (to anal and oral levels), reaction formations, very marked passivity, clinging and dependence, turning of the aggression against the self, and withdrawal into illness. This group of defenses is mainly directed against his phallic oedipal wishes for both parents as well as against his aggressive drives. This defense organization is in any case far from effective at present, resulting in anxiety and symptom formation.

4. *Secondary Interference of Defenses with Ego Functions*

It is not difficult to see how such a vast and excessive use of these types of defenses have led to an interference with his schooling and learning processes. His marked passivity plays a specially important role here.

Arthur's tendency to control his aggression, partly by means of turning it against himself, seems to interfere with his motility leading frequently to falls and accidents, where he hurts himself. The function of speech is interfered with by his oral aggression and the defenses against it, particularly in a given set of circumstances, i.e., when he has to read in a loud voice at school.

C. *Development of the Total Personality (Lines of Development and Mastery of Tasks)*[5] *or Age-Adequate Responses*

GENERAL COMMENTS

For didactic and methodological purposes we have artificially isolated the drive development from the ego development and have assessed each independently. Under this heading we now aim to see the whole personality, reacting to what Anna Freud has called *life*

5 At present, one of the aspects of our research program on the Developmental Profile consists of the application of a number of *developmental lines* to our cases. This has been suggested by Anna Freud (1963) who points out: "Far from being theoretical abstractions, developmental lines, in the sense here used, are historical realities which, when assembled, convey a convincing picture of an individual's personal achievements, respectively of his failures in personality development."

task. This reaction is partly dependent on the stage of development reached at any given moment. Life tasks are situations with which the child is confronted at different stages of his development. Many of these are common to every one, but some may not be so usual or apply so generally.

Examples of life tasks that will confront children at different times are: going to nursery school at three and a half years; the birth of a sibling; the death of a close relative; hospitalizations (of the child himself, the mother, etc.); separations from the parents; moving house, etc.

We expect that the child's reaction differs at different ages, according to the means the child has acquired through the course of development to deal with such situations.[6] In these situations the personality as a whole reacts to the particular life task under consideration. The child as a whole adapts himself to the new situation and during this process makes use of all the resources at his disposal.

We can learn a great deal about each individual child. We can obtain information about his ego development and his capabilities, the sorts of defense he can mobilize, his capacity to tolerate frustration, his possibilities of sublimation, of toleration for anxiety and his ways of dealing with it, his ability to accept substitute or neutralized gratification with enjoyment, the progressive forces present in him as contrasted with the regressive ones and so on.

CASE ILLUSTRATION

In Arthur, the age-adequate achievements are lacking in the main. He has remained closely attached to the family (one positive element here is his ability to go biking with a friend). He prefers the family (both father and mother) to look after him and his body as if he were a small child.

The relationship to the parents, particularly to the mother, has remained highly sexualized. His interests in literature are sexualized.

VI. Regression and Fixation Points

GENERAL COMMENTS

As previously described, we look here for signs that reveal fixation points in pieces of significant behavior, fantasies, and in certain symptoms.

[6] An excellent example of what is meant here is given by Gauthier (1960).

In some cases the fixation points will show themselves as precipitates in the character structure. Observation of the different imprints which the various libidinal phases left on the character structure can be very relevant. They may manifest themselves either directly as the characteristic traits of any given phase or through corresponding reaction formations, for example, excessive cleanliness instead of dirtiness.

The relevant material is classified under the subheadings: Oral, Anal, and Phallic.

As has been mentioned, there is a link between this heading and drive development. It is obvious that the various aspects of the Profile are intimately connected. Therefore there is a constant need to correlate the material recorded under each heading and to consider how each completes and qualifies the other. This process of correlation helps us to think in an organized fashion. In addition and even more important, each section provides checks of the material in the other sections, and the sections pose questions to one another, questions that are relevant to the consideration of the case. This brings out apparent or real contradictions in the material. It constantly forces our minds to translate clinical observations into our conceptual frame of reference and vice versa.

In working with the Profile, the following questions and thoughts occurred to me in relation to the heading Regression and Fixation Points: what, if any, will be the difference between fixation points coming about as a result of deprivation and frustration (extreme cases being institutionalized children) and those which are a consequence of excessive gratification (those overwhelmed by stimulation or intense seduction)? Is there any difference in diagnostic or prognostic significance between these two possibilities?

Deprivation or frustration experienced early in life will under certain circumstances severely damage the child's possibilities for development, and these damages may not be reversible. What will be the counterpart of intense deprivation if we are dealing instead with excessive gratification or stimulation? Will the outcome be similar or even comparable?

Deprivation (intense frustration) or excessive gratification, when it occurs later in life and development, does not seem to have the same significance once a certain stage of development has been reached. After this point it looks as if, in some cases, intense stimulation (excessive gratification) is a more dangerous element than frustration as far as further development is concerned.

A further observation of interest in regard to fixation points is that these points may be almost all that remains of later levels and stages of development, once massive regressive processes have taken place (both on the ego and libidinal sides). Generally, the existence of strong fixation points is a potentially dangerous situation, because when faced with obstacles during later stages of development the libido that has remained behind pulls back the forward-moving libido.

In one of our cases we could observe that this whole process had been reversed. In view of this experience it might be justified to assume that fixation points also exert a forward pull (in this case, toward development) on the libido which, due to regression, has gone back to the very earliest stages. If further observations and clinical material were to confirm these speculative thoughts, we would be forced to add a new dimension to the function of fixation points. Side by side with their potentially pathogenic role in cases of neurosis, in other cases of more severe regressions and disorganization of the whole personality we would have to view fixation points as anchorage points in stages of higher development that had to be abandoned. They would not only be indicators of the stages reached, but would favor (by their "pulling" attraction in the descriptive sense) the forces of recovery. If this is the case, the presence of the fixation points in severe cases of regression would have prognostic value.

CASE ILLUSTRATION

As already pointed out, Arthur has very important fixation points at the oral and anal levels to which part of his libido has regressed.

Oral Level: According to the mother, Arthur slings his food down, eats at an abnormal rate, and is always hungry. He still sucks his thumb when he is at home. He is supposed to have bitten the side of his wooden cot so that the wood was chewed away. At three he used to bite other children at the nursery. Now he screams and yells and has an inhibition of reading in a loud voice at school.

Anal Level: The mother described the toilet training as difficult. Arthur retained, and still does, his bowel movements. He has bowel movements only at home, and he constantly comes home with his pants soiled. He is said to be obstinate and to have a violent temper that may well be the imprint of this phase of development on his character. The relationship with the mother has a sadomasochistic character.

Phallic Level: The relationship with the mother is still highly sexualized. He giggles and says "ooh" when he sees his mother not fully dressed. He is always making jokes about girls and laughs about nude pictures with his mother. Arthur's battle at the oedipal stage is still going on; as a result of this, part of his libido has regressed to the previous phases. It is also noticeable in the intensity of his positive attachment to the father, which has defensive aspects but which is undoubtedly linked with the intensity of his bisexual conflicts and therefore primary in character. The father himself plays an important role in this connection: he bathes Arthur on week ends.

VII. Dynamic and Structural Assessment (Conflicts)

general comments

This heading is subdivided into (a) External, (b) Internalized, and (c) Internal Conflicts.

(a) Much of the material that one feels tempted to include under External Conflicts belongs in fact in Section III, Family Background and Personal History, and in Section IV, Possibly Significant Environmental Influences. Entries under this subheading are prominent in the Profiles of those cases in which a final structure of the personality has not been achieved (superego). The conflicts are between id-ego agencies and external authority figures. This may be due to the child's age who is still too young to have completed his structural development, but it applies equally to those cases in which an arrested ego development makes final structure impossible, figures in the outside being used both as ego and superego auxiliaries. A similar situation is present in certain cases of defective superego development, in which the conflict takes place with external figures or with society (certain types of delinquent, etc.).

(b) The subheading, Internalized Conflicts (between id, ego, and superego), is of great significance. In itself it indicates that a final development in the structural sense has been reached. Fear of external authority has been internalized and has become fear of superego.

Guilt feelings appear and become the measure and expression of tension between the ego and superego. The presence of guilt in the material is a pointer to the existence of the superego as a functioning mental agency.

The internalized conflicts must be described in metapsychological terms, and a dynamic, economic, and structural analysis must be made of the conflict or conflicts involved (either of a libidinal or aggressive character). For this purpose it is necessary to refer back to the information examined and collected under the other headings, mainly those under defenses and fixation points, describing which drives are defended against and so on.

(c) The subheading Internal Conflicts is meant to cover conflicts between opposite drives—masculinity and femininity, activity and passivity, etc.

The assessment of this is not always an easy task. The older the child the more difficult it can be to sort out how much belongs to the initial bisexual conflict, how much to environmental influence, and how much to a defensive attitude developed at the time of the oedipal relationship and a consequence of castration anxiety. Nevertheless, in many cases it has been possible to complete the sorting out successfully.

One is reminded here of what Freud said: "in both sexes the relative strength of the masculine and feminine sexual dispositions is what determines whether the outcome of the Oedipus situation shall be an identification with the father or with the mother. This is one of the ways in which bisexuality takes a hand in the subsequent vicissitudes of the Oedipus complex" (1923, p. 33).

In view of Freud's statement, it is clear that the outcome of the oedipus situation will itself be a pointer to what the original bisexual constitution was like. This can be shown with clinical material and observation. Moreover, in the area of the drives the child is not as open to environmental and external influence as he may be in other areas (ego development).

The process of sorting out thus becomes more feasible. When we are confronted with an apparently passive-feminine identification in a boy we can always ask whether what we observe is the result of the original bisexual constitution or rather the outcome of external influences, or perhaps the result of defensive measures brought about by castration anxiety, or of an early feminine identification. Freud gives us an answer in the passage I have quoted. The passive-feminine identification was possible and is the outcome of the oedipal situation in a particular child, precisely on account of the strong feminine element in his constitution. If this had been otherwise, in spite of everything this possibility would not have been open for him. Similarly, an early feminine identification (implying a true modification of the ego on the basis of the identification) is only open to those children who have an original bisexual constitution which facilitates such an outcome.

On the other hand, one must realize that in relation to this problem, as anywhere else in the Profile, the interaction between endowment and environment cannot be overlooked or underrated. The concept of complemental series" is as valid in regard to bisexual constitution as anywhere else. The influence of the environment is more prominent precisely in those cases which have a weaker endowment (e.g., a boy not strongly endowed with masculinity, and consequently with a relatively strong feminine element in his bisexual constitution).

In working with the Profile we found that, in order to evaluate the problems belonging to this particular subheading, a good developmental history is a great asset. In it we will look for pointers to the nature of the bisexual constitution, particularly (if it is possible) to its character before defensive measures against castration anxiety had the chance to exploit the basic bisexuality conflict and to form a final picture in which it may be more difficult to discern how much is the outcome of defense and how much is primary.

The possibility of an early identification of a passive-feminine character (with the mother, for example, before the phallic phase), as a consequence of, let us say, compliance with the wishes of the mother for a girl, will not be open if a strong masculine element is present. If it does occur and is an identification (with subsequent ego modification), this fact again constitutes a pointer to the marked bisexual conflict of the particular case. One has to distinguish certain types of "as if" identification, which are the result of compliance, from true identification. In the former, the child's drive, strivings, and fantasies remain masculine.

In the developmental history data about all aspects of the child's behavior since early life, his physique, his voice and speech mannerisms, the way he walks, his body language in movements, facial expressions, the way he runs, climbs, the way he asks for things, the way he reacts in different situations, his games, and so on, may be possible pointers to his original bisexual constitution.

CASE ILLUSTRATION

(a) *External Conflicts:* While Arthur's conflicts are mostly internalized, there are some conflicts with the external world that play an active role in his actual pathology and stage of development. This is due to the amount of seduction and external interference with his development (factors already referred to at different points).

(b) *Internalized Conflicts:* These are libidinal and aggressive in character and mainly centered around the oedipal situation (both mother and father aspects playing an important role), as a result of which part of his libido is now back at oral and anal levels. As mentioned previously, not only the positive oedipal attachment to the mother but the strong oedipal attachment to the father must be noted here. Part of it is defensive, but part is no doubt linked with the intensity of his bisexual conflicts and primary in character. Arthur's conflicts at the oedipal level are frequently expressed in anal and oral terms.

(c) *Internal Conflicts:* There are numerous hints of conflicts between opposite drives (male, female; passive, active). In both cases these conflicts seem to be partly of a primary character and partly a defense against anxiety provoked by one of the elements of the pair of opposites.

VIII. Assessment of Some General Characteristics

GENERAL COMMENTS

This heading has four subsections: (a) Frustration Tolerance; (b) Sublimation Potential (Capacity to Accept and Enjoy Substitute or Neutralized Gratification); (c) Over-all Attitude to Anxiety; (d) Progressive Forces versus Regressive Tendencies. It will be noted that these are mainly, though not exclusively, of great prognostic value. For this reason, they have been singled out from other areas and headings where they might belong. The prognostic value of these subsections relates to the possibilities of further normal development, to treatability by the psychoanalytic method, and to long-term prognosis.

(a) Frustration Tolerance is not always easy to assess. (This heading overlaps to some extent with the two following ones, which are in some ways related.) The lower the capacity of any child to tolerate frustration, the worse he is equipped for life. Frustration tolerance refers to the immediate reaction that follows the postponement or total lack of fulfillment of an instinctual wish. When trying to assess a child's frustration tolerance we cover three points: tolerance in regard to the frustration (i) of libidinal drives, (ii) of aggressive drives, and (iii) of failure when engaged in neutralized activities. It should be kept in mind that frustration tolerance varies at various times in life, from practically none at birth and in the child's early life, to different levels at some later stage. When, for example, regression to the oral phase occurs, the level of frustration tolerance will be very diminished. It must be taken into account that the tolerance of frustration may be different in relation to different component instincts.

(b) Sublimation Potential—The Capacity to Accept and Enjoy Substitute or Neutralized Gratification—is a measure of an important safety valve for mental health. Those who have a good capacity in this area are safer in life.

In most cases the material available for diagnostic purposes gives one some impression of what the child looks like in this area. Accounts of the child's behavior, usually given by the mother, generally suffice for this purpose. In addition, descriptions of work and behavior at school may be useful. The presence of sublimation is another pointer.

(c) Under the heading Over-all Attitude to Anxiety, as far as possible a metapsychological description of the facts should be given. In one sense this heading is the other side of the picture described under Internalized Conflicts. There a metapsychological account of the conflict situation was asked for. Here, we want to know about the rearrangements that have taken place, precisely as a result of that conflict, in the structure of personality and in character formation, viewed in dynamic, economic, and structural terms. In short, what is required here is the rearrangement brought about as a result of the conflicts and defenses used in the structure of personality and in character formation, as well as an estimate of the child's basic attitude toward anxiety.

There are great variations in the amount of anxiety which different children can tolerate without resorting to symptoms and defenses.

If the child can meet anxiety in an active way, this is a positive factor and he is in contrast to those who will either regress or develop phobic symptoms.

(d) Looking at the Progressive Forces versus Regressive Tendencies, we make an attempt to obtain a feeling of the underlying general tendencies in the child. There may be a tendency to progress and develop in spite of external difficulties and stresses, or the contrary may be the case. Many pathological manifestations can be absorbed by a strong impulse to development.

CASE ILLUSTRATION

(a) *Frustration Tolerance:* Arthur has a relatively low capacity for the toleration of frustration.

(b) *Sublimation Potential:* So far there is no evidence of his having a high sublimation potential, though the real picture here may be somewhat blurred and interfered with by the undue stimulation and seduction on the side of the parents.

(c) *Over-all Attitude to Anxiety:* Arthur tends to withdraw from situations where toleration and mastery of anxiety are required. This can be observed in the reading inhibition he developed when having to read in a loud voice at school (at home his oral aggression breaks through in shouting and yelling) or in his regression to earlier levels of drive discharge and gratification, resulting from castration anxiety and intolerable oedipal strivings.

His over-all ego attitude to this type and amount of anxiety is inefficient; the result has been symptom formation and a tendency to restrict the ego, in spite of very high potentialities.

(d) *Progressive Forces versus Regressive Tendencies:* There is a pull back, a tendency to regress to more primitive levels of libidinal development and more primitive sources of libidinal gratification. This has involved, on occasions, the temporary regression of certain controls and ego functions already achieved when the frustration period sets in (i.e., speech).

IX. Diagnosis

GENERAL COMMENTS

In this section we are only concerned with a broad formulation of the type of disturbance. Broadly speaking, we can distinguish between normal development and its variations, neurotic (i.e., regressive processes in development), atypical (i.e., arrested processes in development), and psychotic and borderline (i.e., malignant processes).

CASE ILLUSTRATION

Arthur belongs in group (3) of our provisional classification (A. Freud, 1962), showing neurotic conflicts with regression to the anal and oral levels, symptom formation and marked ego restrictions.

DISCUSSION

This section of my paper is devoted to some general considerations and comments concerning the Developmental Profile and the subject of diagnosis.

After using the Developmental Profile for a period of about a year, the diagnostic discussions of a number of cases revealed that it meets the requirements for these procedures. Diagnostic discussions are of necessity limited in time, as far as any one case is concerned, after which a diagnostic decision is attempted. However, this time limitation, so necessary for obvious reasons, has certain dangers.

The Profile meets some of the shortcomings of ordinary diagnostic evaluations in a more appropriate way. It forces us, from the very beginning, to pay attention to and cover each and every area of the personality. A case must be seen as a whole, due attention being paid to every aspect. In this way we avoid some of the dangers implicit in the ordinary procedure, particularly the tendency to focus on a particular symptom or striking piece of behavior. Important as this symptom or piece of behavior may be for the assessment of a child, they should not be considered in isolation, in which case they might acquire quite a different diagnostic meaning and significance. They must be viewed in the context of the whole personality, as part of a total structure, because they can be properly assessed and qualified only in this context.

As far as the time invested in elaborating a Profile is concerned, it can be said to be negligible. Since the Profile is truly a way of thinking and of organizing clinical observations and material, metapsychologically and within the conceptual frame of psychoanalysis, it can be built up as soon as one has finished reading the material available (i.e., social history, psychiatric interview, etc.). I have already commented on the fact that the classification of material under different headings is done for didactic and methodological reasons. The analysis of specific areas, for the time being artificially isolated from other areas with which they are closely interconnected, is only the initial step. This must be followed by the synthesis that the Profile represents.

The Profile is meant to be an extremely dynamic and alive picture of a given person. This requires the selection of relevant clinical material, which will convey meaning and imbue the Profile with liveliness. For those who want to achieve this, an important warning must be given: this is not to work from the headings to the material, a procedure which will never make a Profile, but rather the other way round, from the clinical material to the headings. Working in this way the clinical material will tend to classify itself whenever it is a relevant piece of information under a given section. Frequently, the same piece of material will "place itself" under several headings, making a different and valuable contribution to each and throwing light on the particular personality being examined. This makes the Profile meaningful, dynamic, and alive.

If, on the other hand, one "feeds" the headings simply because they exist, if one goes from the heading to the clinical material, one may be able to collect much information under each heading. But this is static and at times meaningless information. The Profile will lack that integrating thought process that is necessary for the construction of a meaningful picture of a person. It will also lack that which enriches the Profile and ourselves by teaching us to correlate our theoretical model, our conceptual frame, with clinical observations and vice versa. In short, the metapsychological approach is missing, and the process of trying out every possible angle in our own mind is lost. The finished Profile constitutes, after all, nothing more than a summary of our mental activities while reading the material, a sort of summary of our mental exercises in correlation, in assessment, in the translation of clinical observations into theoretical concepts and vice versa.

It may have been noticed that the headings belong to different levels of concept formation. They are hierarchically different and collect and organize the material at different levels of conceptualization. I have mentioned several times that a close relation exists among the different headings, and consequently of course among the clinical data that are classified under these various headings.

Furthermore, some headings are built up mainly on the information which has already been analyzed in several of the others. For this reason the information which is given in and analyzed by the different headings is not all at the same level or in the same conceptual category. Some headings collect the material in a rather simple way, others organize it at a more complex level of concept formation; and finally when we arrive at the summit of the Profile, we have the metapsychological formulations.

The Profile highlights the various areas of conflict, at times giving a very clear picture of the intensity and magnitudes of the forces involved. It permits us to make some quantitative assessment (in relative terms) of the magnitude of the drives, present as the result of a person's endowment, and to make comparisons with other cases. In this way a clearer understanding of the economic aspects is possible.

A good developmental history not only helps us to achieve all the purposes mentioned, it also allows us to understand the vicissitudes of the drives at various developmental stages; vicissitudes which are the result of the interplay with forces and figures of the environment, and later the interplay with the inner representatives and heirs of these external figures and conflicts.

With the information available at any time during the course of treatment, or after completion of treatment, a Profile can be constructed which may be compared with that obtained at the diagnostic stage on the basis of the information then available. This enables us to check on how far our diagnostic assumptions, our understanding of the case, and our predictions were correct, and how much of what later emerged in treatment was visible at the diagnostic stage, and so on. It allows us to check whether our metapsychological assessment of the material at the diagnostic stage was correct and whether it coincides with the assessment we could make after several years of analytic treatment.

The results obtained by the application of the Profile in this way have been satisfactory and instructive. The comparisons of Profiles obtained at the diagnostic stage and after the completion of treatment have shown us that the Profile pin-points at the very beginning the child's basic personality structure and main conflicts.

We then examined a number of cases in which we knew our

initial diagnostic assessment to be incorrect or incomplete. The Profile was applied by a worker familiar with its use, but he had no knowledge of the particular case. Again, we were impressed by the results and regretted that no Profile had been available at the diagnostic stage of these cases. The analysis of causes of failure in the diagnostic procedures, in the light of knowledge gained after the analytic treatment of these cases, will lead to improvements.

The Profile constantly feeds back information that can, in its turn, improve our diagnostic techniques and our evaluations of the material. The very nature of the Developmental Profile provides checks on the reliability of our different sources of information (mother, father, etc.). We do not rely as much as we did in the past on a particular account given about a patient and on the accuracy of that account. Rather we rely on the internal picture we construct with all the information about the conflicts and the structure of a given personality. This picture must fit with the one familiar to us from our experience with neurotic, atypical, borderline, or psychotic pictures. Our ideal is to achieve a positive diagnosis. As in general medicine, we attempt to construct a syndrome in which all the symptoms and signs must correspond to and fit with what we know about neurotic conflict or atypical cases. For this purpose we follow the role played by the drives, by the different structures of the mind, the mechanism of symptom formation, defenses, the degree of maturity of the systems involved, etc. (the medical equivalent being anatomical, anatomopathological, physiological, and physiopathological considerations, etc.). The whole clinical picture thus arrived at must be properly delimited from others and must be internally consistent. If it is not, the Profile highlights contradictions and inaccuracies and permits us to trace them back to their sources.

Furthermore, the Profile poses questions which must be answered in order to resolve such inaccuracies and contradictions; it asks for more information on specific points, before a correct judgment can be arrived at. In this way the Profile checks itself or rather leads us to do the checking. If we obtain an incomplete picture of the structure of a neurotic conflict we will be warned to look more closely and to be prepared for a diagnostic surprise of one sort or another. For example, we may have a child with neurotic conflicts similar to those which any other child might have. But in addition, this child has, within certain limits, a faulty or defective ego. We will see the usual picture of neurotic conflict, but also that the child is not able to deal with the anxiety and the conflict situation in quite the same way as other children with normal egos do. This child will be in greater distress, more overwhelmed by his anxiety, and more helpless. The problem here may be a quantitative one, the ego not being able to cope beyond a certain point.

I have mentioned before that the Profile can be applied at any given point during the course of treatment, yielding a cross-section of the personality at that particular moment. It follows that the Profile is thus a useful tool for the assessment of the progress of analytic treatment. Applied at the end of treatment it provides an assessment of changes brought about by treatment.[7] The Profile evaluates the results of treatment by scrutinizing the inner changes and the structural rearrangements brought about by the analytic treatment rather than by assessing certain particular external manifestations. This method examines closely the changes in the defensive systems, the disappearance or diminution of the original conflicts in terms of the relative magnitude of the forces involved, the processes of sublimation that have been favored by the treatment situation, and the like. It also takes into account the ego's new capacities and techniques for dealing with anxiety. In short, it tries to highlight the structural, dynamic, economic, and adaptive rearrangements that may have taken place as the result of analysis.

In a number of cases we have repeated the Profile at the end of treatment (psychoanalytic treatment five times a week for a period of two, three, four, or more years).[8] It cannot be overemphasized that the inner picture may be very different from the one based on an assessment of external manifestations, which can be very mis-

[7] At the panel on the Curative Factors in Pyscho-Analysis (1961), the question of how to improve our assessment of the results of treatment was posed. In her answer, Anna Freud referred to the potential uses of the Profile. [For a specific application of Profile considerations to problems of termination, see van Dam et al. (1975).]

[8] The material utilized here consists of the reports made by the therapists on the treatment. At Hampstead we make written reports on every child in analysis at weekly and bimonthly intervals; in addition, each case is presented at least once a year to the general staff meeting. After completion of the analysis a summary of the treatment is prepared by the child's therapist. This material is available for research purposes.

leading. This is well brought out by the case of Arthur whose Profile has been presented here.

Arthur was eleven and a half years old at the beginning of his treatment. A Profile was made with the material recorded after three years of analytic treatment and subsequent follow-up. A superficial assessment might give the impression of a very much improved child, with no apparent trace of the conflicts and anxieties that had brought him into treatment. However, a closer examination, making use of the Profile, showed that most of the main conflicts and anxieties remained even though they were no longer as apparent as at the diagnostic stage.

He is now nineteen years old. His passivity and his tendency to revert to it as a consequence of castration anxiety or disappointment were seen at the diagnostic stage and are still present though they are less transparent. The diagnostic Profile also revealed a disturbed mother-child relationship. At present his relationship to his mother is still a highly sexualized one. His school problems and his learning inhibitions (in spite of his high capacities) are no longer present in their original form, but he has renounced his ambition of becoming an engineer and is at present undertaking a training well below his capacities. His difficulties centering around his aggression are still present.

Arthur's neurotic conflicts and symptoms are no longer as apparent as they were at the diagnostic stage. It seems that he has achieved a more stable equilibrium. However, he has paid the price of having to maintain a number of ego restrictions and limitations. He has also developed a number of rather undesirable character traits. He has not solved his conflicts by inner change but rather avoids them. Thus his interest in girls tends to lead to failure, to fear of competing, and to retreat into passivity. When another boy appears he simply withdraws. Similarly the decision that Arthur has made to enter his father's business is apparently not based on a healthy identification with the father but rather seems to be the outcome of a passive submission to the father's wishes.

We believe that time will confirm the expectations we have concerning the use of the Profile as a research tool. It has already proved its usefulness in many ways. The collection and comparison of large amounts of material obtained from specific cases and many different ones may prove valuable as a means of validating many theoretical assumptions and propositions.

In the experience of those who have worked with it, the Profile has stimulated, improved, and trained our thought processes in the field of psychoanalysis. We consider it to be of value in the training of candidates. It helps the student to learn the metapsychological approach. It sharpens the capacity for translating clinical observations and material into concepts, and helps us to use our theoretical formulations in the scrutiny and evaluation of clinical observations.

It may prove to be the basis on which an analytic classification of childhood (and adult) disturbances can later be built. It brings to such a classification not only a balanced view of the interaction of heredity, endowment, and environment; it also includes the developmental aspects, and the point of view of normality. All of these are basic considerations in any attempt at classifying or evaluating childhood manifestations, either normal or pathological.

Moreover, the genetic point of view has been given its proper place within the Profile. We can thus avoid the frequent mistakes that can occur when the genetic approach is taken further than it can really go, particularly at the diagnostic stage. When treatment has given us a much deeper understanding of the case and the forces and influences operative, it becomes possible to fill the gaps that may exist in this area.

9

A DIAGNOSTIC PROFILE OF PSYCHOPATHOLOGY IN A LATENCY CHILD

DALE R. MEERS
(1966)

Foreword by Reginald S. Lourie, M.D.

The child presented in the Diagnostic Profile that follows has suffered from a seizure disorder for at least six years. This Profile is *not* intended as a differential assessment of an organic as contrasted with a hysterical dysfunction. The child continues under independent neurological supervision during his ongoing psychotherapeutic treatment.

The purposes of this paper would *not* be served if it were considered as an extension of the discussion of organic versus psychogenic etiology of epileptic or seizure disorders. However, at the present stage of the child's treatment (and continuing diagnostic assessment), it is essential to consider the nature of the convulsive disorder as it affected the boy's defense organization, ego capacities, and neurotic solutions to conflict. It is hoped that the treatment will clarify whether, or to what degree, neurosis has made use of a convulsive potential. If hysterical features were to emerge during treatment, if psychotherapy were to disclose a hysterical etiology (which might accompany an organic predisposition), such questions might eventually be examined in the light of analytic documentation.

Clinical experience has consistently underscored the desirability of psychotherapeutic help for many of the patients suffering from emotionally enhanced seizure disorders. In the present case, the

---

The author is a Research Associate at Children's Hospital, Washington, D.C., a guest lecturer and research student with the Baltimore Psychoanalytic Institute; he was formerly a research assistant and a student of the Hampstead Child-Therapy Clinic, London, where he received his training in child analysis.

Dr. Lourie is Director, Department of Psychiatry, Children's Hospital of the District of Columbia.

psychopathological symptomatology might be ascribed, ultimately, to an organic seizure condition and a concomitant intolerance in the ego organization. The structure of both symptomatology and pathogenic defense organization, as evidenced in the following Profile, make it clear that the *form* of the disorder is that of a childhood neurosis which has moved toward encapsulation in a character disorder. That the origins of psychopathology may have roots in an organic impairment is hardly an irrelevant question. Quite the contrary. If true, organic dysfunction is an even stronger reason for psychotherapeutic intervention to help the child cope with atypical neurological dysfunction that complicates and burdens an overtaxed child who adapts by psychopathological means.

The merit of the Diagnostic Profile derives from the clarity of a conceptual biopsy, an ordering of symptoms and developmental data that are both complex and otherwise obscure in the wealth of usual historical and analytic detail. As an *illustration* of the utility of the Profile for the incisive assessment of complexities of childhood disorders, the following paper is a helpful clinical contribution, as is the Profile itself.

R. S. L.

The Research Origins of the Profile

There are four papers that form an indispensable background to the present paper and the use of the Profile in general. A summary of these papers would be an exhaustive commentary on psychoanalysis—and would also do gross disservice to theoretical and clinical formulations that are already concise and renowned for their clarity. The first of these is Anna Freud's classic "Indications for Child Analysis" (1945) in which she stressed the need for a change in emphasis from clinical considerations of manifest childhood symptomatology to an assessment of the impediments to the child's maturational progression. In that paper Anna Freud also discussed the appropriateness and timing, the essential need for diagnostic justification of psychoanalytic intervention in the child's life.

In "Assessment of Childhood Disturbances" (1962), Anna Freud continued and extended a number of formulations and considerations that lend themselves to effective diagnosis, based on the integrated structure of a psychoanalytic "profile of development." A major subsection of the Profile was given more detailed explication in the following year with the publication of Anna Freud's "The Concept of Developmental Lines" (1963). These "lines" provide a specific frame of reference in the assessment of the complex differences, processes, and phases that (may) help differentiate relative normality from varied pathogenic manifestations in childhood.

Clinical and observational data have established that regressions or transient symptoms in particular phases (and ages) of childhood are not essentially pathogenic and that fixations are not unequivocal. Moreover, some expressions of evident and established childhood pathology (which indicate an inadequate resolution of childhood conflict) may be "bypassed" without impeding the mainstream of maturational forces available to the young ego. In Freud's (1916-1917) famous analogy, the question of fixation then involves assessing whether the maturational army had need to leave a regiment to guard against insurrection, or whether a patrol squad sufficed. The concept of "developmental lines" offers a particularly helpful and rewarding conceptual approach with which to evaluate the relative degrees of fixation, regression, or progression in the diagnostic exploration.

The "developmental lines" contain virtues that are not revealed at first blush. There is the explicit need for a diagnostic appraisal of the "age adequacy" of behaviors, defenses, etc. "Age adequacy" could be misunderstood as a static concept, particularly when behaviors (and their modes) reflect strong social and cultural pressures that facilitate (or impede) given drives or modes of their expression (e.g., in the expression of aggression or libidinal forms of gratification). The evaluation of the "age adequacy" of behaviors, i.e., in the context of "developmental lines," permits a bypassing of social and cultural preconceptions or misconceptions of "normalcy" and "pathology." The Profile requires a structured consideration of the ubiquitous processes of biology and psychology operating in all infants and their maturation. *Whatever* the direction or impact of social or cultural stress (manifest in parental-environmental nurture) on the infant and child, a "line of development" exists and permits assessment of its characteristics in that context. Among these universal "lines" are those that lead toward body independence, e.g., from suckling to rational eating, from wetting and soiling to bladder and bowel control, from irresponsibility to responsibility in body management, etc. (A. Freud, 1963, 1965).

In discussing the use and development of the Profile, Nagera (1963) extended the rationale of its structure while providing the first published illustration. The adequacy of diagnosis is obviously not to be measured in the completion of subsections of a formula or Profile. Yet the inception and developmental structuring of the Profile, via prolonged diagnostic research at Hampstead, have "built in" a progression of considerations leading from developmental data to increasingly specific theoretical, metapsychological formulations of explicit diagnostic significance.

The problems of differential diagnosis of childhood disorders are obviously not resolved by the Profile, which is essentially a conceptual tool that can be used with varying degrees of adequacy, depending on the experience of the diagnostician. The Profile does, however, provide for a "fail-safe" (in the vernacular of the day) to the degree that the diagnostician must relate his clinical observations back to the structure of psychoanalytic, developmental metatheory. As Anna Freud has underscored in her most recent work, *Normality and Pathology in Childhood* (1965), the assessment of childhood disturbances continues to be complicated because, among other reasons, we know so little of "normal" variations of maturation.

It is of importance to restate the Hampstead staff's caution, in this regard, that the Profile was developed from the study of psychoneurotic conflicts of childhood, vis-à-vis (what is known of) "normal" ego-drive development. As a diagnostic research tool, the Profile has undergone significant internal modifications. It has been considered less a "finished product" than an experimental research tool designed for specific types of assessment.[1] The Profile's utility for assessments of other forms of pathology has been extended to adult neuroses (A. Freud, H. Nagera, and W. E. Freud, 1965), the study of impulse disorders (Michaels and Stiver, 1965), atypical and borderline children (Thomas et al., 1966), etc. Its value for teaching, with reference

[1] My own (limited) familiarity with Hampstead's Profile work derives from attending Diagnostic and Profile Research Committee Meetings during my last two years of training there.

to both analytic diagnosis and conceptualization, seems to have very rich but still undocumented or unexplored possibilities.

Nagera's clinical elaboration, in the first published case presentation (1963), is authoritative and representative of the succinct character of Profiles at the Hampstead Clinic. The relative scantness, however, of his published clinical material in the body of a conventional Profile is misleading because there is no indication of the wealth of data available to the diagnostician. It may be helpful to note the convention and practice at Hampstead, viz., that extended data derived from diagnostic interviews of parent and child, projective and psychometric reports, school reports, etc., are used as the explicit base for the skeletal "profile." Since all research staff review precirculated diagnostic data in their entirety, the Profile itself can then be kept succinct and dispense with extensive documentations.

In settings other than Hampstead, and particularly for research publication, the scantness of data in the body of the Profile (i.e., presented *without* extended documentation) poses a problem of credibility. The need to extend the internal documentation of the Profile, i.e., in other settings, had been anticipated by the principal investigators.[2] The present extended paper is somewhat of an experiment as to the degree of documentation necessary to insure the adequacy of diagnostic credibility. The wealth of data in the case that follows is somewhat unusual, i.e., for a first Profile of a child. While it draws on two months of twice weekly treatment, it still remains evident that a considerable amount of relevant data is lacking—and in fact may be unobtainable without the depth provided by analytic treatment.

This broaches the additional research value of the Profile in the area of diagnosis and systematic investigations of the etiology of psychopathology, related defense organization, etc. As Nagera (1963) has noted, such research in London has included the diagnostic *reassessment* of a child during or on completion of analytic treatment. The comparisons of second and third Profiles of the same child, over varying periods of time, provide for increasing accuracy and corrections

2 I am particularly indebted to Dr. H. Nagera (London), one of Hampstead Clinic's principal investigators, for his many helpful suggestions on the first draft of this paper and for his comments on the historical development of Profile research.

Special thanks are also due to Dr. J. Waelder-Hall for the opportunity of presenting this paper at the postgraduate child analytic seminar (Baltimore Institute).

of diagnosis via the depth of data provided in the child's analysis. Heinicke (1965) has made use of the Profile to research questions of effectiveness of treatment, etc. In the present assessment, two considerations led to the use of the Profile: (1) the great complexities of differential diagnosis in a latency age boy with both manifest neurological and psychopathognomonic symptomatology, and (2) the potentialities for research, i.e., if the child concerned should enter analytic treatment.

Gottschalk (1956) noted a particular diagnostic difficulty where in "certain types of paroxysmal activity, variously called 'psychic equivalent seizures,' 'affective epilepsy' . . . and so forth, it may become impossible to differentiate between epileptic experiences (and behavior) and nonepileptic experiences (and behavior). This is especially likely to be so when the presumed seizure activity involves complicated and highly integrated patterns of behavior and psychologic processes" (p. 352). The present Profile has attempted this type of differentiating assessment; it also led to the child's start in analytic treatment. The research value of the Profile necessitates second and third (if possible) reassessments. The publication of such extended documented material poses two problems: one expository; and the second, that of protection of the patient's anonymity. These considerations have led to some essential nonclinical distortions, which, hopefully, will not unduly complicate the reporting of future diagnostic reassessments of this case.

Diagnostic Profile

Ian F.

Age: 11 years 6 months (at start of treatment)

Sources of Information:

Psychiatric interview, Dr. A., Date: Current
Social history, Miss B., Date: Current
School history, Miss B., Telephone report, Date: Current
Intelligence test reports, Dr. C., Date: Current
Dr. D., Date: 5 years earlier
Neurological notes, Dr. E., Consultation records covering two years.
Psychotherapeutic treatment notes and interviews with parents, author's records.

I. Reasons for Referral

Ian's parents have been concerned about his well-being since the age of eighteen months when he was hospitalized with a convulsive episode that lasted three hours. Subsequently, between the ages of four and five years, Ian's aggression and behavioral difficulties were sufficiently trying that he was referred for psychiatric evaluation. At age six and a half (following the death of a sister, Gwen) Ian had his first psychomotor seizure. While neurological examinations and EEGs were negative, the clinical picture was classically that of a petit mal attack and he was started on anticonvulsants. At about age nine, Ian developed facial and neck twitches or tics accompanied by nauseous stomach sensations. These were considered neurological corroboration of the diagnosis of psychomotor seizures, and Ian's anticonvulsant medication was subsequently experimentally modified and increased to date.

During the year preceding this referral, Ian's school grades dropped markedly. Moreover, he became increasingly provocative and aggressive with peers and negativistic and rebellious with his parents, particularly his mother. The neurologist concluded that such increase in aggression might have accompanied an increase in medication.

The crucial determinant of the parents' decision to seek psychotherapeutic help was this increase in Ian's negativism and aggression, accompanied by the mother's despair that she could no longer cope with her son. In addition, the parents also feared that Ian's emotional difficulties were ruining his academic opportunities in one of the city's best schools. The parents were intelligent and insightful in their conclusions that whatever the intrinsic, organic or neurological nature of the boy's difficulties, he needed psychotherapeutic treatment. They had become increasingly aware of their son's impairment and distortion of his "self image," particularly evident in his repeated, perhaps manipulative, "I can't help it, after all I'm sick in the head." It is also clear that the parents were concerned about the possibility that organic damage might be progressive and that it could lead to psychosis. A referring psychiatrist had added to the parents' concern by his suggestion that the seizures might be hysterical and that the mother might have the greater need for therapeutic treatment.

II. Description of the Child

Ian is a rather handsome and impressive boy who is tall and well built for his age. He has raven black hair, a dark complexion, and is the more striking for the unexpected blue of his eyes. Ian stands in slightly exaggerated erectness, as if in awareness that someone might be looking at him. His rather handsome appearance is marred by an expression that is often "suspicious" and perhaps sullen; yet Ian can also relax into a gracious and warm smile when secure. In his initial treatment interviews, Ian's tics were constantly evident. His efforts to disguise them were frequently more bizzare than the tics themselves, e.g., strange movements of the head, twisting or poking at his eyebrows, etc.

It is apparent that Ian shares his parents' attitudes toward dress and personal grooming. He has come to his sessions from school, usually dressed in well-pressed slacks, clean shirt, a Windsor knot in his tie, well-polished shoes, etc. At other times, when coming from home, his garb may be casual, but in such instances his sweaters and trousers are in excellent taste and quality, suggesting a familiarity with the best of men's shops. Ian is also impressive and immediately so, for his precocious and pleasantly direct attitude in relating to adults (e.g., schoolmasters, psychiatrists, his therapist, etc.). Ian seems to expect that he should know and should be held responsible for his behavior. In this he seems consciously to anticipate adult evaluation and criticism; his expectation of adverse judgment is evident in his guilt reactions and self-recriminations (e.g., in not studying, in misbehaving, etc.). One senses a measure of insincerity in the boy's confessions, as if he had discovered a technical means of circumventing adult punishment by pseudo self-castigation.

III. Family Background and Personal History

The father's family has enjoyed relative wealth, impeccable repute, and considerable status as owners of extended estates in the English midlands. Mr. F. recalls his parents as being infinitely gentle, kind, and mutually tolerant. His father in particular was considered by the family as *not* second in place to the angels. Mr. F.'s only brother seems of some significance to this history because of his indirect impact on Ian, of which more will be said later.

Mr. F. was graduated from Oxford before World War II, following which he worked a short time on the family's estates. Abandoning this position, apparently precipitously, he secured temporary employment at an Austrian ski lodge. Thereafter, Mr. F. returned to graduate school where he studied philosophy. During his graduate college years, Mr. F. met and married Ian's mother. The sequence of subsequent events is not clear, but it appears that Mr. F. also taught at Oxford, served in World War II as a lieutenant in Navy intelligence, and at some point began his work with a government ministry where his activities were secret to the family, and by inference were exciting and dangerous. Mr. F.'s past and present work schedule has been predictable only for its irregularity; i.e., the family expects that he will be called away from home at night or for days on end. His present position has permitted a greater degree of stability.

Mr. F.'s appearance is distinguished, not least by his 6′4″ height and the consonance of his excellent physical proportions. He has handsome, though somewhat "pretty" features, set off by a shock of hair as black as his son's. In manner, the father appears reserved but quietly interested and alert. He is an intellectually insightful person who has long suffered from migraines and more recently from an acute depressive episode. On this occasion, approximately two years preceding this referral, Mr. F. entered psychotherapy which both he and his wife agree was of considerable help to him. From his therapy, Mr. F. notes that he dramatically identified with his own father who has always considerably influenced his life. As a result Mr. F. feels he has led an "as if" existence in which he "played at being in school," "played at marriage," "played at having an occupation," etc. He has agreed with his wife's accusations that he is and always has been far too passive. Mr. F. also noted that he felt he was different from others in his own incapacity to love with affection and intensity. He has always fought clear of emotions of any sort, e.g., consciously exercising self-controls even when viewing an emotional film or play. Mr. F. states that in years past he has had only two alternatives in coping with his son: (1) by mimicking his own father's gentle, superior, and benevolent attitudes; or (2) by treating his son as another adult. Mr. F. felt that his own therapy left him somewhat freer in his relationship with his son, in permitting greater expression of both fondness for Ian but also of legitimate annoyances and grievances.

Since Mrs. F. is most volatile and explosive, Mr. F. has been motivated over the years to intervene intellectually between mother and son, trying to mitigate the mother's apparent severity and discipline. Because of his own emotional isolation, Mr. F. could rarely give Ian much affection and had hoped that his wife, on Mr. F.'s urging, could recompense the boy in this way.

The father's depressive episode may relate to the death of his own father at that time. The paternal grandmother is still alive and family correspondence seems regular. There is no known family history of psychopathology or neurological disorder. The paternal uncle warrants comment because Ian links his own intensity to the time when this man's wife melodramatically deserted. The aunt absconded with her two sons, secretly taking them to France by airplane without warning either the children or her husband of her intent. She is castigated in the family as an evil woman who deserted for the only and express purpose of "catching a millionaire" (which she did). The elder son of that marriage, Ian's cousin, developed a stutter at that time; Ian notes feelings of murderous rage whenever he is reminded of his aunt by stutterers whom he hears today.

The father's contribution to Ian's misbehavior should be illustrated. During Mr. F.'s momentary absence, Ian burned pages of a school book in the family study in front of his mother (who had been reading there). When she intervened with both anger and anxiety, Ian wrestled with his mother, threw her to the floor, and when she just lay there he snarled, "Well! Have you given up on me again?" When the mother allowed herself tears (for the second time in her life in front of Ian), the boy contemptuously kicked her where she lay and walked out of the room. Mrs. F. was furious, outraged, and frightened. After her husband's return, she waited until her temper was under control and then told him of the event. The father was very angry and ordered Ian to his room where Mr. F. then remained to talk with the boy. Thereafter the father returned to Mrs. F., full of admiration for Ian's "keen insight." Ian had told his father he felt apologetic, yet he knew he would do it again (this was insight!). Ian was concerned about his mother's forgiveness, and the father told Ian that when Christ was asked how many times He would forgive, He replied not only forty times over, but as much more again if necessary. Mrs. F. wanted understanding and protection for herself, not a comparison with or a fate similar to that of Christ. But she listened to her husband's unimpeachable Christianity and was eventually won over to the view that it was her responsibility to go to her troubled son and both forgive and kiss him so that he could sleep untroubled that night. Such incidents suggest a mutually unconscious collusion of father and son in which Ian perpetuates some of the aggression that the father denies in himself.

The mother's background sounds as explosive as the father's seems serene. The maternal grandmother in particular is eternally present, both in fact and in fantasy. She is described as a controlling, insidiously devouring woman who takes and holds everything she can. There is one maternal uncle, a source of continuing shame and humiliation. He is described by Ian's mother as a "professional psychopath," a drunkard, drug addict, a troublemaker, etc. He reputedly never "escaped" mother and the latter nominally continues to pursue, and in reality occasionally secures, the uncle's temporary psychiatric institutionalization. Mrs. F.'s aversion to (and fear of) psychiatry is identified with her experience with one of her brother's psychiatrists. Mrs. F.'s protestations that she had nothing to do with her brother's illness are sufficiently excessive to be suspect. One is immediately impressed with some sense of unconscious guilt as well as with her concern for this brother. The uncle's importance to Ian is of long standing, both because of the boy's incipient fear that he may have inherited some genetic defect and secondarily because of the mother's invidious and continued comparisons. She has harassed Ian over the years, telling him that he would be just as incompetent, incapable, or in need of institutional care, i.e., if Ian did not do as mother instructed. The mother is somewhat abashed in such self-reporting, but it is abundantly clear that she has felt that such "shock tactics" would be one of the only real ways of deterring her son from misbehavior. She does not recognize the fact that such comparisons serve only to frighten Ian and provide him with rationalizations.

It is known that the maternal grandmother lived in London when Ian was a toddler and that she occasionally cared for him then. Later she lived in the family's home for several years where, from Mrs. F.'s point of view, the grandmother was a constant source of chaos in the family. It is of interest to note that the increase in Ian's hostility and aggression at home coincided with the mother's insistence that the grandmother move and find residence elsewhere. Ian indicates that he likes his grandmother very much, but separately notes to his mother that he needs help to protect himself from her excessive needs for hugs and kisses.

Mrs. F. is very tall, and is as attractive and equivalently well proportioned as her husband. She is invariably smartly dressed, well groomed, and her appearance is strikingly handsome, though not "feminine." Mrs. F. describes herself with nominal amusement as emotional, explosive, and strong-willed. (Her family and Ian's therapist would rather agree.) She also describes herself as most loving and interested in her husband and son, implying by this an ambivalent, erotic intensity. She feels that she is unsure of her maternal capacities and is consequently manipulable by innuendoes that might touch on her adequacy in this area, where she feels sensitive and guilty. Mrs. F. also feels that her husband is much more intelligent than she is and that she should follow his advice even when she is emotionally in profound disagreement. She bitterly resents her husband's "inability to be active and masculine," particularly in family matters where discipline or control of Ian has been important (from this statement one can draw a clear inference about their sexual relationship). Whatever difficulties may exist between the parents, they leave the impression of a fundamental and mutual respect, with an apparent reciprocity in their individual psychopathology which binds rather than divides them.

Sexuality was openly and excessively discussed in the house, in the "liberal and progressive" mood of the times. There have been, for example, detailed discussions of the approaches for intercourse in the matings of Ian's white rats. His surviving sister, Fiona, discusses her beaus' sensual overtures to her with the mother, but in Ian's presence. The mother has confronted Ian on the question of whether he masturbates, etc. The father has occasionally showered with his son, and Ian has felt free to walk into the bathroom of the parents, regardless of whether his mother or his father is there. This may be the more important since the parents have noted Ian's precocious move into puberty, evident in the boy's pubic hair and genitals. The father has insisted, as earlier noted, that the mother give more physical, intimate loving to the boy than she would prefer. She has accommodated in such matters, nominally only under duress.

The violence and intensity of feelings in the home, particularly between mother and son, will be noted elsewhere. The mother's temper, as well as Ian's, has precipitated innumerable quarrels over everything in the gamut of possible mother-child difficulties. While verbal discipline is common, isolation is more so. Physical discipline has included forcibly washing Ian's mouth out with soap, hitting him on the head with a broom handle, hitting him in the face, etc. This picture of violence within the family is deceptive, however. The violence is more impulsive than studied. Outside the home, the mother presents a most poised, socially presentable, and smart appearance. She is indeed an attractive person who seems to enjoy meeting others, going to teas, taking art lessons, etc. In other than family matters, the mother's poise and keen interest, her slightly caustic humor, are undoubtedly social assets that make her a well-accepted guest and friend.

Siblings: The F.'s first daughter, Fiona, is nine years Ian's senior. During her college years, she worked in biological and psychological sciences and seems to have a spurious knowledge of Ian's early neurological difficulties. Fiona is presently professionally employed and lives semi-independently in the family's house. Fiona's influence on her parents seems to be considerable; e.g., she apparently gives psychological direction or instruction to her parents. Little is known of her significance to Ian's early years or to his present life. So far as is known, Fiona has suffered from no psychological or neurological disorder.

The second child born to the family was another daughter, Gwen. When Gwen was eighteen months old, Mr. F. was assigned to Greece and the family moved to Athens. Shortly after their arrival there, Gwen suffered from encephalitis and was hospitalized with a convulsive seizure. Her subsequent slow development resulted in extended neurological examinations. Gwen had suffered brain damage and was left permanently mentally retarded. By the time of Mrs. F.'s next pregnancy (with Ian), Gwen was sent to an institution (the family having returned to London). The sister did not return home again, and Ian knew of her only as his sick sister who had to live in an institution because she was "sick in the head." Only at Gwen's death, when Ian was six years ten months of age, did he ever see her, i.e., when she was returned home for her funeral. Ian was described as having been most upset, sorrowful, feeling tricked by his parents that he had not had the opportunity of seeing his sister in life (when in fact she had not been far from home). It should be further noted that Gwen had always been openly considered the mother's most loved and special child, though physically absent. Whatever ambivalence the mother must have felt for this damaged daughter, any rejection or disavowal seemed encapsulated by an overcathexis and restitutive undoing.

Friends: Parents, schoolteachers, and Ian agree that he has no intimate friends, yet that he has reasonably good peripheral relationships. There is apparently one boy slightly younger and much smaller than Ian whom he likes best. Little is known of their common interests or activities. At school, Ian is characteristically shy, reserved, indeed embarrassed if asked procedural questions by his teachers. Yet Ian is not rejected or teased for his shyness, though the mother reports considerable fighting with school peers during the previous year. The teacher does not confirm this, but rather thinks the parents have preconceived feelings and err in oversimplifying Ian's difficulties. Ian indicates that his size and athletic skills make him a much-desired participant in team sports; e.g., Ian is one of two boys who have been given special consent to play with the older ones in the school's regular competitive football matches. Ian's success at team sports is not matched by any direct friendships away from the structured and supervised team companionship. His occasional visits to the homes of acquaintances brought requests that he be permitted to stay overnight. Ian has never been successful in this because of his sleep disturbance (not a referral symptom); Ian becomes extremely unhappy and anxious because he cannot fall asleep away from home. Few boys call on Ian and still fewer ask him back for a second time.

Personal history: It is to be recalled that the parents decided to institutionalize Gwen when the mother became pregnant with Ian. Since she was the mother's favorite, it can be surmised that the pregnancy with Ian was not an unmixed blessing. Mrs. F. was troubled by indigestion and nausea; her delivery, however, was short and uncomplicated. Ian weighed seven pounds at birth and appeared to be a healthy and normal infant. He was described as a fussy baby in that he spat up considerably, though he ate well. He was not breast-fed. Troubles with formula occurred between ten and twelve and a half weeks; he had continual diarrhea, which stopped with a changeover to skim milk. Bottle feedings were gradually replaced with a cup at age six months. Nothing is recalled as to his teething. There are no feeding disturbances, and there were no indications of maternal discomfort in Mrs. F.'s indirect allusions to orality, e.g., that the boy continued sucking his thumb until the age of two.

It is not without significance to Ian's oral needs, however, that the mother reported that Ian had difficulties which she described as related to sleep. Ian was left to "scream himself blue with rage." When, at the suggestion of others, Ian was brought down with the other children or adults and held, the mother reports (without insight) how surprisingly pleasant the child could then be. One may conjecture here as to the mother's early attitudes and fears regarding her infant son: she described him not as having been unhappy, but as having been "in a rage." It is quite clear, by inference, that the mother describes herself as unresponsive to her son's earliest infantile needs, and as expecting her son to be hostile and aggressive.

Ian is further described as having been a very active and determined infant and toddler, with early developmental achievements, e.g., walking at nine months and walking independently on the stairs by fifteen months. By age eighteen months, the boy was already memorizing and reciting nursery rhymes. The mother recalls with curiosity and surprise her own failure to capitalize on Ian's obvious intellectual precocity as a means of preparing him for the dramatic changes that then occurred in his life at that age.

At age eighteen months, Ian was left for a week with his maternal grandmother while the parents packed and made their farewells in preparation for yet another assignment in Greece. Ian rejoined his parents when they boarded ship in a milieu that was anything but "home," a situation which must have been fraught with all the additional tensions occasioned by the confusions aboard ship and the proprioceptive discomforts induced by a sea voyage. The parents found Ian inseparable, crying, and screaming if they tried to leave him alone, e.g., for dinner. Moreover, he would not nap and refused to sleep away from the parents at night. It is not clear whether the parents attempted to use phenobarbital at this time, as they did later. By the end of the voyage, separation anxiety had not abated and sleep had become a chronic problem, with Ian keeping the parents up progressively later until two, three, or four o'clock in the morning.

In Athens, housing was difficult and the father's assignment took him away almost immediately. At their hotel, Ian gorged on food and finally and most pleasantly (to the parents) went to sleep. This left the parents with the impression that they could have one quiet meal together before the father left. Leaving a "do not disturb" sign on the door, the parents left the sleeping infant and dined at leisure. On their return, they found several frightened and very worried maids in the hall outside the door from which came the sound of Ian's voice screaming in panic. The maids, who feared to trespass, reported that the screaming had continued for some thirty to forty minutes. The mother recalled that when she entered the room it seemed impossible to her that one small child could have vomited so much. She felt intuitively that this situation was all too much, horrifically, like the time years before when her daughter had fallen ill (also at age eighteen months and also in the same city). The mother rushed Ian to the hospital. En route, Ian began to have a seizure that continued for three hours. The mother indicates that the convulsions were not controlled by medication and that her son was kept on the critical list in the hospital for the next two days. The hospital investigation of the convulsion indicated that the boy had no fever; neurological examinations and EEG were also negative. The mother's account is not clear, but it appears that following discharge Ian was returned to the hospital for outpatient examinations on at least two occasions. Attempts were made to use phenobarbital to facilitate repeated EEGs, and these precipitated acute panic reactions ("he was given enough to knock out a horse and it didn't faze him"). Attempts to examine Ian were apparently traumatic to both mother and child. Yet Mrs. F. later indicated to Ian's neurologist that the boy was kept on phenobarbital until the following year. There are no known sequelae to this episode.

While still in Athens, before the age of three, Ian was hospitalized for a tonsillectomy. However real or distorted, Ian recalls this as having been done under local anesthesia and insists that he recalls the surgeon dropping his tonsils in a wastebasket while his mother left the room in anxiety. It is of significance that Ian developed a devouring interest in dinosaurs, a thorough knowledge of their classification, and a preoccupation with them that was so intense as to concern his later nursery school teachers. It should also be noted that Ian had kept a "transitional object" throughout these years. It was abandoned in Greece, when his mother refused to take his "filthy blanket" back to London. The family returned there when Ian was three (during treatment it was learned that Ian still, episodically, demands his mother's silk scarf as a precondition to sleep). The return voyage to London was also problematic and difficult, with abortive attempts to quiet Ian's anxiety and excitation with phenobarbital. Little more is known of the boy's next year, during which time the family resettled in London.

The mother recalls little of Ian's habit and toilet training. She suggests that she was less demanding of him than she was of his sisters, and that he "may have been a bit delayed" in bowel control, becoming clean between the ages of eighteen and twenty-four months. Given the "normal negativism" and independence of this phase of development, and given the mother's present, demonstrable rage reaction to Ian for even looking disagreeable or in disagreement with her, one can only surmise that the mother's memory of toilet training has been expurgated. Ian, at this late date, remembers surprisingly more than is typical. At age four to five years, he reports that he was frequently constipated and afraid of letting go. On one particular occasion his mother insisted on giving him two tablespoons of castor oil. Ian lost his control completely and felt terribly ashamed. He has since concluded that his early constipation must have derived from his fear, viz., that if he ever relaxed, he would lose control and all his feces or insides would come out. He also recalls and describes with precision his mother's using enemas on him. (The mother separately volunteered that she did not think she had ever given the boy an enema. One may question whether this is the mother's repression, or whether there are anal, sexualized fantasies of the child involved here.)

At about age five, Ian was physically abused by an older boy in his neighborhood, who repeatedly picked on him. The parents were concerned that Ian had provoked such attacks (and there is an inference of sexual assault suggested by Ian in his psychiatric interview; i.e., Ian described masturbation as that which little boys are forced to do by bigger, older ones who take them off alone). Details are limited, but it appears that from the age of five, Ian persistently attacked his own peers. There are also reports that at the same age he was in various types of trouble with his parents and that he may have been a firesetter as well.

As a consequence, Ian was referred for psychiatric diagnostic evaluation at five and a half years. He was tested by a Dr. D., who administered both projective and psychometric tests. The latter indicated a high intellectual potential, with a Binet (L) I.Q. of 136. Ian was grossly fearful of aggressive impulses and dangers. His castration anxiety was exceptionally open, with the boy holding his hands over his penis during much of the examination, yet somehow finding it possible both to unzip his trousers and to unbuckle them so that he had to ask for help from the examining psychologist at the end of the session (counterphobic?). Mrs. F. remembers some of Ian's interview, particularly his "three wishes." Ian had wanted a new mother, a toilet tank, and something else the mother could not recall. Ian was given the toilet tank for his backyard, but not psychotherapy. The installation of the toilet tank is recalled by both mother and Ian as giving rise to considerable amusement and pleasure, with the neighborhood children as frequent visitors who came to play with it and Ian. In line with this interest, Ian also became a precocious reader and owned an encyclopedia set of his own. His keenest interest was in the study of waterworks, internal plumbing, etc. (such interest has continued to date, but at a vastly more sophisticated level; Ian now studies "water hydraulics").

As previously noted, Ian's sister Gwen died when he was six years ten months of age. He saw her for the first and last time at the funeral. Some two weeks later, as Mrs. F. recalls, she was sitting at dinner and asking Ian his multiplication homework—when he had his first psychomotor seizure. The mother gives a very graphic description of her son's behavior, a classical neurological picture of a petit mal seizure. During the following two years, Ian apparently had six or seven similar seizures. The neurological examinations that followed included some four or five EEG's, all negative with the exception of one that seemed a bit "suspicious." Increases and changes in medication were followed by initial abatement in the seizures, which invariably returned shortly afterward. Medication was progressively increased over many months with dosages of Meberal, and eventual substitution of this by Mysoline, always accompanied with dosages of Dilantin. Ian's present dosage is 1000 mg. Mysoline, plus 200 mg. Dilantin taken thrice daily.

With the change in medication there may have been a modification of seizures or their manifestation, e.g., the first appearance of his tics. It is clear that Ian began to develop more extended difficulties with his sleeping during this time and that he became more explosive and more provocatively difficult with his parents. The neurologist expressed concern that medication might be responsible for the explosiveness, but could see no relationship to the sleep disorder. It should also be noted that Ian was undergoing orthodontic treatment during these times and there was concern that massive doses of Dilantin might adversely affect his gums. Ian also suffered from a diaphragmatic hernia, diagnosed about age nine and a half, and surgical correction remained a continued threat. Eventually Ian was hospitalized at age ten and the hernia was corrected under a general anesthetic, but without surgery (via oral, esophagal probe).

The family is Anglican and Ian is a very religious child, which he partly exploits in asking for parental (if not Divine) absolution. At the mother's persuasion, Ian had continued a childhood practice of sharing his confessions of the bad things he had done during the day, i.e., until age eleven. The parents had been concerned that Ian should not have to feel guilty. Ian seems to exploit his parents' sensitivity by using his "confessional" maneuver to manipulate his parents, knowing that if he "confesses" he will not be punished, i.e., directly. But it is also evident that the parents have been frustrated and angered by this behavior, and have punished the boy indirectly for different, otherwise acceptable behavior. Ian evidences the normal range of conventional moral values for a boy his age. At school and at others' homes, Ian's reaction formations seem well maintained; he appears honest, compliant to the interests and needs of others, cooperative, respectful of others, sympathetic, etc.

The dramatic difference in Ian's attitudes and regressive values is evident only at home. The aberrant nature of his misbehavior and particularly his open aggression impressed the parents as evidence of gross psychological disturbance. Detailed information of the mother's interactions, her seductive attitudes, and her provocations need to be assessed, however. To illustrate, Ian made a snide comment concerning his sister and the mother involuntarily slapped his face. Hurt, humiliated, and angry, Ian ran up the stairs shouting choice and unkind things at his mother. At the top of the stairs, Ian paused to pick up his baseball, turned and gestured as if he would throw the ball at his mother. At this juncture, she smiled and sarcastically suggested that Ian throw it; and with this she turned her back and started to walk away. Ian, in fact, threw the ball and hit his mother. The pain was apparently considerable and the mother found herself in tears, something that she had never permitted herself in front of the boy. Ian was shocked and dismayed by his mother's behavior, begged her forgiveness, and was a model child for a short while thereafter. Whatever the mother's ambivalence to her son, whatever her seductions, the degree of Ian's provocations cannot be minimized. Ian is a constant tease, and a not-too-humorous, rather sadistic mimic.

With the increased behavioral difficulties at age ten, Ian's parents asked for a psychiatric re-evaluation. While psychotherapy was recommended, and the question was raised as to the mother's need for therapeutic help, the consulting psychiatrist did not have sufficient time free to accept Ian. Further modifications and increases in medication were made that summer on a neurological basis, with Ian's seizures again diminishing, particularly at a time when he was separated from his parents and spending his vacation on one of the family's estates. While his seizures abated, Ian reportedly threatened a kindly adult with violence and was involved in many provocative disputes with an older boy. These incidents seemed important since the inference was that Ian provoked in such a manner that it was he who would be punished. Ian ran away from the family estate, hiking and hitchhiking some 30 to 40 miles to rejoin his parents. The seizures re-emerged at home and the last psychiatric referral was made to Dr. A., and then to me.

Ian was initially resistant to treatment, e.g., forgetting to leave school in time for his appointments, being "disturbed with school matters" and running away from school instead of coming to treatment, etc. During the first two weeks of therapy (he was seen twice), Ian acted out considerably; e.g., mutual, nude exhibitionism with a neighbor boy, smashing a window at home, threatening his father with a prized saber, etc. Treatment was then increased to two appointments per week; the immediate result was complete cessation of acting out at home. Ian has since come to his treatment sessions with verve and enthusiasm. He has viewed his treatment as an introspective "detective story" in which he searches his experiences and memories for clues to the origins of his difficulties, for pieces of his own jigsaw puzzle. Ian has displaced some of his provocative teasing of his mother into his treatment sessions, where he enjoys and now openly delights in intellectual torture of his therapist. But Ian is also able to look at himself somewhat intellectually, lamenting his lack of friends, his humiliation in his sleep disorder, and considerably enjoying the ready acceptance he has found in his therapist. Treatment is of interest and acceptable, i.e., so long as this does not reach too far or come too close to Ian's most sensitive areas (e.g., feelings of humiliation, worries over toilet matters, questions of his sanity, etc.).

IV. Possible Significant Environmental Influences

Ian's neurologist, a most experienced specialist in childhood disorders, was unequivocal in his conclusions that this boy suffered from an organic convulsive disorder, petit mal in nature and idiopathic in origin. What had struck me, however, was the fact that Ian had never been seen by the neurologist during a seizure and that the clinical description of such seizures had been largely provided by the mother. What is also suspected, but not clear, is the degree of Ian's suggestibility, his readiness or potentiality for physical expression of maternal suggestion of his illness.

It may well be that Ian's seizure condition derives solely from an organic dysfunction. But Freud's comments seem of particular interest in the diagnostic assessment, viz., that it is "quite right to distinguish between an organic and an 'affective' epilepsy. The practical significance of this is that a person who suffers from the first kind has a disease of the brain, while a person who suffers from the second kind is a neurotic. In the first case his mental life is subjected to an alien disturbance from without, in the second case the disturbance is an expression of his mental life itself" (1928, p. 181).

The neurological evaluation and diagnosis cannot be improved on. Yet it would seem desirable to consider Ian's developmental history with a view to assessing alternative psychogenic contributions to his seizures. Whether organic or psychogenic (or possibly a combination of these), there are a number of "significant environmental influences" (1) which may have lowered a neurological-psychological seizure threshold, or (2) which have predisposed the ego organization toward hysterical discharge processes and interrelated psychopathological defense organization. Whatever theoretical orientation might be emphasized, the same basic environmental influences seem relevant:

1. The mother's early (and continuing) incapacity to respond to her son's needs as an infant, e.g., letting him scream "until blue in the face." The mother's projection of her own aggressive expectations seems paralleled, in this respect, by her intolerance of passivity and her need to provoke aggressive responses in her son.

2. Separation from the parents at age eighteen months for one week, followed by the immediate loss of the home environment, and consequent disequilibrium aboard ship (separation anxiety seems specific and related to sleep disturbances).

3. Accumulative fatigue and anxiety during the ship's voyage; plus excitation due to the ship voyage, sharing of parents' bedroom, change of language, etc.

4. Acute anxiety attack in hotel, with screaming, vomiting, etc., in absence of parents. Possible cyanotic asphyxia from screaming and consequent aspiration of vomitus (?) with consequent convulsion.

5. Hospitalization of Ian, with further separation, acute anxiety of both child and mother (in the absence of the father).

6. Attempts at both massive medication with phenobarbital and electroencephalographic examination; consequent manic-hyperactive response.

7. Tonsillectomy at age two and a half, same hospital (?), local anesthesia (?).

8. Further exacerbation of separation fears with change in home, environment, ship voyage, return to London; acute anxiety reactions and panic; attempts to quiet him with phenobarbital on board ship; age three.

9. Impact of mysterious, exciting, and dangerous implications of father's occupation and nighttime absences.

10. Parental attitudes are particularly suspect. There is an impression that they feared Ian's convulsion in infancy might have left him damaged, like his sister. Parental overindulgence at present suggests possible overindulgence in infancy so that age-appropriate

expectations were inconsistently demanded. The mother also expected her son to be similar to her "professionally psychopathic" brother and has long viewed Ian as potentially defective, e.g., in his lack of control of rages. One suspects that the mother compensated for her ambivalent aggression by inconsistent, restitutive overindulgence. This is consonant with the tentative view of her needs for anal-sadistic battles, evident in her own comments that she cannot "keep her hands off Ian, either in anger or affection."

11. The physical attacks on Ian at age four or five appear to be symptomatic (because of provocations) rather than precipitating causal experiences. Yet it is possible that the child experienced a sadistic or sexual attack. Ian's account of anal assault by the mother during his phases of constipation could be true or might represent fantasies relating to anal-sadistic sexual wishes.

12. The sister Gwen existed as a phantom, an ideal, best-loved child who was absent *and* "sick in the head." The potentialities for identification with the sick or dead sister are facilitated by the actual facts, and by the family folklore of the remarkable coincidence in which Ian suffered his infant convulsion at the same age and the same place as the dead Gwen. It hardly seems fortuitous that Ian's first seizure occurred within two weeks of his sister's death and his first and only view of her.

13. Hospital and medical examinations, electroencephalographic investigations, and the various pharmaceutical medications have all been environmental interventions and probable stresses. The significant ages would appear to be eighteen months, three years, six and a half years, and rather continuously since then. Ian seems to have handled his later neurological and medical examinations comfortably, but it is evident from his treatment that he fears that he is "brain damaged" and potentially insane, a boy whom the best doctors and the best medications have been unable to cure.

14. The date of diagnosis of Ian's diaphragmatic hernia is not clear. One wonders if this is coincidental with the increase in the boy's seizures two years ago.

15. Equally obscure are the inferences that Ian's paternal grandfather died two years ago, that the father suffered a concomitant and prolonged depression, and that the maternal grandmother was rejected from the family household.

V. Assessment of Development

A. *Drive Development*

1. *Libido*

(a) *With regard to phase development*

There seems no question that Ian has reached the phallic stage of psychosexual development and has made tenuous advances into latency. Phenomenologically, the latter is evident in Ian's relatively adequate academic competence, his active and interested participation and skill in particular group sports, his capacity to relate (under structured circumstances) and take at least minimal pleasure in some age-adequate activities with peers and adults other than his parents.

Such progression, however, is not secure and Ian's capabilities remain partly dependent on his being reassured via the supervision of adults. Ian's schoolwork also breaks down, sometimes completely, when the mother insists on supervising his homework. He is more successful when he isolates his schoolwork and arranges to remain in school in the afternoons to continue studies under the more benign supervision of a teacher.

The tenuousness of Ian's freedom from oedipal, sexual and aggressive drives is clear, even to the mother who notes her son's unusual interest in her and feels his provocations have an odd aura of sensual sadism. One clearly sees the existence of libidinal fixations in the anal phase in Ian's beginning references to toilet problems, his difficulties over enemas and constipation, and more particularly in the ease of regression in which he provokes and fights with his mother (as a love battle).

The evidence of oral fixations is not clear. The history notes an early yet transient feeding difficulty. More suspect are the reports that the child was left to scream in times of need. Ian presently attributes his having orthodonture treatment to self-damage caused by prolonged thumb sucking, i.e., until age two years. There is a long history of oral, medical interventions and it should also be recalled that the vomiting at age eighteen months preceded the first convulsion. If there is a hysterical contribution to Ian's seizures, then the boy's oral and labial tics and mouthings, plus his nauseous stomach feelings, should be questioned as derivatives of oral fixations. It is equally clear that the more dramatic oral traumata occurred during or after the anal phase of development. Whether such oral assaults were experienced or understood as a consequence of anal retribution (upwardly displaced) or whether they may have reinforced a more primitive oral fixation is anything but clear.

Ian's characterological and defense organization, however, is predominantly anal. His history of continuing interest in waterworks, toilets, etc., indicates the existence of excremental sexual fantasies, and permits the inference of fixation, and perhaps regression, from phallic to anal expression of libidinal phase dominance.

(b) *With regard to libido distribution*

(i) *Cathexis of self:* While Ian is not hypochondriacal, his seizure condition has greatly contributed to an intense self cathexis, both of his body and his psychological self-awareness, self-judgment, etc. Despite this high cathexis of the self, it does not seem positive or pleasurable. He makes high demands of himself, e.g., that he should be well dressed, scholastically superior, etc., yet he obtains little gratification from his successes. On the contrary, Ian gives the impression not only that he feels he is organically defective or damaged, but also that his standards (introjects) are so perfectionistic that whatever the adequacy of his real-life performance, it is never quite good enough to leave him pleased or secure with himself.

(ii) *Cathexis of objects:* Ian's cathexis of his objects is relatively normal, i.e., it shows no evidence of borderline or psychotic processes. There is a neurotic, psychopathological unevenness of cathexis, however, since Ian views his objects as potentially dangerous or threatening to him. There is an intense ambivalent cathexis of objects, particularly during his regressions, which are markedly reminiscent of the toddler stage of development; e.g., he expects his parents to accept his violent aggression not only without objection, but with love and forgiveness.

2. *Aggression*

(a) *Quantity of aggressive expression*

Ian appears to have a relatively normal endowment of aggressive drives, but his history suggests an abnormal degree of reactive aggression from infancy onward. This could relate to the mother's ambivalence and need to stimulate aggressive, masculine responses (which she finds so lacking in her husband). Both the developmental and the current history are replete with incidents in which the mother helps to perpetuate ongoing, sadomasochistic battles over even the most incidental of matters. Ian's experiences at age four or five when he attacked his peers has the sound of an abreactive, passive-into-active defense in which he enacted on others what he had experienced himself (the attacks on him by the older boy). Yet this behavior is also described by the parents as having been provocative. In this sense, Ian's very early behavior fits a general pattern of sadomasochistic provocations which may have continued from infancy onward.

While Ian's aggressive outbursts have the appearance of quantitative abnormality, one might better view these outbursts in terms of imbalance in that aggressive fury is defended against in most social situations, yet is afforded too frequent, too prolonged expression at home (where the father remains Ian's apologist). Ian notes, for example, that by the age of five he was quite prepared to set fires in ashtrays, throw over chairs, throw knives on the floor, all as manipulations to insure that his mother would return home from a cocktail party when he was in a fury and wanted her.

As noted earlier, in structured situations such as football games, his aggression is effectively directed. It is only at home that Ian has "let himself go" and demonstrated his negativistic fury in fierce and vulgar arguments, in physical battles with his mother, etc. His relationships outside of the home have remained relatively free of such outbursts, although during the previous summer there were indications that Ian's fears and aggression might be carried over into other areas of his life as well.

(b) *Quality of aggressive expression*

Ian mimics his parents' attitudes when he speaks of his "violent feelings." While using a vocabulary of violence, he speaks with a bland and sometimes humorous affect. It is not clear whether Ian parrots and makes jokes of his parents' expectations that he should feel terribly upset and aggressive over incidents which might otherwise seem trivial in everyday life. At other times, he speaks almost melodramatically of his evil deeds and attacks (e.g., of running his father through with a saber) when in fact the incident was more one of Ian's fantasy and *not* one of action. While such behavior has the appearance of a "breakthrough," as if it were psychotic, it gave the clinical impression of a contrived dramatization and a perverse reversal of values, which could be related to parental acting out. In illustration, the father tends to see all of Ian's misbehavior as expected and forgiven from its inception, even his breaking of windows, throwing the mother to the floor, etc. The mother, in dramatic contrast, seems to see any small indication of teasing or refusal as tantamount to rebellion against established authority. Ian's *modes* of expression of aggression are as unbalanced as the quantitative expression. In fact, he has been unexpectedly violent over relatively trivial matters. On the other hand, he has accepted inappropriate discipline of himself as being logical and desirable. One is left with the confused impression that, for this boy, aggression in any form may at one time be devastatingly horrible and at another time have little significance because it will be excused no matter how inappropriate.

(c) *Direction of aggressive expressions*

There is lack of aggressive reaction toward persons who have in reality actually deprived, hurt, or demeaned Ian. He rarely permits himself to express openly or appropriately a legitimate grievance or annoyance. Yet he berates himself at such times for his horrible tempers and anger, which in fact have not been expressed. It is not surprising to find that Ian is devoutly religious and prays to God for help with his rages (and also melodramatically and manipulatively exhibits his religiosity to his parents). It is clear that Ian provokes people in such a way that they are bound to direct aggression toward him. His excitement, evident in treatment, suggests a masochistic overdetermination. When Ian does express aggression directly, it is usually inappropriate, disproportionate in its intensity, and more often directed toward his mother (as a scapegoat?).

Freud (1928) believed that hysterical convulsive disorders involved a massive turning of aggression against the self. Bartemeier (1932, 1943), discussing and extending Freud's views on the hysterical features of convulsive disorders, noted that the superego may use an existing tendency to seizures as a means of directing aggression against the self. Ian's seizures could represent such a turning of aggression against the self, but this cannot be documented at this time.

B. *Ego and Superego Development*

1. *Ego Apparatus*

Ian's ego apparatus (his endowment of physiological and sensory equipment facilitating ego functioning) seems to be intact. If his seizure condition has an organic basis, one would hypothesize transient and perhaps global impairments of the entire ego apparatus. Yet studies such as those of Peterson et al. (1950) suggest that patients with hysterical convulsive disorders have full recall under hypnosis for events occurring during the time of the seizure. Whatever the etiology of Ian's seizures, they do not seem to have affected his basic progression and relatively normal development.

2. *Ego Functions*

Ian has been tested on both the Stanford-Binet and the WISC, at ages five and eleven. In both instances, his performance was at the superior level. Until a year and a half ago, his school performance was most adequate in a competitive setting with high standards. The impairment of intellectual ego functions seems to be of psychoneurotic origin and his difficulties in this area seem to be affected especially by his mother's concerns.

Ego functions such as control of motility, integration and synthesis, may be impaired by Ian's seizure potential. It is noteworthy, however, that he has never injured himself physically during a seizure and (so far as is known) that he has never been observed having a seizure other than in the presence of his parents. (However, see also Section 4, Secondary Interference.)

3. *Defenses*

Ian's relative honesty, cleanliness, pity, and compassion, etc., are clearly and firmly established. One would consider them well-established reaction formations if it were not for the fact that Ian seems to derive little or no *pleasure* from the gratification of these opposite-drive tendencies. One may conjecture that Ian cannot tolerate or find pleasure in himself (excessive standards or extreme punitiveness of the superego?) or that the urgency of the unconscious aggression is so demanding and unsublimated that he pays a constant, defensive price in keeping alien aggressive impulses in check.

Projection of aggression is in pathological evidence, with Ian misconstruing unstructured or ambiguous situations (or comments) as evidence of anger and potential rejection of him (e.g., by teachers, friends, therapist, etc.).

Ian "panics" when he is unable to sleep away from home; he fears that something will happen if everyone else in the house goes to sleep before him. He is afraid he might die from accumulative fatigue when he is unable to sleep; his environment seems alive with aggressive and hostile undercurrents. Treatment suggests that there is an excited malice in the boy's midnight interruptions of his parents' sleep, in his telephone calls asking them to bring him home when he is unable to sleep at a friend's house. While the behavioral characteristics of Ian's sleep disturbance support the mother's conviction that it originated at eighteen months (in connection with separation anxiety), Ian's fantasies that mothers kill fathers and abandon them (for millionaires) suggest that the sleep disturbance also incorporates a projection of the boy's own anger and death wishes toward his father. One should also consider that the mother may be explosively aggressive, that she may reinforce Ian's fears of an extremely aggressive world. Such factors provide Ian with a rationalization for the appropriateness and intensity of his own feelings, thereby masking both Ian's provocations and the indigenous base of his own projections. On the other hand, Ian's extrafamilial school milieu is quite benign; yet Ian carries his own internalized, defensive attitudes into his peer relationships, which are independent of the reality of his problems with his parents.

Denial of affect and *intellectualization* are two defenses that seem to be characteristic modes of Ian's coping with everyday matters. He rarely permits himself to experience age-adequate feelings in an appropriate manner. He functions as a rather "feelingless" young man who intellectualizes and reviews his behavior from a psychological distance. While Ian's use of defensive intellectualization has the appearance of a precocious adolescent reaction, it seems developmentally related to his parents' extensive intellectual expectations of their son; i.e., they treat him as if he were an adult. There are also indications of obsessive ruminations that possibly reinforce introspective intellectualization, as a means of controlling drive activity.

Regression is another characteristic defense, which is particularly in evidence at home, under stress. In public, Ian functions rather well, e.g., at school or when adult friends are visiting his home. He successfully avoids and withdraws (with phobic characteristics of anxiety if he cannot avoid painful situations), and retreats physically to his home where he may then regress emotionally to anal-sadistic behavior. In this, he is petulant, demanding, torturing; and he expects complete acceptance from his parents no matter what he has done. Fearing even worse behavior, the parents have accepted, if not reinforced, such regressive and infantile behavior.

Identification with the aggressor is clear in Ian's mimicking and provoking of his mother, his therapist, etc. His behavior seems to have a degree of conscious purposefulness when he denigrates and cynically exploits or exhibits his parents' shortcomings by adopting inappropriate behavior which they have in fact exhibited to him. Ian's misbehavior is a parody of his mother's lack of control, and with it he mimics and cynically exploits her guilt.

Ian's earliest history also supports the view that aggressive identification may be syntonic (and not altogether defensive), e.g., as an effective mode of coercing his parents to give him care and attention. His ability to identify has been effectively used in learning by anticipatory trial actions.

Ian's defenses are not characteristic of his age, and the lack of joy or self-confidence suggests that sublimations are possible only to a limited degree. His defense organization does not seem adequate to the task of coping with excessive aggressive and sexual conflicts (partially influenced and exacerbated by provocations and seductions of the parents). The two characteristics of turning aggression against the self and identification with the aggressor may relate to a masochistic, sexual conflict, but this is obviously speculative.

4. *Secondary Interference with Ego Functions*

Ian's reality testing, e.g., of the benign or malignant nature of situations or people, is significantly impaired, and in this respect there is clear evidence of interference with ego functioning.

Ian's school performance was transiently impaired at about age five, when he was said to have been obsessionally concerned with dinosaurs. Academic functioning, however, remained relatively free thereafter until about age ten, and since then it has varied considerably and dramatically. Cognitive functions, as demonstrable via psychometric tests, remain relatively free. Ian's intellectual capacities seem impaired predominantly via the mother's concern or interventions. Preliminary exploration of Ian's underlying fantasies (in treatment) suggests that full exploitation of intelligence is impaired by a fear of success and an inhibition of exhibitionism. Ian fantasies, for example, that he is a genius whose success could be so overwhelming that either he would devastate his competitors, or they would be so fantastically jealous, envious, and hostile that they would murder him for his success. Ian's fantasy life fits in with Sperling's theoretical formulations of petit mal in children. In discussing psychogenic headaches, petit mal and epilepsy, Sperling (1953) suggests that "*petit mal* is interpreted as an instant cutting off from functioning of those parts of the mind which serve the perception and execution of stimuli from within and without, because perception of certain stimuli would lead to an explosive reaction endangering the life of the patient and that of the people in the environment" (p. 252).

C. *Development of Total Personality (Lines of Development and Mastery of Tasks or Age-adequate Responses)*

1. *From Dependency to Emotional Self-Reliance and Adult Object Relationships*

Ian appears to be having a very difficult time consolidating himself in latency (Stage 6). There is much evidence of attempts to establish mutual and reciprocal relationships with a select group of boyfriends and responsive teachers. Such relationships are not secure and may break down when Ian meets with frustrations that are amenable to misconstruction, e.g., when an acquaintance fails to telephone, when there is a relevant criticism of schoolwork, etc.

Not unrelated is Ian's difficulty in maintaining his academic work, particularly when his mother tries to help him. The most dramatic disturbance of object relationships is Ian's incapacity to cope with his parents. The intensity of the battles between parents and child is sufficiently dramatic to obscure the more fundamental fact that Ian has been unable to establish age-adequate and conflict-free relationships outside of the family.

While Ian has been described by his parents as a self-reliant, emotionally self-contained and independent boy, the developmental history documents other features as well. Separation anxiety, clinging, and inability to separate were manifest at eighteen months and thereafter. The use of a transitional object, "the filthy blanket," cannot be unrelated to Ian's present, though occasional, need for his mother's silk scarf as a prerequisite to going to sleep. Similarly, Ian's inability to sleep away from home, his fear of being the first to go to sleep, his self-isolation from peers, all reflect on his dependence.

2. *Toward Body Independence*

(a) *From suckling to rational eating:* Ian's earliest history is equivocal but suggestive of inconsistent oral gratifications and complications. Historically later oral traumas have been noted. Whatever battles may have evolved in the family's eating patterns or traditions, it appears that Ian's attitudes toward food and eating have now approximated those of the parents and are age-adequate. He seems free from notable food fads, battles over meals, and readily and appropriately can eat away from home, seemingly at any time or place. This may overstate the case, since Ian is also most egocentric and can hardly envision that he should eat at any time or place that he might dislike. In the selective, benign environments in which he is cared for, covert oral problems could readily be disguised. However, it appears that Ian has moved relatively completely into rational eating that is uncontaminated by psychological conflict.

(b) *From wetting and soiling to bladder and bowel control:* Ian became dry and clean at about age two. So far as is known, there have been no regressions (encopresis or enuresis) when he was ill, emotionally upset, and during or after seizures. His attitude toward cleanliness, neatness, etc., seems Spartan. It is not surprising to find Ian volunteering the information that it was appropriate for his mother to have washed his mouth with soap when he first used "dirty words." Whatever developmental battles may have occurred in the line toward independent bladder and bowel control, it is evident that these controls are both secure and age-adequate.

(c) *From irresponsibility to body management:* The history of Ian's precocious motor abilities and his aggressive, nominal independence are consistent with his present capacities. Ian seems completely responsible and fully capable of his own body management, including responsibility for intake of medications. If there is anything unusual, it is in the excessive independence rather than in the failure to take responsibility for body management.

(d) *From egocentricity to companionship:* When conditions are favorable, Ian seems to relate well and to accept the mutual needs and interests of other children. He is unable, however, to do this under stress, e.g., in groups lacking adult supervision, when visiting away from home, etc. It is clear that Ian relates to other children at least as temporary helpmates in sustained activities such as group sports and occasionally on an individual basis in play. Ian's treatment material suggests a yearning for peer relationships and a sorrow that he cannot maintain friendships. He is somewhat aware of the reactions of other children to his own joking provocations. It is also clear that he has a capacity to identify with other children as "objects in their own right," as persons whose feelings and wishes he would like to acknowledge and would like to respect. The parents' and Ian's reports suggest that he began a more secure step in his social relationships about a year and a half previously. This evidence indicates that Ian had reached Stage 4 on this line of development, however tentatively, and that his present inability to accept or reach out for companionship and friendship derives from a neurotic interference.

(e) *From the body to the toy and from play to work:* Assessments of this developmental line take into consideration the earliest cathexis of the infant's body, the extension of cathexis to the mother and to inanimate objects such as "transitional objects." Stage 3 describes the toddler who may cuddle and maltreat symbolic objects with a full range of expression of his ambivalence toward them. In Ian's case, one is impressed by the fact that his episodic regressions are to this stage of development. However, I hesitate to use the term "regression" because his developmental history clearly indicates that such behavior has persisted from early infancy onward. Ian's use of his mother's scarf, however, is not syntonic and gives rise to shame. This need does seem regressive and is consonant with developmental fixations in a very early stage at which "transitional objects" are cathected as an extension of the mother.

Ian's toys, his hobbies, and his physical activities in sports are aggressive and phallic in nature and are used to express and work through transient fantasies. He has extensive sets of toy soldiers and battle equipment, and in his play with them he usually identifies with the Nazi and Russian armies, identifications which are consonant with other manifestations of his sadomasochistic and aggressive impulses (which are not adequately neutralized). His pleasure in and capacity for task completion and problem solution show a clear, however tenuous, move into Phase 5. As noted earlier, Ian is dissatisfied with his capacities to function adequately and is hypercritical of his performance. He leaves the impression that he is grossly insecure as to his capability in functioning, therefore turns to his objects for reassurance, and when this is lacking, regresses to earlier stages under stress.

Many of Ian's achievements seem based on counterphobic dynamics, e.g., his study of water hydraulics, the collection of sabers and guns, etc. He has obviously mastered the drive controls and achievements necessary for such activities, but the autonomy of such secondary ego functions is not well established and he seems to lack an adequate degree of neutralization and sublimation, both prerequisites for the ability to progress from play to work.

3. *Assessment of Correspondence between Developmental Lines*

There is a high degree of consistency in an overall evaluation of the different developmental lines. On the side of ego development, there is a uniform and marked precocity and early achievement beyond age-adequacy and expectations. But equally consistently, one finds Ian unable to make use of his excellent endowment and ego skills. He is not satisfied with himself; he shows an inadequate capacity to separate from his parents; a limited capacity to maintain age-adequate relationships with peers; and a marked restriction in the progression from play to work.

VI. Regression and Fixation Points

The early developmental history, though ambiguous, suggests that Ian received inconsistent care in relation to his early oral needs.

The history of oral traumas, dating back to eighteen months, continues through the latency period. Since the child's early years were symptom-free, the degree of orality implicit in Ian's psychomotor seizures may in fact have stemmed from retrospective trauma, or may otherwise reflect an upward displacement of anal and phallic fears of damage.

The mother's known attitudes to and intolerance of aggressive activity or "insolent disregard" of her wishes must be considered along with the fragmentary evidence of early fixations. It is particularly striking that the mother fails to remember her son's habit training when Ian so vividly recalls his extended troubles with constipation, laxatives, and enemas. It is clear that Ian was precociously active and aggressive, presumably before the advent of habit training. Given his particular assertiveness of independence, along with the normal negativism of the average toddler, one can only conjecture on difficulties of toilet and cleanliness training. Dominant defenses and character traits suggest anal fixations, which were perpetuated into phallic and (fragmentary) latency development. Both the neurologist and Ian's therapist have noticed the interesting and continuing fact that the boy's aggressive outbursts become more extensive and frequent when he is *less* subject to seizures. This permits the inference, as one possibility, that the psychomotor seizures are a regressive, primitive psychophysiological response which occurs when anal-sadistic behavior is checked. Whether Ian's symptomatic mouth movements, tics, and nauseous stomach feelings reflect early oral fixations or are merely a concomitant of primitive psychophysiological reactions is quite unclear.

The mother's comments on Ian's phallic development are largely negative; i.e., she does not remember exhibitionistic, protective attitudes; competitive play initiated by Ian with his father; genital masturbation, etc. Yet the psychological evaluation of Ian at five years six months is striking in its emphasis on the boy's phallic anxieties. At that time, the boy's projective materials were predominantly concerned with aggression and castration fears. Ian's concern for a toilet tank could reflect regressive anal preoccupations; or, if considered along with his extended interest in waterworks, it might be better understood as reflecting his concern about phallic potency. We know from the father that he asked, if not seduced, his wife to indulge the boy in intimate and caressing body care. Ian's continuing sadomasochistic, highly exciting and sexualized aggression with his mother indicates an anal-sadistic manifestation of phallic drive development.

In the attempt to assess the question of regression, one should recall that the first psychomotor seizure occurred in the middle of Ian's sixth year, shortly after he saw his dead sister. It will be recalled that she was the mother's favorite child who was "sick in the head." I suspect that this trauma may have precipitated further regressive tendencies at the very time Ian was making peripheral and tenuous movements into latency.

VII. Dynamic and Structural Assessments (Conflicts)

A. *External Conflicts*

This section of the Profile is customarily used for much younger children, i.e., prior to the internalization of conflicts. Some of Ian's behavior is sufficiently bizarre or aberrant to indicate that only limited or inadequate introjections (in terms of superego formation) may exist. In view of the open and regressive conflicts within the family, some of Ian's reactions have the quality of external conflicts with the parents. From the parents' point of view, these are external conflicts because the boy is "psychopathic," without conscience.

B. *Internalized Conflicts*

Ian has deliberately broken windows in front of his parents, "deliberately worked himself into rages," melodramatically threatened his father with a sword, etc. All such behavior has been described as if it were nonconflictual and did not induce anxiety or guilt. These features led the parents to compare Ian with Mrs. F.'s "psychopathic" and often-institutionalized brother. Ian's behavior in treatment has illustrated, in minimal fashion, some of the characteristics the parents have alluded to, i.e., his slyness and manipulative provocations. Ian adds further support to this impression by purporting that he does things because he wants to be bad; i.e., he wishes me to believe that he is consciously controlling and directing his temper tantrums (which is highly questionable).

When this type of behavior is juxtaposed with the developmental history of Ian's provocative attacks on older and larger boys and on his mother, one is left with a different impression, viz., that Ian feels impelled to precipitate trauma, which he is eternally expecting and fearing. The boy's aplomb after such incidents has the quality of a ritualized, parentally induced attempt to intellectualize or rationalize, to find reasons for behaviors and rages that are otherwise inexplicable. This is further complicated by Ian's unconscious sadism which colors his attacks. In this respect, he is aware of a partial truth, viz., that he does want to hurt, ravage, and revenge himself upon his parents.

The superego is fully structuralized, but is archaic in its sadism and intensity. The evidence for this statement is derived from several sources. Ian's reaction formations, his religious orientation and fears, the general adequacy of his moral values and standards, all are maintained independent of his parents or setting. Moreover, his depressed moods, his constant self-devaluation and sadistically cruel innuendoes as to self-damage and inadequacy indicate that aggression has been turned against the self (via the superego). The apparent lack of guilt in Ian may be explicable in terms of the parents' behavior; viz., their solicitation of Ian to confess his misdeeds so that they could mitigate his guilt. One suspects an externalization of the superego, in which the parents either absolve or punish him so that Ian escapes responsibility, anxiety, and guilt.

The developmental history is consistent with the view that structuralization occurred early, and self-control, via introjection, was an early and dramatic necessity for a child who seemed to have felt overwhelming concern both for his own rages and those of the environment.

C. *Internal Conflicts*

Ian has been a vigorously active child since birth. Whatever passive drive endowment he may have, it is little evident today, except perhaps in his symptom formation, e.g., in his dependent inability to separate from his parents at night. Ian's controlled activity has the hallmark of a defense against passivity and indicates a pathological resolution of his passive-active tendencies. Such attitudes are relatively age-adequate. The pathological implications derive from the developmental history and the clear evidence that this boy has warded off passivity since earliest childhood.

His masculine-feminine conflicts are of a similar nature. Ian is a most "masculine" boy who permits himself few behavioral characteristics that might imply anything "girlish." He acknowledges that he sometimes cries to himself in despair and anger, but he considers this to be a bit "babyish" and not feminine. Ian's inability to sleep in the home and bedroom of school friends could reflect a defense against passive, feminine tendencies. While his father is a passive-appearing and gentle man, he is also as dynamically coiled and powerful as a steel spring. Ian emulates his father's silent superiority and strength, and shares with him a rather pious but implicitly contemptuous attitude toward girls and women. This attitude is age-adequate for Ian, and the pathological implications are inferred only from the implacability of defense.

VIII. Assessment of Some General Characteristics

A. *Frustration Tolerance*

The mother has always believed that Ian had little tolerance for frustration and cites his earliest screaming "until blue in the face" in illustration. While the dynamics of that particular parent-child interaction is suspect (e.g., the mother's intolerance of passivity), the history does suggest an early developmental impasse in which Ian did not have a gradual and easy introduction to frustrations that were within his capacities to cope. The mother seems to have been consistently unable to respond appropriately in gauging the child's capacities at each developmental level and she seems to have permitted excessive frustrations and then overindulged in compensation. Ian has developed a view according to which his tempers are all rages, his hungers are all famines, his loves are all passions, etc. He seems, unrealistically, to judge his needs as potentially overwhelming. Yet this overstates the problem, since Ian has established that he functions reasonably well in a benign atmosphere away from the parents. Moreover, the parents have also strongly suspected that Ian's tempers and allusions to his seizures may have a highly melodramatic undercurrent, and be used by him as a manipulative control of them.

It will be recalled that the father, in particular, has expected Ian to act like an adult, and Ian seems to have adopted this attitude with regard to his own behavior, particularly when he is away from home. Ian shows an age-adequate degree of frustration tolerance in postponing direct gratification, e.g., in deferring free play for hard and continuous practice in football games; saving pocket money for deferred plans in weeks to come; etc.

Frustration and anxiety tolerance are not always easy to distinguish. Moreover, Ian's frustration tolerance may have a masochistic quality, and some of his frustrations and suffering may be unnecessary. The boy seems to obtain a measure of self-esteem regulation in a stoic ideal of being strong and tough (perhaps like his father). He has coped most adequately in the area of his physical illnesses requiring many neurological examinations, orthodonture treatment, hospitalization and correction of hernia, etc. There is little question that he can and does cope with many more frustrations than most boys his age. His inability to cope in other areas and his "babyish" reactions to hurt and frustration have a regressive and neurotic coloring that is dramatic for its contrast with his otherwise excellent adequacy.

B. *Sublimation Potential*

Where Ian's psychopathology does not distort his perception, where the environment is benign, his progress seems to have been fairly constantly progressive. He has clearly demonstrated his capacity for displacement of drive energies, and his learning capacity is relatively free of id invasions. His work, however, seems relatively joyless; and his humor, when it emerges, is more often sadistic (practical jokes). His activities are controlled, competent, and "neutralized." Ian is capable of directing a considerable degree of psychological effort to secondary-process activity, but much of this leaves the impression of defensive activity.

The conceptual distinction between sublimation and the defense of displacement is not an easy one to make, particularly with the limited evidence available in the case of Ian. As Anna Freud (1948) has noted, when viewed from the side of the id, sublimation involves a displacement of sexual and aggressive energies to noninstinctual aims and implicitly involves a loss of pleasure. She also notes, however, that sublimation "brings great gains: the flow of instinctive energy into socially adapted behaviour widens the scope of the child's interests, transforms otherwise dull and uninteresting tasks into interesting and fascinating pursuits, and—as every teacher can observe—thereby improves the child's ability to work and play and quickens his intelligence" (p. 28). Robert Waelder (1964), commenting on Anna Freud's formulation, has noted that "all later papers by various authors emphasize merely the desexualization of the drive without noticing the concomitant sexualization of the respective ego activity. Thus, sublimation appears in these later publications as a net gain from the point of view of the ego; actually, the implicit sexualization of the ego entails the danger that the ego activity in question may be embroiled in the conflict to which the drive has been subject. The ego is somewhat in the position of a nation that has called on another nation for help—an action which may have its immediate rewards but also its perils; the ego has marshaled the mighty support of an instinctual drive, but that is not always a comfortable ally to have."

Ian's sublimation potential seems constantly threatened by contaminations of aggressive and sexual drives which he cannot adequately displace. This is evident in the boy's recurrent difficulties with schoolwork, in his need to isolate himself in social relationships, in his preoccupations with intellectual processes intimately connected with instinctual conflicts.

C. *Overall Attitude to Anxiety*

Both the parents and Ian indicate that he suffers and experiences little anxiety. The only indication that Ian might have such feelings concerns his abortive attempts to stay overnight in the homes of friends. He (blandly) told me that he was "panic-stricken." Yet his description of thoughts, feelings, and behavior during such occasions leaves doubt that he actually suffers much anxiety, as contrasted to that described by other patients. Rather, one gains the impression that Ian has scant tolerance for anxiety and defends himself phobically against any circumstance or situation in which anxiety might arise. He has been free to withdraw from most anxiety-producing situations, returning to his home and parents. There is some evidence that he resorts to obsessional rumination to handle anxiety when either self-esteem or physical circumstance has limited the possibility of physical withdrawal. In his regressions to tantrum behavior at home, Ian does *not* give the impression of a child whose ego is completely wanting in intrinsic strength to cope with anxiety, but rather that his compliant and perhaps seductive environment has indulged him to such an extent that he has had little reason to cope with anxiety by means of internal resources.

D. *Progressive Forces versus Regressive Tendencies*

Ian's aggressive and defiant behavior at home, which brought him to treatment, has been seen by the parents as a regressive trend. Preliminary indications from the boy's treatment, however, indicate clearly that Ian had begun to withdraw from his mother's seductive and aggressive demands that he share his intimate secrets with her, that he confess, etc. He knew very well that his deviant tantrum behavior maneuvered his parents into a psychiatric referral for him. In a restrictive sense, such deviant behavior then constitutes a "progressive tendency," a use of acting out to precipitate outside intervention in a developmental impasse. This view is supported by Ian's enthusiastic response to his treatment. He has been quite concerned about his "babyishness," his inability to stay away from home. He has been even more concerned that he might be "mad" and beyond help. He is a hurt and lonely boy in search of better solutions. His regressive tendencies and family battles have been a way of life, providing both excitement and pleasure, yet this has not been totally syntonic for Ian. Large for his age, Ian is growing rapidly and already showing secondary sexual characteristics. His pubertal growth and concomitant sexual drive activity may facilitate progressive movement. But there is little question that Ian's psychopathology is most pronounced and that his defense organization is maladaptive and regressive.

IX. Diagnosis

The openness of Ian's aggression with his mother is understood as a peculiar derivative of his fixations, his neurotic conflict, and the mother's seductiveness. There is no evidence of atypical, borderline or psychotic impairment. While there is evidence of possible organic complications, this does not imply a destructive, degenerative process that affects mental growth. One is impressed with the fact that Ian has a lot to cope with, both because of his fear of organic damage and because of the constant reality that he might have a seizure and that he must take anticonvulsant medications.

What seems to have been a psychoneurotic behavioral disorder of essentially oedipal nature has now settled into a less easily recognizable symptomatology. Ian's intense and sexualized tie to his mother (in particular) indicates a faulty resolution of his oedipal conflict. Ian's move into age-adequate latency is obviously hindered by his powerfully ambivalent ties to his mother; in addition, a secondary complication derives from his archaic superego which denies Ian pleasure in his achievements and demands punishments that infantilize and damage him. One also suspects that he has identified with the brain-damaged sister. Ian's infantile neurosis seems to be in the process of becoming encapsulated in a character disorder, in which there is ego-syntonic phobic avoidance of anxiety- or frustration-producing situations. The externalization of responsibility (superego) and the parents' readiness to justify and rationalize Ian's deviant behavior (as due to organic damage) have facilitated a beginning character structure that has the hallmarks of a delinquent or impulse disorder.

Psychotherapy has now continued for three months, with two sessions per week. Ian has settled into a secure and reasonably effective therapeutic relationship. His behavior in school and his academic performance are temporarily undisturbed, probably because he now studies in the school building, thereby neutralizing the mother's interventions. Ian's tics have (temporarily?) disappeared. Behavioral difficulties at home have markedly diminished but gradually begin to invade the treatment situation, where Ian likes to provoke, test, tease, etc. As one would expect, the emergence of these transference reactions has drained much of Ian's neurotic impulses to act out at home. The treatment problem becomes one of determining whether twice weekly treatment can control the development of negative transference aspects and permit sufficient intellectual insight so that at least some defensive readaptation might be accomplished. It seems highly questionable that the neurotic problem can be adequately worked through in nonintensive treatment, which provides only a very limited possibility to break the circularity of parent-child excesses of overstimulation. At best, one would anticipate that progressive maturational forces (alone with nonanalytic treatment) might facilitate more effective encapsulation of the neurotic process.

Analysis would be the treatment of choice. Ian seems highly motivated and accessible to therapy. In considering analysis, his obsessive, ruminative insightfulness constitutes a resistance to treatment, but taken in conjunction with his excellent intelligence it is also an advantage.

The timing of this referral was not ill-advised. Ian presented the picture of a boy who was almost prepared to abandon his limited relationships with peers and the social standards which he had previously maintained effectively. For Ian, the danger seems to have been the extension of sadomasochistic battles with his parents to other relationships and the acceptance of such behavior as normal (epileptic), and approximating the behavior of his "psychopathic uncle."

The seizure condition and continuing heavy medication have undoubtedly put additional stress on Ian's strained resources. However, his difficulties do not date from his first seizure episode or from the increases in his medication. Rather, the developmental history gives clear clues as to the inception of difficulties, i.e., separation anxiety, with a persistent developmental impasse in the parent-child relationship. Even if medication could alleviate further seizures, the diagnostic picture is that of an encapsulated psychopathological debility which impairs the child's psychological functioning and potentials for emotional, sexual, and social development.

However clear the neurological diagnosis, the presenting symptoms are not incompatible (given the developmental history) with a hysterical exacerbation (if not hysterical origin) of a latent neurological dysfunction (Gottschalk, 1956). In this regard, one is reminded of Freud's observation that a patient's susceptibility to specific modes of tension discharge might well be based on prior illness that would lay down certain psychophysiological patterns. The introductory months of psychotherapy have made it clear that Ian is exceedingly concerned about his "damage." In this regard, whatever the boy's "seizure potential" may be, he suffers from a sense of damage and a feeling of incapacity which has caused long-standing anxiety and is now an integral part of his neurotic problem.

10

ASPECTS OF THE CONTRIBUTION OF SIGHT TO EGO AND DRIVE DEVELOPMENT

A Comparison of the Development of Some Blind and Sighted Children

HUMBERTO NAGERA, M.D., B.Sc. and
ALICE B. COLONNA, M.A., B.A.
(1965)

This study is based on six blind children observed in our Unit for the Blind. It is an attempt to organize and describe by means of the Profile headings what was learned during "periods of observation," analytic treatment, and Diagnostic Profiles about this group of children. For each of the children a Developmental Profile[1] was prepared and discussed in the Profile Research Group at the Hampstead Clinic.[2]

At the time of the assessment the children ranged in age from four to eight and a half years; four of them were between five and six years; one was four, and the other was eight and a half years.

We are especially indebted to Anna Freud, Dorothy Burlingham, Ilse Hellman, Liselotte Frankl, Ruth Thomas, Joseph Sandler, John Bolland, S. Fahmy, Martin James, Moses Laufer, Hansi Kennedy, Doris Wills, Marion Burgner, Elizabeth Model, Pat Radford, Lily Neurath, and many others who either have greatly contributed to group discussions or have been responsible for the preparation of the Developmental Profiles of the cases selected for this study. Special mention is due to Dr. Ehud Koch who helped with the collection of material and its organization for a pilot study on the subject.

[1] See Anna Freud (1962) and Nagera (1963).

[2] The Group consists of more than thirty members including psychoanalysts, psychiatrists, child therapists, psychologists, psychiatric social workers, teachers, etc. All members are also analytically trained. The specific observations included as illustrations in this paper were made by Alice B. Colonna, Marion Burgner, Hansi Kennedy and Barbara Bank.

A brief description of the children's history of blindness follows:

George (5;3 years).—Pregnancy was normal, born in hospital. Nothing was said to the parents about eyes at this time, though, according to the father, there was no pupil present in the left eye from birth. First seen at Moorfields in December, 1957 at age 2 months, when examination under anesthesia showed that he had a mass in the right fundus and the left eye was large and prominent with a raised intraocular tension and hazy cornea. It was thought that the right fundus picture was not that of a neoplasm but probably of developmental or inflammatory pathology. The tension of the left eye remained high and the globe increased; therefore, in March, 1958, the left eye was enucleated. Histology of the eye showed a chronic endophthalmitis. Since then, the right eye has been kept under observation regularly; the mass in the right eye showed no change in size and tension was normal. It is difficult to assess accurately George's visual acuity at present.

Joan (4;6 years).—Totally blind as a result of high concentration of oxygen. Born prematurely (thirty weeks). Retrolental fibroplasia.

Gillian (4;6 years).—Retrolental fibroplasia, blind from birth. Born by Caesarian section. Mother very ill during pregnancy, child's weight at birth 3 lbs.; spent nine weeks in oxygen tent. When the child was ten weeks old the mother was told that Gillian was blind.

Helen (4;6 years).—Helen was born prematurely (at twenty weeks), had little sight afterwards, remaining sight was lost when she had measles, at age of three. Mother had three miscarriages, but Helen was the first pregnancy. Weight 2 lbs. at birth; in an incubator for 102 days, at which time she weighed 5 lbs. and was taken home. When she came home her mother went to a home for a week.

Winnie (7 years).—Congenital cataract. Born one month premature (weight 6 lbs. 1 oz.) (not in oxygen tent).

Janet (8;6 years).—Blind from birth, pseudoglioma, eyes removed at four months.

Speaking very generally, we have had the opportunity to observe two very different possibilities of development among children who are born blind (and we include here as well children who may have become blind very early in life, perhaps soon after birth). In a small number of such cases their development, in spite of their blindness, does not seem to lag much behind the development of sighted children. Their ego processes, their drive development, their object relationships are not too far behind those of the sighted of similar ages. In another very distinct group, one finds blind children whose developmental processes are atypical. They lag behind in different degrees in the different areas, giving in some extreme cases the impression of a marked mental retardation. These two types are the two extremes on a scale with all sorts of possible combinations in between.

The cases we are referring to in this paper belong mostly in the second group; they show a specific clinical and developmental picture which they have in common with many other blind-born[3] but which is by no means representative of the developmental possibilities of all the blind-born children.

We further believe that the study of these two different groups of children born blind may teach us a great deal about how and by what means some overcome their handicap and find effective alternative ways to a degree that brings them closer to the level of the sighted. Even when the blind grows up under the most favorable circumstances (which are rarely encountered) in terms of ego endowment, good early mothering, reasonable environmental conditions, favorable object relations, etc., there is a point at which the development of one or another ego function clearly requires a contribution from the side of vision. When that contribution is not available, a disruption in the development of a specific function ensues. In turn, the insufficiency of these functions or of other aspects of the ego leads to further developmental interferences in all areas in which such functions are a necessary prerequisite. A somewhat similar point of view was expressed by A.-M. Sandler (1963) and by Fraiberg and Freedman (1964). It seems to us that this state of affairs can be somewhat alleviated by the environment, its handling of and attitude to the blind and their problems. It can make a positive contribution to the blind child's development by teaching him directly and at the right points the suitable alternative ways and means of compensating for the lack of sight. Left to itself the ego of the blind may never achieve this or only through long and painful detours and at much later stages. It may well be that some of the differences in development of the two groups of

3 See, for example, some of the cases reported in the recent literature by Omwake and Solnit (1961), Segal and Stone (1961).

blind we are describing are related to these very factors.[4] Thus, the observation of the means by which the blind child's ego finds alternative solutions can give us clues to the kind of teaching and handling required at the different development points at which help may be needed to stimulate further development.

In our study we have made special efforts to single out those aspects of development and personality of blind children which are specific to them, and those in which they differ somehow from sighted children. In this way we hope in time to be able to understand the nature of the contribution sight makes to normal ego development and how much blindness can distort it. Though our study is based primarily on the six children described above, we have also checked relevant material of a large group of other blind children to verify certain aspects of our formulations. These formulations are nevertheless to be considered as tentative. The study of more cases will either confirm or modify them. With growing insight into the developmental processes of the blind new formulations may become necessary.

As previously stated, we shall present our formulations in terms of the relevant headings of the Developmental Profile introduced by Anna Freud (1962).

The Drive Development of the Blind

Libidinal Development

All the cases studied show that the blind develop in this area at a much slower pace than the sighted child.

Helen's Profile at five years eight months showed that even at that age there were no significant signs of her being in the phallic phase and no indication of oedipal development. There is a great deal of oral activity that finds direct expression in the sucking of objects and in the way she devours food and drink. She sometimes spits them out. Drooling is still observable. Anal messy behavior is noted in her intense enjoyment in pouring water or powder on the floor in a provocative manner.

Janet, at eight and a half, showed no signs of latency. The material contained only tenuous indications of her having reached the

[4] We are planning a close study of the group of blind children that develops more like the normal in the hope of clarifying some of the problems here posed.

phallic phase, but oral and anal activities are still very prominent, including rinsing of her mouth and spitting; she does a great deal of mouthing (which is partly an ego exploratory activity); anal masturbation was noted during her analytic sessions. She pulls at her knickers and skirt and places her index finger in her anus. She comments on smells and noises, frequently passes wind and once soiled herself in doing so. There are endless and repetitive games and fantasies of other children soiling and wetting themselves and having to clean up the mess. Water play is accompanied by fantasies of mother forcing her to defecate and of other children soiling and wetting and being smacked.

Even more striking perhaps is the fact that this group of blind children, in marked contrast to the sighted children, seems incapable of leaving behind the previous phases when a new developmental move occurs. The move into the phallic-oedipal phase does not at all imply that drive gratification and autoerotic activities pertaining to the anal and oral phase will tend to disappear or even to recede notably into the background. On the contrary, marked activity of the anal and oral stages is always observed simultaneously with the newly found phallic-oedipal forms of drive gratification. This can best be illustrated in the case of Winnie.

At the time she came into analytic treatment (at the age of three) there were clear manifestations of active libidinal interests on the anal and oral levels of libidinal development. After five months of treatment, Winnie progressed into the phallic-oedipal phase, as the following material illustrates. Envy of little boys made its appearance and began to be openly expressed. She made clear what she wanted to do to them by attempts at dismembering dolls with much giggling. The dolls previously called "girl doll" were now "boy dolls." On one occasion when her envy of boys was verbalized, she strutted around the room with a boy doll held between her legs, saying, "Look what I got stuck up my fanny." She expressed wishes to sleep with her brother-in-law, Martin. Nevertheless, and in spite of this move, there remained a great deal of anal and oral concerns which were expressed in her fear of messing, her discomfort due to constipation, her use of anal swearwords, and her attempts to seduce her therapist to "smell" her fanny. Similarly noticeable were her strong ambivalent (anal-sadistic) feelings toward objects.

It may perhaps be concluded that blindness can so much interfere with finding new means of gratification both in drive discharge and ego activities that any form of gratification once experienced is not easily abandoned or left behind, even when further developmental steps are taken by the blind child; all earlier forms of gratification remain ego syntonic. We shall come back to this point.

Cathexis of Self

Self-esteem Regulation. In this area our group of blind differs from normally sighted children in that the blind have a more marked and presumably longer period of dependence on the external world in order to maintain the cathexis of themselves at a level compatible with well-being. In many of the children we have studied and observed in our Nursery for the Blind, this extreme dependence upon the object world is further shown in an inability to maintain their own self-esteem and cathexis of the self when the object world withdraws cathexis from them.

When Winnie's mother was depressed, Winnie suffered a loss of the feeling of well-being and tended to become immobilized, particularly so at the nursery, where she also retreated from interaction with the other children. However, she showed very different behavior in the treatment situation, where she was able to enjoy a one-to-one relationship with the full attention of the therapist concentrated on herself. Thus, she was often verbal and active in treatment, while in school she appeared withdrawn and involved in manneristic gestures.

Cathexis of Object. It seems clear from our observations that even apparently retarded blind children can reach object constancy and can relate to the object world on that level. On the other hand, they may not completely leave behind the other phases and will sometimes relate to and use the objects on a need-fulfilling basis. Indeed, they tend to move forward and backward from the one to the other phase quite frequently.

They sometimes give the impression that they readily and easily exchange objects, even for unfamiliar ones, as if object constancy had not been properly established.

A more careful examination of the facts will support the view that, owing to the lack of sight, the blind child experiences extreme anxiety when someone is not nearby to protect him. The blind child, fully aware through experience of the very many dangers around and of his inability to care for himself in the absence of a protective object, tends to cling to anyone present when the familiar or dearest objects are not available, for whatever reason. It is presumably this attitude, which in fact serves self-preservation, that leads to the false impression that some blind children are not attached to their objects on the level of object constancy. We have noted that the blind group we studied shows a strong tendency to comply with the wishes of their important objects and especially with those of the mother. This is carried to extremes that are hardly observable in sighted children of the same age.

Aggression

We have formed the impression that these blind children show a tendency to inhibit any form of overt expression of aggression against those objects on whom they are dependent. The fact that they do inhibit aggression in this specific way may not be apparent to the casual observer who may easily gain the impression that the children's behavior is quite aggressive. This misunderstanding of the real circumstances is due to two factors.

First, many of these blind children are still largely at the anal-sadistic stage of libido development. Winnie, for example, was fully at the anal-sadistic stage and behaved accordingly; it is true that descriptively, i.e., to an observer, behavior of this type may seem extremely aggressive, but it is in fact the phase-adequate expression and type of relationship of children in that phase. The extreme ambivalence of the anal-sadistic phase allows us to see, for example, the child's expressions of love followed by violent biting. It may be profitable to distinguish this type of phase-adequate expression of the aggressive drive from aggressive behavior as a more organized type of response which is phase independent; the blind child's inhibition is of the second type.

The second factor concerns the child's relationship with other children. In Winnie's case one must take into consideration that on the line of development "from egocentricity to companionship" (A. Freud, 1963) she has not yet developed any empathy for other children's feelings; consequently they can be used freely for the expression of her strong ambivalence. This type of aggressive behavior must be distinguished from the later forms where the aggressive act is carried out with full awareness of its effect on the other child.

Although Winnie was able to express open aggression to the therapist in the "permissive situation" of the treatment, it was not quite the same in relation to other objects or in other environments. In the nursery, for example, Winnie rarely made aggressive assaults; during a period in which she was unusually destructive in her sessions (throwing bottles, breaking glass, lashing out at the therapist, etc.), she was described at the nursery school as moving less freely, with a bad posture, "as though she were carrying the cares of the world on her shoulders," and indeed she presented the picture of a depressed child. Similarly, she rarely expressed openly aggressive, hostile impulses toward her mother. On one occasion when she did, after playing out having been nagged by her mother for making too much noise, she said, "What have you done with your mummy, did you throw her in the muck bin?" The next day, she snuggled up to the therapist and said, "But I wouldn't really do that; I'm a helpful girl, I help mummy."

In this way, she behaved very much as other blind children do, that is, with a marked inhibition of the expression of aggression. This is due partly to the fear of losing the favor and love of the object, a fear that is immediately transformed into a fear of annihilation caused by the extreme dependence on objects for reasons of safety.

In Winnie's case we noted that it was important for her "to hear" the result of her aggressive actions (breaking objects, glass, etc.), but we have not been able to confirm that this applies generally to other blind children. Some instances of very disturbed behavior which takes place in moments of regression provoked by current difficulties at home, in school, etc., may be wrongly interpreted as object-directed aggression. In fact, some of these manifestations are the panic reactions of an overwhelmed ego; they lead to disorganized behavior and other primitive expressions of the infant stage such as crying, throwing things at random, etc.

The Ego of the Blind

The consistent and systematic study of the personality of a number of blind children, by means of the application of the Developmental Profile, has forced us to conclude that there is an unwarranted readiness to interpret their peculiarities of behavior, fantasies, symptoms, etc., in the same light and on the same basis as those of sighted, normal or neurotic children.

Thus, we proceed in our assessments as if the blind were ordinary children except for their lack of sight. This may be so when the loss of sight has taken place late in the child's life, when his development in every direction may have been fairly well advanced. Clearly, when the child's lack of sight dates from birth or early babyhood, drive and ego development proceeds in atypical and distorted ways. The correlations valid for the sighted between surface (behavioral material) and depth (unconscious determinants and meaning) are not directly applicable to the blind. Many of the pointers, indicators, clinical evaluations, etc., on which we can rely with a fair degree of certainty in assessing the sighted child's personality and neurotic conflicts are unreliable instruments in the evaluation of the blind.

Many of the blind children we have studied tend to show a marked fear of animals and noises. Helen feared dogs, horses, birds, and noises. Janet feared thunder, rain, wind, trains, drilling machines, dogs, etc. When these fears occur in sighted children of a comparable age, they can be taken as a sure indication of an area of disturbance, of specific conflicts, of clear defense activity and symptom formation. In the sighted child of a given age, the presence of fear or phobic avoidance of certain animals such as birds, horses, dogs, etc., entitles us to assume that the animal stands for the oedipal rival and that the fear of being attacked by it is the result of the child's projecting his own aggressive feelings onto the hated rival.

In the case of the blind it is frequently very difficult to determine how much of the above behavior or symptomatology is the result of defense activity against the drives, i.e., the result of conflict, and how much is in fact appropriate adaptive behavior (in terms of survival) in a child who lacks vision. Here one has to remind oneself that when a blind child hears a barking dog he cannot see whether the dog is big or small, whether it is playful or hostile, whether it intends to bite or not.

The same viewpoint applies to the blind child's unusual degree of clinging to and dependence on the object at an age when he would normally be expected to have outgrown this type of relationship. In the sighted of the same age such clinging constitutes a clear indication either of important fixation points at the oral level or of defense activity directed against certain specific conflict situations. In the blind this extreme clinging and dependence, as already mentioned, are characteristic for a long period of life. Rather than being the result of defense activity, they may be another sign of the complex pattern of ego adaptation to a sighted world.

Other pieces of behavior characteristic of the blind, like their withdrawal (into fantasy or otherwise), their passivity, etc., can be understood in a similar way.

The sighted adult who has learned to cope with the ordinary conditions of his immediate environment experiences "fear of reality" only in the face of true danger situations. For him, it is practically impossible to imagine the state of extreme helplessness and anxiety of the blind child, for whom a great deal of the external world represents dangers that he is ill equipped to master. The blind child is swamped by constant waves of anxiety derived from an unending variety of occurrences which are incompletely understood or wrongly interpreted.

This state of permanent alertness to external dangers which have to be mastered seems to occupy the child's mind to a degree which outweighs the importance of the internal dangers, represented by the impulses and other drive representatives. Compared with the dreaded hazards of the environment, the inner world is a source of safety and gratification to the blind child. It is this combination of factors (fear of the external, retreat to the internal world) which may explain the marked delay in the mastery and control of drive activity which we observe in our blind children.

On the other hand, the children's fantasy life seemed extremely limited in comparison with the richness of imagination and fantasy production of the sighted (either normal or neurotic) of similar ages, a fact which may be due, of course, to the comparatively low level of ego development of the group of children studied. Fantasy production, as a well-known prestage of neurotic symptom formation in children and adults, usually represents the withdrawal from an unpleasant external reality which interferes with processes of drive gratification. The blind children, in spite of their most unpleasant external reality, cannot afford to withdraw from it. Only constant surveillance, with the alternative senses at their disposal, will avoid unpleasant, hurtful experiences. Consequently many of their mental activities consist of attempts to master through repetition and in imagination the many painful situations which they have experienced.[5] No less important is the fact, mentioned above, that the blind child allows himself a great deal of direct drive gratification which may make the function of fantasy less vital for him.

As regards the development of certain ego functions in the blind, it is important to note that their ego performance can be extremely unreliable even in cases of reasonably well-established functions. Most important in this respect is the ease with which anxiety can become overwhelming and traumatic and result in the temporary collapse of otherwise well-established functions.

Thus it was frequently observed that when in distress, danger, or extreme anxiety, many of the children would become immobile. Winnie, for example, became immobile to the extreme of being rigid. This immobility may well be a response learned very early in order to protect themselves from further pain, damage, or dangers.

Immobility in blind children was observed as well when they were introduced to a new environment. For a short while they tended to remain still in order to orient themselves, perceiving and collecting as much information as possible through the appropriate sense organs, especially the ear.

In the cases studied, walking started at any time between thirteen months and three years, the parental attitude to the child being a significant factor in connection with this function. Winnie started walking at thirteen months. She did not crawl but used to turn round and round on her behind, then pulling herself up. The father used to help her by walking alongside. Helen began walking at eighteen months without previous crawling. She was given a large doll to push and in this way began to walk. George walked by twenty months; Joan at two years without having ever crawled before; while Janet did not sit up until she was two years, crawled at two and a half years, and walked at three years of age.

[5] D. Burlingham (1964) has pointed to a piece of behavior that is often misleading. To the casual observer the blind children frequently appear to be fully withdrawn into passivity when in fact behind this façade there is an extremely active listening and a close attention to what goes on in the environment.

The following examples illustrate the blind child's use of ego functions in the service of adaptation to the world around him.[6]

Winnie relied on other sensory modalities to orient herself in and explore the environment, and for her own stimulation. Her reliance on tactile sensations was great (e.g., feeling the bumps on the windowpane, stroking a new object with her cheek). She also used her head as a drum knocking an object against her temples, which would seem to involve both tactile and auditory sensations. She enjoyed being barefooted and explored her environment in this way. Her awareness of surfaces was seen in her recognition of certain streets with cobblestones. Her hearing was most acute: she would aim objects correctly at the therapist when she wanted to throw them; she felt more at ease when she heard the therapist knitting and thus was assured of her awake presence; she derived much pleasure from hearing the sound of glass breaking; she would knock two objects together and listen for their sound. Smell was also important to her: she could locate the local bakery by means of the smells. Smell was at the same time sexualized as can be seen in her request to the therapist, "Come, smell my fanny." Throughout the treatment, she often sought close physical contact by sitting on the therapist's lap and asking for love, which suggests that the total surface of her body was a major receptor of stimulation.

Helen showed and made use of a very well-developed sense of hearing. She was able to tell when the paper boy was coming down the road long before her mother could hear him. She was also clearly attracted to her mother's powder and scent.

George compensated for his lack of vision mainly by means of auditory and tactile senses. In addition, testing, mouthing, and licking (very frequent in blind children) were used by him when he was five years old, in a manner similar to the ways of a sighted toddler.

Memory seems to serve the blind well. In practically all the cases studied and in many others observed, this function showed itself as adequate and helpful. Not infrequently it served purposes of orientation, as shown in Winnie's trips with her therapist to the local shops. Things recalled for such purposes were memories of smells experienced, of noises heard, of texture of surfaces felt (cobblestone surfaces, etc.).

[6] D. Burlingham's (1964) paper contains an interesting account of the development of hearing in the blind and the role of the relationship to the mother. See also D. Burlingham (1961).

Contact with the object world through words plays a particularly important role in the blind. In the cases here studied the acquisition of speech was not precociously developed and the timetable for the beginning of talking ranged roughly from eighteen months to three years of age. George began talking at eighteen months; Helen was fairly fluent by two and a half years; Winnie was talking by two years; Janet talked when she was three years.

It is a well-established fact that certain forms of thinking and the development of several other ego functions are dependent largely on the acquisition of a proper imagery, and of adequate symbols, on the basis of which thought processes of an ever-increasing complexity and quality are possible.

The synthetic and integrative functions of the ego are very dependent on the intactness of these processes, which are essential for the proper understanding and mastery of the world around us, making further ego development possible on that basis.

It is likewise well established that words are the essential units, the required symbols, on the basis of which the above-mentioned processes can take place. Quite clearly, whatever interferes with the child's ability to acquire such symbols may bring aspects of his ego development to a near standstill and be responsible for sometimes creating the impression of extreme backwardness. Extreme examples of such cases can be observed in children with congenital deafness. When they are taught to lip-read and to talk, dramatic improvements often take place in their ego development, and with it in their object relationships, in their understanding and mastery of the world. This happens because words as symbols have become available for thought processes and for the performance of functions which are contingent upon secondary-process thinking of a certain quality.

Although the blind child's disadvantages in this area is not on a par with that of the deaf, there is some evidence that lack of vision interferes with the ability to acquire and make use of words as symbols. Many essential elements of these "word symbols" can be contributed only by sight. For this reason the concepts abstracted by these words have no real meaning for children blind from birth. "Dark," "light," and the whole range covered by words describing "color," etc., belong in this category. No other sense can convey suitable alternative information to clarify these concepts and abstractions. It is not difficult to imagime how many limitations are thus imposed on the mental processes of the blind. A few observations from our Nursery for the Blind can exemplify some of these problems.

Gillian (six years) was in the lavatory. "Put the light on, it's dark."
Teacher: "What do you mean?"
Gillian: "You know, it is cold and horrible."

Matthew (age four), playing hide and seek in the cupboard, called out, "It's all dark in here." When asked what he meant, he answered, "Well you know, all cold and rainy."

In a still larger group of words the contribution of sight may not be as fundamental but nevertheless important enough to render these symbols somewhat insufficient when compared with the equivalent symbols of the sighted.[7]

Whatever ego functions are dependent on the availability of the right kind of imagery of symbols are thus limited in a proportional degree. The imagery of the world of sighted people is of necessity in many ways inappropriate for the blind. Nevertheless, it seems that in spite of the absence of the visual contribution to many of these "word symbols," alternative compensatory means are finally found so that these symbols become useful elements in the performance of the complex mental processes for which these basic units are required. This need not imply that they finally become identical with the same "word presentation" of the sighted. Experiments on blind adults (from birth) who have recovered sight in adulthood through certain operations have shown that they are unable to pick out objects by sight, to recognize or even name them, even though they know all about them and their names by touch. As Young (1960) points out:

> At first he only experiences a mass of colour, but gradually he learns to distinguish shapes. When shown a patch of one

[7] "A word is thus a complex presentation . . . ; or, to put it in another way, there corresponds to the word a complicated associative process into which the elements of visual, acoustic, and kinaesthetic origin enumerated above enter together. A word, however, acquires its *meaning* by being linked with an 'object-presentation,' at all events if we restrict ourselves to a consideration of substantives. The object-presentation itself is once again a complex of associations made up of the greatest variety of visual, acoustic, tactile, kinaesthetic and other presentations" (Freud, 1891). The quotation appears as part of Appendix C, Words and Things, attached to Freud's paper "The Unconscious" (1915, p. 209), because the last section of that paper is based on these views expressed in *On Aphasia*.

colour he will quickly see that there is a difference between the patch and its surroundings. What he will not do is to recognize that he has seen that particular shape before, nor will he be able to give it its proper name. For example, one man when shown an orange a week after beginning to see, said that it was gold. When asked, 'What shape is it?' he said, 'Let me touch it and I will tell you'. After doing so, he said that it was an orange, when he looked again at it he said: 'Yes I can see that it is round'. Shown next a blue square, he said it was blue and round. A triangle he also described as round. When the angles were pointed out to him he said, 'Ah, Yes, I understand now, one can *see* how they feel'.

Further evidence supporting the limitations we are describing is presented by the indiscriminate use of words that can be observed in many blind children. They use words in a "parroting fashion" without having a proper understanding of their true and complete meaning.

For example, when Janet was nine she frequently used words such as "contradict" and "nuisance," without knowing their meaning, obviously having taken them over from her mother. Matthew (four and a half) was washing the stuffed bunny and said that at home in the bath when soap gets into his eyes its stings. "They are delicate," he said, adding, "I wonder what delicate means?"

The occurrence of word parroting long before the child grasps the corresponding abstract meaning of the words shows how much longer it takes the blind to assimilate many of the concepts symbolized by words.

Not all words represent the same level of abstraction; many are more concrete than others. The blind learn the concrete first and more easily than the abstract. Though there exist noticeable individual differences in this respect, in general the blind children show a certain tendency to concreteness in their verbalized thoughts and some difficulty in the formation of abstract concepts. Similarly, abstract concepts are readily concretized.

Wendy, for example, shows concern with the meanings of "wearing out" and "worn out" as used with regard to people, objects such as toys, feelings, etc. She worried whether worn-out people are discarded like worn-out music boxes.

Peter at around five years of age was gingerly fingering dough. He said, "Squeeze it; can he squeeze it? Will it hurt?" On another occasion he tried to open a peanut, saying, "That hurts it." He then stopped the activity.

Matthew (at around six years of age) heard at home the story of *Pinocchio*. He asked at the nursery what "conscience" is. "Can you really hear a little voice when you do something naughty?" He decided to try it out and with a serious expression tore up a paper napkin. He then pushed over a chair and said, "I still can't hear it."

These limitations help to explain why, in many cases, the blind children are not able to master and fully understand the world outside; large areas of it remain sources of intense fear and anxiety.

Nevertheless, at some point of development, some of these limitations disappear or are reduced to a minimum compatible with performances on the ego side more similar to the level of performance of the sighted. We have no doubt concerning the usefulness of the close study of how, when, and through what means the ego finds alternatives and compensatory ways that finally to some degree help overcome its original limitations. Such a study will throw abundant light on many developmental processes undergone by the ego. It will also clarify and establish the essential elements that must combine to bring about the performance of more complex ego functions.

It is our belief that the ego of the blind must first find alternative means of coping with some of the problems described in this paper before it can turn to the rather primitive drive organization and establish appropriate controls over drive activity. In many blind this seems to happen at a much later stage than in the sighted. At this later point the ego can make use of alternative sources of gratification and find sublimatory outlets. Exactly when this happens should be determined by detailed study and analyses of blind adolescents and adults.

The Superego Structure

The whole question of how the superego structure as a controlling agency develops in the blind deserves a study in its own right. We are limiting ourselves to highlighting some striking differences between sighted and blind.

First of all, in the group we have studied, it is very difficult to find signs of guilt when specific transgressions occur, even at ages when such signs are plentiful in the sighted. For example, the blind children engage freely in a great deal of autoerotic activity and drive gratification corresponding to all sorts of levels, as pointed out above. These activities are performed openly in the presence of adults; on the whole they seem to be ego syntonic and free of guilt.

It is also important to point to an apparent contradiction in these children's superego development. In the sighted child the process of internalization of external demands (leading to superego precursors and in due course to the final establishment of the superego structure) is assumed to start when the child's awareness of the importance of the object forces him to give up drive gratification, out of concern and fear of the loss of the love of the object. The blind children, in spite of their extreme dependence on their objects, do not seem forced (by fear of loss of the object's love when his disapproval is incurred) to internalize prohibitions and commands or to give up the multiple and primitive forms of autoerotic activities and drive gratifications to which they cling so tenaciously.

Development of the Total Personality
(Lines of Development and Mastery of Tasks)

A marked retardation and unevenness in the development of the total personality as shown on the Lines of Development seems to be the normal picture in this group of blind children. This is in part due to the lack of sight which implies interference with development in every area and in part to environmental interferences such as pity and overprotection. We anticipate that the study of the blind in terms of the "Lines of Development" (A. Freud, 1963) established for sighted children will throw some light on certain aspects of ego development, especially on the contribution made to that development by the organ and the function of vision.

It is also possible that for an independent assessment of their development we shall have to set up entirely new standards permitting us to explore the possibility of different interactions between the expressions of drives and the severely handicapped ego and superego structures.

Regression and Fixation Points

This is another area where we have become aware of the fact that the behavior and symptomatic manifestations of sighted children, usually taken as indicators and pointers to the levels at which they may be fixated, are not always applicable to the blind.

Thus, the intense mouthing observed in most blind children up to a very late age cannot be taken as a sure indicator of a fixation on the oral level. Mouthing in the blind, quite apart from the oral drive gratification, must in some of its aspects be considered as an auxiliary exploratory ego function. A very similar situation exists with regard to the prominent use of the sense of smell. It is, of course, not an easy matter to distinguish between drive and ego activity in this respect.

We suggest that one should try to note whether an organ is used by the ego in a limited way to compensate for the lack of vision (as in the exploration of objects through mouthing). In this case the activity will cease when this purpose has been accomplished; otherwise it will continue well past the exploratory phase and show an impulsive, instinctual quality.

Another example is the frequent touching inhibition of the blind which as an indicator of fixation to the anal phase does not have the same value it has in the sighted.

There are many other important differences between blind and sighted children with regard to fixation and regression. For example, it is very difficult to establish where phase dominance lies in the blind, since drive activity remains spread through all levels of development and the ego acquiesces in this state of affairs. The picture is further complicated by the extreme readiness of the blind children to regress temporarily from higher to lower levels of gratification as soon as any difficulties arise. In fact, the group we observe gives the impression of moving backward and forward far more readily than sighted children would in similar circumstances.

On the other hand, it is not quite correct to refer to what we have been describing as "fixations" proper, since it may well be that the reluctance to give up earlier forms of gratification is due to the immense and constant frustrations experienced by the blind; these make the ego more tolerant to the obtaining of gratification by whatever means possible. In fact, we have the impression that if sight could be restored (which would lead at once to a better balance between pleasure and frustration, etc.), very many of these earlier forms of gratification would disappear, a development which could, of course, never occur in the case of true fixations.

The constant shift in functioning from one level to another (with backward and forward moves), for example, in relation to external events, tends to support this view.

Dynamic and Structural Assessment (Conflicts)

External Conflicts

Owing to the extreme and very prolonged dependence of the blind child on his objects, the "external type" of conflict is perhaps more prominent than it is in the sighted. The blind need a longer period of time for internalization to take place and even then they seem to remain to some extent dependent on the approval of the outside world. They are more likely to have conflicts between the wish for independence and self-assertion and the ever-present realistic need for continuous support and protection from the objects. The outcome of such conflicts frequently seems to be extreme passivity and a readiness to comply with the demands of the object out of the fear of loss of love or fear of annihilation.

Internalized Conflicts

Blind children of the age group we have studied may show some superego precursors. They have internalized some of the environmental demands that have thus become their own. For example, they may take over from the environment the command to become clean and dry and make it into an internal concern. On the other hand, it has been noted that in blind children it is not easy to come across clear examples of "guilt" when transgressions of these or other commands do occur.

Although at the present time we cannot be more specific, there is no doubt that there are important differences between this group of blind and the sighted in the process of internalization as well as in the ego and the superego (or its precursors), as shown by the apparent "lack of guilt." On the whole internalization probably starts later and takes longer in the blind than in the sighted.

Assessment of Some General Characteristics

Frustration Tolerance

It is very difficult to evaluate the blind child's reaction to frustration. On the one hand, a great deal of direct drive gratification occurs all the time, a circumstance that would indicate low frustration tolerance; on the other, there is little doubt that in their dealings with the external world they are constantly exposed to and must tolerate excessive frustrations owing to their blindness and the resultant helplessness.

Sublimation Potential

It seems that the tendency to cling to any form of gratification that has been experienced previously, the general tolerance of the ego in this respect, etc., are factors working against whatever capacity or potential these children may have for sublimation. Moreover, the need for close bodily contact with the objects may further interfere with the blind child's capacity to sublimate or to accept substitute gratification.

These statements are true only up to a given age. Random observations of blind adults seem to point to the fact that at some stage there occur important economic and structural developments and rearrangements in the personality of the blind (partly described under the Ego section), which sometimes allow satisfactory sublimations to take place.

Over-all Attitude to Anxiety

This is an area of special interest in blind children (see under Ego Development).

Because of their readiness to develop anxiety to a traumatic degree in times of stress, the function of anxiety as a signal is frequently overruled. At such moments the children tend to look for very close bodily contact with the object. It seems that up to a comparatively late age the children's anxiety, as observed in our group, is aroused mainly by their inability to deal with, understand, and master the external dangers and the external world.

Progressive Developmental Forces versus Regressive Tendencies

In this group of blind children the material seems to point to a very marked backward pull exerted by the regressive tendencies. We have already mentioned the need to cling to old forms of satisfaction which does not make it any easier to take progressive steps into new phases. Although progressive tendencies are seen, development on the whole takes place at a slower and rather retarded pace; certain environmental attitudes, such as overprotection, etc., may further obscure the true state of affairs concerning the blind child's potentialities in this area.

11

COMMENTS ON SOME ASPECTS OF SELF AND OBJECT REPRESENTATION IN A GROUP OF PSYCHOTIC CHILDREN

An Application of Anna Freud's Diagnostic Profile

RUTH THOMAS
in collaboration with
Rose Edgcumbe, Hanna Kennedy, Maria Kawenoka,
and Lilian Weitzner

(1966)

The four children whose analyses and Profiles form the basic material for the following discussion were chosen from a large group of atypical children resident in the High Wick Hospital where care and study are devoted exclusively to this type of child.[1] After a period of residential care these children (ranging in age from seven to ten years) were considered to have developed sufficiently to be amenable to a modified form of analytic therapy. In addition to being able to walk, dress, feed themselves, and perform highly co-ordinated activities, they had acquired a degree of verbal ability sufficient to insure some basis for verbal communication.

They had in common an extreme primitiveness of instinctual behavior and very uneven ego development, which precluded the diagnosis of mental defect. The various descriptions of such children in the psychiatric literature indicate that we are far from under-

---

[1] High Wick is a hospital under the National Health Service, and is under the general and psychiatric direction of Dr. George Stroh. To Dr. Stroh, Dr. Tischler, and the staff of the hospital we are heavily indebted for information and detailed observations outside the scope of the analyses.

standing the contribution of organic, genetic, dynamic, and environmental factors to their disturbances.

General Comments on Diagnosis

The diagnosis of childhood psychosis is made on the basis of: (1) highly unusual or bizarre behavior; (2) speech disturbance indicative of confusion of thought or thought disorder; (3) grossly disordered relationship to people. Furthermore, when these abnormalities are present, their frequency and intensity warrant the diagnosis of psychosis; they readily differentiate it from neurosis. Three discernible groups can be identified under the heading of psychosis:

1. *Early infantile autism* (to which none of the four children belong) is characterized, usually, by absence of speech, and when speech is present, it has a specifically automatic quality. There is extreme withdrawal and preoccupation with sameness (repetitive manneristic activity).

2. *Childhood schizophrenia,* a term which is here not used as synonymous with either "psychosis" or "autism," but which denotes a syndrome not unlike schizophrenia in later life, with periods of marked regression, withdrawal, and thought disorder. (Lucille belongs in this group.)

3. *Traumatic psychosis.* Children in this group (Basil, Norma, Stanley) have suffered psychological traumata of such frequency and severity that their experiences can reasonably be understood to be of primary importance in the causation of their disturbance. In this sense, these children can readily be differentiated from the autistic child, whose basic perceptual defect causes experiences of everyday life to assume the quality of trauma, and who defends himself against this by complete withdrawal. Other features that seem to be characteristic of the "traumatic" psychosis are excessive demandingness and relative absence of pleasurable experiences.

The children have been grouped together in a single research unit at Hampstead although they show a diverse adaptive potential and divergent learning achievements. They are identical in retaining archaic, grossly pathological ego attitudes which dominate their primitive capacity for object relations and preclude the maturation of feeling states which have meaning for the child and are recognizable by others. This paper focuses on what these children have in common—i.e., a level of primitivity and immaturity which persists and remains largely intractable—although in other respects they have diverse characteristics which preclude their classification into a single pathological entity.

Background Material

We do not feel that we have broken new ground in our analytic approach to these children. Our results show only partial success in two of the four cases. Our discussions, doubts, and dilemmas concerning the modified analytic approach we deemed appropriate at the time we undertook treatment have been described previously (Kut Rosenfeld and Sprince, 1965).

In what follows we present a brief description of the children's histories and symptomatology; to these we have added a survey of the areas in which analysis with our present techniques was effective. Three cases have been terminated because we felt that they could not be further influenced by our present techniques; the fourth, Basil, still continues in analysis and we have recently begun to approach his deepest pathology by more flexible attempts to reconstruct his earliest years. In his material appeared some indirect clues to which we feel we have been insufficiently alerted. Our openness to this new approach is largely a result of writing this paper and is in part due to a closer study of the work of D. W. Winnicott. The limited treatment results do not affect the validity of the observations, though the contributions of the various genetic factors to the disturbances of each child have been only slightly clarified as a result of our work.

Basil was a thin, hyperactive, mulatto child with closely cropped curly hair and light brown skin. His bearing demanded attention at all times; he was extremely alert, spoke precisely, giving accurate descriptions, but usually with a flat voice and affectless facial expression. He was placed in residential care in his seventh year, following the final breakup of the marriage between his middle-class white Jewish mother and his Jamaican Negro father. He was found to be unmanageable in this residential center and was eventually hospitalized at High Wick at the age of seven years two months. He began treatment at the Hampstead Clinic when he was nine and a half years old and is now almost fourteen.

At eight years, tested with the Revised Stanford-Binet Scale, Basil scored an I.Q. of 100; at thirteen, tested with the Wechsler Intelligence Scale for Children (WISC), he showed an I.Q. of 118 on the verbal scale and 97 on the performance scale, with an I.Q. of 109 on the full scale. The most prominent features were the extreme scatter of scores on the subtests and the marked differences between the verbal and performance results. Basil was unable to find a logical and reasonable solution to tests that had an emotional and interpersonal impact. His perception of situations was distorted and his pseudo affects were apparent. The psychologist was left with the impression that Basil had a mask or cloak of normality which would be vulnerable if he encountered emotional demands. It was felt unwise and inappropriate to undertake an EEG for this reason.[2]

Basil was absorbed in a fantasy world, isolated from other children, and showed no affection. He often threatened to bite or strangle his younger sister. His behavior varied from rigid overcontrol to complete breakdown of control with acute and unbearable anxiety attacks. Primitive play with urine and feces evoked no shame in him, and he spent much time in isolated play devoted mostly to digging holes. The bizarreness of his fantasies was apparent in his notions of the body. "Why does my nurse not turn her head right round, so that I could use it as a wheel? Why can't I squeeze your breast and get all the spaghetti out?" He was demanding and fastidious about food. He made frequent use of neologisms and concrete thinking. There was some compulsive head jerking and smelling of objects. He sadistically manipulated other children to act out his aggressive fantasies, while he withdrew to avoid retribution.

Much of Basil's early family life had been stormy, chaotic, and traumatic enough to account for his deviant ego development. He was a premature baby, weighed only 4 pounds at birth, although his delivery was normal and he was never in an incubator. His mother alternated between turning all her affection and care on him and depressive withdrawal from him. From earliest infancy until the beginning of treatment he had periodically shared his mother's bed and had experienced her embraces and her excitement as highly seductive.

In the hospital his attachment to three staff members represented separate aspects of these frustrating infantile experiences. From one

[2] Dr. David Buick of High Wick Hospital undertook the testing of all children, and Dr. George Stroh was responsible for the diagnostic findings.

he would accept a caretaking role, and apply to her for help in his activities or general assistance; from another he demanded erotic gratification in the form of body contact and sexual gratification; and a third he overwhelmed with tormenting and teasing manifestations which she found almost unbearable. During his sojourn at High Wick, he longed ardently for his mother's visits and had idealized expectations of gratification which broke down with each real encounter. Their meetings were either stormy and upsetting to both or involved each in marked overcontrol, giving an unreal quality to their relationship. He strenuously avoided initiating an erotic contact with his mother always fearing a rebuff. The analytic work revealed that he usually sought erotic contact with others when he felt particularly unloved and unwanted by his mother, and that the crucial and damaging experience for him had been not the actual or fantasied seduction by his mother but the repeated experience of loss of a close and intimate relationship that was entailed in his experiences of being subsequently "pushed out of her bed."

Throughout his early childhood there were intense quarrels and violent scenes between his parents, often resulting in his father staying away for prolonged periods, or his mother leaving the home with Basil, frequent moves to new houses, and placement in day nurseries and nursery schools, all situations which he was unable to master and react to adaptively. In the analysis it emerged that Basil had interpreted the many observations of parental quarrels and fights, as well as the final separation of his parents, as mother pushing father out and not letting him return. In this way, he was identified with his father, suffering or anticipating the same fate. He brought many vivid memories of being confined to a cot while witnessing parental fights; he felt excluded, shut out, and isolated. Later, these experiences crystallized into fears of being abandoned, deserted, and forgotten.

There was, of course, also material indicating his conflict over loyalty, his being forced to take his mother's side in the conflict; his fear of his own violent and aggressive wishes, which would make him attack his mother as his father had done and lead to loss of love and abandonment; and his masochistic involvement, which made him wish for father's role of victim. In all these memories and reconstructions two features always emerged: the fact of being immobilized, either physcially restrained or panic-stricken and "frozen"; and the painful realization of being left out and "forgotten." The former became the basis for massive sexualization of anxiety, and the latter led to a lifelong attempt to defend himself against the pain of feeling unloved and unlovable.

The most traumatic event of his life leading to massive ego

regression occurred in his sixth year. The birth of his sister, when he was four and a half years, temporarily improved the marital relationship, but for Basil it entailed yet another separation from his mother and forcibly reaffirmed again his precarious position in maintaining his mother's love and affection. At first, he attempted completely to deny his sister's existence, later he became violently jealous and aggressive toward her. The mother's third pregnancy two years later led to the father's final desertion. In desperation, Mrs. B. sought refuge with the paternal grandparents in Jamaica. After a nightmarish journey in which Mrs. B., near term, traveled alone with her two children across stormy seas, they found only horrible, squalid conditions, and grandparents who were severely rigid and brutal guardians. Basil was left with them for some weeks while his mother traveled to the city awaiting her confinement. His two-year-old sister was left with other relatives, but for Basil it looked as if his mother was taking her and leaving him behind, and later returning with two children. On her return she found Basil like a "terrified animal." He had been beaten, starved, and restricted; he crawled on all fours, wetted and soiled.

He remembered many painful experiences in Jamaica. The analytic material revealed his great distress over not knowing his parents' whereabouts and his gradually mounting hopelessness of ever seeing them again. At first, he made attempts to run away and search for them; later he gave up all hope. His isolation, loneliness, and sadness were accentuated by the frequent punishments of being locked up all day alone in a room, and the thoughtless or deliberately cruel attitude of his guardians who would not even allow him to keep his mother's letters. The other children in the family were hostile and antagonistic toward the intruder and took delight in taunting him about his mother never returning again. This he took as confirmation of his own fear and doubt.

Basil's memories of his early life consisted of a series of frightening and painful events with the ever-recurring theme of "feeling all deserted, feeling all alone, and waiting and waiting for something or someone who never comes."

The main experiences of loss in his life at different periods, together with the cumulative fantasies with which he imbued them, were worked through extensively and in great detail. This work gave a marked impetus to his ability to attend normal school and reach secondary school entrance standard. He now travels alone in London and meets unexpected situations sensibly and without acute anxiety. He is living at home with his mother and siblings and is moderately adjusted. Nevertheless, the core of his personality with its focus on irremediable loss and emptiness remains untouched. He has some intellectual understanding of and regret for the emotional impact his unreasoning demands make on people, and to a great extent he is able to control himself to meet their expectations.

He has hardly ever talked about good experiences or indicated that he has such memories as well. Yet we know that he was not an unloved baby. At times, he was the center of his mother's whole life and on occasions he even replaced her sexual object. In many ways his mother overestimated his achievements, particularly his artistic productions by calling him her "Leonardo." The father, too, when present, took great interest in his development, and played and talked to him, although he often did so on a level above the child's functioning.

The analysis is now oriented to the "false self" (Winnicott, 1960a), which his accomplishments may well represent, as distinct from the real self, which the emotional demands of both parents kept from developing. It may still be possible to clarify his problem further if we can gain a deeper understanding of the primitive introjective processes to which his immature ego may have resorted in his attempts to cope with the intense feelings with which he was surrounded, and of which he was sometimes the focus, but which were not geared to his needs. In the father's relation to him, there was a demand for precocious learning; in the mother's, for precocious feeling; intermittently he was dropped altogether from a relationship. He has recently become aware of the intense hatred which his mother feels for him, though he has still much to learn of its history. We still have to determine the extent to which the damage he has suffered is reversible.

Stanley was a first child born when his father was abroad. Even after the father's return he had little contact with the child. During Stanley's first year the family lived with indulgent grandparents whose handling is said to have contrasted strongly with the admittedly strict and critical attitude of both parents. Stanley's highly phobic mother did not impress workers with any spontaneous warmth, and both parents felt gravely threatened by Stanley's disturbance.

Stanley was a full-term baby and was bottle-fed from the beginning because his mother's milk was insufficient. He sucked well and is supposed to have thrived. It is not easy to form a picture of his babyhood. He is said to have woken crying most nights until he was two years old; he delighted in teasing his mother and would scratch and tear wallpaper. (At the same time, both parents had the impression of relative normality until the birth of David, when Stanley was three.) He sat up at nine months, walked at eighteen months, and was clean and dry at three years. His speech development was slow and he began to talk only at three years. He did not like to be held and showed no signs of affection. After David's birth, Stanley began to follow the parents around and would not sit down. The circumstances of the birth were unusual: the father delivered the baby at home in the absence of a midwife. Stanley was unprepared for David's arrival and for the first time in his life was looked after exclusively by his father. During labor, the father was forced to leave Stanley alone in his high chair, where he was very quiet.

The severity of Stanley's disturbance struck the parents when at the age of five he was expelled from school as unmanageable. A child guidance report at this time described him as hyperactive, often talking to himself, repeating unintelligible phrases, living in a fantasy world, and unable to relate to other children. When he was admitted to High Wick at six, he was very anxious; he talked only in shouts; there was much blinking, spitting, and drooling; he used many neologisms; and he was afraid of physical contact with adults.

Stanley was able to complete an intelligence test only at the end of treatment (when he was nine years nine months old). By then, his I.Q. on the WISC was 110 (verbal), 116 (performance), 109 (full scale). In comparison with an earlier testing there was an increase of 23 points in the verbal I.Q., and of 11 points in the full scale I.Q.

When at age seven and a half Stanley came to treatment, the confusion of pronouns was no longer in evidence, but his need for neologisms and word distortions soon came to the fore. However, the main initial impression was that of a tremendously anxious child. His anxiety proved to be severe both with regard to intensity and spread. Stanley had innumerable fears and was easily overwhelmed by them.

Stanley was in treatment for over two and a half years. His material, reflecting the fragmented way in which his ego functioned, was often disjointed. He communicated by actions, which frequently were provocative and aggressive. There was, however, one theme which kept returning and on which much work was done—the trauma of his brother's birth and the fears of the birth of yet another sibling. The prevailing anxiety was undoubtedly that of being immobilized and unable to reach his mother. This was complicated by Stanley's feeling that as his father came and went from the kitchen to the bedroom, boiling kettles and using scissors, murderous attacks on the mother were in process. His wish to investigate was acted out in the Clinic in excited running from one room to another. At this point, he became highly interested in things electrical and preoccupied with getting electrical shocks. Nevertheless, he developed great skill in handling electrical appliances, had a large assortment of electrical power points, plugs, and batteries, and would think out innumerable combinations of these. His inventiveness was often striking. The noise made by his apparatus was of great concern to him and so was its movement. If he managed to set an assembly in motion, he was greatly excited. Some working through of the birth experience was possible, but it was limited by the fear his memories aroused in him, exacerbating his intense castration anxiety. His object relations remained at a strongly sadistic level. The absence of basic tenderness indicated a partial arrest at the level of very early part-object relationships, an arrest which the analysis was unable to touch.

One of Stanley's most prominent fears was that of being abandoned by his parents. Placement at High Wick appeared to be its immediate cause, but underneath it were painful memories of helplessness, loneliness, and exposure to frightening, incomprehensible events. His way of coping with this fear was to reject his love objects. He could be helped to the extent of recognizing some love for his parents, but his need to provoke rejection remained strong and led to a premature termination of treatment. However, Stanley had improved sufficiently to be moved from High Wick to a boarding school for neurotically disturbed children.

When *Norma* came to High Wick at the age of four years and eight months she looked like a two-year-old. She spent most of her first months rocking on all fours and moaning. She did not speak and usually refused solid food. She made a primitive relationship with her housemother, first adopted a creeping gait like a small disabled animal, then began to walk and after six months to speak. She has made steady progress in speech though it was still somewhat retarded and bizarre. She had an aortic systolic murmur loudest medially of the apex. EEG and X-ray were normal. There was a hypochromic anemia, which responded readily to oral administration of iron, and recurrent eczema, first evident during treatment.

Norma was an unwanted child and her mother is said to have attempted abortion. The parents were unmarried and led a stormy, unstable life. The delivery was normal. The mother found the idea of breast feeding repulsive, and all the children were bottle-fed. Norma took the bottle well and never refused feedings.

When Norma was four months old, her mother became pregnant again, attempted suicide, and the pregnancy was terminated. The mother was depressed for at least the first year of Norma's life; she did not want to be bothered with the baby, but somehow managed to feed and change her. Norma cried a lot and was given a bottle whenever she cried, for whatever reason. She was mostly left to hold the bottle herself. Various attempts were made to give her solid foods, but Norma consistently refused them, would not allow a spoon into her mouth, and would not swallow. Her mother returned to bottle feeding for the sake of peace, and this continued until Norma was four and a half years old.

The mother remembered little about Norma's infancy. There was apparently little attempt to play, and no babbling or other sounds apart from crying and yelling. Norma sat at four months, stood at about one year, and walked at about fifteen months, without previously crawling. But she preferred to stand rocking from foot to foot in one favorite corner, from which she disliked being moved. She was frightened when she was taken out of the house. She would not approach people and pushed them away when they approached her; she screamed and struggled when she was picked up. She would not sit on her mother's lap, and resisted or rejected anything her mother tried to do to or for her. Toilet training was attempted at age two, but abandoned as hopeless.

An examination at two and a half years revealed no physical abnormalities. When Norma was three and a half she went to a day nursery. She gradually lost her fear of leaving the house and began to run about more normally instead of standing and rocking. The nursery eventually managed to get her to eat solids, when she was four and a half. She began to make sounds, but there were still no words. She often had tantrums and screamed a lot. Gradually she understood and obeyed commands given in a casual voice, but resisted anything said abruptly. Norma's development was erratic, with alternating periods of progress and regression, which made her mother despondent. When Norma was referred to High Wick her mother was relieved and openly expressed her hostility for the child. For the last three years the parents have not visited or shown any interest in her.

Norma's psychotic behavior became increasingly apparent as her speech developed and her motility improved. Treatment was commenced at the age of seven and discontinued four years later. In the early years of treatment, aggression was manifested in unpredictable outbursts of diffuse destructiveness directed at anything within reach, including herself. In the course of treatment aggression became more specifically object-directed and was often traceable to frustration, disappointment, or anxiety. These affects were sometimes aroused by external circumstances, but more often by the failure of objects and herself to do away with her internal sensations of tension and discomfort.

For Norma, the most distressing and intolerable aspects of her disturbance were her inability to deal with physical and mental sensations of tension and unpleasure and her striking paucity of pleasurable experiences. She seemed, indeed, to seek unpleasure rather than pleasure, centering attention on her anxieties and worries, only rarely appearing happy. In the course of treatment, she acquired some slight capacity to remember past pleasures and anticipate future ones, and to use these to exclude feelings of unpleasure from consciousness. But she could do this only in periods of optimal functioning. Under stress she became unable to seek, remember, or anticipate pleasure.

When Norma entered treatment, body boundaries were firmly established so that she could differentiate self from objects, but objects were sometimes confused with each other. Other related differentiations had not occurred. She could not distinguish between physical and mental states, so that psychic pain and unpleasure tended to be experienced in terms of hurts and ailments, a tendency reinforced by her physical condition. She could not distinguish between her own feelings and those of her objects and believed their feelings to be identical with her own. These differentiations began to appear during treatment, but they were always precarious.

From indiscriminate use of all available objects Norma moved to definite preferences on the basis of the object's capacity to fulfill the roles of need satisfier or auxiliary ego; eventually she began to discriminate between objects on the basis of function, e.g., between therapist and housemother. At first, people were often viewed as dangerous, at best harmless. For years her projected aggression interfered with all moves toward new objects and turned even a beloved object into a focus of terror. She slowly began to develop limited trust and the wish to be fed and to enjoy her food. Her need to provoke the repetition of rejection was always paramount. Her communications moved slowly from primary-process thinking to an unstable use of secondary process; she had organized memory though never of pleasant experiences.

Norma's aggressive attacks stemmed mostly from her fears of being deserted and left homeless. She felt she had damaged herself and destroyed her penis and that without one she could never be acceptable. Her wish for a penis led to endless attempts to find substitutes in long hair, high heels, and body attachments, and to much curiosity not only about external body protuberances but about internal organs as well. She finally acquired an extraordinary though distorted knowledge of physiological processes. While all attempts to deal with her penis envy proved abortive, her preoccupation with the inner states of her body led directly to her feeling of emptiness. Her therapist's main concern, therefore, became that of establishing herself as a trusted object who could support and supplement Norma's inadequate attempts at defense against her greedy and destructive wishes to engulf her objects.

Norma developed new ways of displacing aggression onto toys and of substituting less dangerous forms of attack, e.g., squirting water instead of scratching. She would also withdraw from situations which aroused anxiety; and when she had failed to control herself, she externalized her destructiveness onto creatures she invented. Having torn her dress she explained, "A birdie pecked it." Later, she invented a jumper-caughter—a creature who caught and tore her dress—laughing mischievously as she elaborated about "glove-caughters" and "sock-caughters."

There were some indications of reaction formation and primitive identifications: as she cared for her dolls she said she wanted to be a housemother to look after them.

Much of Norma's anxiety was contained in her "worry words," about which she complained bitterly because she could not get them out of her mind and felt constantly forced to say them, so that they punctuated her conversation and interfered with her thinking. These worry words changed frequently and could sometimes be traced to an anxiety-provoking situation; e.g., "dolly" became a worry word after a refusal to let her have another child's doll. Usually the word and the anxiety soon became detached from the original context, and even if the therapist succeeded in discovering and verbalizing the original anxiety, this did not dispel it. On the contrary, it seemed that Norma's worry words were used to encapsulate and make manageable incipient panic attacks which threatened to overwhelm her. These mostly derived from comparatively harmless events to which she had attached terrifying fantasies. Reconstruction of the original situation served only to revive the panic and the ego's experience of being overwhelmed, and in no way mitigated the fantasy content.

Norma's reparative efforts increased concurrently with the recovery of a degree of internal control. She used vast quantities of tape, sticking plaster, glue, staples, and string in "mending" and strengthening toys. But if these materials ran out, as they often did due to her extravagance, she would be thrown into a state of panic (Winnicott, 1960b).

On the whole, Norma disliked ordinary toys because they were too fragile, preferring to make things for herself. She revealed an extraordinary creativity and ability to manipulate unlikely materials. For example, she could make weird but convincing people and animals out of bits of plastic stuck together with tape. In time she began to use this ability to overcome disappointment at the refusal of toys belonging to other children; e.g., she envied Stanley his possession of a guitar, and made herself one out of tins, tape, and elastic bands.

In these activities Norma demonstrated her fear of her own omnipotent destructiveness—in her endless search for indestructible toys and materials. She rejected paper, cardboard, plasticine, and cloth because they could be torn or squashed. She usually settled for tin and plastic, with wire, tape, and sticking plaster to fix them together. But there were days when she rejected one thing after another, accompanying her frantic search with wails of "But it might break." She endlessly asked repetitive questions about how strong things were and thought up circumstances in which they might break.

The therapist attempted to supply Norma with the ego functions she lacked, to anticipate, delay, and control actions. The child not only used her therapist for this purpose but took over some of these functions for short periods as if she herself had developed them. Finally, it was possible to approach Norma's feelings of emptiness and their psychic content and to elucidate her confusion between penis and breast. In the context of her eating problems, she expressed the idea that animals have udders to give milk to their babies, while humans have only milk bottles. Then she remembered that ladies have breasts, but patted her genital to show where. She then pointed to the proximity of genitals and udders in animals. Shortly thereafter it was possible to reconstruct the young child fumbling for the propped bottle which forever escaped her.

While much further work was done to support her defective ego functioning, it finally became apparent that these gains were not cumulative. It seemed that Norma made progress on the basis of some inner belief that she would achieve her satisfaction and fullness if she imitated the thought processes and verbal formulations offered her by the therapist. This process did not lead, as it can in the normal child, to autonomous ego functioning which persists in the face of frustration and dissatisfaction. It was at such points that her forward steps revealed their "as if" quality, and there was a massive retreat into miserable and destructive behavior which could not be dealt with.

Norma was tested on the WISC shortly before termination and achieved a prorated verbal I.Q. of 85, which was considered to be a reliable estimate. Her ability to cooperate was limited, and her efforts to involve the tester in her confused inner states resulted after several attempts in only a partial test score. Norma is still enuretic at night. She has attended the High Wick School and can read, write, count, and do simple sums. She can do her own laundry and will help prepare meals and wash up and do housework adequately as long as she is able to contain herself emotionally.

Lucille began treatment at the age of seven years three months. Tall and slender, she was an attractive blonde child, with blue eyes, which frequently had a vacant, dreamy, unfocused expression. In contrast, her movements were direct, purposive, determined, and markedly agile. She usually looked clean, but even when she wore skirts, her appearance lacked feminine softness, probably because of her wiry build. Usually isolated from other children, she could be found alone preoccupied with making a mess with sand and water, eating it, or cleaning it away. Her play was accompanied by a constant monologue, directed to herself or the doll in a scolding, admonishing tone, or describing her intent in the play. At these times her voice was deep in pitch, forceful, loud, quite different from the tone she used for communication. Although she frequently appeared to be oblivious of activities or events about her, she was in fact very perceptive and alert to almost all that occurred on the hospital grounds. She was obsessively preoccupied with hammers and brushes, which represented people.

Lucille was a first and only child (two subsequent pregnancies ended in stillbirths), born to an intelligent, quiet, withdrawn, working-class couple. There was evidence to suggest that they both warded off depression with difficulty. Excessive cleanliness was a feature of the mother's personality. After a difficult delivery without any birthcry, Lucille developed inhalation pneumonia followed by bilateral atelectasis. For the first few days Lucille vomited every feed; later she was a lazy feeder and did not suck easily. She did not sit up until ten months of age. At the same time she was very active bouncing up and down and able to undo the straps of her harness. She learned to walk at about sixteen months, but her motility was uncertain until the age of two and a half years. At four years Lucille's speech was a repetitive, incomprehensible jargon and at seven and a half years it was still abbreviated, telescoped (with reversal of you-I pronouns), and represented condensation of desires, thoughts or broken memories. She became dry but not clean at about fifteen months. Later on she became constipated and passed a motion only after days of irritability ending in violent tantrums. This condition persisted with intermittent, more normal periods until after treatment began. We know that she sat on the pot for long periods and her mother used suppositories. Extremely low frustration tolerance and panic states were expressed in tempers in which she attacked herself as well as others.

All these difficulties with the child made the mother "feel inadequate," and from the latter part of the first year of life the parents gradually became aware that something was wrong.

At five and a half years Lucille was hospitalized for neurological examinations and EEG, which was performed both waking and asleep under Seconal. The findings suggested a local lesion in the left occipital area, without any signs of a gross lesion. X-ray revealed a mild degree of asymmetry of the vault of the skull only, the right frontal bone was more prominent than the left. The relevance of these findings to her mental state was doubtful. There was a marked psychotic overlay. Continued hospitalization was recommended. Psychological tests administered at five and a half years yielded an I.Q. of 71 on the Stanford-Binet Scale and an I.Q. of 89 on the WISC.

In the first year of treatment primary-process thinking was extant; crude instinctual drives, both libidinal and aggressive, were expressed directly in speech, body language or function, and play activity. Her material revealed that she had been traumatized by the primal scene, and that she had a severe touching problem arising from anal masturbation, followed by soiling and playing with her feces. The touching prohibition extended to a variety of things and bodily functions, which were damaging because they were dirty. She attempted to reproduce these activities, which were "allowed" to the parents in displaced fashion, but always precipitated disasters. It appeared that Lucille was dominated by a basic sexual fantasy of danger, freely moving from danger in the present to danger in the past. Causality and time, two concepts vital to the development of ego boundaries, were lacking. Treatment helped her to distinguish between the inner and outer factors contributing to stressful events, to sort out cause and effect, and to anticipate unpleasant experiences, and deal with them in more adaptive ways.

At eight and a half years she was given a toy tortoise with which she remained preoccupied for a long time. Identification with animals was a prominent feature in Lucille's treatment; she often gobbled up cat food and other inedibles, prior to gross destructive attacks on animals. The gift of the tortoise occurred in the second year of treatment at a time when she was extremely depressed following the death of another child cared for by the same housemother. Lucille's despair was increased by the housemother's depressive reaction and inability to turn her attention to Lucille. The tortoise to which she clung, symbolized for her a roof over her head, a permanent and safe place to retreat to. It also epitomized the oneness with her object which she despaired of finding and also her magical wish for self-sufficiency. The failure of her present relationship with her housemother provoked feelings of intense emptiness, helplessness, loss of identity, and a need to preserve the object by incorporation. However, it is doubtful whether this child was ever able to internalize a satisfying object representation; therefore she remained dependent on the external object or its symbol as a replacement. In Lucille's case there never developed the reciprocal relationship between mother and child so essential to provide the affective experience necessary for development (Spitz, 1957).

In Lucille's early life, a cat had indeed been the recipient of her mother's spontaneous attention and affection. The mother remarked: "I felt more for my cat than I was able to feel for Lucille." The "sibling's" death at the hospital now confirmed Lucille's jealous destructiveness and recalled events not long past when she had killed small animals as if they had been the cat who she felt displaced her and received her mother's affection. More recently she was fascinated by a housemother's tortoise protecting itself from attack by withdrawing into its shell, which also provided a home.

Her aggression was constantly provoked by the feeling of not being adequate and loved for herself, and she defended against this anxiety by greedy demandingness and gobbling. She fended off loneliness and emptiness by an attempt to create body fullness, both through eating and anal retention. Later, she demanded eardrops (suppositories) to dissolve the hard, painful wax. It would seem that the infantile, archaic sensory modalities were still highly cathected.

At the time of the rival child's death, despite her intense suffering, Lucille finally organized herself to function, to tidy up, and to engage in constructive activity. She responded more to the personal situations of other children and the housemother. Internally, however, she was even more alone, for she identified only with the ordering aspect of the therapist. Without libidinization, the control she evidenced was insecure and undependable, and she became self-destructive.

The level of object relations moved during treatment in the direction of establishing a symbioticlike attachment with efforts to avoid, rather than incur, pain. At this stage, the you-I confusion decreased, and she began to use the you-I pronouns correctly. The therapist was the gratifier of drives, but, more importantly, she became that part of the ego that sorted out and integrated past and current perceptions of repeated traumatic experiences. The relationship was not libidinized and the therapist did not become a unified, consistent object.

As an alternative to this process, Lucille endowed her chosen objects with sexual and aggressive intent or conceived them like herself as lifeless and "dead." To get the object, she had to be dead, like the missed child, a fantasy which she verbalized. In defense against this anxiety, she requested enemas or tried to fill herself up with grass. She pushed her arm through a window in her need to achieve somatic discharge, precipitate punishment, and achieve a sense of aliveness.

As treatment progressed she perceived her own defects and her inability to identify with more capable children. She thought there was something physically wrong with her head, and, as in the past, saw herself cast out by the housemother as the fecal, smearing child. She requested that the object function as a protector, but the basic model was that of being eaten up. She denied the destructive aspect when she asked if her housemother would swallow her so that she would be in her tummy and then come out again in bowel movements.

Her object relations remained unaltered at the end of treatment and when treatment had to be discontinued, she became totally regressed and withdrawn.

The Purpose of the Profile

The treatment of these children was undertaken at the Hampstead Clinic by trained child therapists under my general direction and supervision. Problems of transport made it possible to see the children only four times weekly. The therapists submitted weekly reports on each child and attempted a more integrated summary of their work at two-monthly intervals. A comprehensive report on each child was submitted at the end of two years of treatment. These reports were read and discussed by Anna Freud and myself as they appeared, and the longer comprehensive reports were read and discussed at general clinic meetings. They were also discussed by the Study Group for Borderline Children whose members have used this case material together with other material available on borderline children attending the Clinic for different studies. This material has also been discussed by the Profile Group.

The aim of the Profile is to present a comprehensive metapsychological picture of a child in which the analyst's thought processes are broken up into their component parts. Profiles can be drawn up at various junctures, at the preliminary diagnostic stage, during analysis, and after the end of analysis, or as a follow-up. "At the diagnostic stage the Profile for each case should be initiated by the referral symptoms of the child, his description, his family background and history, and an enumeration of the possibly significant environmental influences. From these it proceeds to the internal picture of the child which contains information about the *structure* of his personality; the *dynamic* interplay within the structure; some *economic* factors concerning drive activity and the relative strength of id and ego forces; his adaptation to reality; and some genetic assumptions (to be verified during and after treatment)" (Anna Freud, 1962, p. 151; see also 1963, 1965).

Our attempts to use the Profile for the clarification of the problem presented by borderline children led to two findings. On the one hand, the Profile enabled us to highlight aspects of the children's chaotic development and reaction to treatment. On the other hand, the apparently more significant characteristics also appeared in a wide variety of other diagnostic categories in which the disturbance arose in the earliest infantile period. These characteristics therefore did not differentiate between a gross disturbance such as our children manifest and other severe disturbances with arrested development where the children nevertheless show greater adaptive capacity and lack psychotic features.

We have, therefore, studied manifestations of behavior and functioning which seem significant for the group and for which the Profile does not yet make provision or does so only by implication which we now attempt to define. The aim of this report is to indicate our attempts to modify the Profile where it has not proved a fine enough sieve to differentiate between the degree of disturbance we are studying and lesser disturbances which are better understood. We have chosen for discussion only those aspects of the Profile on which our work has recently concentrated for their potentiality in understanding these peculiar difficulties and which have an overriding significance for our chlidren. It is hoped that such understanding may eventually contribute to a clearer discrimination of the processes of earliest ego growth and the factors on which this depends.

Aspects of the Profile Selected for Discussion

A. Family Background and Personal History (Profile Point III[3])

1. Only two of our cases show evidence of gross disturbance in one or both parents, though none of them would qualify as normal. In a third the mother reports her outstanding inability to relate to this particular child from birth, though the mother herself is not a

[3] Points A and B of our Profile headings and their immediate subheadings represent the original plan of the Profile, while the subheadings "Cathexis of Self" and "Cathexis of Objects" represent modifications deemed necessary for the description of the group of children under discussion.

grossly disturbed person. While the parents of the fourth child are highly anxious and have debilitating neurotic symptoms, their social adaptation is constructive and well within the norm for the population.

2. All children showed early feeding disturbances and derivatives of these persist.

3. Speech was uniformly delayed in all children, and all continue to show some disturbance of this function.

4. Two of the children are reported to have shown an abnormal degree of erratic and aimless activity early in life and this has persisted to a large extent; in a third, these manifestations developed later, a fourth was a constant rocker well beyond the period when this activity usually subsides. Three of the children had a history of sleep disturbances and excessive crying fits from an early age, unduly prolonged beyond infancy.

5. History and analysis reveal that the children were exposed to potentially damaging experiences at a very early age. While the traumatophilic features of this type of child are well known, the experiences referred to do not permit the inference that they were initially self-engendered.

6. They all are now in a hospital because their families were unable or unwilling to cope with their unmanageable behavior.

At present we are not in a position to assess the importance of any one of these features, or to suggest that singly or together they may account for the peculiar and far-reaching character of these children's disturbances. The comparative data do, however, highlight one factor. In the histories of more normal children we are used to finding a dynamic interrelatedness in a succession of symptoms, one giving place to another with the growing age and maturity of the child. For example, in neurotic children an early disturbance in feeding or habit training may clear up totally and be replaced by a learning inhibition or a school phobia. Phobias arising in the phallic phase may be directed to a changing series of situations as one phobic object is replaced by another. This does not happen in these children. The intractable survival of erratic and aimless behavior and the persistence of early feeding and sleeping disturbances are manifestations which may come to have some etiological significance when they are better understood.

B. Assessment of Development (Profile Point V)

1. DRIVE DEVELOPMENT WITH REGARD TO PHASE DOMINANCE[4]

The presenting picture is an overlapping of phases with oral, anal, and phallic manifestations and no evidence of latency. The bulk of libido is active in primitive forms at the oral and anal stages. Its quantitative distribution is difficult to evaluate in the present state of our knowledge. Crudely impulsive oral manifestations in action and fantasy are common in this group, though finger sucking is absent; the object relations of all four children are partly tied to this phase by fantasies of incorporation and primitive identificatory mechanisms. Unintegrated phallic manifestations exist in all cases, without phallic dominance, and without the appropriate developments in ego and object relations. In only one case, Basil, is there an area of structured ego functioning akin to what we expect at the phallic stage. Nevertheless, in this child the archaic ego attitudes seem to have persisted from a very early age; they are isolated to some degree from his structured development but intensively color all his feeling attitudes. While there is some evidence that instinctual development is open to influence by the process of analysis, the general picture is one of arrested libidinal development.

While this picture can be found in a great number and variety of unrelated disturbances, the degree of arrest and its intense and unremitting character are outstanding in our cases.

2. DEVELOPMENT WITH REGARD TO DISTRIBUTION OF LIBIDO AND AGGRESSION

a. *Cathexis of Self*

(1) *The self as a body*

In children who move unpredictably back and forth between various levels of maturity, it is not possible to draw clear-cut lines of development between the self as a psychic entity built on a firmly demarcated body image with recognizable experiences of pleasure

[4] In Anna Freud's Profile the development and distribution of libido and aggression are treated separately. In applying the Profile to psychotic children, we have not separated libido and aggression because to do so would suggest a greater degree of differentiation than is apparent from our observation.

and pain, and more archaic forms of body experience which we have learned to attribute to the developing infant. In following the transitions of our children's self experiences we encountered the following confusions:

1. A confusion of inner emotional states with body fullness or emptiness.

Lucille described another child in these terms: "She's got motions in her; that makes her happy." Lucille also envied children who were given suppositories or enemas for the same reason that in this way they achieved fullness. When she felt lonely and neglected, she ate dirt and plasticine. Basil constantly craved for food supplies and measured his feeling of well-being by the supplies available. He was anxious about defecating because: "You never know when you sit on that hole what will happen. Everything may fall out and you'd find yourself being a skeleton with nothing but a bit of skin holding you together." Urinating, bleeding, and even crying were experienced in terms of breaking apart. His concern over losing part of himself by coughing or sneezing reached a climax in a session when he had a bad cold. He spent the whole hour trying to ascertain whether it was safer to blow out the mucus through the nose than to pull it up and keep it, and which way would secure replacement. This fear extended to his genitals. "If you are a daddy and don't want to make a baby, can you save the seed? What happens if you lose it somewhere?" While these confusions are often found in the fantasies of adult neurotic patients, the latter are highly developed formations in contrast to those of our children which appear to reflect early developmental stages and belong to the pleasure-pain series. In the adult neurotic, feelings of fullness and emptiness frequently denote pregnancy fantasies, and fears of loss of body content are related to the threat of castration. These children's experiences and their meaning can be differentiated from the more mature fantasies of the adult neurotic only on the basis of the contexts in which they emerge and the level of interpretation to which the child responds. For example, only when Lucille's feelings of fullness and Basil's fear for his viscera and genitalia were interpreted as reflecting the loss of an object did the children accept the therapist's understanding. While the possibility is still left open that these expressions were overdetermined, several years of analysis intervened without their more extended meanings appearing to have any validity for the children.

2. A confusion of inner emotional states with peripheral sensations.

When Norma felt content she described herself as having a "tender and delicate face." She thought her therapist had "different kinds of worries, nice tender ones." When she was angry she had to whisper because her therapist "had tender and delicate ears." Her angry feelings were constantly confused with a noisy impact on her "delicate ears." She sometimes felt she had square ears. Round ears were soft and delicate, square ears were painful and belonged with angry feelings. Once when she was afraid of being cross during an anticipated visit, she asked for a swimming cap to protect her hair. In this context the cap was to prevent her having feelings which were experienced as a hurting head. Once she repudiated the need for a therapist in these words: "Don't want feeling doctor. Want dentist. Don't talk about feelings. Talk about teeth, upper teeth, lower teeth, baby teeth." Anger was often experienced as a splinter in her throat. Uncomfortable feelings of being to blame were described thus: "They make me feel not so pretty, a buzzing in the head."

When Norma was upset or disliked something for its emotional impact, she referred, quite out of context, to its sensory and not to its emotional qualities. "No-like puppet-panda. It has rough edge. What panda eats? Neck too rough, hurts my finger." She showed the hurt finger and then had an itchy toe. She connected these hurts with the bites of a crocodile whose "bumps" intrigued her. "Why it have bumps on skin? Who made teeth, will teeth bite? Ladies have bumps. They have brown spots [breast aureoles]."

In two additional confusions *the integrating attempts at defense* against states of disintegration are more evident.

3. A confusion of the state of well-being with the possession of symbolic bodily attachments.

In spite of the apparent relation of this material to phallic anxieties, interpretation at this level resulted only in an endless proliferation of fantasy, while interpretation at the level of the child's need to replenish "bodily emptiness" brought about some resolution, though only temporarily.

Norma tried to attach rubber tubes to her genitalia and fitted flippers to her feet. She made herself breast appendages and added high heels to her shoes. She made a complete study of the entrails of birds and (by inquiry) of humans, to persuade herself that she was not empty inside. Ultimately it became clear that she equated these appendages with the functioning of a constantly replenishing breast. It was possible to reconstruct early feeding situations in which her bottle was propped and she constantly lost contact with the nipple. At this point she gave up her use of body appendages.

4. A confusion of the state of well-being with the possession of a symbolic object which could be kept within the body orbit by vision.

Basil made the transition from the Clinic to the waiting car which conveyed him to and from treatment by placing a box of chocolates in the back window of the car so that it could be seen from the treatment room, and in reverse by placing notices in the Clinic windows which could be seen from the car. These devices helped him to retain a feeling of self without "falling apart" as he moved between car and Clinic.

Relatively normal children also utilize symbolic objects in their attempts to defend against anxiety caused by loss of their objects. The degree of their anxiety usually indicates the intensity of a highly ambivalent object relationship. To Basil, however, the therapist appeared not as a person but rather like a known experience which acted, for the period of her presence, as a skin holding him together and preventing him from breaking to pieces. What he feared was a complex of *bodily* sensations which felt like breaking to pieces physically, because the holding-together-therapist experience or alternately the holding-together-car experience was lacking. However we may conceive of the dynamics of this situation, it must be distinguished from the normal child's experience of defense against an imminent *affective* state linked with a whole object relationship.

These confusions seem to arise in a futile attempt to organize organic and peripheral sensations into an abiding sense of a bodily self. They significantly lack the experience of emotional states with specific *quality* as we know them, and are characterized by an intense, diffuse form of excitement. Basil expressed this as follows: "I feel like electricity inside. What I need is a fuse box to give me warning before I get too excited and wild. Getting excited is like breaking in two."

Norma also drew attention to the exaggerated *quantity* of her inner states. "Not hurt much—little hurt not hurt." It would be possible to deduce that the quantitative element and its overwhelming, unorganized character as well as its quality as excitement are responsible for the sense of "hurt" in all the children.

It is not possible to link this diffuse state with a particular level of instinctual need. Excitement at the various instinctual levels seems to manifest itself at the *more integrated* levels of the children's functioning.[5] But the diffuse state is accompanied by the most intense and ungovernable anxiety and gives rise to aggressive reactions of great magnitude. Some children feel threatened with bodily disintegration, some are driven to wandering, some to killing animals, some to violent attacks on themselves or others; the person attacked may be an uninvolved person.

There is evidence that these outbreaks follow ineffectual attempts to obliterate feelings. Norma, for instance, often wished she were dead, which to her meant not to have any feelings. But the feeling of being dead was also unpleasant. This primitive mechanism of obliteration could be traced more clearly when greater maturity of feeling was evident following some analytic intervention. Norma treated more normal feelings of anxiety and depression as if they were foreign bodies which could be shaken out of her system. She was then given to standing on her head to rid herself of them. Only much later when Norma could recognize the value of the human object were we able to observe these primitive reactions give place to recognizable defense mechanisms.

Lucille could say at a later stage in her analysis when her housemother left the hospital, "We'll talk about anyone but not Miss B. She's not nasty but we won't talk about her."

There is evidence that the child's perception of emotional states is replaced by the perception of organic and peripheral sensations and represents a partial arrest at a primitive form of pre-emotional experience. This primitive state is superseded only when a certain level of object cathexis and ego development has been reached. As a result

[5] All the children masturbate, some anally; none make use of finger sucking. We are reminded that autoplastic modes of discharge are influential in maintaining whatever psychic unity the child may have achieved (Anna Freud, 1954, p. 61). The absence of finger sucking may be a significant diagnostic feature in pinpointing the absence of a basic form of object relationship without which normal integration cannot be achieved.

of this development the experience of excitement is tamed and can then assume the function of a signal of anticipated instinctual activity.[6]

When first encountered prior to analytic intervention the sensory experiences described seem to bypass the existence of the human object. It is as if the children were unaware that satisfaction had anything to do with the human person and as if the feeling experiences that would be appropriate in this respect were unknown to them. In Mahler's term (1952), they operate at a stage of primary body narcissism.[7]

6 ". . . in comparison with unconscious ideas there is the important difference [between unconscious affect and unconscious idea] that unconscious ideas continue to exist after repression as actual structures in the system *Ucs.*, whereas all that corresponds in that system to unconscious affects is a potential beginning which is prevented from developing. Strictly speaking, then, and although no fault can be found with the linguistic usage, there are no unconscious affects as there are unconscious ideas. *But there may very well be in the system Ucs. affective structures which, like others, become conscious.* The whole difference arises from the fact that ideas are cathexes—basically of memory-traces—whilst affects and emotions correspond to processes of discharge, *the final manifestations of which are perceived as feelings.* In the present state of our knowledge of affects and emotions we cannot express this difference more clearly" (Freud, 1915, p. 178, our italics). The "affective structures" to which Freud refers may have some correspondence to built-in systems regulating organic and peripheral discharge. These systems may antedate the period at which the oral erotic zone is dominant and may act as an overflow system of discharge even after that zone has been established. They appear to continue to characterize the psychotic child's experience of affect and may belong to the undifferentiated id-ego described by Hartmann (1952). In discussing this footnote, Anna Freud pointed to the need to consider the question: under what conditions does the child return to experiencing affect in terms of bodily sensation after having already achieved the capacity for normal and appropriate affect.

7 "The newborn and young infant gradually must be brought out of this tendency toward vegetative splanchnic regression, out of the tendency to lapse into this exhausted, semistuporous state, into an increased sensory awareness of, and contact with, his environment (Greenacre, 1945; Spitz, 1946). In terms of energy or libidinal cathexis this means that a progressive displacement of energy quanitities from the inside of the body (particularly from the abdominal organs toward the periphery of the body) has to occur so that the perceptual conscious system, as Freud calls the surface of the body, the peripheral rind of the ego, containing the sense organs, may receive cathexis. The turning from predominantly proprioceptive awareness to increased sensory awareness of the outer world occurs through the medium of affective rapport with the mother. The baby's libido position thus proceeds from the stage of fetal narcissism to primary body narcissism, a stage in which representation of the mother's body plays a large part" (Mahler, 1952, p. 287). In the children we describe, both the visceral cavity and the sensory surface would appear to have retained an archaic form of cathexis which in the earliest stage of the analysis seemed in no way connected with the felt need for an object. They solicited the caretaking functions of the adults to deal with their disturbance in an adventitious way, if at all, much as they might ask for a minor cut to be bound up.

The children do not have internally consistent object relations at any one time, and they unpredictably move back and forward between different stages of object orientation (see "Cathexis of Objects"). There is, however, a considerable uniformity in their *more archaic* states which appear side by side with some disparity in their ability to take up more advanced positions. What is abundantly clear is that at this point they all seek and can verbalize a demand for a state of homeostatic equilibrium which is felt as deriving from different sources at different times.

The following sources seem to approach but not fulfill the desired state of balance (fullness): (1) soothing sensory stimulation; (2) primitive instinctual gratification at all pregenital levels; (3) the continuous presence of the object who, the child expects, will be totally responsible for instinctual gratification and control and for the elimination of undue excitement.

Basil stated: "I don't want a therapist. I want someone there all the time. I want to be *looked at* all the time."[8] Norma expressed this wish in terms of being a baby monkey clinging always to the body of a mother. At times of intense excitement she would say: "Hold me I am so bad." We have called this *the stage of the object as auxiliary ego*. Provided the object fulfills the child's conditions, there is almost no recognition of the object's identity. Even her physical appearance is readily mistaken (see "Cathexis of Objects"). Basil always asked for his "therapy" on arrival, not his therapist. When told of an impending absence, he would say: "Then who will give me my therapy?"

The children's attempt to maintain a state of mental equilibrium is doomed to failure, because this attempt is based on an archaic model of feeling which is out of harmony with their more advanced instinctual and physical development and their uneven ego states. Instinctual pleasure is necessarily transitory and is in these children insufficiently reinforced by pleasant memories of past gratification and the assurance of future ones. The model, however, seems to presuppose the activation of memory traces involving some good experi-

[8] This statement recalls to the observer—though not to the child—the role of the mother as watcher and executor of the child's wishes when the child becomes capable of locomotion (see Spitz, 1957). At this and earlier phases the child may conceive of the situation as being held together by the mother's look.

ence with an object. With growing frequency and for lengthening periods they become aware of this in analysis.

Norma once linked the "dead" feeling with the absence of an object. She described a dead bird she had found as follows: "Dead Mummy bird. No baby. The baby all finished, 1962. Dead Mummy bird, 1962." On a later occasion she had been able to maintain her sense of well-being for some days, but it vanished as soon as she experienced some disappointment in her therapist. She described the change in this way: "Now my baby [herself] all dead. All the magic gone." In the course of treatment she moved from collecting transitory and unconnected symbolic objects which were inevitably lost, to amassing a large collection of silver paper which she used sparingly and with discrimination so that she would always have some for future use. As treatment progressed there was an increasingly spontaneous and continuous recognition of the value of the human object and the specific emotional states generated by loss. However, an unusually great or unexpected threat of loss could always revive the diffuse manic type of excitement with its threat of disintegration and total loss of control. In Basil's case we have become sure only now that his sense of physical emptiness can be replaced by feelings for an object, or by states of feeling with a recognizably normal quality, which are capable of reinforcing his self-love. On separating from his mother on an occasion when they had both been pleased with his adjustment at home, he said, "Today, I would not have cried even if she had not given me any chocolate. I thought it was the chocolate last week I missed but it was not."

While all the children achieved a small vocabulary for describing feeling states, we were cautious in judging this new facility as representing a true change in emotional experience because of their easy adoption of adult patter.

We have confined this account to the descriptive level. In two of our cases, treatment failed to enable the children permanently to obtain greater specificity and more varied quality in their emotional states. Moreover (except in the case of Basil, who is known to have developed more mature instinctual and ego positions), we do not know why object cathexis has been kept at so low a level. We have few definitive clues to whether the primitive way of experiencing emotions arose in a retreat from the object because of pain and frustration, and if so, why it was so total. Spitz (1945, 1957), in his observations of hospitalized babies aged nine months to one year and a half, records the manifest unpleasure which they evidenced at the human approach and the rotating avoidance movements of the head which this engendered. Spitz specifically connects this rejecting reaction with a dislike of rising tension intruding on a pathological state of lethargy. The institutionalized children described by Provence and Lipton (1962) ultimately failed to avail themselves of the object only with regard to some aspects of care. For example, they did not expect help where the normal child would do so. In Provence's children this feature sometimes proved irreversible. We still know too little about the irreversibility of early damage due to defective care. Our own material is too scant to answer the question whether our children's gross ego disturbance is inborn or acquired.

(2) *Psychic image of the self*

While disturbances of body feeling took priority in the children's cathexis of self at the commencement of analysis, the self also existed as a psychic representation in which other features derived from a variety of instinctual and ego states emerged. While these features varied from the magical to the more or less reality-syntonic, they contributed to the small degree of self-esteem which the children maintained.

(i) Elements Deriving from Fantasies of a Primary Narcissistic Character

The ability to verbalize feelings of omnipotent self-importance arising in fantasies of *magical action* appeared in the most developed of our cases and was absent in others. We are inclined to attach some benign prognostic value to this aspect.

In treatment Basil felt he should never wait. The car should be waiting for him, the road clear, and the therapist on the doorstep to receive him. Fog and traffic jams were experienced as personal affronts and reacted to by an increase of omnipotent thinking. "I felt like opening that door, stepping right out and turning myself into a giant and pushing all that traffic out of the way." He planned to write letters of complaint to the bus companies and often did.

When Stanley opened the Clinic door and saw the sun shining

he felt he had brought this about. He also felt it specially shone for him. "Every time we come into therapy, the sun shines." Stanley maintained some self-esteem through the bravura with which he brandished aggressive and libidinized *words,* in a meaningless and omnipotent way. These words had a demoralizing effect on adults and children alike and when other children adopted them, Stanley's self-esteem was increased.

In Norma's psychopathology, a masochistic self-blame for all the catastrophes which occurred in the hospital was an outstanding feature. She constantly ruminated about her imagined part in causing illness and used this "worry" to present herself as needing care from her objects. The most intractable aspect of this feature was embedded in masochistic self-love generated by her belief in the magic of her aggressive *thoughts.*

Basil came back from a holiday saying everything had been fine. After he had expatiated on this for some time, his therapist said she had some doubts because he was involuntarily shaking his head, which, she said, must be a *magic gesture* to keep him feeling good and happy. Basil replied, "But it helps me," adding that his mother had been ill and he had met her new boyfriend. The head-shake immediately diminished to a token, and finally disappeared some weeks later. *Magical wishes* at one time dominated Basil's view of himself. He referred to himself as the most popular boy in High Wick and drew attention to himself everywhere without discrimination.

(ii) Elements Deriving from Objects

All the children maintain what sense of well-being they can by demanding constant tokens or gifts from their objects. This is an endless and disappointing process, bringing only transitory satisfaction.

It was important to Basil that he should collect as many things as possible to put in his locker. When the locker was full, he felt "full." It was best when the things were quite new and intact. He locked them away so that no one should damage them or even touch them. He would finger them himself with satisfaction and show them off to others. He collected books but neither read nor used them himself. The mere quantity and newness were sufficient. He kept his bike, a birthday gift from his mother, locked away while he competed for the use of the hospital bike, which he would joyously crash into the fence; he never did this with his own bike.

Norma emphasized that the indiscriminate and valueless things she collected from her objects kept her "safe." Unlike Basil, she kept them only for short periods. Her growing ability to retain the good memory of the giver could be measured by the time it took to lose or destroy them.

Stanley collected valueless objects with the aim of having more and more.

All the children collected words from their special caretakers, often with little understanding of their meaning. These collections were subject to considerable flux and were tenuously dependent on the child's growing object relations. It was often possible to trace the current importance of a human object to Norma by her temporary selection of words.

In the early stage of his analysis, Basil asked his therapist for a cash register. This gift brought enduring and exceptional bliss. To him, it represented all he desired of a love object: it was a machine and thus entirely under his control; it could be locked away and was therefore always available; it lent itself to living out in concrete symbolic form his wish for continuous oral supplies. Since the contents could be used over and over again, the danger of loss of content was eliminated. The extent to which his well-being depended on it became apparent when he labeled his locker "Basil, with cash register." Basil went through a stage of hoarding pocket money, thus giving himself "fullness" and safety. Much later he employed his pocket money to buy objects which he protected and made use of and which he was willing to share.

Lucille was for a long time preoccupied with the gift of a toy tortoise. This symbolized to her (by transitory identification) a roof over her head which would be permanent and a safe place of retreat. It expressed her wish for magical self-sufficiency as well as her sense of unrelatedness and also epitomized the oneness with her object which she despaired of finding.[9]

[9] In a discussion, Anna Freud suggested that the stages in cathexis of self and objects made explicit in this paper in order to capture the particular qualities of psychotic functioning might be retained in the Profile and be assessed in all children. While in psychotic children, these archaic phenomena have a rigidity and gross inappropriateness to age, in other disturbances they manifest themselves in a more fluid and transient

(iii) Elements Deriving from Ego Activity

(a) *Modification of behavior.* While all the children appeared to mature in response to the opportunity for object cathexis afforded them, the tenacity with which they adhered to their accomplishments was uncertain. After a period of analysis these appeared to be rigidly tied to the wish to please and thus retain the object through conformity to its wishes. Their achievements had little cathexis in their own right, and their retention was therefore subject to the extreme vicissitudes of the children's object relations, the nature and level of which changed unpredictably.

At a time of great depression, Lucille could tidy up at the end of the hour when help was not forthcoming from the therapist, at the same time reminding herself that she could not have the object with her always. Her activity, however, had the quality of a performance she was demanding of herself out of fear of loss of the object's care and attention. Her identification with the ordering aspect of the object appeared libidinally incomplete—a barren imitativeness.[10]

Norma was cross with her nurse, shut herself in her bedroom, soiled her bed, and smeared the walls deliberately. While she showed anxiety about this when she came to therapy, the fear of disapproval and not shame was the outstanding emotion.

It sometimes appeared that the children had occasional insight into this discrepancy in their make-up.

When Norma had been particularly provocative and was later prepared to be more compliant, she would cover her face with a mask and ask how pretty she was now.

When conformity was established it tended to be a blind conformity in which the adult's demand was in no way mitigated by the child's ability to judge time and circumstance.

Basil's mother was cross because he came home in winter without his scarf. Basil now insists on wearing a scarf when going home, no

---

fashion. The extent to which they have been retained in the personality or returned to at a later age should facilitate quantitative and qualitative comparisons and sharpen the differential diagnostic features between types of disturbance. Blind children also collect seemingly valueless articles and these collections appear to be aimed at raising their self-esteem. The collection of words is also a feature of the adolescent's attempt to obtain oneness with his objects.

[10] We are, however, reminded of a remark which Ferenczi is reported to have made: that all morality begins in an act of hypocrisy. This could with justification be amended to all sublimations begin in such an act.

matter what the weather. "My mother will be cross," he says to any protest.

Sometimes one had the impression that as a result of behavioral modification the children were for long times more anxious and lonely and not more self-esteeming or self-sufficient.

Norma, whose aim is to be adopted by her aunt, exerts the most painful self-control in the period prior to her visit and is ridden with anxiety and fear of being unable to please. Her efforts produce greater certainty in the adults that she will be able to behave well, but they produce no such certainty in her and relatively little pleasure. On the other hand she has recently "lit up" when her therapist has been genuinely able to praise her.

It has become a feature of therapeutic technique to show the children from time to time their advances and encourage their pleasure in this. Basil and Stanley both became able to take stock of their development and gain a measure of self-esteem. However, it is doubtful whether in either child this improvement would altogether outlast a failure in the support they are afforded by their special objects.

(b) *Maturation of skills.* While the ability to learn and perfect new skills varied, the children had certain features in common which at their age were unusual.

They showed an unusual degree of selectiveness as to the person with whom they would exercise these skills; this selectivity is normally observed in the second year of life and again later in the latency child's division of home and school activities which he keeps apart.[11]

Lucille would make things only with her therapist and her teacher. The libidinal aspect of the process seemed to be confined to the presence and participation of the object and did not adhere to the process itself.

On the other hand, the content of the construction was often

[11] Anna Freud noted, in a discussion, that these children represent an extreme version of the general dependence of learning on the presence of a love object. However, in this group there is a massive discarding of learned skills in the face of object loss, more basic and excessive than in younger children and in depressed patients. In Lucille, the loss of her therapist precipitated the loss of the moderate gains of the analysis which were never recovered.

used to add a libidinal element which the child experienced as missing in the object relationship.

In a period of depression, Lucille insisted that the therapist make for her a tiny swimming boat with a baby figure in it, which gave her real pleasure and filled out her empty relationships.

The vicissitudes of the object relationship were reflected in the fluctuation of effort directed toward the skilled activity.

On her return from holiday to High Wick Norma attempted to ride a bicycle and wanted to learn to skate. This was clearly an attempt to recapture her High Wick objects and keep them with her and when this did not succeed she attempted to destroy her bicycle and the word "bicycle" became phobic.

There is often a short and unusually productive period following a setback in Norma's relationships. When her housemother left, she made her first attempts to read and write which were very successful. This lasted only a few weeks, however. Recently she said: "When I feel bad, I work so as to feel better. I am in a rush to learn to grow up."

The attempt to displace libidinal cathexis in the direction of sublimation is made all the time and with some success, but far from age-adequately. It is not clear whether more than one feature in the psychopathology contributes to this. It is a peculiar quality of the children's object relationships that they continue to exist at many levels simultaneously and that the tendency to total withdrawal is never completely absent (see "Cathexis of Objects"). We may postulate a special quality of the libido, an adhesiveness or inability to give up primitive libidinal positions, whether for reasons familiar to us in connection with the concept of fixation points, or because of some quantitative lack in the libido itself or a constitutional imbalance between libidinal and aggressive drives. We would then have to postulate a pathology of the drives which impedes ego development and reality orientation.

On the other hand, Loewald (1951) describes how the child's attitude to reality and his ability to build boundaries between his inner and outer world bear the imprint of the stages of his relation to his object. While the primary narcissistic identity with the mother constitutes a libidinal motive force for the ego's striving to progressive differentiation and unification of reality, it is also the source of a threat to perpetuate and re-establish this position and engulf the emerging ego into its primary narcissistic unity, "the unstructured nothingness of identity of 'ego' and 'reality' " (p. 17). Hartmann (1956) states: "The transition from 'egocentric' thinking to recognizing the relativity of qualities depends on the insight into the relativity of the 'me' " (p. 42).

Basil, the most advanced of the children has still clearly stopped short of this phase of development. His housemother reports on a journey to the Clinic: "Basil was reading a book, so I was talking to Norma. She was going on about her worries with words. I said they didn't worry me as I had too much to think about. Basil looked up and said, 'Yes, you think about me don't you.' "

We might also postulate that the extreme difficulty these children have in displacing libido in the direction of sublimations and in maintaining them is evidence of a primary deficiency in the ego, an ego which is unable to lend its energies to maintain the positions the children constantly begin to take up and just as constantly fall back from.

Norma appears to verbalize some such feeling when she says, "Wind me up [like a clockwork toy] so that I go," and, "I am in a rush to learn to grow up." Sometimes Norma also seems to be paralyzed by the effort she makes toward reality orientation.[12]

Our observations suggest that in these children growth occurs under great stress, proceeds slowly, and that they experience much less pleasure in their accomplishments than normal children do. While their self-esteem owes a little to their growing skills, the

12 In a discussion, Anna Freud suggested that such eagerness to reach a higher point of development at a time when ego control was not adequate to the achievement was analogous to a child vainly trying to establish urinary control for the sake of the object when he is not physiologically equipped to do so. In our children, however, the search for homeostasis through the use of and cooperation with the object, not object love in itself, is the prior and more pervading need. Martin James raised the possibility that a very early experience of being dissociated from the mother might be a relevant factor. He was reminded of those mothers who did not respond to the infant's needs but rather encouraged the infant to perform in a way that would satisfy their own needs—a situation which sets up a dystonic experience for the baby, interrupts the mutuality of the mother-child relationship, and prematurely emphasizes for the baby his separateness from his environment. Joseph Sandler stressed the distinction between behavior aimed at reducing and discharging instinctual tension and that geared to securing well-being from the object. In these children the instinctual side was secondary to the ego's need to attain and preserve feelings of safety and integration afforded by the presence of the object. It was not a true libidinal cathexis of the object.

limited nature of these skills is also the source of great anxiety and disappointment. When they suffer the additional stress of object deprivation, constructive activities disappear and the cathexis of the self diminishes.

At a time when her therapist was absent because of a prolonged illness Norma appeared dressed in a towel the former had left behind. Asked who she was, she replied, "Nobody." Whenever anyone left her, she assumed a transitory identity by wearing portions of their clothing.

At present the following hypothesis seems most valid to us: the fulfillment of ego potential for which the children strive unavailingly and which they lose so readily may depend on a primitive stage of mother-child relatedness which for unknown reasons was never achieved. Without this, the libidinization of ego functions and their consequent maturation does not take place. In Basil's case, there was considerable achievement, manifesting itself in an age-adequate scholastic competency. Nevertheless, the original maternal unrelatedness, which may have been less in degree than in our other cases, persists in his insatiable emptiness and sense of persecution whenever he experiences normal frustrations. Our uncertainty about the adequacy of our analytic techniques still leaves open the problem whether the damage sustained is reversible. We might expect different degrees of reversibility in different cases of early damage.

(c) *The ideal self.* At the onset of treatment the children show no evidence of any wish *to be* something different from what they are. The emphasis is altogether on *having* something which they endow with the power of altering their uncomfortable states of psychic tension. This varies from the need for special food (Basil) or presents of token objects with symbolic value to permanent attention from the desired object for purposes of maintaining homeostasis and instinctual equilibrium. The emphasis throughout is on the attempt to find means of dissipating internal states of discomfort.

The wish *to become* other than they are emerges in all the children during treatment. While the wish to retain an object as a constant source of supply comes into existence at an early stage in treatment, the fact that the object can be retained in memory is the child's first introduction to the need for change in his own internal functioning as the only solution to his problems. Gradually he voices the need to live in an ordinary home with a permanent object; with this emerges the wish to be normal, expressed differently by each child. They all become *intellectually* quite clear that this involves the ability to control behavior without distraction from their chaotic emotions.

The ability *to anticipate* a state of well-being, however vaguely defined, is at first not related to *intentionality* in which self-direction is a governing force. It is rather related to being given something or possessing something or having something done to them in a way which will produce a magical result. This attitude, characteristic of the stage preceding structuralization, implies that change can be initiated only by an outside agency.

Norma still wishes to reach her ideal by *magical means.* She frequently asks to be "wound up" like a clockwork toy, so that she will "go."

Basil at first felt that living at home would magically endow him with normality. However, when he visited his home, his chaotic behavior made the family and him equally unhappy. Only much later did he set himself the aims of self-control and maintenance of unaggressive behavior, and then became very critical of those who could not live up to this standard. It is still doubtful whether he has established a libidinal cathexis of these ideas for their own sake as distinct from the advantages which they buy, namely, praise and an assured welcome.

Stanley's ideal is attached to the wish to attend a "normal" school, a wish that is overdetermined. "To have a normal school" is partly a residue of the need to possess a talisman as an aid to instinctual equilibrium. It has also some of the qualities of a phallic idea; at the same time it acts as a defense against his oedipal fears which manifest themselves on visits home. Nevertheless, this ideal contains elements of the wish to become different and thus motivates his growing self-control, though the latter is not yet adequately cathected. A short comparative study of his development in this respect is of great interest. At the onset of treatment Stanley could not tolerate any mention of "when you were little." This seemed to have the effect of undermining his present abilities and to expose him to regression. It acted like a threat to his self-regard in the present as if the words would magically reduce him to "littleness." But recently when he asked for some string to take home as a memento of his therapist, she refused, saying, "Now you can remember me." Stanley agreed, saying, "Do you remember when I used to make timetables to remember you?" He referred to a much earlier time of great emotional upset when he despaired at the end of each session of ever seeing the therapist again and marked off the intervening time on a chart, in an endeavor to combat his feeling that the absent object no longer existed. The stabilization of his object representation was now clearly linked with the stabilization of self boundaries and the ability to contemplate changes in the self without the fear of dissolution. These changes would therefore appear to have laid a foundation for encompassing *a time concept* in relation to the self. This development must be central to the ability of maintaining distance from the self as a changing or growing entity without experiencing a threat of dissolution, and would therefore lend momentum to the growth of the capacity to make and tolerate judgments about the self. It is apparently an important step in the abandonment of primary-process thinking. This development must be a necessary first step in the process to which Hartmann (1956) refers as achievement of "the relativity of 'me.' " This seems to be an area in which the libidinal cathexis of the object and the cathexis of ego functions are closely interrelated.[13]

[13] Anna Freud noted that the phenomena under discussion represented an area in which the move from primary- to secondary-process thinking could be studied. Behind Stanley's belief in the magic of words was his fear of any reference to a past self and this thought was of the order of a dream representation which depicts a time of being little as an image of someone *now* little. Joseph Sandler added that Stanley's later development showed a growing capacity for thinking in relative terms. This dimension, also described by Piaget, appeared to involve a move from an egocentric mode, operating on a "here and now" basis which precluded the possibility of imagining a different self, to a stage where the child could step outside himself and view himself in relation to his objects and his environment. The authors noted that the step from egocentricity initiated in Stanley and others a tolerance for the revival of memories and anticipatory thinking about future states. (On the other hand, Basil's ready translation of words into concrete things was a mode of thinking which interfered with his capacity to view himself from a distance.) It was generally agreed that the hierarchy in the development of various functions and their interdependence was a vital consideration for further study. The variability of functioning in our children gives the impression that a function might be available in one activity and not in another and, conversely, that a defect in one function might disturb other functions in a particular area of operation but not have such effect in other areas. Anna Freud noted that the egocentricity and the concrete use of words were part of the primary process. The question she posed was: what are the specific features of the move from primary- to secondary-process functioning; and with regard to the present discussion, when does a child learn to use words in a

The reverse of this process, the loss of cathexis of ego functioning, could be studied in Norma at a late stage in treatment when she was threatened with the loss of her therapist.

Norma became afraid she would get "lost" on the long journey to Hampstead. Since she was driven by a hospital attendant she was clearly referring to a sense of inner "lostness." As she talked about how she could tell people where she lived and ask for help, and wondered how dumb people managed who could not speak, the threat of overall loss of ego functions was clear.

The decathexis of elementary ego functioning was often the prelude to a deeper withdrawal of libido which threatened the body self.

Norma was pleased to be thought sensible enough to visit the village hairdresser for the first time. She had also achieved a dry bed and was praised for this. However, she wanted the nurse to stay and talk to her and when this was not possible and she was left alone, she pulled out two front teeth and showed the blood-stained bed to the nurse on her return. The teeth were not loose and she must have exerted considerable force in this attack on herself.

The sequence would appear to be that the child felt threatened with homeostatic failure through impending withdrawal of libidinal cathexis of ego functions and of the self image, and demanded the presence of the object to hold her together. A refusal led to a cathexis of ego functions and body image with undiluted aggression, and a temporary loss of boundary between self and object.

The instability of the cathectic processes and their unpredictability can be judged by two observations almost contemporaneous with the above, but in complete contrast to them.

At one stage of treatment Norma began to verbalize the discrepancy between what she was and what she would like to be. She said: "I don't like myself because myself is not as nice as other people's." In a recent anxiety state she said, "I shall go to my room and leave the 'moany' Norma there." Here she manifested an intentionality that was directed as much to pleasing herself as to pleasing others.

---

nonmagical way and to see himself in relation to objects. She felt that the individual features of the primary process are probably lost at different times; it was her impression that the magical use of words was abandoned before the egocentric attitude was given up.

Norma rode her bicyle so far ahead of her housemother that the latter was disturbed. "When we came to the town, Norma managed everything so well that I relaxed. She picked up on this in my tone of voice and said 'Now you like me again.' " Norma was able to maintain her ego functioning in a difficult situation and for some considerable time, in spite of her feeling that the object was failing her.

In so far as the children have learned to tolerate a deferred wish to become something different and to anticipate and work for its fulfillment on the basis of seeing the need for internal change as a precondition of gratification, their stage of ideal formation approximates that of the child between three and five years of age. Hartmann (1939) underlines the importance of anticipation in the development of the reality principle and secondary-process thinking. However, the capacity of our children to abstract and maintain libidinization of the ideal is so limited that their strongest efforts toward control and direction have a precarious and tentative quality. Even so primitive an ideal formation, however, can act as a temporary organizing element in the psyche and an elementary source of integration of short duration.

So far our observations seem to suggest that there is a capacity for ego development which is not being consistently used. We are not able to say what the limits of this capacity are; indeed, our evidence covers only the most primitive forms of development and in minimal quantities. The maintenance of this development may well require more complex ego functioning of which the children show no evidence. We are used to observing a similarly unstable cathexis of ego processes in very young children.

Our observations also suggest that to the extent to which we are able to influence object cathexis in a positive fashion, this minimal ego development can be discerned, but not necessarily maintained.

b. *Cathexis of Objects (*Profile Point Vb)

The very varied states of object relatedness which we shall describe should be considered a course over which the children move in two directions, i.e., progressively and regressively. The direction in which they will move at any one moment is quite unpredictable. The initial more primitive stages were more obvious before treatment and appeared later with less frequency and for shorter periods, and the later stages which emerged in the course of treatment were sometimes held to more tenaciously. At later stages it was possible to trace the reasons for regression in terms of a frustrating experience, anticipated or undergone, at other points there seemed to be a fluctuation of defense for unknown reasons, leading to the reinvestment of more primitive positions.

(1) *The tendency toward dissolution in the object*

The precariousness of body boundaries appeared most frequently in children who approached the object for physical comfort and almost immediately withdrew in panic. At times neither Norma nor Lucille could stay in the treatment room close to the therapist but withdrew to the garden. The child seated herself on a mat as if to define her own limits, and the therapist sat near. Confusion of the I-you pronouns appeared in most children, and in Norma and Lucille the *confusion of psychic identity* with that of the object was a massive one.

At a time of great anxiety Lucille used to feed her therapist with a spoon, simultaneously opening and shutting her own mouth.

Norma would ask to be fed with candy from her therapist's mouth, in the mouth-to-mouth position.

Norma asked for a tiny doll to be taped to her hand. When this was done, she burst into tears as the concrete manifestation of the fantasy undermined its reality and she tore the doll off.

At times of severe strain when Norma felt she was "Nobody," she dressed in a towel belonging to the therapist.

These manifestations differ from the role play of normal children in that any interference precipitated an anxiety attack and a state of confusion. There appeared to be a partial fusion of self and object images; this fusion was paramount in the maintenance of the child's equilibrium, but was also perceived as a danger.

(2) *Symbolization of the object in the inanimate and the non-human*

We refer here to the intensive investment of a thing with a quality of relationship normally confined to a person. The attachment appears to be to a *function or functions of the thing* which, because it represents human functioning as it exists or as the child desires or imagines it, appears for a time to create a profound feeling that we expect to see only in relation to the human object. At its most primitive level the particular thing invested differs from the transitional object in that it gives no immediate sensuous gratification, such as is given to the child who is attached to a piece of shawl or an article of mother's clothing; it is not cuddly and it does not smell.

Spitz (1957) states: "As we have shown by experiments, no distinction is made [by the three-month-old child] between animate and inanimate surround as long as both possess certain primitive Gestalt attributes" (p. 122).

The totally inhuman Gestalt of our children's symbolic objects may therefore mark them out as representing traces of a very early phase of not-I representation. At the slightly more mature level of their personalities which seems to coexist, it may be part of a defensive maneuver to avoid the sensuous element in objects which threaten the stability of their primitive self images.

Basil's cash register was used for its indefinite capacity to feed and be fed into, to control and be controlled by, for the idea of gratificatory functioning, but not for immediate sensory gratification. It related primarily to homeostasis.

In fact, the symbolic object seems at times to be explicitly chosen because it is incapable of directly stimulating feeling of a sensory type. At other times the emphasis appears to be on its incapacity to suffer damage and become the object of aggression.

Although humanlike toys were available, Lucille for a long time used blocks and beads to symbolize people. She remarked, "These things have no feelings." What could be involved here is the residue of the most primitive not-me, inanimately conceived, "holding-mother" necessary for homeostasis. In normal children, this element does not appear so markedly in their earliest toy selection, although it may be thought to appear in the baby's play with spoons and other functional hard objects. It is usually not noticed because of the preference for the sensuous soft object where the sensory gratification of the "holding-object" has become a markedly discriminated feature, invested with value. Our children's disinterest in and aversion to such soft toys may mean that the inanimate, "holding-object" world has to be established as a necessary foundation for attachment to the sensorily gratifying and finally libidinized object world. Their tendency to touch and fondle live human creatures is always tentative and slight. Either the children lack the development to value this type of gratification or they defend against it by some form of obliteration. There is a further possibility that the toy which is not sensuously gratifying represents a memory image of the dissociated, ungratifying mother. Our material does not allow us to do more than formulate these hypotheses.

It would be important to differentiate in this area the dynamics of the normal developmental displacements involved in the move to the transitional object and ultimately to the toy (infancy) and the hobby (latency and postlatency). The normal advance through play with material having human characteristics or relationships (dolls) to hobby activities involving identification with a functioning human object is an attempt at partial, not total decathexis of earlier satisfactory forms of object relationship. In this respect our children differ significantly from normal children, and this difference probably is at the basis of our doubts concerning the stability of our children's play accomplishments; these have a compulsive, repetitive quality even when they embrace quite marked skills, and appear to have some of the quality of hobbies.

When Lucille's housemother gave her two teddies, Lucille said, "Jean did not know that you wanted a metal tortoise that can't be broken."

Basil played with the window for hours, and then said, "Do you like the window more than me?"

There is no doubt that these objects are cathected at the expense of cathecting humans.

Norma asked for a little object to take with her to keep her safe, "Something that would not break or crumple if washed or tear or get dirty." She selected a little tin bowl but was afraid it might get dented if banged.

Even when the cathexis of the human object was central, it was still in the nature of a cathexis of functioning. The children initially reacted to the treatment and to Clinic personnel in terms of a person's function and not to the person herself. The emphasis was not on the object as libidinal provider.

At the time of the cash register, Basil still asked for his therapy and not his therapist. When Basil had been coming to the Clinic for several months, needing a drink one day in the absence of the receptionist who dispenses the drinks, he turned to a very dissimilar therapist and said, "Is she the orange-juice lady?"

When Lucille's treatment had to stop, it was the treatment not the therapist for which she grieved.

More nearly related to the transitional object, though still lacking in sensuality, is the symbolization of the human part or appendage, used as a substitute for the human object.

Lucille's fantasies often referred to people such as Mr. Leg, Mr. Trouser, Mr. Mouth, giving the impression that such external aspects were all she had been able or willing to encompass.

The idea that people were like things was implicit in Norma's comment on the death of a child: "Why could she not be mended?" The same notion was carried over to her self image when in periods of depletion of self cathexes, she asked to be wound up like a clockwork toy. She still saw herself as made up of pipes like a drainage system. "You pour water in and wee comes out. You need a plumber to unblock you and clear the blockage."

In its primitiveness, this stage has some affinity with Provence and Lipton's institutionalized babies who cathected the bottle before the human object. This statement is certainly an oversimplification, and consideration must be given to the fact that our observations were made when the child was in the company of an adult of whom he was perceptively aware and whom he must have minimally cathected. Nevertheless, our children have an overriding preference for the inanimate and impersonal, which differs fundamentally from the usual displacement of cathexis from the human to the inanimate object. The difference is apparent in the emphasis on safety as distinct from comfort and gratification. The anxiety appears to concern survival.[14]

[14] In assembling our material on this aspect of the children's object relations, we were impressed by the parallel it offered to Tausk's theoretical formulations concerning the origin of the "influencing machine" in adult schizophrenics (1919). His major premise is that the ultimate delusion was preceded much earlier, possibly in childhood, by states (not noticed by observers) in which changes in self and object representation were experienced, rationalized, and otherwise defended against. Tausk's formulation is given an almost slow-motion exemplification by our children. The "estrangement" from the whole body or from a specific organ arising from the perception of its libidinization is exemplified in the cases we have quoted (see, for instance, Norma and Lucille). Subsequent persecution by the "thing" world was shown by Norma (see below), though the defensive mechanisms involved were not identical with Tausk's adult cases. In fact,

The cathexis of the inanimate object represents a retreat from the human object or a fixation at the stage of the most primitive human relatedness; the "thing" elicits no sensuous feeling and its cathexis may sometimes represent a part-way defensive stage in the process of becoming "numb" or "dead," i.e., in the process of emotional obliteration. In Norma, this was most apparent; interest in an inanimate object always coincided with the emergence of a somatic symptom, and was a prelude to the state to be next described, in which the object world was conceived as wantonly depriving and destructive. It would appear, therefore, that there is a secondary anxiety—secondary, that is, to the fear of annihilation—that concerns the dominance of the child's destructiveness toward the human object who fails to meet the child's needs. The retreat to an inanimate world is difficult to maintain, and the double defense of obliteration and somatization finally proves inadequate in the face of internal pressures. The result may be a violent aggressive attack which represents renewed contact with a revitalized but unbearable world.

(3) *Perception of the object world as hostile*

As a result of analysis, the children's need for the object was revived, but they also became demanding and insatiable. Hartmann, Kris, and Loewenstein (1946) describe the young child's normal development in terms of a widening series of satisfactions which begin with sensory and instinctual gratification, embrace satisfactions from the object relationship, and increasingly include satisfaction from his own activities. The absence of satisfaction as distinct from zonal pleasure was a marked feature of the children we are describ-

---

all the children were preoccupied with a machine and its makeup in some specific and compulsive way, but the degree of pathology was often veiled by the fact that these were children at play. Norma constructed a cardboard phonograph which operated by string, and Stanley became expert at electrical wiring. The frustrations involved in these activities gave a veneer of realism to the underlying persecutory feelings. The positive aspects of the mechanical thing were also usually evident. The machine and the thing represented an estrangement from self and object representations, linked together by the process of identificatory thinking (see below). Important changes in instinct theory formulated by Freud in the year immediately following the publication of Tausk's paper and the development of psychoanalytic ego psychology in the intervening years invalidate Tausk's premature explanation of these phenomena. Moreover, while ego regression from established positions of maturity can clearly be seen as deriving from instinctual regression in adult schizophrenics, age-adequate ego functioning has never been established in our children.

ing. For a very long time we had no evidence that they could experience satisfaction. They very rarely expressed pleasure and then only momentarily. When they admit satisfaction now, it is often in a reminiscent mood where the events referred to are in the past.

Lucille said, "You once let me sleep at the other house. Do it again. Take me to tea, get me a koala bear, buy me a cardigan" (all past gratifications).

But even this type of reminiscence is rare. The children remember their deprivations infinitely more than their satisfactions.

Norma said, "When I am feeling bad, I can't remember any nice things at all."

The most outstanding need for the object is as a provider of more and more things which promise satisfaction. When provided, they prove inadequate and for the most part harmful in the child's view.

Norma's demandingness at one point started again. She wanted to invade the other rooms, to equip herself with innumerable objects which were now "necessary." However, each was discarded as too vulnerable, and she started a moaning complaint because "they" did not provide differently. In this context, "they" referred to the unknown makers of objects, not the known people who provided them more immediately. "Why do they make needles that prick? Or airtoys that break? Why don't they put a solid stopper on glue pots? Why rubber? Rubber reminds me of airtoys and balloons that prick and go empty." She could not bring her airtoy to the Clinic because there were too many scissors to prick it. Plastic which was provided reminded her of paper which tore. At this point she threw away her precious collection of silver paper and asked: "Why did you get it for me?" She attempted to make an airtoy with tape and plastic, but the air escaped and it emptied. Finally, she turned on the therapist and asked: "Why don't you get me something interesting?" It was as if the whole inanimate world now lacked the power to afford pleasure. At this point Norma's thoughts ran to clockwork toys that go when they are wound up, humans that have inside works like lungs and a heart that ticks, and from time to time she asked to be wound up. Although she had maintained herself at a higher level for several months, Norma and her therapist appeared to be helpless observers of the dissolution of her inner world.

Stanley's therapist wrote to him when he was ill, saying what a nuisance he had diarrhea. Stanley's reaction was: "Why you say it? It is a silly word. If you write it, it makes me say it. Why you say I am a nuisance? Don't write me letters."

When Basil rang his therapist and she was absent, he later asked, "Did you not answer because you knew it was me?"

Basil does not believe that his siblings were also placed in an institution. He complained: "Perhaps they are at home while I am here." His mother does not lie to him.

Stanley said, "This is more than I can stand. Why does everything go wrong with my life and not with my brothers?"

Stanley asked, "Why am I left-handed? Why me?"

It is the overall appearance of being in a bad world that is so outstanding a feature and which amounts to a total depletion of satisfaction and at times of pleasure, except for the more primitive autoerotic ones.

The anxieties aroused in the context of killing and being killed were maximal at times of illness. On at least one occasion the endeavor to deal with this anxiety gave rise to a hallucinatory experience.

Lucille's therapist visited her when she was ill in bed. Lucille became immediately out of control and screamed for her to leave. She later compared this experience with that of taking LSD, which she had once been given.

In the neurotic child, "the hostility of the world" can be understood as the result of projection arising in the context of destructive wishes in a state of gross dissatisfaction. However, the mechanism in our children appears rather to be an uncontrollable externalization brought about by the tenuousness of boundaries between the self and the external world. Moreover, while projection is effective in maintaining a libidinal position, this mechanism of externalization may again result in entirely emptying the self of feeling. Its aftermath may be a series of anxiety attacks which lead to chaotic functioning of catastrophic dimensions, and continue for days on end, often followed by a period of placid functioning.

The wish to be devoid of feeling carries with it the obliteration in memory of the immediately provoking situation which becomes unusually difficult to ascertain. It is a feature of the children's analytic development that this technical problem lessened and a temporary change in their ego capacity to maintain the relationship between feeling and precipitating event ensued; their new capacity to communicate this link decreased for a time the outbreak of anxiety attacks.

(4) *The object as auxiliary ego*

At earlier stages of our contact with the children the feelings of emptiness and depletion were massive and the object was needed to ensure that an identity was retained. At later stages the prevailing fear was to be overwhelmed by instinctual impulses rendering the ego helpless against desires to attack and kill. The children's fear of being unable to protect themselves or their objects against destruction was realistic and had to be constantly guarded against.

The fear of total helplessness was at its worst when change of any type was imminent. This situation provoked the most archaic defenses.

Prior to going to camp, Lucille made plans to meet the unknown situation. Finally, she bedded herself down on the floor of the treatment room, saying, "I in camp." Her last defense was always to take to bed as a safe place where she would be protected and could indulge in autoerotic activities.

This imminent helplessness could be studied as the children waited to be called into the consulting room and as they waited to be collected after treatment. The waiting period was minimal, usually a matter of minutes, but precipitated great anxiety, often complete lack of control, and sometimes destructiveness.

At first nothing helped Basil if the therapist or the attendant collecting him was not with him in the waiting room. Chaotic functioning would break out in an instant. Even when the therapist was present, Basil was difficult to control, the prevailing anxiety being that no one would come and he would be abandoned. Later, the therapist's presence reassured him. Still later, he was able to reassure himself by envisaging where the attendant would be. "I did not panic because I knew she would now be coming up the hill."

The nature of the help demanded was the practical one of controlling outbursts due to anxiety, but it had to have the quality of omnipotence. "Help me, stop my worries, stop me hurting." The magic was assumed to reside in the adult and was beyond the power of the child.

Following her attacks on animals and children, Norma feared to repeat these events and said, "Please help me." Following a failure of her parents to visit, Norma made houses for beetles, but in installing them they were inevitably killed. She then placed the hands of the clock at three and at seven, three being the time of her session and seven her bedtime (safe times).

The interrelation of the various forms of object orientation we have just described offers a considerable challenge to our understanding. It is clear that the instinctual forces involved are mediated by a primitive ego organization, about which we know comparatively little. Moreover, the likelihood is that the ego is not only primitive in the area of object relations but also defective in some unknown way. It is clear that the main mechanism is not projection, as it would be in other types of object disturbance to which we are accustomed. According to our observations, the sequence of experiences is as follows: the world becomes dead through a failure to find the object at the level of psychic need; the child also feels dead; the world and the self then become replete with an undiluted form of terror which is dangerous to the self and the objects. But in the aggressive outburst, both child and object come alive again. A primitive need to survive plays an inescapable part in the sequence.

The trend away from the object and the far-reaching obliteration of feeling also seem to derive from an anxiety concerning survival.

(5) *Safe object relations maintained by identificatory thinking*

Alice Balint (1943) describes a process whereby the very young child transforms a strange and consequently frightening world into one that is familiar and enjoyable—identificatory thought,[15] a process which is employed for the purpose of avoiding what is unpleasant and obtaining what is pleasurable. In this type of thinking, the primitive pleasure ego plays a greater part than in objective thinking. The basis of the earliest identifications is not resemblance

[15] The term as used by Alice Balint has no relation to the mechanism of identification; in a discussion Anna Freud suggested a more apt description: that the child maintains a primitive state of animistic thinking.

to the object but the manner in which the object enters into relation with the child's instincts. Identificatory thinking forms a bridge to the external world and to object relations. Alice Balint postulates that "we are able to know the external world only as something akin to the ego [in our terminology, self]" (p. 320).

Much of our children's relation to the anxiety-provoking aspects of the world is expressed in terms of this type of thought. They deal similarly with the anxiety-provoking aspects of their own experience, seeking through an animistic link with their objects to give acceptable meaning to what otherwise lacks it.

Thus, Stanley's therapist wrote: "Ever since I have known Stanley he has envisaged a unity of feeling and experience between us. He would ask if I had washed my hair when he had washed his; if I had been to the barber when he went; if I was upset because his housemother left; even whether I was jealous because the curtains were higher than he. He resented all proofs of my separate existence. When I took out a handkerchief, he asked why, because he didn't have a cold. When I commented on his father being a policeman, he asked, 'Is your's one too?' "

Basil constantly asked about the adult's tastes; he was distressed and felt rejected when they did not coincide with his. To him, this appeared as if he was unliked. He commented: "It is good if people want to be like you, because it means they like you."

Much of the children's use of language, which gives an inaccurate view of their advancement, can be understood as a superficial identity with their close objects. The aim of the general parroting of words and phrases is to keep this safe link with the adult. It is often difficult to know how much the children understand words they use and how much is imitative repetition.

Concerning his dislike of his new escort, Stanley commented: "That's because I'm not used to her. What does used mean?"

In the context of her own sadness, Lucille always repeated explanations her therapist had given her. Their meaning was less important to her than the fact that they were the words the therapist would use in this context. For example: "Don't be disappointed if you can't have it"; "You don't need two crocodiles"; "Jean's sad about Joy dying. She'd be sad if you died." She reminded herself that she could not have the therapist to herself and tidied up as the therapist would wish her to. At the same time she seemed to be more alone suggesting that this identificatory link with the therapist's rational and ordering aspect was in some way libidinally incomplete. It had the quality of a performance she demanded of herself, but it did not lead to a state of satisfaction.

The following examples indicate a more advanced stage where the children hover, as it were, between the world of egocentric thinking and true awareness of the object. Perceptual discrimination is available in problematic situations, but belief in it is uncertain. Hence action is still conflicted.

Norma reported, "I saw a man walking under a bridge and he wasn't frightened." Bridges are frightening to Norma, but this observation surprised rather than reassured her.

When a housemother was upset, Norma commented, "Poor Mrs. M., are you sad? Shall I break something for you?" On this occasion Norma ended up by spontaneously helping to dry the dishes as a consoling action, but she was clearly uncertain which line to take.

(6) *Ambivalent object relations, with development of defense mechanisms*

In the course of treatment, the ability to retain the object as both loved and hated developed in varying degrees in different children. It was always precarious and the degree of the regression from it differed from child to child. On the whole, the trend was toward maintaining this state of orientation; for a time the ego functioning on which it hinged could be increasingly depended on, though only in limited areas.

Sometimes Norma expressed her ambivalence by alternately being tender and cross, at times hitting the therapist while using a caressing voice. This state was reminiscent of a year-old baby. At other times she manifested some distance from her aggression with changed modes of adapting herself to it. She said: "I saw a little girl with a bicycle and was jealous. It worried me and I had to run away." When the therapist asked where to, she replied: "In here to you." She would cross the road to avoid difficult experiences but usually told the therapist about them with a clear ability to define her conflict.

Basil, who used to fight his way through his weekends at home and was overcome with jealousy and demandingness, now says (and acts upon it!), "If there is any quarreling, I shall take a book and go to my room."

Occasionally a child developed empathy with the deprived object in areas strictly limited by his own experience of deprivation.

Norma was always upset by the traffic jam at the roundabout on her journey to the Clinic. One morning she said, "Poor lorry driver when he held up." She was also sorry for girls who have no penises and for boys who cannot have babies as girls do.

Gratitude for and pleasure in what was done for them began to emerge, if uncertainly.

Norma took pleasure in what the therapist gave her and said, "You nice to me." She then began to make presents for other people.

Important objects were more clearly discriminated: the child noted not only their appearance and functions but also their individual qualities and characteristics which he was ready to understand and react to.

Basil said: "I don't tell my housemother about anything nasty. I tell you the nasty things because you can help me."

"Why is my mummy so impatient and cross? She never used to be. When I do something for her, why does she always ask more and more from me?"

Acceptance of the object's sensory and emotional states led to transitory attempts to protect it.

Norma asked, "Shall we close the window if you cold?" When she wanted a gift at the store and the therapist was short of money, Norma was concerned whether the therapist would have enough to buy a pineapple for herself as well.

When his therapist had eye trouble, Stanley asked, "Shall I put you to bed?"

Norma's frequent visits to the lavatory on walks were disconcerting to her therapist and caused some resentment in shopkeepers. Gradually Norma learned to anticipate her problem and to avoid the unpleasantness.

The ability to contain aggression by expressing it verbally in critical statements based on reality and even to indulge in a macabre type of humor about it emerged surprisingly often.

Basil and Stanley now consider the effect of their own behavior on their parents and with growing accuracy are capable of discriminating between those aspects which they have induced and those for which they have no responsibility.

Norma after an argument with her housemother said the next morning: "Bloody God! Twilley's not dead yet." She then went into a variety of descriptions of how Twilley could die. She might stick a knife in her. Asked if this would work, her housemother replied, "Would you like to try?" Norma burst into laughter and said: "You teasing me." Norma now speaks of her own death in the same macabre way. She does not feel certain whether she will have a cross on her grave. This bizarre and unfeeling speech has to be compared with the terror of dissolution for its positive aspects to be apparent. The child's continuing fear of being overwhelmed by aggression is only too clear. However, Basil's recent statement, "What's the good of being good if it doesn't lead anywhere," has a ring of normality about it.

Summary

We have confined this report to our observations on the self and object representations of a group of four children in analysis. Our attempt to systematize these has of necessity made use of formulations which derive from our understanding of the earliest stages of ego development. The distribution of instinctual forces in self and object representations is in these children mediated in part by a primitive ego organization which utilizes archaic modes of functioning and which nevertheless shows some small capacity for development under the stress of a modified analytic process, though not always predictably and only for limited periods of time.

We may formulate the following unstable advances:

1. The synthesis of body states into recognizable feeling states which from being meaningless and tormentingly detrimental to homeostasis, now take on the significance of signals of need.

2. The gradual acceptance of a priority of cathexis of the human person as a satisfier of need.

3. Some rudimentary acceptance of a reciprocal feeling relationship with the human object (observed in the development of limited empathy, gratitude, protectiveness, and the wish to give). Neverthe-

less, this advance still seemed to be carried out in the face of a severe arrest in the area of self and object relationships, in which, for long periods, feeling states were in abeyance or defended against and in which preoccupation with the inanimate was an unusual feature. When for internal reasons, these defensive activities failed, there appeared a trend toward animistic thinking with the denial of differences between child and adult.

In Norma and Lucille, this arrest seemed to affect their whole ability to relate. In Stanley and Basil, a larger area of their personalities seemed capable of operating independently of this arrest, though the disparity between the two levels was always grossly evident and remained so.

Being in analysis which involved a close and continuous opportunity to relate has undoubtedly helped the children to communicate and made possible the detailed observations we have recorded. Without the analytic contact, the children could not have verbalized their inner states so clearly and intensively. Nevertheless, we are aware that our clinical approach influenced scarcely more than the uppermost neurotic features of these children's disturbances. In Basil and Stanley, their social awareness and to some degree their ability to conform have advanced, but there has been no advance in the level of their most basic object relationships. In adolescence this may well prove disastrous. We are considering whether a different clinical approach aimed at reconstructing the failure of early environmental holding might be more effective in cases such as theirs.

Norma and Lucille came to us at a much lower level of integration. We do not yet know whether this could have been influenced by a different technique. The experience of the staff of High Wick, where the children receive constant intensive care from a single object, and where allowances for regression in a permissive environment are made, does not lend support to the idea that the children would improve merely by devoted care given over a prolonged period of time. Our findings as set out in this paper suggest that the arrest in development involves in all cases a failure in relating at the most primitive ego levels prior to structuralization. However, our data do not permit us to determine whether this failure is due to an innate lack of potentiality or neurological defect or to a deficit in the earliest "holding environment."

12

FREQUENCY OF PSYCHOTHERAPEUTIC SESSION AS A FACTOR AFFECTING THE CHILD'S DEVELOPMENTAL STATUS

CHRISTOPH M. HEINCKE, Ph.D.
With the assistance of
Joseph Afterman, M.D., Marian Bradley, B.A., Leah Kaplan, M.S.W., Anneliese F. Korner, Ph.D., and Jean Moore, M.S.W.
(1965)

The primary purpose of this publication is to present a series of hypotheses relating to the differential status (outcome) at the end of treatment, and at two points following treatment, of children seen once a week as opposed to those seen four times a week. The hypotheses are derived from the results of a pilot study exploring the effect of frequency of treatment in psychoanalytic child therapy. Future publications will attempt to clarify the differences in the therapeutic process of the two groups.

Despite much clinical experience indicating the importance of the frequency with which a child is seen, there are few studies which explore the differential outcome of children seen at varying frequencies. Arthur (1952) deals mainly with process considerations, but does suggest that the less frequent treatment is not likely to

---

This study was planned while the author was a Fellow at the Center for the Advanced Study in the Behavioral Sciences, and was initiated at Mount Zion Hospital, San Francisco, under grants from the Rosenberg Foundation and the National Institute of Health, Grant M-2948. It is being completed at Reiss-Davis Child Study Center, Los Angeles, with the assistance of a grant from the Grant Foundation.

We particularly wish to express our gratitude to Rocco L. Motto, Norman Reider, Anna Maenchen, Barbara Carr, Elise Greenhouse, and Dorothy Habben for their generous help in carrying out this project. Without the support of the school systems involved this study would not have been possible. Finally, we are much indebted to Sheila Speilman, Rosemary Ginn, Diana Hager, and Roselyn Katz for their devoted assistance.

reach the fundamental sexual conflicts and is thus likely to be "ineffective in a symptom formation which is based exclusively on a primary sexual fantasy."

The effects of frequency of treatment on adults has been investigated (Imber et al., 1957; Lorr et al., 1962; McNair et al., 1964), but these studies are limited in that twice a week represents the most frequent treatment studied.

Starting with a given theoretical and technical approach to child therapy, namely, that associated with Anna Freud's teachings, one group of seven to ten-year-old boys was seen once a week and another group was seen four times a week. This variation in frequency cannot be considered a simple independent factor. Despite the use of the same general technical approach, the nature of the material produced is soon different; therefore, the utilization and assimilation of this material are different. This in turn leads to variations in the further emergence of material, etc. (Bibring, 1954). Yet it was felt that the characterization of the cluster of independent process variables associated with differences in frequency and its effect on outcome was the first step in a long-term research strategy. It was anticipated that examination of the differences in the process could then suggest which are likely to be the most significant correlates of variation in frequency. For example, it has been hypothesized that the specificity, affect intensity, and variety of the transference phenomenon may well be one such significant correlate.

The findings of this study are based on the experience with ten children. Four of these were seen four times a week and six once a week. Two of the once-a-week children moved from the area, leaving four in each group. Two psychoanalytic child therapists trained at the Hampstead Child Therapy Clinic in London treated the children. One therapist saw three pairs of children and the other one. Both had had four years of child psychotherapy experience with children seen on a once- and five-times-a-week basis. All the mothers were seen once a week by a psychiatric social worker or other therapist, and where appropriate the fathers also were seen.

The children were all judged to be suitable for psychoanalytic treatment in that permanent and severe symptom formation of a predominantly neurotic character and the retardation of ego and libidinal growth were associated with permanent regressions and fixations (A. Freud, 1962).

Cases were assigned so as to insure that one group was not over-represented by the more severely disturbed or by certain qualitative constellations (for example, a defensive organization subject to deadlock versus lability). Individual variations are likely to defy matching of groups of cases; as demonstrated elsewhere (Heinicke, 1965b), however, the two groups of children did not differ at the beginning of treatment on any of 45 clinical dimensions which do differentiate them after treatment.

The two samples of four boys are also characterized *and do not differ* in regard to the following:

1. They were between the ages of six years, eight months and ten years, five months.
2. The main reason for referral was a learning disturbance linked to a psychological disturbance.
3. Their difficulties could not be readily linked to the influence of organic impairment or psychotic process.
4. They were either threatened with being held back or had been held back in school.
5. Their rate of academic growth in reading, spelling, and arithmetic was below the national average.
6. They scored a Verbal I.Q. of 91 or better.
7. They came from intact business or professional families.
8. All treatments were terminated at the request of the parents and with the consent of the therapist.
9. The length of the therapies ranged from one and a half to two and a half years, the mode being two years for both groups.

The subsequent sections of this presentation are organized to describe the following: (1) the assessment of each of the children at the beginning, end, one year and two years after treatment; (2) the use of the Developmental Profile (A. Freud, 1962) to integrate the information derived from these assessments; (3) an example of a set of three Profiles from the case of Steven; (4) the generalizations describing the hypothesized differential development of the two groups.

The Method of Assessing the Child's Developmental Status: The Profile as an Indication of Psychotherapeutic Outcome

Anna Freud (1962) has suggested that Profiles drawn up at various junctures can among other things serve "as an instrument to measure treatment results, i.e., as a check on the efficacy of psychoanalytic treatment." Comprehension of what is to follow requires familiarity with the Profile (A. Freud, 1962, 1963; Nagera, 1963). Characteristics which make it especially suitable as an indication of therapeutic outcome should be highlighted. Most important, any indication of child psychotherapeutic outcome must deal with the fact of the child's potential for development. Although it is meaningful to study changes in the latency child's adjustment to school and peers, these diagnostic signposts are not as stable as the adult's capacity for work and love. The Profile is based on the assumption that "the capacity to develop progressively, or respectively the damage to that capacity, is the most significant factor in determining a child's mental future."

Previous experience suggests that it is essential to base the assessments of therapy on a variety of sources of information (Cartwright et al., 1963; Rosenfeld and Novick, 1964). By providing a common framework and language, and by insisting that all inferences are made within the context of all the material, the Profile makes the integration of descriptions as well as case comparisons both possible and clinically meaningful.

It is further assumed that to arrive at an adequate assessment of the developmental point that the child has reached, and what his growth potential is, the total diagnostic material must be formulated from different metapsychological points of view: dynamic, structural, economic, genetic, and adaptive. An assessment based only, for example, on the child's ego strength is likely to be misleading.

The Procedure for Obtaining the Information

The procedure used to gather the diagnostic information has been essentially the same throughout our work, but the experience did suggest slight changes which have in fact been incorporated into a second project.

Following an initial Clinic intake interview with the parents, at which time a preliminary assessment of the suitability of the case for psychotherapy was made, the mother began seeing the therapist assigned to her, and Joseph Afterman saw the child in two psychiatric interviews. The contact with the parent initially provided an elaboration of the statement of the problem, further developmental history, and the collection of information on the family and other aspects of the environmental situation.

At the end of his contacts with the child, the psychiatrist prepared him for the testing to follow, and certain tentative recommendations were made to the parents.

The battery of tests administered by Anneliese Korner consisted of: The Revised Stanford Binet, Form L; the Wide Range Achievement Test; the Rorschach; parts of the T.A.T. and Michigan Picture Test; and the Draw-a-Person Test.

To provide yet another independent source of information, visits were paid to the school for lengthy discussions with the teacher and related personnel. These interviews were structured to the extent that an effort was made to gather detailed information on the child's academic achievement, his relationship to peers, and his behavior in the classroom.

If after these various assessments the child and the family were felt to be suitable for the services offered by the Clinic, then the child began seeing the child therapist, and the parent or parents continued to see the therapist who did the intake interview.

After a year of treatment the tests of reading, arithmetic, and spelling were again administered by A. Korner, and a school visit was once more made at this point. Immediately after the end of treatment the child was first seen by J. Afterman, and then given the total test battery by A. Korner. A school visit was again arranged and the parents were seen at least once by their child's therapist to discuss the findings of the terminal assessment.

A year after the end of treatment the child's therapist saw the child at least once, the parent or parents were seen by their therapist, the total test battery was again administered by A. Korner, and another school visit was made. At the end of the assessment the child's therapist again met with the parents to discuss the findings.

The procedure for the second follow-up, two years after the end of treatment, was the same as for the first follow-up, but this time it was felt that the children would not be sufficiently motivated to take the tests. Reading test scores comparable to the Wide-Range Achievement Test were, however, available from school records.

Methods of Recording the Information

The method of recording the various diagnostic clinical interviews was essentially the same as that used to describe the therapeutic sessions with child and parent. Immediately following each session the clinician dictated the following into a tape recorder:

1. A description of the patient's general mood, appearance, and approach to the session.
2. A detailed chronological account of the session, including a careful description of the nature of the therapist's interventions and the patient's reactions to them.
3. The therapist's over-all understanding of the session: how the session relates to previous sessions and what he anticipates in the future.
4. The therapist's personal feelings about the session and the patient.
5. A summary of the changes observed in the patient.

In regard to the school visit, a detailed account of what transpired was given as well as some evaluation of this information.

All the data from the psychological test situation were recorded as suggested by the instructions accompanying the test.

Modes of Data Analysis: Interpretations by the Psychiatrist and Psychologist

In addition to providing a process account of his contacts with the child, J. Afterman prepared the following for each child at the beginning and end of treatment:

1. A running interpretative account of each of the significant items in the sequence of the diagnostic interview.
2. An integrated evaluation of each diagnostic contact, which considered both the child's history and certain salient facts known about the child's present circumstances. As it turned

out, the theoretical guide lines developed for this purpose were very similar to those suggested later by the Profile.

For the beginning of treatment, J. Afterman also ranked the children in terms of the level of ego integration exhibited.

A. Korner summarized her psychological findings for the beginning, end, and year after the end of treatment in an extensive report which included the following subheadings: an evaluation of cognitive functioning; an evaluation of scholastic skills; separate sections on the interpretation of the Draw-a-Person Test, the Rorschach, and the Apperception tests; a series of general comments; and finally a diagnostic summary.

Using the assessments based on the psychologicals, A. Korner also rated the children in terms of the following dimensions: the level of ego integration, progress as opposed to regression in phase development, and the over-all capacity for forming object relationships. Her rankings on the first of these correlated perfectly with those made by J. Afterman on the basis of his findings and also correlated significantly with the rankings made independently by the therapists. Although it was planned to repeat these ratings at the end and after treatment, limitations in resources confined us to the write-up and interpretation of the test results.

Integrating the Total Findings: The Profile

The Profiles for the beginning and end of treatment were constructed by the therapist some time before the first follow-up took place;[1] those based on the follow-ups were done soon after those assessments were made. The primary focus of these Profiles was to derive a cross-sectional and integrated statement of the child's developmental status and potential. It was assumed that at this point in research the most reliable and valid conclusions about a child were based on all the material available at a given point in time.[2] This approach would point to the essential variables and change in variables. It is then possible to develop ways of assessing a certain

1 The Profile was not available when the project being reported on was begun. The procedure in the current project is to have both therapist and diagnostic psychiatrist write a Profile shortly after each assessment point.

2 The reliability of the Profile construction and ratings based on them has been studied in a variety of ways and found to be satisfactory (Heinicke, 1965b).

function and changes in it by using one source of information or test.

Having formulated all the Profiles, it was possible to compare those for the children seen once as opposed to four times a week and to formulate hypotheses reflecting the differences in developmental status and potential at a given assessment point.

As will be seen, few striking differences were noted at the end of treatment, but the children seen four times a week did show a greater spurt in their growth during the two years after treatment. Before turning to these group differences, the Profiles written for a nine-year-old boy, Steven, are given below. He was seen four times a week for a period of nineteen months. His mother was seen once a week, and his father also had some contact with a therapist.

Steven's development illustrates well both the general and specific hypotheses formulated on the basis of the group comparisons. This is not to imply that the development of the other children was identical; very important variations did exist.[3]

The Profiles on Steven: A Child Seen Four Times a Week

REASON FOR REFERRAL

Steven's family was referred by a private psychiatrist following the parents' request for help because of Steven's failure to progress in school. Aged almost nine, he was at the time in the low third grade; although he had repeated half a year, he was a year behind in reading and spelling, and somewhat behind in arithmetic. In the classroom he was hyperactive, lacked self-control, had a short attention span, and was constantly seeking approval from the teacher.

DESCRIPTION OF THE CHILD

Steven is lightly built with dark, close-cut hair and slightly protruding ears. Appropriate boyish dress, a generally pleasant appearance, a shrewd, observing, intelligent look, and a warm smile together gave a likable impression. While he was at first solemn, his darting inquisitiveness anticipated the liveliness and movement which were to follow. His occasionally widened brown eyes and tentative explorations communicated fright, but a manly and seemingly confident approach was also apparent.

[3] Copies of the set of Profiles formulated for Gordon, a child seen once a week, are available on request from the author.

FAMILY BACKGROUND AND PERSONAL HISTORY

Steven is the third child of a professional family. At the time of referral, his two older sisters, Jennifer and Barbara, were fourteen and eleven years old, and his brother, Michael, was five. The family lived in the suburbs of a large metropolitan area.

Some of the salient facts from his developmental history are as follows. The pregnancy with Steven was unplanned but an easy one; the mother felt good during the whole time. Steven was very active intra-uterine, and this excessive activity carried over into his babyhood. It made him a sharp contrast to the other children in the family, who were all very quiet. The mother nursed him for two months, but this proved unsuccessful because of her nervousness and his frequent spitting up. Because of his overactivity and his continuous vomiting she also found it very difficult to care for him and stressed particularly how difficult it was to keep him clean.

With the exception of a slow speech development, his second and third years were remembered by his mother as much more favorable. He walked at the usual time, but even though he could at one and a half years of age say simple sentences, he slurred them so badly that only his mother could understand them. It was not until the age of four that others could also comprehend what he was saying. Toilet training occurred "over night" when Steven was two and a half, and after it was completed, she took him everywhere with her. The mother reported she was very proud of her first son, thought he would be her last baby, and spoiled him a great deal.

The picture again changed during the third year. The mother first of all, recalled that while she was giving Steven a bath, the father for some reason hit her. Steven, too, remembered this incident and later admitted that this was a great source of fear for him. At about three and a half when the mother was pregnant with the younger brother, Steven started to suck his thumb. Shortly after this he would sit or sleep on his hands to restrain himself from thumb sucking since this was strongly prohibited by the parents. It was also at about three and a half that his mother remembered getting very angry with Steven, screaming at him and hitting him because he misbehaved. She then begged him to forgive her by saying: "Help me be a good mummy by not doing these things."

When Steven was four and a half, the younger brother was born. Steven had been babied a great deal up until this time and now all this suddenly stopped. His father reported that while the mother was still in the hospital Steven told the neighbors that she was not going to bring the new baby home, and that the baby had died. Prior to the birth of the baby, Steven had had a room to himself. After the birth, he shared a room with Michael and about the same time became terrified of noise and cried a great deal. He was especially frightened by the street noises when put in the parents' bedroom in the front of the house for his nap. At about the same time he was put in nursery school, where he was a problem because of his overactivity.

In kindergarten Steven attempted to use scissors, broke out in a sweat, and was unable to do it. The teacher pictured him as being a very fidgety, active child who had difficulty listening and was unable to sit still. His speech was careless, his diction bad, and his homework poor. Toward the end of the term, he became more relaxed, more attentive, and a better worker, but then relapsed to a state of lack of self-confidence. He missed some school in kindergarten and the first grade due to tonsillitis. He missed much less school after the tonsils had been removed. Most important, despite being sent to bed at 7:00 o'clock, he seemed to be always tired.

The reports of his first-grade teachers indicate that he still could not use scissors and had difficulty writing. He dawdled and was disorganized. "He wanted to do a good job but just couldn't seem to concentrate," one teacher reported. He daydreamed, and chewed and dropped pencils frequently. His weakness was both in number work and in the recognition of written symbols. Beyond this, he was reported to be a good sport, friendly, and respectful of the rights of others.

Of particular significance in his seventh year was his having to repeat part of the first grade again and also being hit by a car. Although the car threw him some distance and he was unconscious for a few minutes, he was not seriously hurt. Almost exactly a year before this, his maternal grandfather had been killed in an automobile accident. Being held back in school depressed Steven because he wanted to continue to be with his five favorite friends. His second-grade teachers reported that he was still having trouble concentrating and still could not use scissors. He was reading in the low second reader, but had a small vocabulary, could not attack new words, and would skip over things. In contrast, it was reported that his number work was improving. It was during the second grade that he was referred for testing by the Guidance Service, but this was not followed up. Although Steven at times resented authority and criticism, he was never a behavior problem, and was well liked by his peers. By the beginning of the third grade he had become a little less popular, however, because he was pushing the smaller children around. The teacher felt that this was his way of trying to deal with the fact of being held back.

Just before the start of treatment, his mother reported that he was very high-strung, unable to sit still, but yawned a good deal when reading. He would know a word in the morning and forget it by afternoon. The parents had stopped their unsuccessful attempts to tutor him in reading, but the father would still sometimes sit for two hours at a time and try to "drum arithmetic into his head." He was still having trouble with fine skills, but rode his bicycle well and had just passed his swimming tests.

Likely to be of significance in Steven's development were the following past events:

1. The mother's inability adequately to feed a very active baby.
2. The mother's negative reaction to the messing associated with his feeding.
3. The father hitting the mother when Steven was three and a half; this was very likely representative of frequent parental conflict.
4. The mother's explosive outbursts at an uncontrollable child; these outbursts were very likely repeated frequently.
5. The excessive doting on and exhibition of her "last" son; i.e., Steven.
6. The birth of Michael and the impact of being "dropped" at the age of four.
7. Being held back in the first grade and the simultaneous loss of five friends.
8. Being hit by a car on the anniversary of the death of the maternal grandfather.

The rest of the Profile written at the beginning of treatment and those formulated at the end and one year after the end of treatment are given below. To emphasize the development over time, we present the conclusions drawn for each of the major subsections of the Profile at each of the three time points.[4]

POSSIBLY SIGNIFICANT ENVIRONMENTAL INFLUENCES

At the Beginning of Treatment

The impact of Steven's parents overshadowed all other current events. Mrs. A. was constantly impelled to intrude into Steven's life. Angry at being treated like a stupid little girl and terrified that her son would be found wanting, she burst into the therapy room. Equally conducive to Steven's poor differentiation was her constant push to organize. To deal with her feeling of hopelessness, she insisted that Steven and her husband "get on the ball." She said that they were alike in many ways and depreciated both with

[4] Limitations of space have prevented presentation of the extensive descriptive material on which the Profiles are based.

accusations of their being "hopeless" when her attempts at organizing them had failed. This hopelessness was very likely linked also to previous feelings of hopelessness about her brain-injured younger brother. Her maternal organizing could, of course, be of great comfort; its sudden disappearance when her rushing literally exhausted her and she failed, for example, to pick Steven up on time led to serious disruption. Or turning the tables, she would plead with him to help her control herself and keep her from spanking him when he had been provocative and thrown his toys all over.

Threats of divorce and actual mutual attacks further challenged any anticipations of an "expectable environment." Neither the masculine nor the feminine model would appeal: the father was derided for not making enough money and had once been kicked out of the house. In turn he would suddenly hit his wife and call her stupid. Although Steven enjoyed being "her little man" and lying in bed with his mother, both her expectations and the threat of a father who actually hit him and cut his hair would be terrifying.

Yet, the father wanted his son to succeed, and thought he would, in fact, make it. Similarly, the mother's affection, caretaking, and feeding were clearly supportive. Her tendency to withdraw this support either because she was angry with her husband and displaced this anger onto Steven or because she unconsciously wanted to motivate him to "get on the ball" would, however, again lead to angry helplessness. Especially threatening was her tendency to give to Michael at the very moment when she was depriving Steven.

At the End of Treatment

Without underestimating the importance of factors like school environment, the nature of the impact of the parents on Steven again seems most important. The mother's need to intrude, to organize, and depreciate Steven had become less urgent. Able to perceive his increasing ambition, she could relax and instead encourage his independence by promising him a bicycle if he did all his work. The implicit supervision became more obvious as she tried "drilling him" to get even further ahead. This time she realized that too much pressure was useless. Many of her efforts to organize the best school experiences for Steven were also realistic. Most beneficial was her obvious pride in his achievement and her ability to encourage rather than curb his curiosity.

Still likely to be disruptive was the contrast between her organizing of his activities in response to his needs and the insensitivity shown when she would, for example, keep him waiting. This in turn was a function of her own disorganization. Although she had increasingly turned to pleasurable activities of her own and thus had less need to pressure her husband and son, she still had difficulty integrating her activities so as to avoid paniclike rushing or suddenly deserting others. While the father could still be provoked by Steven's "fooling around," he increasingly took pride in his son's successes.

Much of the open marital conflict had now ceased, so that the constant modeling of mutual denigration and victimization had lessened. A greater affectionate closeness allowed Steven to confess in their presence that his father had often terrified him.

A Year After the End of Treatment

Reports from the teacher and the material of the mother's interviews indicate that the mother had become even more aware of the futility of constantly pushing Steven. Interestingly, during the year she had been able successfully to resist the pushing of her own mother. She mentioned what great pleasure she took in Steven's achievement, did have realistic ambitions for his future education, and gave great support to a difficult project which Steven himself had decided to pursue.

There were still fights between the parents, but these were now more adequately resolved. During their joint interview with the child therapist they were more harmonious and affectionate with each other as well as the therapist.

As a model of organized ego functioning, the parents were still wanting. They arrived late for their interview because the mother had to finish the laundry. Many items of their clothes needed sewing, and the father several times got up to look out of the window at passing fire engines—like Steven, he could not sit still.

Otherwise benign trends in the parental impact as noted at the end of treatment continued in the year after treatment. Particularly noteworthy was the affection shown Steven by both parents.

ASSESSMENTS OF DEVELOPMENT: DRIVE DEVELOPMENT

At the Beginning of Treatment

Libido: Phase Development.—While Steven had reached the phallic phase, dominance on it had not been attained. He was chronologically in latency, but very little behavior appropriate to this phase was evident. His development had advanced sufficiently to take a positive oedipal stance; as Tramp (in the story) he had a secret love relationship with Lady. Yet these and other phallic advances were constantly subject to massive regression to earlier phases of development.

Libido: Distribution.—The quality and quantity of Steven's narcissism were such as to make a primary defect unlikely. Yet the quantity of the secondary narcissism was minimal. His tendency to split his body image best represented the lack of an integration necessary to experience a sustained self-esteem. In a moment of confidence he could challenge the therapist to a game of checkers and penetrate his "back line," but the least indication of possible defeat led to a fantasy of Humpty Dumpty. Unlike Humpty Dumpty, Steven's feet left him before "the great fall." His general ease in moving from aggressor to victim is also illustrated by the above. Similarly, he shifted from being clever to crazy, and boy to girl.

Given moments of sufficient integration to experience self-regard, the quantity of secondary narcissism derived from his ego achievements was nevertheless very limited and dependent on the reactions of others. He knew he could solve arithmetic problems, but even this skill was disrupted as he tried to demonstrate it to the diagnostic psychiatrist. All achievements were constantly subject to extremely sadistic external and internal evaluations. Without losing touch with reality, the constant shift in self representations offered a way out of this intense pressure.

The love reserved for the first son had, however, been sufficiently internalized to alleviate the above devaluation. In so far as this involved comparison with an encroaching younger brother and the retaliation of a jealous father, this source was again likely to be uncertain.

Object Libido.—Steven's ability to initiate object relationships represented his most advanced asset. He could express sufficient trust and affection toward both paternal and maternal figures to arouse the initial reaction of being likable. He was aware of his power to be his mother's little man and to elicit feminine reactions of "cute." Similarly, he expected that like his father, other men would be interested in promoting his development.

But if the above represented an advance to the oedipal level of object relationships, the regression to the preoedipal level was more impressive. As such it was consistent with the rest of his libidinal development. Any continuing relationships and particularly the involving passivity were likely to be flooded by monsterlike representations. Thus, he needed a mother who fed him good food and who provided the protective organization of daily life, but this was overshadowed by the representation of a devouring, intrusive, demanding, and overwhelming figure. Similarly, any competitive approach to a male was likely to be overwhelmed by representations of a hitting paternal monster. To this regressive construction of his object world, Steven reacted by passively complying or defying, by a variety of escapist tactics to keep from being tracked down, and by a magical longing for less monsterlike figures. Yet the most frequent reaction to his expectations of being victimized was to provoke just this by unwittingly or purposely disrupting things through his constant discharge. The teachers liked Steven, but they preferred to get rid of this uncontrolled, nonproductive "handful."

In contrast, his approach to his peers was accompanied by benign object expectations very likely modeled on his trusting relationships with his older sister, Barbara. But his younger brother, Michael, and other younger children were viewed as an interference, and had to be either denigrated (stupid, feceslike, etc.) or defensively bossed around.

Aggression.—Initially inhibited and passive, Steven very quickly expressed a great deal of aggression. Consistent with the regression to all levels of libido development, its quality derived from all phases. He was furious that he had been kept waiting by his mother, was preoccupied with time-bomb explosions, and defensively enacted how he would murder the therapist.

Although directed outward, the aggression initially tended to be a part of a general explosion rather than taking the form of a specific wish to injure; much of the aggression was also turned inward. "He invited murder." His feet were blown off by the time bombs, and it was he who had lost so often that he didn't mind anyway.

At the End of Treatment

Libido: Phase Development.—Steven (now ten and a half years) had achieved dominance on the phallic phase and increasingly showed behavior appropriate to late latency. A definite progressive quality now characterized his libidinal development. Yet on occasions when his competence was threatened these advances were still subject to regression to previous fixation points.

Libido: Distribution.—Steven's various self representations had been sufficiently integrated to provide a stable focus for considerable secondary narcissism. The tendency to split his body image was no longer present. A feeling of having changed as a function of treatment was focused on feeling older, being different from his brother, and no longer being the victim of family pressures.

It was particularly the feeling of making progress in reading that would counter his previous "I can't make it." Yet if given difficult problems he was still inclined to vacillate between "Am I not wonderful" and complete helplessness; too often the adult still had to judge for him which of these self feelings he should accept.

His object relations also provided much narcissism. He had shifted from being a victim to holding his own. He could compete effectively with his father and could desire independence without being motivated by a need to escape a devouring mother. When confronted with the diagnostic psychiatrist he asked a number of challenging questions.

Least narcissism was still likely to be derived from superego sources. He still saw himself as one who "just can't help fooling around" (masturbating) and taking forbidden things (snitching cookies). To deal with his guilt he again had to be the feminine victim.

Object Libido.—Steven's ability to initiate and particularly to sustain a variety of object relationships had continued to develop and was now more consistent with the rest of his development. Although he was in some ways more reticent (and this was consistent with a move into latency), his capacity to express trust and affection was considerable. For the first time his teacher was experienced as an approving person; he tried hard to please her. He still viewed his brother and other young children with some contempt, but he tended either to overprotect them or leave them alone.

However, most important in accounting for the greater trust, as opposed to his previous need literally "to jump over the fence" and escape, was the change in his image of his mother. In fantasy it represented a change from a devouring monster tracking a small car to a normal-sized woman. He told of a boy who left his mother and went to camp because she insisted on treating him like a little baby. In another story a boy felt sorry he had broken a gift that his mother had given him. Both a greater independence of and sensitivity to the mother are implied by these stories.

Steven could now take a competitive stance, and the expectation of a castrating attack from the father was minimal. The former dread was further eased by Steven's ability to transfer the problems of oedipal rivalry to the boy-girl friend area. His stories reflected the acceptance of giving up the oedipal object and being chosen by a girl friend.

Yet there were still occasions when his inability to finish a school report gave him the feeling that he would never be able to succeed either in relation to the competition with the father or the oedipally tinged expectations of the mother. On these occasions he was forced to get the mother to coerce him and the father to shake (castrate) him in order to ease his guilt and depression.

Aggression.—Little aggression was now evident in the manifest picture. That seen took the form of provocative complaining and not doing his work in relation to specific people: his therapist, father, and mother. It was thus directed outward, but was also likely to incur punishment. As before, the content of these provocations derived from all three libidinal levels: the angry complaint of not receiving more help, the defiant failure to perform, and the fooling around linked to masturbation.

A Year After the End of Treatment

Libido: Phase Development.—Steven had achieved dominance on the latency phase and showed prepubertal interests. Signs of regression were temporary and were not likely to impede his further libidinal development.

Libido: Distribution.—Although there had been no striking qualitative changes in the integration and essential components of his total self representation, the quantity of secondary narcissism had increased further.

Although revealing less about his self feelings, and this would be consistent both with his age and the nature of the follow-up, what could be inferred indicated considerable change. He drew a picture of a boy approximately his age who was characterized as "building racers" and "doing well in his schoolwork." At the beginning of treatment he depicted a racing car escaping from a devouring feminine monster; during the follow-up interview he built a very fine, confident-looking racing car. The implication of an enhanced forward-moving body concept was supported by the fact that he had become a good runner and one of four team captains in his physical education class. Also new was the fact that he could tell a story about an eighteen-year-old boy who was considered "cute" by a sixteen-year-old girl. Other material supported the inference that Steven was increasingly aware of and accepting of his prepubertal status.

Similarly, being chosen by his class to decide questions of "the just punishment" would provide external support for his feeling "of being one of the boys." These "boys" included the five friends he had lost once because he had been held back.

In comparison with other sources of his narcissism, least was still derived in relation to superego sources. As indicated above, he could arbitrate in questions of fair play, showed the inner control necessary to be a captain, and did now finish all his academic work. Yet both in relation to the therapist and the mother his provocative "fooling around" suggested the previous image of: "I am a dirty boy who masturbates and doesn't work." The quantitative force of this fantasy was, however, greatly reduced.

Object Libido.—The progressive trends seen at the end of treatment had been consolidated further into normal object relationships. Fantasy material suggested that the mother was still seen as overpowering and demanding and the father as a forbidding as well as denigrated sexual rival. Such inner object representation could account for the need to "fool around" rather than work and succeed; but this provocation was now rare. Other observations pointed to his ability to withstand the mother's intrusion and depreciation and to his ability to reciprocate affection. This same affectionate charm was also seen in relation to his teacher. Similarly, a very realistic acceptance of his father's strengths and weaknesses had replaced the earlier image of a castrated yet physically explosive monster. Consistent with these changes was his tendency to distance himself and be independent of both his therapist and his parents. At the same time his observation of and sensitivity to the needs of others had also developed further.

His feelings for his brother continued to be both affectionate and defensively superior. He still had to tease and provoke "the little fellow" who had deprived him, but the nature of their fights was such that the mother did not feel impelled to punish Steven.

Underlining the progress in his object relations was his age-appropriate interest in the opposite sex. Although he still needed to keep his distance—and this is consistent with behavior seen in latency—his stories to the projective tests revealed a heterosexual interest: his boy and girl characters had amorous interests.

Aggression.—Manifest aggression had declined even further in the year after treatment. That directed toward peers appeared to be age appropriate. The re-emergence of occasional attacks on his little brother and the near emergence of anger toward the therapist's remaining patients revealed his former anger at not being the favorite one. It was in turn related to some evidence, on the fantasy level, of oral sadism.

Anger about not receiving more from the therapist and his parents could also be inferred, but the fate of this particular anger was now one of inhibition rather than explosion or turning it against the self.

Sadistic components could also be seen in his conception of intercourse. In occasionally provoking the parents by fooling around, he might have been inviting an attack, but, as indicated previously, these provocations were extremely limited.

ASSESSMENTS OF DEVELOPMENT: EGO AND SUPEREGO

At the Beginning of Treatment

Both the quality of his functioning (e.g., the hypermotility) and his development (e.g., the late onset of speech) suggested the diagnosis of some mild brain damage or a constitutionally based defect in the ego apparatus. Even the initial formulation did not, however, stress this explanation.

Rather, an emphasis was placed on the interruption of ego integration and differentiation. In all situations he moved rapidly from an initial inhibition to increasing motility expressed via gross and fine movements. This hypermotility was used for purposes of discharge, as a defense, and as a symbolic expression of certain conflicts. Invariably he enacted what he talked about. As he put it: "I can't sit still and think." When he spoke about a volcano, he made explosive noises. Such heavy reliance on motility was not coupled with a high degree of efficiency and differentiation of this function. He misarranged picture sequences, even though he could verbalize the solution correctly. His visual-motor deficiency was expressed graphically through a WISC obtained at school on which he earned a performance I.Q. of 79 as compared with a verbal I.Q. of 113. Even his perceptions were mobile in that on the Rorschach he rarely saw the same things twice. The constant shift in his thoughts and feelings affected his orientation in space. At the Clinic he consistently went in the wrong direction. His time sense was also poorly developed; he frequently had to ask what time it was. To avoid being passively subjected to stress he substituted his own stimuli for the ones offered. Since such defensive maneuvers are more difficult in auditory recall tasks, his extremely poor performance on these tasks may in part be accounted for.

His vocabulary, verbal facility, and judgment were generally above average. This could be associated with a generally effective reality testing. However, by too often having to act out his thoughts and by becoming what he talked about, he made a condensation which blurred his differentiation of what is inside and what is external. At the beginning of his second session he could very accurately portray how like a sly fox he had outwitted his mother. The observation of her weak points was most realistic. On the other hand, as he enacted the military defense of a hospital containing one ill, damaged, soldier, the enemy was suddenly everywhere.

While a variety of images and impulses were available, the pressure for discharge allowed little adaptive cognitive elaboration or the adaptive use of a variety of specific affects. His capacity to bind tension was in general weak. His archaic fantasy in particular suggested considerable primary-process intrusions in his mental functioning. This fluidity could also be considered potentially consistent with Steven's capacity for humor and his ability to observe his own predicament. About a drawing, undoubtedly a self-portrait, he remarked, "If his eyes were not lopsided and his body not crooked, he would look like a regular person."

Ego Ideal and Superego.—Behavior indicative of well-integrated superego or ego-ideal representations and the associated appropriate signs of guilt and shame were not in evidence; there was little consistent inner control. The operation of extremely sadistic injunctions could be inferred in relation particularly to academic failure, aggression, cheating, and masturbation. To defend against his drives,

Steven relied heavily on the object world. He clearly wanted to succeed, but could not consciously experience either the intensity of his shame or show realistic concern about his academic retardation. Rather, responsibility for the initiation of academic or any other activity was left to the mother and teacher. Similarly, he depended on the adult world (parents and teachers) to stop his disruptive and provocative activities.

Defense Organization.—A great variety of defenses were apparent as Steven made an effort to deal with quantitatively overwhelming drives and internal and external demands. At best, their work resulted in a labile equilibrium; at worst, the primary process colored all expressions, and could result in further defensive steps leading to a fragmented body image.

Some defenses were age adequate: inhibition (of fantasy aggression), repression (forgetting the unpleasant), passive to active (keeping mother waiting), reversal of affect (he was glad, not sad, to miss a session), displacement (from person to toys), and identification with the aggressor (he beat up some kids at school). Although these defenses suggested normal functioning, they were unevenly deployed and appeared in the context of more primitive ones. Thus, the inhibition and repression represented an unstable hold and were overwhelmed by the excessive and primitive use of defensive identifications: Steven became, and motorically enacted, varying partial identities either to represent or to ward off. At times the connected discharge was directed at his own body image—suddenly he would hit his head; or it was projected outward (his parents became aggressive monsters). Obsessional ordering was attempted in relation to anger toward his mother. He hoped for magical solutions to his academic problems. When about to lose competitively, he could only disrupt the whole game and create a cloud of confusion. The pervasiveness of regression in all these defenses must be emphasized. Avoidance also played a key role in the equilibrium reached; he avoided discussion of his failure at school or denied that he cared.

The interference with ego achievements associated with the above defense constellation was extensive. The avoidance and his dependence on external control would make him unable even to confront the academic task. Even when he could be cajoled to initiate a task like reading, the pressure toward the use of defensive identifications, regression, and the associated defenses was such that he could not sit still, not take in, not remember, not think clearly.

At the End of Treatment

In contrast to Steven's initial status, gross signs of a lack of ego integration were now absent. The performance I.Q. rose 23 points to 102 and was thus less discrepant with the verbal I.Q. which remained essentially the same, 114, as opposed to the previous 113. With the exception of his drawing, his eye-hand coordination had improved greatly. There were many indications of a more orderly and consistent approach to tasks, but other observations pointed to the continued variability of cognitive functioning; e.g., although his visual memory had improved, he still had great difficulty with material presented orally.

The decrease in his hypermotility represented the most dramatic change and played an important part in improving the level of ego integration. In the test situation he worked with great persistence for more than three hours without getting restless. The teacher reported that for the first time he could sit still in class and attend; the gains he made in the five months before the end of treatment had brought him to grade level in reading and arithmetic. Thus, his verbal and conceptual facility was enhanced in part because he was no longer as frequently overwhelmed by a primary-process type of diffuse motility and fantasy discharge. He could reflect, ask very relevant questions, or just talk.

As this discharge and the associated pressure to avoid any type of passive experience became less intense, his ability to distinguish between inner experience and outer reality became more pronounced, and his orientation in space was much more adequate. His comments about school, treatment, and the nature of his own changes revealed his power to observe others, a considerable ability to observe himself, and the ability to seek information from others to confirm or disconfirm his observations. For example, he very pointedly asked the diagnostic psychiatrist why he had not continued working with him after their contacts at the beginning of treatment; or he could realize that not reading as a way of getting even with the parents was also self-punishing.

Consistent with the above was the greater ability to bind affects and to elaborate on ideas and fantasies. While the strong color cards could still arouse archaic imagery, secondary process now prevailed in that the images were elaborated on as part of a scientific-space theme. Similarly, his stories to the T.A.T. cards were longer, more complicated, and more interesting. The greater tension-binding capacities led to some suppression of affect, but this very fact made possible a shift from chaotic discharge to the adaptive use of a variety of feelings. As his therapy drew to a close, he could express sadness and anger at being left, disappointment that his wish for magic had not been fulfilled, and yet also gratitude.

Not perhaps surprising, regression to the previous level of ego functioning occurred as his adequacy was too overwhelmingly challenged. When tackling the I.Q. performance subtests, Steven once more became restless, and on occasion became what he was working on. Thus, when assembling a car, he seemed suddenly to become a "Dauphine" and made horn noises. These regressions were, however, limited in frequency and could in the context of sufficient integration conceivably become an asset in creativity.

Ego Ideal and Superego.—The evidence for integrated and benign inner controls was now considerable. Clear-cut internalized ambitions to get a college diploma were coupled with a high level of realistic concern and persistence. Although he was still more than usually sensitive to the possibility of being shamed academically, only occasionally was this associated with a chain of failure leading to further failure.

Signs of sadistic superego representations were no longer as obvious. Guilt about challenging his oedipal rival, about masturbation, and in relation to defying his mother by not performing academically could be inferred. At certain moments the only way for Steven to reach some sort of equilibrium was to have others push, punish, or discard him, but most of the time he had sufficient self-discipline to pursue his work at home and in school. The anger about not having been the therapist's favorite and not having received the magical gift also aroused his guilt, but these affects were again experienced in the context of the quiet functioning of other inner controls.

Defense Organization.—Regression to previous libidinal fixations was at the end of treatment still noticeable. Whenever he was confronted with object loss, this tendency combined with other defenses: the need for the magical gift; the resort to passivity and its provision of food and sleep; a babylike crying appeal for help; provocatively inviting or doing the discarding; denial of all affect or the reversal of it; and turning the passive being left into active leaving.

Defensive identifications were also still evident, though greatly diminished. For example, in relation to conceptions of intercourse he was either the victim or the attacker. Similarly, the full implications of active masculine success were at times avoided. He provoked the adult to hit and push him and externalized: the therapist must choose the game during the last session just as his parents must make him do the homework. It was particularly this avoidance and provocation that still exacted a price in decreased adaptation and enjoyment.

Defenses of a most primitive sort diminished greatly or disappeared altogether: aggression to the self, a tendency to split the body representation, obsessional mechanisms such as doing and undoing, and crude forms of denial and projection. Most important, the defensive use of motility and a tendency to disrupt the total situation gave way to the age-adequate use of inhibition and conformity and resulted in an equilibrium which only occasionally was subject to regression and lability.

A Year After the End of Treatment

Although Steven's gain of 10 points on the verbal I.Q. and the maintenance of essentially the same level of performance I.Q. had resulted in considerable discrepancy (124 versus 99), there were no indications that the variability in his functioning had increased. Though by no means always predictable—and in this he fell below what would be expected for his age group—his total performance was more reliable than the previous year.

As at the end of treatment, there were no gross signs of a lack of ego integration. The level of tension-binding capacity continued to show gains and the mobility of images was not observed. There was no longer any evidence of confusion between what is inside and what is outside. The primary-process type of diffuse motility and fantasy discharge was now confined to a few instances: mouth noises, accidentally falling off a chair, and difficulty in handling a pencil.

There was instead much evidence of secondary-process functioning. His vocabulary was average. The quality of his thinking and judgment was realistic, though at times variable. He could sit still, attend, and perform verbally in front of the class. Although it was not evident in the psychological test situation, the teacher observed that he could remember material presented orally. Rather than dosing stimuli himself, he was more alert and thus more realistic.

Parallel to these signs of greater integration and efficiency were indications of greater inner freedom. His imagery was more lively and less pseudoscientific. The construction of a car during the follow-up interview with the therapist was based on a very creative plan. He could experience a greater variety of affects including sadness, enthusiasm, embarrassment, pride, affection, and disappointment.

New also was his clear-cut ability to plan, organize, and persist in relation to academic and other tasks. Having successfully completed his work he could take pride in it. The strength of his academic ambitions had definitely increased, but it had also become more realistic. He could accurately assess the extensive gains he had made in all three academic subjects, and was realistically planning his preparation for college.

His general self-awareness had definitely been advanced; at the same time he could more readily assume the other person's point of view. For example, he could empathize with the psychological tester in terms of the problems she was having writing down all his responses.

Ego Ideal and Superego.—Excessive guilt and the tendency to externalize control and provoke punishment had declined. There was still evidence in his fantasy expressions on the tests that he could be provocative about getting things done, and that he felt guilty when his sexual curiosity was aroused. Behavior with the therapist indicated a short-lived temptation to externalize and a tendency to provoke punishment for having indulged in masturbation, but there was no evidence of guilt about curiosity. On the contrary, it was openly expressed. Remnants of guilt in relation to anger about not "being the favorite" and not receiving sufficient oral supplies were still evident.

His total development was, however, suggestive of more benign inner controls. Illustrative was his ability to assume leadership in peer situations involving justice and fair play.

Defense Organization.—While a tendency to regress to mouth noises and passivity was still evident, the recovery was rapid. Similarly, he would express a wish for magical aid, but then dismiss it and proceed with the task.

Various passive to active maneuvers related to the loss of the object were still evident. His needing to know the time at the end of the session and some indication of having to run away suggested that he still had difficulty parting from significant objects. It was hard to evaluate at the time whether this was a specific residual in relation to the therapist or a more general problem with its associated defenses.

The defensive use of movement, various defensive identifications, provocative behavior, and the denial of affect, though once prominent, now occurred infrequently. In contrast, conformity with certain adult standards was observed more frequently. For example, Steven now tried to please the tester.

In summary, a balanced, age-adequate organization of defenses was operating effectively enough to lead neither to deadlock nor to lability. When regressions occurred they tended to be temporary and no longer resulted in the serious impairment of functioning seen at the beginning of treatment.

ASSESSMENTS OF DEVELOPMENT: TOTAL PERSONALITY

At the Beginning of Treatment

From Dependency to Emotional Self-reliance and Adult Object Relationships.—We have already cited Steven's dependence on external control to initiate any activity or to curb his instinctual life. In his move toward adult relationships he was still predominantly at the ambivalent anal-sadistic stage. Yet in his ability to find his way around his neighborhood and separate from his parents, he showed self-reliance appropriate for his age.

From Suckling to Rational Eating.—Although Steven had no feeding problem, there was evidence both of some irrational attitudes toward food and of battles with the mother. He reacted particularly strongly to her efforts to force him to eat foods reminiscent of the male genitals (e.g., two brussel sprouts).

From Wetting and Soiling to Bladder and Bowel Control.—Although complete sphincter control had been achieved, Steven had not internalized the standards of cleanliness usually found in his age group. He spilled food at the table, and often left his room in chaos.

From Irresponsibility to Responsibility in Body Management.—Given his very protecting father and mother, it was difficult to assess whether Steven had voluntarily endorsed the rules of hygiene, or whether he simply complied with requests made. Although he had at the age of seven been hit by a car, there was no indication that in health or safety matters he needed any particular protection.

From Egocentricity to Companionship.—Steven had had five good friends in his second school year, and related to them as partners. After he had been held back, the picture had changed. He still participated actively in games with his former friends, but with the younger children he was bossy, and was not liked because he was too loud and uncontrolled.

From Body to Toy and from Play to Work.—Least progress had been made in his capacity to work. There was little persistence and pleasure in the finished product. While he had made some academic progress, particularly in arithmetic, this was more a function of maternal pressure than of intrinsic interest. He had no hobbies, and even his play initially offered him little satisfaction. He could delay long enough to use material in the enactment of a fantasy, but the subsequent wild destruction left no finished product except discharge. Having carefully set up a fort, a wild car suddenly crashed through everything and left a shambles.

Although all aspects of Steven's development had been affected by his disturbance, there was considerable discrepancy between his ability to work and his development from egocentricity to companionship.

At the End of Treatment

From Dependency to Emotional Self-reliance and Adult Object Relationships.—Although Steven's general level of independence and quality of peer associations placed him well into latency, there were still occasions when he relied on the adult world either to initiate an activity like a report or to help him deal with his oedipal and masturbation guilt. Equally important, however, was the fact that he was actively attempting to move away from the constant protection of his parents.

From Suckling to Rational Eating.—Although the evidence for oral fixations persisted, indications of irrational attitudes toward food, battles over food with the mother, and unusual food habits were missing. His development in this regard was age appropriate.

From Wetting and Soiling to Bladder and Bowel Control.—In so far as his cleanliness habits were now well within the range of behavior expected for his age, Steven was progressing normally on this developmental line.

From Irresponsibility to Responsibility in Body Management.—There was no evidence that Steven was either excessively irresponsible or responsible in the care of his health and safety.

From Egocentricity to Companionship.—Both his old and new friendships were now characterized by partnership and by a considerable variety in the activities that were shared. On the basis of classroom observations, the teacher stressed that Steven was now capable of putting himself in the other person's place.

From Body to Toy and from Play to Work.—Steven had made the greatest progress on this developmental line. He persisted in his academic work and enjoyed the end result. Various classroom projects and peer games were approached with much enthusiasm. While he had no hobbies, he did now enjoy reading a book. His occasional need to be mobilized and limited has been mentioned previously, but even this deficit was not so great as to detract seriously from the general conclusion that the total congruence in development and functioning was now considerable.

A Year After the End of Treatment

From Dependency to Emotional Self-reliance and Adult Object Relationships.—Steven's self-reliance had in the year after treatment developed further. While the rare invitation to be coerced and the implication of dependency were still in evidence, indications of psychological independence were much more frequent. He could realistically criticize the father's efforts to help him, but at the same time he indicated very clearly that he intended to pursue the father's profession. He could not only resist the excessive help of his mother but in fact make suggestions which helped her. Taken together with his developing interest in the opposite sex, as well as slight indications of rebellion, these signs of psychological independence now placed him in the preadolescent phase.

From Suckling to Rational Eating.—Little change had occurred, but the previous progressive development was consolidated further.

From Wetting and Soiling to Bladder and Bowel Control.—Little change had occurred, but the previous progressive development was consolidated further.

From Irresponsibility to Responsibility in Body Management.—Little change had occurred, but the previous progressive development was consolidated further.

From Egocentricity to Companionship.—Little change had occurred, but the previous progressive development was consolidated further.

From Body to Toy and from Play to Work.—In what had always been the weakest area of his development, Steven had made more progress than might be expected in a year's time. Not only did he take responsibility for completing his work, but he clearly derived pleasure from being, for example, the best arithmetic student in the class and having gained more than a year in all subjects since last tested a year ago. There were instances when he would still get out of his seat or provoke the parents by not starting his homework until midnight, but these occasions were rare.

Given the above advances, and reviewing the absolute level as well as potential progress on all developmental lines, one can conclude that the congruence in Steven's total development was now considerable.

GENETIC ASSESSMENTS

At the Beginning of Treatment

Steven was both firmly rooted in the phallic phase of development and regressing to all previous libidinal levels. From his initial contacts conflicts around the activity of masturbation could be inferred. During his therapy session he played a solitary game of cards, built up and reduced the piles, and then suddenly noticed a gap in the card sequence. From this beginning his play soon revealed the tremendous regressive pull to earlier phases.

First to appear in the material and certainly central in emphasis were the intense conflicts around the birth of his brother and the regressively linked conflicts generated by feelings of deprivation. In an opening statement he told the psychiatrist that there are some things he does not know and other things he does know. He knows about borrowing, tried to subtract 9 from 5, but could not do so. The numbers were obvious references to how the birth of his brother (now five years old) had taken much of his mother's love away from him. Similarly, he was furious and became depressed because his mother could not get him to his hour on time. The emergence of intense death wishes and the return of thumb sucking at the time of Michael's birth as well as Steven's earlier overactivity and vomiting provided independent evidence for these fixation points. The constant mouth noises and vocalizations as well as the indistinct speech of his second year further underlined the importance of the oral fixation. While looking through a book on evolution he named words and filled the interstices between words with "dum-de-dum." An example would be: "There's a plant-eater—dum-de-dum—eats plants—dum-de-dum—bit one. . . ."

The repeated repetition in play of his being made unconscious in a car crash pointed to great anxieties about being the victim and the manifold meanings this had for him. In the context of a constant confusion about "he"and "she" and the associated intense castration and bisexual anxieties, the monsters (overwhelming forces) took different forms; regressive aspects as well as references to past trauma could often be inferred. A hurricanelike mother, looking more male than female, threatened to overwhelm and swallow everything. The mother's past appeal to Steven to help her control herself seemed relevant, but this overwhelming woman was herself subject to attack: "She is going to be blown to smithereens; a bomb goes right into her belly and she is going to die." In a different context, he recalled the father's attack on the mother while she was giving Steven a bath.

While anal regressive components were suggested by the overwhelming display of sadomasochism and the constant explosions, the evidence for regression to the oral phase was greater. The "sexual" cards of the Rorschach evoked associations suggesting oral-incorporative notions. Castration anxiety was largely experienced in archaic forms involving a fear of being devoured. For example, he saw a monster who would suck in and eat up anyone who came close to any of its orifices.

At the End of Treatment

As at the beginning of treatment, conflicts in regard to the activity of phallic masturbation once more constitute the starting point for the genetic assessments. While the quality of the fixation points preceding this developmental point was also similar to that seen at the beginning of treatment, the quantity of regression was greatly reduced.

Although he had made great strides in actively competing and being curious, there were other times when instead of confronting the task he again had to "fool around." This could consist either of actual masturbation or such derivatives as fooling around with his friends rather than working. The anal regressive component was suggested as he still was afraid of being tracked down for this "dirty" activity. Conceiving himself as "Bumface" he regressively invited the coercion of his mother to make him produce a school report.

Fooling around was also linked to cheating in the sense of depriving Daddy-O of his strength and thus becoming the "king around the house." While the various meanings and consequences of this wish had come up in treatment, the regression to a feminine identification still occurred and was associated with Steven's wish to incorporate the father's phallic-oral strength. The guilt deriving from both this biting wish and the positive oedipal one, as well as the longing for and dread of the passive feminine position still drove Steven actively to provoke the father. He told the therapist of accidentally coming across some of his father's M & M candies, and how he could not resist stealing some. The next day the father called. Steven had been "fooling around," refused to do his homework, and simply refused to understand the difference between M and N. In desperation the father had finally shaken him. Indicative of the potential for recovery from this crisis is the fact that not only did Steven finish the report, but in his contact with the psychiatrist immediately after treatment he had the letters of M and W upside down but then made the correction.

Without being able to see all the regressive links, residuals of the earliest fixations could be seen in his concern of why he was not the favorite son of the parents; the regression to passivity and oral noises also emphasized the earliest fixations, but, as indicated, these regressions were limited to stressful occasions, and recovery was adequate.

A Year After the End of Treatment

While both the regressive potential and the importance of phallic-oral fixations could once more be delineated, their force had further decreased and tended to be temporary in their effect. This is well illustrated by the hour held with the therapist.

After openly expressing his curiosity about the therapist's greatest secret, he momentarily began to provoke the therapist by "fooling around" with a microphone rather than dictating with it as he had done previously. He inhibited this impulse and a tendency to regress to the earliest phases appeared: he complained about the therapist's junk (toys) and then threw himself on the couch. Again, this was short-lived. The temporary nature of this regression to passivity could be inferred, but the evidence from the psychological tests indicated that a residual of sadistic conceptions of intercourse and the dread of femininity were also likely "to make him get up." Continuing with the sequence of the hour, after an interruption by the mother, Steven turned to building a racing car. He expressed the wish for help in designing it, indicated the tinker toy set was a gyp because there were not enough parts, but then quickly relied on his own resources. As he ran into difficulty in building a very masculine-looking car, there were other familiar signs of regression to the oral phase: he again made some mouth noises and talked of some pills that his father had given him; but the noises quickly stopped, and he expressed his independence of his father by saying (quite realistically so) that the pills had done no good. The positive progressive phallic move was once more underscored as he finished the car and took great pride in it.

Finally, the parting from the therapist once more stressed the regression to the earliest fixations as well as the ability to recover. Had the therapist fired his previous secretary? By implication he was asking why he had been fired and why was he no longer the parents' favorite? He took a gun off the shelf, but then returned it. The emergence of anger was this time inhibited. He clearly had difficulty ending the hour, but he could for the first time shake the therapist's hand.

DYNAMIC AND STRUCTURAL ASSESSMENTS

At the Beginning of Treatment

Steven was at referral subject to each of the three major types of conflict. The external conflicts can be related to the previous account of significant environmental events. Steps in the direction of autonomy were likely to be met by maternal organizing, depreciation, or intrusion. Moves toward phallic dominance encountered the physical blows of a jealous father. A constantly charged and disorganized family atmosphere did little to further Steven's internal integration.

Yet the internal conflicts were more prominent. In the previous section we have stressed the many regressive links between the phallic and oral phases. A hysteric structure is suggested. A phobia in relation to being in certain rooms had developed at one time, but neither this nor the signs of an obsessional solution were adequate to check the regressive force. Chronic defects in ego integration and differentiation had appeared early in Steven's development, and have been stressed in distinguishing his difficulties from a simpler neurotic structure.

In further trying to account for the failure of the above-mentioned neurotic solutions, one could emphasize the intensity of certain incompatible drive representatives: the intense ambivalence toward his mother and brother, the complete inability to balance passivity and activity, and the extensive fluctuation in age and sex identities.

Yet the sheer intensity and number of internalized conflicts were impressive. He showed great interest in the potential love relationship between Lady and the Tramp, but then became most concerned with the accident depicted in the story: Tramp is pinned down by the dogcatcher's wagon. He then told of a dog that was sent to the pound for fooling around. Fooling around referred not only to masturbation but also to not doing his homework and being restless. All were subject to injunctions analogous to the mother's hurricane yell of "Get on the ball," and the father's impulsive hit on his head. Any effort to move forward psychologically, that is, to achieve successfully or to compete, was thus likely to encounter such dangers. More specifically, to know or attempt to find out the adult secrets was clearly forbidden.

However, regression activated other conflicts. Salient were the injunctions against the oral sadism experienced toward his mother and that felt toward his brother, the intruder, who took away his favored position. When his mother brought him late for his first therapeutic hour he could at first only indulge in obsessional counting, but this soon gave way to a provocative messing; the invitation to be punished would help him with his guilt and also allow the forbidden wish to "kapuih" all over his mother.

Steven portrayed his dilemma dramatically when the hurt soldiers in a jeep could move neither forward nor backward; in front and in back they were hemmed in by monsters.

At the End of Treatment

In so far as the mother could be aroused to coerce him into performance and the father to shake him for cheating and fooling around, so Steven's conflicts clearly had an external component. Similarly, moments of family disorganization in basic routines would stimulate feelings of helplessness.

In delineating the structure of internalized conflicts and associated incompatible drive derivatives, those remaining at the phallic and oral phase of development were again central. If completing a school report still signified competing with a castrating father, then he still had to fool around so the father would be invited to turn him into a victim. In this way he controlled the powerful father by identifying with the masochistic rather than the sadistic partner in intercourse. To provoke the mother to coerce him into performance and punish him for his dirty masturbation again led to the unacceptable masochistic feminine position.

Regression from these phallic conflicts to earlier levels also activated conflicts, which, taken together with the above, would still give him the feeling of being hemmed in. An attempt to obtain oral strength from his father once more spelled femininity. To seek regressively the position of the favored son stimulated the ambivalence felt toward mother and brother and the guilt he experienced in relation to oral sadism and anal explosiveness. Rather than be the quiet, passive, little flower girl, he would still prefer to "jump over the fence," or fall off it as Humpty Dumpty.

While the potential for feeling hemmed in was still there, both the elaboration of the phallic derivatives and the lessening of the regressive forces were such as to allow a definite forward move. Internal regulators of his wish to take a competitive stand, of his active exploration of the adult secrets, and of the setting of his academic and other achievement standards were more benign and no longer of monster proportions. As he portrayed it: the army jeep could go back for (oral) supplies, but could then drive forward into the secrets of the night.

A Year After the End of Treatment

Conflicts with the external world would again be stimulated as the mother had to depreciate Steven by invidious comparison with his brother and to intrude into his private life, i.e., burst into his hour with the therapist. Yet she had become painfully aware of her actions, and the occurrence of these external conflicts was rare. The impact on Steven of the parental disorganization was now less clear, but it was still likely to have some effect.

Even though the major emphasis was now on the adequate resolution of internal conflicts, signs of inadequate resolution at both the phallic and oral level remained. A story told to the T.A.T. card showing a couple embracing best focused the residual of Steven's conflict. He identified the characters as a father telling a son not to go into the swamps. These details as well as the rest of the story suggested former conflicts around penetrating the secrets of the night. Not that his curiosity was inhibited, but the misidentification of the sexes was consistent with his anxiety around identifying with the active masculine role in intercourse for fear that he "might be sucked helplessly into a swamp" and again become the feminine cha-cha dancer. Whether the rejection of, as well as the obvious sexual interest in, the feminine was simply consistent with prepubertal developments or represented a deviancy beyond the normal could be determined only in further follow-up. Although the provocation to be turned into a feminine victim by the father or mother could well be related to the above anxieties, this provocation could no longer be considered deviant.

Such regression as occurred did stimulate conflicts related to the earliest fixations. Passivity had to be inhibited not only because of its feminine connotations, but because of its link to the residual of oral sadism. Similarly, his longing to be the favorite son could not be expressed because of the anger that would accompany it. By putting the toy gun away he was in a sense rendering himself impotent. On the other hand, he could express his oral longing by eating a considerable amount of food during the psychological testing.

While these observations again point to residuals of conflict suggestive of a hysterical character structure, the total resolution of conflict was now such as to allow for extensive libidinal and ego growth.

ASSESSMENT OF GENERAL CHARACTERISTICS

At the Beginning of Treatment

Given the impact of his frustrating and anxiety-provoking parents, it is not easy to evaluate Steven's own tolerance in these areas. Yet independently assessed, it was clear that he could not tolerate frustrations relating to any deprivation imposed by the mother: the absence of a favorite food, and favoritism toward his brother stimulated an intolerable anger.

Similarly, the anxieties stimulated by any phallic step forward were too overwhelming: curiosity, sexual possession, and any active approach to a competitive situation, but particularly the academic one, were intolerable.

If only by contrast, there did seem to be some potential for sublimation. He had been able to achieve in the motor area; he could swim and ride a bicycle. Furthermore, his arithmetic was nearly at grade level. Otherwise, the areas of neutralized adaptation were very limited.

Finally, although the regressive tendencies far outweighed the progressive forces, there was also no doubt that Steven wanted to escape from an intolerable situation. He wanted to catch up with friends, and expressed an intelligent interest in his therapy: "I guess I am not doing well enough and could improve."

At the End of Treatment

Both qualitative and quantitative changes had taken place in Steven's ability to tolerate frustration and anxiety. He still found it difficult to tolerate the loss of the object and to give up being the favorite son, and had difficulty with anxieties arising out of competition with the father. Not only did the evidence of inadequate tolerance tend to be confined to these areas, but Steven showed much greater powers of recovery: that is, the frustrations and anxieties were quantitatively less overwhelming.

The development of Steven's sublimations and particularly the acceleration of the turn toward neutralized gratification were impressive. He could now derive much satisfaction from age-appropriate attainment in academic subjects, sports, and friendships.

By implication the progressive developmental forces were in ascendancy. His wish to be free of treatment and to test his strength was not only defensive. Moreover, his perception of himself as having changed and his academic ambitions were realistic and reflected an active wish to grow up. Going to college had become one of his goals.

A Year After the End of Treatment

Qualitatively speaking, evidence of frustration in relation to losing the object, not being the favorite, and not receiving the magical gift could still be seen. Similarly, the idea of performing competitively aroused initial anxiety and withdrawal. Yet quantitatively, further shifts had taken place in that the lowered tolerance was momentary.

As at the end of treatment, the evidence of the increasing number of aim-inhibited activities was impressive. Aside from continued and considerable academic progress, he had become a team captain, was an excellent athlete, and actively participated in a summer camp which he attended.

That the progressive forces had further accelerated is indicated by the fact that the wish to grow up was no longer talked about but just assumed—he would be like the friends with whom he had now caught up.

DIAGNOSIS

At the Beginning of Treatment

It is clear that permanent regressions had led in Steven to permanent symptom formation, and to a standstill in libidinal and ego growth. Few progressive forces were in evidence at the time of referral, but the phallic development had definitely been reached, and a wish to move forward again was retained.

The conflicts associated with the main symptom, a learning difficulty, were predominantly neurotic in nature. Developmental deficiencies in the differentiation and integration of ego functions also contributed, however, tc Steven's learning impairment.

At the End of Treatment

Although Steven still evidenced a considerable regressive potential as well as residuals of various types of conflict at all levels of development, their structural interrelation and quantitative force had been changed to the point where permanent symptom formation, impoverishing effects on libido progression, crippling effects on ego growth, and a lack of ego integration and differentiation were minimally present.

Projecting trends initiated during treatment, the therapist expected at the end of it that the predominance of the progressive over regressive forces in Steven's functioning would continue to increase in the year following treatment. It was anticipated that the conflicts specifically related to the terminal phase of treatment had been sufficiently interpreted so that their eventual resolution would aid rather than hinder the progressive forces. It was further anticipated that under pressure he would again tend to regress to crying or negative passive provocation, but that these tendencies would be temporary rather than permanent. It was realized, of course, that this would be possible only if his environment and particularly his parents were as supportive as was the case at the end of treatment.

A Year After the End of Treatment

Steven's functioning fell within "variations of normality." Permanent symptom formation, impoverishing effects on libido progression, crippling effects on ego growth, and evidence of a lack of ego integration and differentiation were quantitatively no greater than would be expected for a boy of this age.

It was anticipated, therefore, that Steven would continue to show the appropriate amount of progress in all areas of development, even though he was to be placed into one of the most advanced classes in his age group.

THE ASSESSMENT OF STEVEN TWO AND THREE YEARS AFTER THE END OF TREATMENT

Further follow-up evaluations of Steven and his family were done two and three years after the end of treatment. At each of these points the mother met with her therapist, Steven had a session with his therapist, a school visit was conducted, and finally the parents were seen jointly by the child therapist. While our formulations focused on Steven as evaluated three years after treatment, the information available from the follow-up two years after treatment was used in making these assessments. If previous assessments had been complicated by the reaction to termination and the accentuated repetition of material seen during treatment, in evaluating the assessments presented below it must be kept in mind that Steven was now thirteen and a half years old. Since in general the Profiles of the second follow-up confirm the results of the assessment done one year after treatment, only selected areas are discussed.

By three years after treatment Steven showed the beginnings of adolescent development. His wish to be independent in his choice of activities and an assertive defiance of his mother were differentiated from earlier behavior exclusively provocative in nature. The adolescent character of his object relationships was underlined by his great sensitivity to his peers. Although he knew he was well liked both as a companion and athlete, and had continued his ways of "fair play," he overreacted whenever one of his many friends left him. Here again one is reminded of his feelings of no longer being the favorite son, but once more we conclude that this type of depressed feeling falls within the normal range of adolescent object relations.

Examination of Steven's superego functioning best focuses both his strength but also potential deterrents to progressive development. He was consciously determined to succeed and there were many indications of the internalization of benign paternal expectations. He would train for the same profession as father, could identify with his religious values and yet compete with him in this area. Most important, he felt support from an inner feeling that the father wanted him to succeed.

While benign inner expectations would also derive from a devoted mother who had high hopes for her first son, there were still some indications that the severity of these demands (now internalized) could potentially hinder Steven's development. He had taken on a great deal of extracurricular activity; although he managed to cope successfully, the strain was considerable. Only a further follow-up could determine how the various components of his superego would be integrated, but the expectation was that the benign aspects would predominate.

The Differential Development of Children Seen Once and Four Times a Week

As the complexity of the case of Steven suggests, the number of different ways that the children seen four times and once a week could be compared is very great. Nor can a presentation of group findings do justice to the unique individual constellations. Considering each of the major sections of the Profile, it could, however, be determined which characteristics were salient in differentiating the two groups of children; those generalizations which could be derived despite important individual variations are stated in the form of hypotheses.[5] Thus the first of these is derived from the material available in the Profiles on phase development (A. Freud, 1962).

Because Steven has been presented in detail, and because he best illustrates the development of the children seen four times a week, the illustrations for this group will be drawn exclusively from his Profiles. The children seen once a week were Gordon, Robert, John, and Philip. At the end of their treatment they were twelve, eleven, ten, and twelve years old.

[5] Further substantiation of these hypotheses is provided by the analysis of the clinical ratings based on the Profiles (Heinicke, 1965b).

PHASE DEVELOPMENT

The children seen four times a week achieve dominance on a more advanced libidinal phase during the follow-up period.

At the risk of oversimplification, it can be said that at the beginning of treatment all children in both groups had achieved dominance on the anal phase and reached at least the phallic phase of development. Regression from this advance was, however, either massive (as in the case of Steven) or extensive. Needless to say, the specific fixation points and the quality and quantity of the regression involved differed a great deal.

By the end of treatment all children had reached at least the latency phase. This was judged by the fact that a considerable number of conflicts at the phallic phase had been resolved, some repression and neutralization of drive activity had taken place, and the extent of regression to pregenital levels had lessened.

That judgments of the phase *reached* do not differentiate the two groups is further supported by the fact that some signs of the pubertal and preadolescent development were seen in both groups. For example, there was some interest in the opposite sex and a growing rebellion and striving for independence.

Examination of the follow-up conclusions revealed, however, that for the once-a-week group this advance had been achieved without adequately resolving the libidinal conflicts of the previous phases. Thus, the once-a-week treatment is likely to facilitate an immediate forward move into latency, but the thrust is limited. In contrast to the four-times-a-week group, dominance in the latency phase had not been achieved at follow-up, and the regression to earlier phases was less likely to be in the service of the ego. Not that Gordon's turning to TV and the icebox after a challenging day at school interfered seriously with his school adaptations, but it was related to a disinclination to get involved in the complications of after-school peer relations. Furthermore, by the second follow-up this picture had changed little.

The lack of dominance in the latency phase was also further defined and characterized by the failure adequately to resolve certain components of the oedipal constellation. As already suggested, this in turn is linked to selected regressions to earlier levels.

Although very likely a function of the particular sample studied, this lack of conflict resolution was most readily seen in two areas. All children could by the time of follow-up assume a competitive stance, but the subsequent invitation to be the victim with its implication for unresolved bisexual conflicts was typically more pronounced in the once-a-week cases. Gordon would very effectively defeat the therapist in checkers, but then suddenly had to lose. In contrast, Steven's tendency to provoke his parents to turn him into a victim was by the second follow-up not only infrequent, but now mainly in the service of asserting his independence.

Another area of difference in the degree of conflict resolution and the associated slowing down of libidinal development involved curiosity and fantasies relating to intercourse and birth. Thus, Gordon could fully exercise his curiosity in many intellectual areas, and could even ask both parents and therapist direct sexual questions. Despite repeated explanations, however, his pregenital fantasies continued to have a disturbing influence on his reality testing and he would then out of embarrassment avoid the issue completely. In contrast, Steven had by the time of the second follow-up sufficiently resolved conflicts relating to these "sexual secrets" to be free both to have a realistic picture of adult sexual relations and to take the first adolescent steps toward participating in this pleasure.

LIBIDO DISTRIBUTION

The children seen four times a week show a greater growth in their over-all level of self-esteem during the follow-up period.

Even though the specific constellations vary a great deal, certain generalizations can be made concerning the children's quantity and quality of self-esteem. None of the children were at the beginning of treatment characterized by the type of defect in narcissism usually associated with psychotic process. Nor had any of them reached the point of depression associated with serious suicidal attempts. Some children's experience of narcissism was poorly integrated. Thus, not only was Steven's over-all level of self-esteem initially low, but his self representations fluctuated too frequently to allow for a feeling of some sustained competence and of a differentiated and relatively autonomous self. He shifted too quickly from boy to girl, clever to crazy, and proud challenger to amorphous Humpty Dumpty.

By the end of treatment none of the children showed this type of deficiency in the integration of self representations. It was, however, particularly the children seen four times a week whose libido distribution was characterized by the following: a feeling that they could attain age-appropriate goals by themselves; a feeling of having changed; a self-consciousness in relation to a total separate self; less reliance on the external world for support of their self-regard and a realistic hope which was most intimately related to a feeling of making progress. It was this *feeling* of making or not making progress *during the follow-up period* that most distinguished the two groups. Steven spontaneously spoke of how he was "doing well in my schoolwork" and already at the end of treatment indicated he felt that he "had changed." Although equally hopeful at the end of treatment, a year later and in a more despondent tone, Gordon felt he "was doing even."

In further assessing the children's self-regard, the experience of being the victim stood out at the beginning of treatment. This took many different forms. The children felt they might suddenly be abandoned; that they had deficient brains or bodies; that they were subject to constant control or intrusion, etc. Although the force of these self concepts had by the end of treatment declined for all children, residuals of feeling the victim were more pronounced during the follow-up period among the children treated once a week.

OBJECT LIBIDO

By the second follow-up contact the children seen four times a week more frequently show the capacity to form object relationships which are characterized by a gratifying libidinal exchange, a realistic give and take, and considerable autonomy.

In discussing the development of the children's object relations we must first of all point out that the group differences are less striking and only emerged late in the follow-up period.

Although the nature of the children's object relationships initially varied greatly, two features were particularly striking: the intense longing to be gratified, which all expressed; and the extent to which they relied on the external object to turn them into the very victim they feared and yet also had to be. Because of their own inadequate ego and superego control, much energy was directed toward getting the externally perceived monsterlike objects to coerce or limit them.

Although all children could by the time of the second follow-up express more affection toward at least one parent, in the children seen once a week, both the longing and signs of ambivalence were more evident. When his family was contacted on the phone, Gordon screamed for his mother only to announce that she was not there; he knew this, of course, all the time. All four children in this group clearly expressed the feeling of things being "unfair" in relation to the teacher. Just as John had felt that his mother always favored his younger brother, so he thought that his teacher favored certain pupils and gave them better grades.

Several further phenomena were linked to the above and by the second follow-up characterized the object relations of the children seen once a week. All were still inclined to provoke a significant figure (mother, father, teacher) to coerce them into activity or limit their instinctual expressions. For example, in his anger that the teacher did not help him enough and yet demanded a great deal from him, Philip reflected feelings previously expressed toward the mother and provocatively got out of his seat until the teacher had to "freeze him" in it.

In contrast, the object relations of the children seen four times a week were by the second follow-up characterized by a greater give and take and a freedom from sadomasochistic involvements. Thus, Steven could accept the guidance and help of his mother, but also for the most part initiate and complete his academic work on his own. Also reflecting greater autonomy was his ability to criticize and even surpass his father without experiencing a retaliation of monsterlike proportions.

The children seen once a week also had developed greater autonomy in certain areas. Thus, Gordon could prepare his own meals and was now very capable of finding his way in the neighborhood. Robert and Philip showed their independence by very effectively serving as a focal point of peer feelings against an "unfair" teacher. As the examples indicate, however, the autonomy shown was at least in part likely to be defensive in nature. Gordon's self-care could be understood in relation to a frequently absent, very busy, "shadowy" mother. At the same time he still provoked her to "lower the boom" and force him to improve the Civics which he was in danger of failing. Similarly, Robert had come very close to being expelled from school.

AGGRESSION

The balance of effective assertion to defensive passivity is greater during the follow-up period for the children seen four times a week.

Despite the individual variation in the quality and quantity of aggression expressed at the beginning of treatment, certain conclusions can be drawn. Not surprisingly, it was initially predominantly related to the pregenital levels. If one thinks of the predominant sources, secondary sources, etc., then one can conclude that the children seen once a week showed little change in this hierarchy, while the children seen four times a week showed considerable change. Thus, although no longer openly expressed, and although the objects involved had changed, the aggressive derivatives that could be inferred from Gordon's behavior during the follow-up assessment were related to a constellation of conflicts very similar in structure to those seen at the beginning of treatment. Central at both points was the shift from an effective challenge of the male rival (at ping-pong or checkers) to the subsequent self-defeat. Similarly, at both points he could express his anal defiance (keeping his desk full of loose papers or not taking a shower after physical education) only to provoke coercion or further defeat. Too often he lost important papers, and his lack of cleanliness was responsible for a lowered grade. Finally, his oral sadism, and particularly his need to defend against it (are there muzzles for humans?), could be inferred from his mouth-opening, eye-widening gestures, and the passivity still present at follow-up.

In contrast, though the pregenital sources of the aggression were dominant in Steven's functioning at the beginning of treatment, by the second follow-up most of the aggression that occurred was related to the effective assertion of a preadolescent boy. He successfully maintained his academic progress in a highly competitive junior high school, and could successfully meet the challenge of a jealous bully in competitive basketball.

It is particularly this predominance of effective assertion and the implications for the neutralization of aggression that during the follow-up characterized the children seen four times a week. The level of effective assertion of the children seen once a week had also increased. Gordon's determined approach particularly in certain cognitive areas or in such matters as collecting and trading coins was impressive. However, the inhibition of aggression and the associated passivity were also prominent and more so than they had been at the end of treatment. He waited for others to initiate things, still expected his mother to get him to catch up in certain courses, and underlined the picture of passivity by feeding himself favorite foods, television, mystery books, etc.

In general, the children seen once a week could assert themselves in some areas more than they had at the beginning of treatment, but the continuance of passivity in other areas of adaptation and particularly those involving the academic challenge was also impressive. Philip could deal with mechanical problems and effectively defy the teacher, but he demonstrated little assertion in the academic area. Robert could by the follow-up play a good game of tackle football and could also effectively challenge the teacher's "fairness"; too often, however, he simply sat, still bit his knuckles, and, as could be determined in a further treatment, was consciously terrified he would explode and get into trouble with the school authorities. John could often actively approach both a sports situation (kickball) and the academic challenge, but on many occasions his parents had to "stand over him" to "get him going." Similarly, too often he simply sat in class and did nothing.

EGO AND SUPEREGO FUNCTIONING

The children seen four times a week make greater progress during the follow-up period in the level of ego integration, differentiation, and adaptation than do the children seen once a week.

If the above represents the most general hypothesis, a series of further hypotheses are given to specify the differences seen during the follow-up period. Before specifying these, however, we should stress the similarities seen at the end of treatment. While certain trends which were to be accentuated later could be noticed, there were few *striking* group differences at the end of treatment. The only exceptions were that the once-a-week children already showed a greater tendency to repress aggressive derivatives, whereas the four-times-a-week children were able to express a greater variety of affects and showed a greater ability to elaborate ideas imaginatively.

There were also a number of areas where striking group differences were not even observed during follow-up. Of these the following ego functions are of particular interest: the level of reality testing, the level of the visual and auditory memory, the quality of space and time orientation, and the level of the large and fine motor coordination. Although the quality of the auditory memory was often the poorest function in this group of children, in general the level of the above list of functions fell within the range of normal variations.

We turn then to a consideration of the dimensions in terms of which the two groups could be differentiated during the follow-up period.

1. *By the time of the first follow-up the children seen once a week show a greater imbalance in their defensive organization than the children seen four times a week.*

Early in our project we had been impressed by the fact that after treatment the underlying conflicts of even the most successful cases had not altered drastically, but the mode of coping with these conflicts had changed considerably. Similarly, it is the extent of balance in the use of defenses that differentiates the two groups being discussed. Rather than the defensive operations being silent and effective, or the child using a number of them flexibly, by the first follow-up the children seen once a week tended to use certain ones excessively. Excessive is judged here in terms of frequency and its nonadaptive consequences. Thus, John's continued tendency to turn the anger felt toward his mother inward could be associated, for example, with repeated accidents, one of which led to the chipping of his teeth. He now looked like the abandoned, starving, injured mouse that he had often felt he was.

Similarly, Gordon's turn toward passivity, indulging himself with food and avoiding the complications of more intimate relationships, was excessive and was associated with his impoverished object relationships.

Finally, Robert was by the follow-up isolating his anger toward an unfair, ungiving mother by experiencing these feelings in relation to the teacher and then provoking her until she had to kick him out of the room or even the school.

In contrast, though the exaggerated use of certain defenses had characterized Steven's functioning in the beginning of treatment—regression, avoidance, and the defensive identifications had been used excessively—by the first follow-up a variety of defenses were employed and none of them excessively.

2. *The defense organization of the children seen once a week as opposed to four times a week was by the first follow-up more dependent on the object world.*

Despite the expected individual variations within the two treatment groups, the children seen once as opposed to four times a week continued during the follow-up period to rely heavily on the intervention and guidance of the external adult objects. This was particularly true in terms of defenses relating to conflicts aroused by the academic challenge. Philip, Robert, and John all relied on the teacher to get them going in a task or to limit their provocations.

The greater level of assertion of the children seen four times a week has already been described. In the context of the present discussion with its implications for superego development, one can add that a more benign set of superego and ego-ideal representations could be inferred from these children's ability to initiate and guide the steps leading to successful academic achievement. They could remember the assignment, insist on doing their work in their own room by themselves, and be less dependent on immediate approval when they had achieved an "A" on a paper.

If the above is a reflection of certain essential differences in the defensive organization of the children, and this in turn can be related to the nature of the ego integration achieved, other dimensions can be thought of as relating to the child's inner differentiation.

3. *The children seen four times as opposed to once a week already by the end of treatment show a greater capacity to elaborate imaginatively.*

Judgments of the child's ability and freedom to elaborate certain ideas were based on such observations as his stories to T.A.T. cards, his play and other creative activities during his contact with the various clinicians involved. Could the child elaborate an extensive and yet coherent story? Could he create, enact, and bring to some kind of conclusion a dramatic sequence? Could he creatively plan a construction and carry it through? For example, during his follow-up hour Steven not only designed a very interesting car but completed it, responding flexibly to such changes as were dictated by the nature of the material. The greater ability to express themselves was also shown in other ways.

4. *The children seen four times as opposed to once a week could already by the end of treatment express a greater variety of affects.*

Although there would again be important differences within the two groups, the children seen once a week showed less feeling and such open feeling as was expressed was of limited variety. Thus, Gordon's disappointment was obvious in his whining though quiet tone, but he could show little open anger, little enthusiasm, little pride, little real pleasure. Even the anxiety about being attacked and scrutinized by the therapist could in no way be openly expressed.

In contrast, Steven briefly showed his anger with his brother, complained openly about not being the therapist's favorite, was obviously pleased to see the therapist, took pride in his achievements, and could laugh both at himself and his mother. This leads to another typical difference.

5. *The children seen four times as opposed to once a week by the first follow-up more frequently made use of a nondefensive form of humor.*

Although the predominantly nondefensive type of humor is not easy to define, judgments were based on whether or not it was used primarily in reference to the needs of the object and the social situation or whether its function was primarily determined by inner needs; for example, the need to express forbidden impulses. Steven's expression of his wish to continue his therapy by saying that it had not helped—he was sorry that the book saying that psychiatry did no good had already been written—was clearly defensive, yet it not only amused the therapist but was also an expression of gratitude. Finally, Steven's insight into his own wish to keep the therapist added a special quality to the humor.

6. *The children seen four times as opposed to once a week by the time of the first follow-up show a greater capacity to observe their own behavior and the motives underlying it.*

In attempting to judge the child's level of insight three factors were considered: (1) Does the child observe his own behavior? (2) Does he have any understanding of his motives for behaving in a certain way? (3) Is this recognition achieved in a context that lends conviction to it and is thus likely to lead to some alteration in behavior?

Steven again illustrates these distinctions. At the end of treatment he told the psychiatrist that he felt that he had changed; that he was older. This was in fact true and not only in the simple chronological sense. Moreover, Steven showed insight into his own motivations. Having been shown his anger about being kept waiting by his parents and how he could get even by keeping them waiting and not making any progress in his reading, he realized with surprise: "But then I would be hurting myself." There is little doubt that this type of insight did contribute to the very real progress he began to make in his reading.

Having given examples of specific hypotheses relating to the ego functioning of the two groups, we return once more to the level of ego integration.

7. *The children seen once as opposed to four times a week by the time of the second follow-up show a less adequate level of ego integration than the children seen four times a week.*

It will be recalled that the two groups did not differ strikingly in the level of ego integration achieved at the end of treatment.

Even at this point, however, the integration achieved by the children seen once a week involved greater strain; a greater quantity of countercathexes was involved. Although the previous signs of mobile discharge and unneutralized aggression were missing, these manifestations were associated even in the previously most labile children with a trend toward deadlock. This emphasis is supported by those differences that did emerge at the end of treatment: the children seen once a week were characterized by a greater repression of aggressive derivatives, less variety in the expression of affects, and less ability to elaborate imaginatively.

Given a quality of integration dependent on countercathexes against aggression and a restricted affect expression, one might expect that either the child's development would be restricted or that the aggressive discharge would again occur under certain circumstances. Both in fact occurred. Many of the findings presented demonstrate restriction in development during the follow-up period of the children seen once a week. With the exception of Gordon, all these children also were on several occasions overcome by uncontrolled aggressive outbursts. Robert once gave in to an urgent impulse to destroy a school wastepaper basket. A primary-process quality is suggested. The total evidence for this type of mental functioning was limited, but it was again more evident among the group seen once a week.

DEVELOPMENT OF TOTAL PERSONALITY

The children seen four times as opposed to once a week made greater progress during the follow-up period in moving from dependency to emotional self-reliance.

It was found that already by the first follow-up the children seen four times a week had made greater progress in moving along the developmental lines from suckling to rational eating, from egocentricity to companionship, and from play to work, as well as showing greater congruence in their total development. It was, however, their development toward self-reliance that seemed outstanding.

In the evaluation of the child's progress, considerations of the libidinal phase reached and the development of object relations are focused on the issue of self-reliance—on the extent to which the child can move from the mutuality in object relations characteristic of the oedipal phase to a sufficient lessening and transference of libido to the community (teacher, leaders, peers), impersonal ideals, and aim-inhibited, sublimated interests (A. Freud, 1963).

Previous findings anticipated the conclusion that the children seen four times as opposed to once a week showed greater self-reliance during the follow-up period. Several observations focused on this conclusion. Not only did the children seen once a week have a much more difficult time in independently coping with the academic challenge, but the evidence of the unresolved oedipal and preoedipal relationships with the parents was much more easily traced. Feeling that his mother had dropped her aspirations for him, Philip was likely to attribute similar characteristics to the teacher.

Although the difference in the development of friendships was not that striking, one example of independence occurred sufficiently often among the children seen four times as opposed to once a week at least to suggest a larger difference. When confronted with a domineering or insulting peer, these children were able to deal with the situation without giving in or becoming excessively belligerent. Although Steven was exposed to the jealous attack of a much larger boy, he nevertheless continued his very successful involvement in a basketball game.

GENETIC, STRUCTURAL, AND DYNAMIC CONSIDERATIONS

The children seen four times as opposed to once a week by the time of the second follow-up (1) show evidence of the previous fixations, but the regressive force of these is less; (2) are characterized by a more neutralized and adaptive form of derivative; and (3) are characterized by character traits which can be traced to previous fixations but which are adequately integrated into the child's functioning.

It is first of all important to note that no generalizations could be formulated about the specific nature of the fixations and the conflicts. The potential diversity may make this difficult in any case and this would be accentuated in turn by the considerable diversity among the children being studied.

Such hypotheses as could be formulated are again most easily illustrated by contrasting Steven and Gordon. It was possible once more to recognize derivatives of the most important fixation points in both boys at the time of the follow-ups. Steven's tendency to provoke his male rival to punish him both for his guilt about masturbation and his wish to defeat him were again evident. Similarly, the dangers of assuming the masculine position in intercourse were portrayed in terms of being "sucked into a swamp." Finally, his passive longing, wish to be the favorite, and the related oral-sadistic conflicts once more emerged. However, where regression to these fixations occurred, it was temporary. More important, not only was the interference of these derivatives with adaptation minimal, but the nature of the total structure was such (and this has been outlined previously) as to allow the inference of considerable neutralization of previous derivatives. By the second follow-up one could still readily observe character tendencies of being provocative and feeling depressed; but even these did not disrupt the general picture of sound ego integration.

At the same time it is clear that fluctuations in the nature of the external impact would either enhance or disrupt the adaptive function of the character traits of any of the children being discussed. Although Steven had by the second follow-up managed to integrate his superego demands for excellent academic performance into a realistic approach to his schoolwork, it was clear that should his mother from her own anxiety again "need to push him," then his adaptation might possibly yield to indications of "I can't make it."

In contrast to Steven and illustrative of the children seen once a week, the residual of Gordon's fixations and former conflicts could quite easily be observed during both follow-ups. His need to attack the therapist and the subsequent self-defeat revealed the active and nonadaptive struggle with the residual of bisexual conflicts. In contrast, his assertiveness on the mathematical subtests of the Stanford I.Q. was most impressive. Similarly, his effective verbal sparring with his father suggested the resolution of oedipal conflicts and the associated neutralization; but in the academic area closest to the father's occupation, the intrapsychic derivatives again interfered with adaptive functioning.

Finally, many of Gordon's character traits were not only related to previous fixations but were less well integrated into his total adaptation. Thus, his independence and inclination to "feed" himself provided a resolution of oral-sadistic conflicts, but because of its associated isolation also impaired the development of his peer relationships. Similarly, his persistent and meticulous saving and trading of coins absorbed derivatives of anal-explosive conflicts. Some aspects of this activity—dealing with the various officials, finding his way around town, learning the value of money—were likely to expand his capabilities, but the excessive concern with one activity and the intense interest in accumulating "piles of coins" were less well integrated and revealed the closeness of pregenital derivatives.

GENERAL CHARACTERISTICS

The children seen once as opposed to four times a week by the time of the follow-up period show less ability to resolve and thus tolerate instinctual residuals and in particular oral-sadistic derivatives.

Although all four indices from the section on the Assessment of General Characteristics—frustration tolerance, sublimation potential, attitude to anxiety, and the balance of progressive over regressive forces—favor the children seen four times a week, it was particularly the inability to resolve and thus tolerate residuals of a biting oral anger that characterized the children seen once a week.

Although one would conclude that the conflicts between the child's oral sadism and equally intense superego counterrepresentations were not completely resolved for any of the children treated, and this fixation point thus exerted a continuing force, its regressive force was more striking in the case of the children seen once a week. The child's total functioning was, of course, considered in judging his frustration tolerance; this characteristic could be observed in many situations. Yet various types of behavior particularly characteristic of the once-a-week children place the focus on the inability to tolerate the biting anger associated with earliest deprivation. In some instances the result was a break-through of aggression. John always felt that he might at a moment's notice be abandoned like a rat, and always experienced intense anger toward a younger brother who he felt was favored; the anticipation of another sibling brought on a renewed and extreme attack on his brother. These attacks were always timed so that he would be the subject of intense punishment. Among other ways, Gordon defended himself against the break-through of oral sadism by constantly "feeding" himself a variety of things from food to TV.

FURTHER CONSIDERATIONS RELATING TO THE DATA PRESENTED

Although it is felt to be an advantage to distinguish between the cross-sectional assessment of the child's developmental status and the study of his therapeutic experience, it is important to stress that the evaluation of the generalizations stated above is very likely to be influenced and possibly changed by the knowledge of the details of the therapeutic process. Findings on the differential development of the process in the two groups will be presented in future publication.

The method of constructing the Profiles and its relation to the generalizations derived also require further comment. During the hypothesis-making stage of a project, the therapist's extensive knowledge and capacity to integrate and highlight the findings are likely to be particularly valuable. Yet the therapist's involvement in the treatment can also be a source of bias. The first check on this bias was the great care taken to make cross-sectional assessments, to document the conclusions reached, and to integrate carefully the data from psychiatrist, psychologist, teacher, tutor, and parents.

Further support for the validity of the findings derived from the Profiles is given by the analysis of test indices derived independently of the therapist. The following indices have been used: the rate of improvement on academic tests of reading, spelling, and arithmetic; the Stanford Binet Intelligence Quotient, the vocabulary score on the Stanford Binet; and indices derived from the Rorschach. These results are presented in detail in another publication (Heinicke, 1965a). One example is given to support a general conclusion derived from the analysis of the Profiles, namely, that few differences in developmental status were noticeable at the end of treatment, but that the children seen four times as opposed to once a week did show greater developmental progress in the period after the end of treatment. The availability of test assessments of the child's academic progress made it possible to compute the rate of improvement during certain intervals of time for reading, spelling, and arithmetic. Comparing the trends for the children seen four times as opposed to once a week, we found that the latter showed a significantly greater improvement in reading during the first year of treatment, that there was no significant difference during the last period of treatment, but that the children seen four times as opposed to once a week improved at a faster rate during the two years after treatment. (See Figure 1; the P <.01 indicates that the difference between the groups could have occurred by chance less than 1 in 100 times.) The same conclusions apply to spelling, but no significant differences were found for arithmetic.

A third major consideration in evaluating the generalizations takes the form of the following question: are the various Profile distinctions essentially governed by one conceptual dimension (e.g., mental health-sickness) and are the various group differences, there-

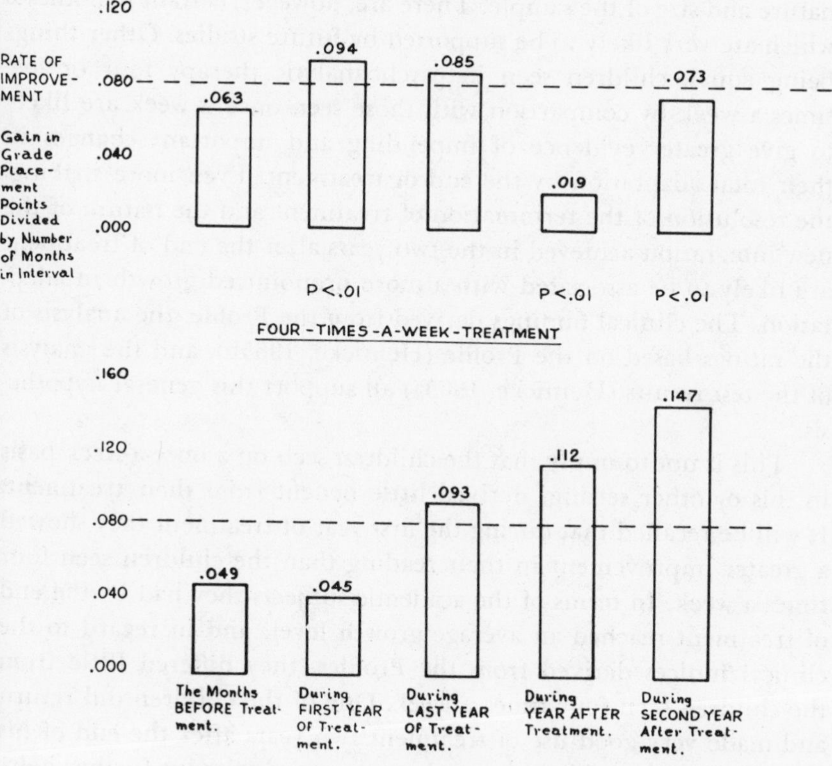

fore, essentially statements of one major group difference? The first answer is that even if this were so, the Profile does insure that all aspects of the child's functioning are considered in evaluating his over-all developmental status and potential. Moreover, various analyses do indicate that many more than one basic conceptual dimension must be postulated to understand the variation in the results presented (see Heinicke, 1965b).

Discussion

As already indicated, the full understanding of the findings reported here will have to await the study of the differential therapeutic process experienced by the two groups of children.

Further limitations on any generalizations are imposed by the nature and size of the sample. There are, however, certain hypotheses which are very likely to be supported by future studies. Other things being equal, children seen in psychoanalytic therapy four or five times a week by comparison with those seen once a week are likely to give greater evidence of impending and important changes in their total adaptation by the end of treatment. Even more striking, the resolution of the termination of treatment and the nature of the new integration achieved in the two years after the end of treatment are likely to be associated with a more pronounced growth in adaptation. The clinical findings derived from the Profile, the analysis of the ratings based on the Profile (Heinicke, 1965b), and the analysis of the test results (Heinicke, 1965a) all support this general hypothesis.

This is not to imply that the children seen on a once-a-week basis in this or other settings derived little benefit from their treatment. It will be recalled that during the first year of treatment they showed a greater improvement in their reading than the children seen four times a week. In terms of the academic subjects they had by the end of treatment reached an average growth level; and in regard to the clinical indices derived from the Profiles, they differed little from the children seen four times a week. One of the children did return and made very good use of treatment two years after the end of his first one, but the other children have managed without further help.

It is clear, however, that any assessment of the outcome of treatment must include adequate follow-up contacts. The impression was that given the average age of these children at the end of treatment, that is, eleven, a two-year follow-up was likely to be a sufficient period of time for the most important effects of the treatment to be integrated into a new adaptation. This does not, however, take account of new and particularly challenging demands of the adolescent development. A further follow-up in early adulthood, therefore, seems necessary.

While the specific form of the accelerated adaptation of the children seen more frequently is likely to vary considerably as the nature of the samples being studied changes, a summary picture of the qualities which particularly differentiated the two groups being studied is of value.

This summary is attempted first in relation to Steven's development. Reviewing the Profile constructed for the first follow-up, it was clear that signs of pathology could still be detected. Many of these were further transformed and integrated by the time of the second and third follow-ups. However, it was particularly by comparison with the children seen once a week that certain positive qualities stood out. There is, first of all, the forward libidinal push as expressed in a sublimated form. The well-designed and executed car with a prominent antenna communicated the quality of ego integration and self-esteem. Where doubt occurred and regression set in, it could be overcome. The implied flexibility is supported by his ability to imagine such a car in the first place. The flexibility was further underlined by the variety of feelings expressed: from the angry complaint of "same old junk" to the pride in his achievement. This very ability to express his disappointment that he had not received the magical gift or was not receiving a "blue print" as well as the ability to tolerate this frustration and to recover from it characterized his functioning and that of the other children seen four times a week.

The nature of Steven's effective assertiveness and independence must also be underlined and may well be associated in part with the type of treatment he experienced. He could develop his own plan, he showed an active but not offensive curiosity, and he could withstand the intrusion of an overly concerned mother. Yet his independence and assertiveness were not associated with aloofness and a lack of humor, as they were in Gordon's functioning. He could express warmth in relation both to the therapist and his mother, and could achieve distance through an appropriate joke.

Once more summarizing, although the level of ego integration was not strikingly different for the two groups until the second follow-up point, by the first follow-up it had become clear that the integration of the children seen once a week was more dependent on the operation of countercathexes, particularly those directed at aggressive derivatives. The quality of the integration was further defined by an imbalance in the defensive organization. Passivity, the tendency to provoke punishment and to turn aggression against the self are outstanding examples of defenses used excessively. In general, these children were more dependent on the intervention and guidance of the adult to maintain their defensive organization. Nor did the resultant constriction in functioning guarantee a continued level of integration; by the second follow-up three of the children evidenced a breakdown in the control of aggression and some primary-process-like discharge.

In contrast to this picture of constriction, the ego integration of the children seen four times a week involved a more balanced use of defenses, indications of more benign superego functioning, and perhaps most important, such indications of flexibility and differentiation as the ability to elaborate an idea imaginatively, the capacity to express a variety of affects, the nondefensive use of humor, and the capacity to observe their own behavior and the motives underlying it.

Consistent with this more adequate level of ego integration, differentiation, and flexibility shown by the children seen four times a week were the increasing indications of sublimation and the neutralization of drive derivatives seen during the follow-up. The evidence here ranges from clinical judgments of the sublimation potential to the rate of improvement in reading and vocabulary.

In terms of their drive development, the children seen four times a week were characterized by a greater assertiveness, particularly in the academic area, and a generally greater progress in achieving dominance on the most advanced libidinal phase. The regressions and associated fixations observed in the children seen once a week were not of such force as to overwhelm the children; they were confined but were less often in the service of the ego. That is, these children neither regressed in an obvious way to former developmental stages nor were they as responsive to new developmental challenges as the children seen four times a week.

The children seen four times a week also showed a more favorable quantity and quality of self-esteem. They were particularly characterized by the feeling that they were progressing and that they could do things on their own.

In terms of the lines of development (A. Freud, 1963), it was the move to greater self-reliance and adult object relationships that differentiated the children seen four times a week. If only by contrast with the general pattern of differences found, in their peer relationships they did not differ strikingly from the children seen once a week.

In terms of certain general characteristics, their ability to tolerate frustration, particularly of their oral longings, and the general preponderance of progressive over regressive forces once more favored the development after treatment of the children seen four times a week.

Once more it must be stressed that the study of both the treatment process and the individual variations is necessary in order more adequately to evaluate the meaning of the differences found. Future presentations will include details of the therapeutic material which characterizes the two treatment situations [see Heinicke (1969), Heinicke and Goldman (1960), Heinicke and Strassman (1975)].

BIBLIOGRAPHY

P.S.C. *The Psychoanalytic Study of the Child,* Vols. 1–25, New York: Int. Univ. Press, 1945–1970; Vols. 26–30, New Haven: Yale Univ. Press, 1971–1975.

S.E. *The Standard Edition of the Complete Psychological Works of Sigmund Freud,* 24 Vols. London: Hogarth Press, 1953–1974.

W. *The Writings of Anna Freud,* 7 Vols. New York: Int. Univ. Press, 1968–1974.

Alpert, A. (1959), Reversibility of Pathological Fixations Associated with Maternal Deprivation in Infancy. *P.S.C.,* 14:169–185.

Arthur, H. (1952), A Comparison of the Techniques Employed in Psychotherapy and Psychoanalysis of Children. *Amer. J. Orthopsychiat.* 22:484–498.

Balint, A. (1943), Identification. *Int. J. Psa.,* 24:97–107.

Bartemeier, L. H. (1932), Some Observations of Convulsive Disorders in Children. *Amer. J. Orthopsychiat.,* 2:260–267.

——— (1943), Concerning the Psychogenesis of Convulsive Disorders. *Psa. Quart.,* 12:330–337.

Bibring, E. (1937), On the Theory of the Therapeutic Results of Psycho-Analysis. *Int. J. Psa.,* 18:170–189.

——— (1954), Psychoanalysis and the Dynamic Psychotherapies. *J. Amer. Psa. Assn.,* 2:745–770.

Bibring, G. L. (1959), Some Considerations of the Psychological Processes in Pregnancy. *P.S.C.,* 14:113–121.

——— Dwyer, T. F., Huntington, D. S., & Valenstein, A. F. (1961), A Study of the Psychological Processes in Pregnancy and of the Earliest Mother-Child Relationship. *P.S.C.,* 16:9–72.

Bowlby, J. (1960), Separation Anxiety. *Int. J. Psa.,* 41:89–113.

Brunswick, R. M. (1940), The Preoedipal Phase of the Libido Development. In: *The Psychoanalytic Reader,* ed. R. Fliess. New York: Int. Univ. Press, 1948, 1:261–283.

Bühler, C. (1953), *From Birth to Maturity.* London: Routledge & Kegan Paul.

Burlingham, D. (1961), Some Notes on the Development of the Blind. *P.S.C.,* 16:121–145.

——— (1964), Hearing and Its Role in the Development of the Blind. *P.S.C.,* 19:95–112.

——— (1965), Some Problems of Ego Development in Blind Children. *P.S.C.,* 20:194–208.

——— (1972), *Psychoanalytic Studies of the Sighted and the Blind.* New York: Int. Univ. Press.

——— (1975), Special Problems of Blind Infants: Blind Baby Profile. *P.S.C.,* 30:3–13.

Cartwright, D., Kirtner, W. L., & Fiske, D. (1963), Method Factors in Changes Associated with Psychotherapy. *J. Abnorm. Soc. Psychol.,* 66:164–175.

Coleman, R. W., Kris, E., & Provence, S. (1953), The Study of Variations of Early Parental Attitudes. *P.S.C.,* 8:20–47.

Darwin, C. (1872), *The Expression of the Emotions in Man and Animal.* Chicago: Univ. Chicago Press, 1897.

FRAIBERG, S. (1968), Parallel and Divergent Patterns in Blind and Sighted Infants. *P.S.C.,* 23:264–300.

——— & FREEDMAN, D. A. (1964), Studies in the Ego Development of the Congenitally Blind Child. *P.S.C.,* 19:113–169.

FRANKL, L. (1958), Enquiry into the Difficulty of Diagnosis by Comparing the Impressions in the Diagnostic Interviews with the Material Elicited in the Course of the Child's Analysis. *Proc. Royal Soc. Med.,* 51(11): 945–946.

FREEMAN, T. (1975), The Use of the Profile Schema for the Psychotic Patient. In: *Studies in Child Analysis.* New Haven: Yale Univ. Press, pp. 117–126.

FREUD, A. (1945), Indications for Child Analysis. *P.S.C.,* 1:127–149.

——— (1948), Sublimation as a Factor in Upbringing. *Health Educ. J.,* 6(3):25–29.

——— (1949), Aggression in Relation to Emotional Development. *P.S.C.,* 3/4:37–48.

——— (1952), The Role of Bodily Illness in the Mental Life of Children. *P.S.C.,* 7:69–81.

——— (1953), Some Remarks on Infant Observation. *P.S.C.,* 8:9–19.

——— (1954), In: Problems of Infantile Neurosis: A Discussion. *P.S.C.,* 9:16–71.

——— (1958), Child Observation and Prediction of Development. *P.S.C.,* 13:92–124.

——— (1960a), Entrance into Nursery School. *W.,* 5:315–335.

——— (1960b), Four Contributions to the Psychoanalytic Study of the Child. Abst. in: *J. Philadelphia Assn. Psa.,* 1:106–112.

——— (1961), In panel: The Curative Factors of Psychoanalysis. Int. Psa. Congr., Edinburgh.

——— (1962), Assessment of Childhood Disturbances. *P.S.C.,* 17:149–158.

——— (1963), The Concept of Development Lines. *P.S.C.,* 18:245–265.

——— (1965), *Normality and Pathology in Childhood.* New York: Int. Univ. Press.

——— (1968), Indication and Contraindications for Child Analysis. *P.S.C.,* 23:37–46.

——— (1970), The Symptomatology of Childhood. *P.S.C.,* 25:17–41.

——— (1974a), A Psychoanalytic View of Developmental Psychopathology. *J. Philadelphia Assn. Psa.,* 1:7–17.

——— (1974b), Diagnosis and Assessment of Childhood Disturbances. *J. Philadelphia Assn. Psa.,* 1:54–67.

——— NAGERA, H., & FREUD, W. E., (1965), Metapsychological Assessment of the Adult Personality. *P.S.C.,* 20:9–41.

FREUD, S. (1891), *On Aphasia.* New York: Int. Univ. Press, 1953.

——— (1915), The Unconscious. *S.E.,* 14:159–215.

——— (1916–1917), Introductory Lectures on Psycho-Analysis. *S.E.,* 15 & 16.

——— (1923), The Ego and the Id. *S.E.,* 19:3–66.

——— (1928), Dostoevsky and Parricide. *S.E.,* 21:175–196.

FREUD, W. E., (1967), Assessment of Early Infancy: Problems and Considerations. *P.S.C.,* 22:216–238.

——— (1968), Some General Reflections on the Metapsychological Profile. *Int. J. Psa.,* 49:498–501.

——— (1971), The Baby Profile: Part II. *P.S.C.,* 26:172–194.

——— (1975), Infant Observation. *P.S.C.,* 30:75–94.

——— & FREUD, I. (1974), Die Well-Baby Klinik. In: *Jahrbuch der Psychohygiene,* ed. G. Biermann. München/Basel: Ernest Reinhardt Verlag, Vol. 2, pp. 119–137.

FRIES, M. E. & WOOLF, P. J. (1953), Some Hypotheses on the Role of the Congenital Activity Type in Personality Development. *P.S.C.,* 8:48–62.

Gauthier, Y. (1960), Observations on Ego Development. *Bull. Philadelphia Assn. Psa.,* 10:69–85.

Gottschalk, L. A. (1956), The Relationship of Psychologic State and Epileptic Activity. *P.S.C.,* 11:352–380.

Greenacre, P. (1945), The Biologic Economy of Birth. *P.S.C.,* 1:31–51.

Hartmann, H. (1939), *Ego Psychology and the Problem of Adaptation.* New York: Int. Univ. Press, 1958.

——— (1952), The Mutual Influences in the Development of Ego and Id. *P.S.C.,* 7:9–30.

——— (1956), Notes on the Reality Principle. *P.S.C.,* 11:31–53.

——— Kris, E., & Loewenstein, R. M. (1946), Comments on the Formation of Psychic Structure. *P.S.C.,* 2:11–38.

Heinicke, C. M. (1958), Changes in Children and the Intensity of Psychotherapy. NIMH Grant Proposal No. MH 02948–05.

——— (1965a), Independent Indices of Development. In: Heinicke (1969).

——— (1965b), Analysis of Clinical Rating. In: Heinicke (1969).

——— (1969), Frequency of Psychotherapeutic Session as a Factor Affecting Outcome. *J. Abnorm. Psychol.,* 74:553–560.

——— et al. (1965), Frequency of Psychotherapeutic Session as a Factor Affecting the Child's Developmental Status. *P.S.C.,* 19:42–97.

——— et al. (1974), Relationship Opportunities in Day Care and the Child's Task Orientation. ERIC, Arlington, Va., Document #ED089871.

——— & Goldman, A. (1960), Research on Psychotherapy with Children. *Amer. J. Orthopsychiat.,* 30:483–494.

——— & Strassmann, L. H. (1975), Toward More Effective Research on Child Psychotherapy. *J. Amer. Acad. Child Psychiat.,* 14:561–588.

Hoffer, W. (1950), Development of the Body Ego. *P.S.C.,* 5:18–24.

——— (1952), The Mutual Influences in the Development of Ego and Id. *P. S. C.,* 7:31–41.

Imber, S. D., Frank, J. D., Nash, E. H., Stone, A. R., & Gliedman, L. H., (1957), Improvement and Amount of Therapeutic Contact. *J. Cons. Psychol.,* 21:309–315.

James, M. (1952), Premature Ego Development. *Int. J. Psa.,* 41:288–294.

Klein, M. (1932), *The Psycho-Analysis of Children.* London: Hogarth Press.

Klopfer, B., Ainsworth, M., Klopfer, W., & Holt, R. (1954), *Developments in the Rorschach Technique,* Vol 1. Yonkers-on-Hudson, N.Y.: World Book.

Kris, E. (1939), Laughter as an Expressive Process. *Psychoanalytic Explorations in Art.* New York: Int. Univ. Press, 1952, pp. 217–239.

——— (1950), Notes on the Development and on Some Current Problems of Psychoanalytic Child Psychology. *The Selected Papers of Ernst Kris.* New Haven: Yale Univ. Press, 1975, pp. 54–79.

——— (1951), Opening Remarks on Psychoanalytic Child Psychology. *The Selected Papers of Ernst Kris.* New Haven: Yale Univ. Press, 1975, pp. 80–88.

Kris, M. (1957), The Use of Prediction in a Longitudinal Study. *P.S.C.,* 12:175–189.

Kut Rosenfeld, S. & Sprince, M. P. (1965), Some Thoughts on the Technical Handling of Borderline Children. *P.S.C.,* 20:495–517.

Lampl-de Groot, J. (1967), On Obstacles Standing in the Way of Psychoanalytic Cure. *P.S.C.,* 22:20–35.

Laufer, M. (1964), Ego Ideal and Pseudo Ego Ideal in Adolescence. *P.S.C.,* 19:196–221.

——— (1965), Assessment of Adolescent Disturbances. *P.S.C.,* 20:99–123.

——— (1968), The Body Image, the Function of Masturbation, and Adolescence. *P.S.C.,* 23:114–137.

——— (1975), Preventive Intervention in Adolescence. *P.S.C.,* 30:511–528.

LOEWALD, H. W. (1951), Ego and Reality. *Int. J. Psa.,* 32:10–18.

LORR, M., MCNAIR, D. M., MICHAUX, W. W., & RASKIN, H. (1962), Frequency of Treatment and Change in Psychotherapy. *J. Abnorm. Soc. Psychol.,* 64:281–292.

MCNAIR, D., LORR, M., YOUNG, H., ROTH, I., & BOYD, W. (1964), A Three-Year Follow-up of Psychotherapy Patients. *J. Clin. Psychol.,* 20:258–264.

MAHLER, M. S. (1952), On Child Psychosis and Schizophrenia. *P.S.C.,* 7:286–305.

MICHAELS, J. J. (1955), *Disorders of Character.* Springfield, Ill.: Charles C Thomas.

——— & STIVER, I. P. (1965), The Impulsive Psychopathic Character According to the Diagnostic Profile. *P.S.C.,* 20:124–141.

NAGERA, H. (1963), The Developmental Profile. *P.S.C.,* 18:511–540.

——— (1964), Autoerotism, Autoerotic Activities, and Ego Development, *P.S.C.,* 19:240–255.

——— (1966a), Sleep and Its Disturbances Approached Developmentally. *P.S.C.,* 21:393–477.

——— (1966b), *Early Childhood Disturbances, the Infantile Neurosis, and the Adulthood Disturbances.* New York: Int. Univ. Press.

——— & COLONNA, A. B. (1965), Aspects of the Contribution of Sight to Ego and Drive Development. *P.S.C.,* 20:267–287.

OMWAKE, E. B. & SOLNIT, A. J. (1961), "It Isn't Fair." *P.S.C.,* 16:352–404.

PETERSON, D., SUMNER, J., & JONES, G. (1950), Role of Hypnosis in Differentiation of Epileptic from Convulsive-Like Seizures. *Amer. J. Psychiat.,* 107:428–433.

PIAGET, J. (1936), *The Origin of Intelligence in Children.* New York: Int. Univ. Press, 1952.

PROVENCE, S. (1966), Some Aspects of Early Ego Development. In: *Psychoanalysis —A General Psychology,* ed. R. M. Loewenstein, L. M. Newman, M. Schur, & Albert J. Solnit. New York: Int. Univ. Press, pp. 107–122.

——— & LIPTON, R. C. (1962), *Infants in Institutions.* New York: Int. Univ. Press.

RADFORD, P., WISEBERG, S., & YORKE, C. (1972), A Study of "Main-Line" Heroin Addiction. *P.S.C.,* 27:156–180.

REIK, T. (1919), *Ritual.* New York: Int. Univ. Press, 1958.

ROBERTSON, JOYCE (1962), Mothering as an Influence on Early Development. *P.S.C.,* 17:246–264.

——— (1965), Mother-Infant Interaction from Birth to Twelve Months. In: *Determinants of Infant Behaviour III,* ed. B. M. Foss. London: Methuen; New York: John Wiley, pp. 111–127.

ROSENFELD, E. & NOVICK, J. (1964), Assessing Deviant Behavior. Read at Michigan State University Workshop on Assessment of Children.

SANDLER, A.-M. (1963), Aspects of Passivity and Ego Development in the Blind Infant. *P.S.C.,* 18:343–360.

SEGAL, A. & STONE, F. H. (1961), The Six-Year-Old Who Began to See. *P.S.C.,* 16:481–509.

SPERLING, M. (1953), Psychodynamics and Treatment of Petit Mal in Children. *Int. J. Psa.,* 34:248–252.

SPITZ, R. A. (1945), Hospitalism. *P.S.C.,* 1:53–74.

——— (1946), Anaclitic Depression. *P.S.C.,* 2:313–342.

——— (1955), The Primal Cavity. *P.S.C.,* 10:215–240.

——— (1957), *No and Yes.* New York: Int. Univ. Press.

Tausk, V. (1919), On the Origin of the "Influencing Machine" in Schizophrenia. In: *The Psychoanalytic Reader,* ed. R. Fliess. New York: Int. Univ. Press, 1948, pp. 52–85.

Thomas, R. et al. (1966), Comments on Some Aspects of Self and Object Representation in a Group of Psychotic Children. *P.S.C.,* 21:527–580.

Van Dam, H., Heinicke, C. M., & Shane, M. (1975), On Termination of Child Analysis. *P.S.C.,* 30:443–474.

Waelder, R. (1964), Personal communication.

Wills, D. (1968), Problems of Play and Mastery in the Blind Child. *Brit. J. Med. Psychol.,* 41:213–222.

Winnicott, D. W. (1953), Transitional Objects and Transitional Phenomena. *Collected Papers.* New York: Basic Books, 1958, pp. 229–242.

——— (1954), Metapsychological and Clinical Aspects of Regression within the Psycho-Analytical Set-Up. *Ibid.,* pp. 278–294.

——— (1960a), Ego Distortion in Terms of True and False Self. *The Maturational Processes and the Facilitating Environment.* New York: Int. Univ. Press, 1965, pp. 140–152.

——— (1960b), String: A Technique of Communication. *Ibid.,* pp. 153–157.

Wiseberg, S., Yorke, C., & Radford, P. (1975), Aspects of Self Cathexis in "Mainline" Heroin Addiction. In: *Studies in Child Analysis.* New Haven: Yale Univ. Press, pp. 99–116.

Young, J. Z. (1960), *Doubt and Certainty in Science.* New York: Oxford Univ. Press.

INDEX